Is Decentralization Good for Development?

Is Decentralization Good for Development?

Perspectives from Academics and Policy Makers

Jean-Paul Faguet and Caroline Pöschl

OXFORD
UNIVERSITY PRESS

OXFORD
UNIVERSITY PRESS

Great Clarendon Street, Oxford, OX2 6DP,
United Kingdom

Oxford University Press is a department of the University of Oxford.
It furthers the University's objective of excellence in research, scholarship, and education by publishing worldwide. Oxford is a registered trade mark of Oxford University Press in the UK and in certain other countries

First Edition published in 2015
Impression: 1

Published in the United States of America by Oxford University Press
198 Madison Avenue, New York, NY 10016, United States of America

British Library Cataloguing in Publication Data
Data available

Library of Congress Control Number: 2015932090

ISBN 978–0–19–873750–6

Printed and bound by
CPI Group (UK) Ltd, Croydon, CR0 4YY

Foreword

Decentralization is everywhere around us. Throughout the developing and developed worlds, both the architecture of the state and the deeper relationship between citizens and governments are being re-shaped by decentralization, devolution, and outright secession. Thirty years ago, academic researchers and organizations like the World Bank and United Nations marveled at the number of decentralization programs across the world. Since then the number of reforms has grown and grown.

Decentralization changes countries in big, deep, and lasting ways because it changes not just financial flows and formal structures of authority, but the fundamental incentives that public officials must respond to. In a centralized system, officials' incentives are "upward-looking" in the sense of responding to the wishes and priorities of officials higher up in government. Their performance is judged, and they are rewarded or not, according to how well they serve the agendas of superior bureaucrats. In a decentralized system, officials' incentives are pointed firmly downwards to the citizens and voters who elected them. They are judged by citizens, and their career trajectory depends on satisfying enough of them that voters choose to return them to office. By changing such deep incentives that operate throughout government, decentralization sets in motion a dynamic that leads to long-term, fundamental changes in public officials' behavior, and public sector decisions and outputs, as well as the underlying relationship between governors and the governed.

These are not abstract theoretical points, but real, tangible, defining features of countries, states, and economies. Just look at the raucous, diverse, colorful—but also stable and legitimate—democracy that federalism underpins in India; compare it to the winner-take-all, brittle, chronically unstable governments that six decades of centralization have bestowed on Pakistan. These countries differ in ways other than decentralization of course. But it is useful to remember that they were governed for centuries by the same British colonial administration, and their politics diverged only at independence when one became a federal, and the other a unitary, state. Think also of Germany vs. the UK, or Spanish South America vs. Brazil, and consider how variations in centralization help shape national economies and the spatial distribution of economic activity.

Big reforms have spawned a big literature dedicated to evaluating decentralization's effects, numbering in the hundreds of published works and thousands of agency reports. But they have mostly ignored questions concerning governance, political competition, stability, and legitimacy, which are highly consequential but methodologically difficult to address, in favor of easier-to-measure, technocratic issues like public investment levels, inflation, fiscal deficits, and education and health attendance. Such second-order issues are also important and worthy of study, of course. But the shift in focus away from the most important effects of reform has had a less obvious, more pernicious effect on our understanding of decentralization. It has pushed researchers and thinkers to assume the perspective of a social planner or policy analyst—the disinterested, benevolent dictator who maximizes some concept of good in society, be it wealth, health, or some other measure of well-being.

Without doubt this is a useful way to approach such questions. But it also serves to divorce a huge literature from the principal concerns of policy makers and politicians: Will decentralization increase or decrease my power and control? Will it get me re-elected? Will it help or harm my party's long-term prospects? Not to mention the principal priorities of citizens: Will decentralization increase or decrease political stability? violence? citizens' rights and freedoms? prosperity? inequality? These are, indeed, the main things that we as development specialists, thinkers, and indeed citizens should be concerned with too. In so doing, the shift in focus makes the majority of decentralization studies—regardless of how rigorous and technically competent many undoubtedly are—less interesting and much less relevant to precisely those people who must lead the difficult changes required to decentralize any country.

When policy makers approach academics for advice about a major, risky reform that seeks to change the shape of government, answering in terms of its second- and third-order effects is a strange thing to do. When these effects are additionally things that policy makers care less about, the effect is downright perverse.

This book is unique in that it turns the tables on an entire field. It examines decentralization through the eyes of policy-making politicians, but with the methodological rigor and theoretical clarity of academics, asking first: Why would politicians *want* to do it? And if they did, *how* would they do it? It then analyzes key issues of governance such as democracy, stability, inclusivity, and state strength. A further three chapters draw the lessons of four decades of reform throughout the world on how best to design tax, transfer, and expenditure systems. Lastly it returns to more traditional, technocratic issues, asking: What happens after reform is implemented? These last four chapters update our knowledge of decentralization's effects on health, education, anti-poverty programs, etc. using evidence from twelve countries across Africa, Asia, and Latin America.

The editors have achieved this synthesis of academic and policy-making perspectives by carefully choosing and pairing authors to write on specific topics. While a few authors are "pure" academics (e.g. Myerson) or "pure" policy makers (e.g. Aiyar), most have a firm base in one camp but maintain an ongoing, vigorous practice in the other (e.g. Bossert, Faguet, Khan, etc.). Five chapters are written by a combination of policy maker(s) and academic(s), four chapters by individuals who significantly span that frontier, two by "pure" academics, and two by "pure" policy makers.

This book is a product of the Initiative for Policy Dialogue's Decentralization Task Force, and was first conceived at a conference held at Columbia University in New York in 2009. Although each chapter has named authors, there is a broader sense in which the volume reflects the collective thinking of all involved.

Bringing policy makers and academics together to think, discuss, and write about common themes has been neither easy nor straightforward. These two constituencies use different languages, are motivated by different concerns, and have completely, utterly different work styles. The authors are trained in economics, political science, public health, and philosophy, and include women, men, old, young, Asians, Europeans, and North and South Americans. But these differences were as nothing compared to the policy-making–academic divide. Breaching it took five years and an enormous amount of work, energy, and dedication.

I hope readers will agree that the effort was worthwhile. The result of my colleagues' labors is an unparalleled synthesis of theory and practice, an analytical memory of key successful and unsuccessful reforms, and a practical guide for those who would decentralize their countries.

Joseph E. Stiglitz

New York, September 2014

Contents

List of Figures

List of Tables

List of Contributors

Editors

Jean-Paul Faguet is Professor of the Political Economy of Development at the London School of Economics and Political Science, and chair of the Initiative for Policy Dialogue's Decentralization Task Force. He has published extensively on decentralization and local governance, including *Governance from Below: Decentralization and Popular Democracy in Bolivia* (2012, University of Michigan Press), which won the 2013 W.J.M. Mackenzie Award for best book published in political science.

Caroline Pöschl earned her PhD at the Department of International Development, London School of Economics and Political Science. Her dissertation explores the relationship between local government taxation and accountability in Mexico. Previously she worked on decentralization, subnational management and taxation at the World Bank and Inter-American Development Bank.

Authors

Mani Shankar Aiyar is a current member of the Rajya Sabha (Indian upper house of Parliament), Chairman of the South Asia Foundation's India Chapter, and Honorary Fellow of Trinity Hall, University of Cambridge. He is former Minister of Local Self-Government (Panchayati Raj), Government of India, and also served as Minister for Petroleum and Natural Gas, and Minister of Youth Affairs and Sports.

Pranab Bardhan is Professor of Economics at the University of California, Berkeley. He has been Chief Editor of the *Journal of Development Economics*, and co-chair of the MacArthur Foundation-funded Network on the Effects of Inequality on Economic Performance. He has also held the Distinguished Fulbright Chair at the University of Siena and the BP Centennial Professorship at London School of Economics.

Thomas J. Bossert is the Director of the International Health Systems Program of the Harvard T.H. Chan School of Public Health. His specialties include health reform, decentralization, social capital, policy analysis, organizational and institutional analysis, human resources policy, public/private relations, community development and project design and evaluation.

Giorgio Brosio is Professor of Public Economics at the University of Turin, where he has taught for 25 years. He is a past president of the European Public Choice Society. He has published widely in the decentralization literature, and has also advised the IMF,

World Bank, and many developing countries on issues of decentralization, federalism, and taxation.

Joseph J. Capuno is Associate Professor at the University of the Philippines School of Economics. His research spans issues of spatial development, local government innovations, political economy of local fiscal decisions, health insurance and financial protection, health and education equity.

Ali Cheema is Senior Research Fellow at the Institute of Development and Economic Alternatives (IDEAS) and Associate Professor of Economics at the Lahore University of Management Sciences. A Rhodes Scholar, he is also a founding director of the Center for Economic Research in Pakistan (CERP).

Vigile Marie B. Fabella is a PhD. student at the University of Konstanz in Germany. She obtained her Master's degree in economics from the University of the Philippines.

Ashley M. Fox is Lecturer in the Department of Population Health Science & Policy at Mount Sinai School of Medicine. She was previously Postdoctoral Fellow in the Political Economy of Health Policy at the Harvard School of Public Health.

Matteo Grazzi is an economist in the Competitiveness and Innovation Division of the Inter-American Development Bank. He previously worked at the UN Economic Commission for Latin America & the Caribbean, and at the Centre for Research on Latin American Studies and Transition Economies Studies of Bocconi University.

Fidel Jaramillo is the Country Representative of the Inter American Development Bank (IADB) in Peru. He was previously Chief Economist and Vice President of Development Strategies of the Andean Development Corporation (CAF), and also Minister of Finance (1988–90) and General Manager of the Central Bank of Ecuador (1997–8).

Juan Pablo Jiménez is Professor at the School of International and Public Affairs at Columbia University in New York. He is also Economic Affairs Officer of the Economic Development Division of the Economic Commission for Latin America and the Caribbean. He previously worked in the Ministry of Economy and the National Congress of Argentina.

Adnan Q. Khan is Research and Policy Director at the International Growth Centre, London School of Economics and Political Science. He was previously a civil servant in the Pakistan Administrative Service, where he served in different districts and ministries, including the ministry of finance.

Stuti Khemani is Senior Economist in the Development Research Group of the World Bank. Her research and advisory work span a diverse range of countries and is published in leading development economics and political science journals.

Aleli D. Kraft is Associate Professor and Director of the Health Economics Program at the University of the Philippines School of Economics. She has published in international and national health policy journals, and collaborated in research work with the University of Queensland.

Bingqin Li is Associate Professor and PhD Convenor at the Crawford School of Public Policy, Australian National University, and Professorial Research Fellow with the Development Research Centre of the State Council of China. Previously she was Lecturer in

Social Policy at the London School of Economics, and Research Associate of the Centre for Analyses of Social Exclusion.

Sandip Mitra is Assistant Professor at the Sampling and Official Statistics Unit, Indian Statistical Institute (ISI), Kolkata, where he has taught for more than 15 years. His research focuses on political economy, micro-finance, poverty, corporate social responsibility, agricultural markets, and official statistics.

Dilip Mookherjee is Professor of Economics at Boston University, and Director of the BU Institute for Economic Development since 1998. He studied Economics at Presidency College, Calcutta, the Delhi School of Economics, and the London School of Economics. He is the author most recently of *The Crisis in Government Accountability: Governance Reforms and Indian Economic Performance.*

Roger B. Myerson is Glen A. Lloyd Distinguished Service Professor of Economics at the University of Chicago. In 2007, he was co-winner of the Nobel Memorial Prize in Economic Sciences with Eric Maskin and Leonid Hurwicz. Dr. Myerson's publications, *Game Theory* and *Probability Models for Economic Decisions* furthered the theoretical research on game theory, information economics, and economic analysis of political institutions. Winner of numerous accolades, including an honorary doctorate from the University of Basel in 2002, he is Fellow and former Midwest Vice President of the American Academy of Arts and Sciences. He was elected Vice President of the Econometric Society in 2006.

Stella A. Quimbo is Professor and Department Chair at the University of the Philippines School of Economics. She holds the Prince Claus Chair in Development and Equity at the International Institute of Social Studies of Erasmus University Rotterdam.

Gonzalo Sánchez de Lozada was born in La Paz, Bolivia, but grew up mainly in the United States, in exile. He graduated from the University of Chicago with a degree in philosophy, and then return to Bolivia to found a film production company, and later a petroleum services and mining company operating in Peru, Bolivia, and Argentina. In 1979 he entered the Chamber of Deputies, was later elected Senator, and then President of the Senate. He became Minister of Planning and Coordination in the administration of President Victor Paz Estenssoro, where he designed the 1985 economic reform that tamed Bolivia's 25,000 per cent hyperinflation, and lay the foundations for economic stability. In 1993, he became the 61st President of Bolivia. He was elected president again in 2002, but was forced to resign in October 2003. He is now the non-executive chairman of a company with mining investments in the Americas and Europe. He has received distinctions and awards as well as honorary degrees from universities in Japan, the United States, and Ecuador.

Abhirup Sarkar is Professor of Economics at the Indian Statistical Institute, Kolkata, where he has taught for 30 years. He has taught and researched in universities and institutions in the US, Canada, and Europe. He is currently Chairman of the State Finance Commission of West Bengal, and also Chairman of the West Bengal Infrastructure Development Finance Corporation, and a past member of the Group of Advisors to the Indian Finance Minister on G20 matters.

Carlos Antonio R. Tan, Jr, currently works for a health policy project in the Philippines. He has published works on economic burden of diseases, impact of water and sanitation, and financial risk protection in *Health Policy and Planning* and the *Asian Journal of Public Health*, among others.

Barry R. Weingast is Senior Fellow at the Hoover Institution as well as the Ward C. Krebs Family Professor in the Department of Political Science at Stanford University, which he chaired from 1996 to 2001. His research focuses on the political determinants of public policymaking and the political foundations of markets and democracy. He is Fellow of the American Academy of Arts and Sciences and recipient of the 2006 William H. Riker Prize in Political Science.

Yongmei Zhang is Associate Professor at the Philosophy and Sociology Institute, Lanzhou University, P.R. China. Her research focuses on rural to urban migration and community development in China's western provinces. Her book *Marriage and Family Life of a Migrant Population* was awarded Second Prize for Outstanding Academic Research Achievement in Gansu Province in 2007.

1

Is Decentralization Good For Development?

Perspectives from Academics and Policy Makers

Jean-Paul Faguet and Caroline Pöschl

1.1 Introduction

Decentralization is at the heart of the policy-reform agenda all over the world. Developing countries as disparate as Mexico, Egypt, Ghana, and India have active decentralization programs in place, citing the need to make their public administrations more efficient, flexible, and responsive. And under the guises of subsidiarity, devolution, and federalism, reform is firmly in the foreground of policy discourse in rich countries too. In 2000 the World Bank estimated that between 80 and 100 per cent of the world's countries were experimenting with some form of decentralization, and its 2004 World Development Report examined decentralization as an instrument for improving public service delivery. Since then, new or deepening reforms have been announced in countries as disparate as Japan, Cambodia, France, Turkey, and Kenya, amongst many others.

Widespread policy enthusiasm has been accompanied by a large literature studying the effects of reform. This literature has changed substantially over the past two decades as economists and policy analysts have employed econometrics and formal modeling to study the effects of decentralization on such issues as education and health services, infrastructure investment, corruption, macroeconomic stability, and growth, to name a few. The decentralization studies of thirty and forty years ago are now often criticized for a lack of academic rigor, and for relying too much on case study and "anecdote." But increasing technical rigor has come at the expense of increasing distance from the concerns and constraints of the policy makers who drive decentralization forward, or fail to. At the simplest level, much of this new literature is now beyond the grasp of practitioners (and many graduate students). Furthermore, the laudable quest for rigor leads technical studies to abstract away from the "details" of how policy reform actually works. Even when methodologically necessary, this has the effect of leaving potentially important aspects of real decentralization reforms outside the purview of academic analysis.

This book seeks to re-unite academics studying decentralization with the policy makers who implement it. It comes out of an extraordinary workshop held at Columbia University in June, 2009 under the auspices of the Initiative for Policy Dialogue's Decentralization Task Force. The two-day workshop brought together academics working at the empirical and theoretical frontier of research on decentralization and subnational government with policy practitioners who have implemented or supported reform at the highest levels of government and international organizations. The purpose of the workshop was not only to exchange ideas, but to marry policy makers' detailed knowledge and insights about real reform processes with academics' conceptual clarity and analytical rigor. The workshop was explicitly structured to facilitate this integration, and this volume is one result.[1]

Synthesis of the perspectives of academic and policy maker naturally shifts the analysis towards questions that the literature has had trouble addressing empirically, but that are of great interest to policy makers and politicians contemplating reform. These are reflected in the structure of the book, which is divided into three parts. Our first focuses on *Decentralization, Stability, and the Strength of the State*. This first chapter asks the question: Why do policy makers decentralize? This has been referred to as the "black hole" of the decentralization debate. Why do national politicians decide to devolve some of their power and resources to others who are beyond their control? Considerations of efficiency or effectiveness are surely insufficient to explain the number and extent of announced decentralizations. We tackle this question head-on, with a chapter by the Bolivian President who decided to decentralize his country shortly after taking power. This is followed by chapters examining how and why decentralization came about in Pakistan and India, and its effects on state capacity and political stability there. A fifth chapter dissects the fiscally destabilizing effects of reform in a number of Latin American countries, and then examines a second generation of reforms that dramatically improved the fiscal situation. The final chapter in this part seeks to answer the question "Does decentralization strengthen or weaken the state?" with a survey of the theoretical and empirical literatures, and some theoretical contributions of its own. All of these are classic examples of questions that are

[1] Another is Faguet, J. P. (ed.) 2014a. "Decentralization and Governance." Special Issue of *World Development*, 53: 1–112.

crucially important to policy makers, but are difficult to address with quantitative evidence.

Once reformers have made up their minds to proceed, how should they design reform? What are the advantages and disadvantages of assigning taxes, transfers, and expenditures to different levels of government? Our second part, *Designing Decentralization: Taxes, Transfers, and Expenditures*, examines these issues through a combination of logical argument and evidence that focuses on Argentina, Bolivia, Canada, China, India, Indonesia, Italy, Nigeria, Peru, and the Philippines, but also ranges farther afield in Latin America and Europe. The authors are senior academics, some of whom have been instrumental in developing the underlying theory, and practitioners with extensive real-world experience.

After reform is implemented, what happens? *Decentralization and Local Service Provision* turns to the area in which most decentralization research has been done—decentralization's effects on the provision of health, education, anti-poverty programs, etc. We present original research by academics working at the frontier of their respective fields. These four chapters by no means cover the full range of "the effects of decentralization." Rather, they update our knowledge in a few specific, important areas in which authors with acknowledged expertise provide new and innovative research findings. Much care has been taken to present their empirical results in a form that is accessible to policy makers, development practitioners, and a wide audience of students from different disciplines. The evidence presented comes from deep studies of China, the Philippines, and West Bengal (India), plus a more summarized survey of evidence from Bolivia, Colombia, Ghana, India, Morocco, Nicaragua, Pakistan, Uganda, Vietnam, and Zambia.

Before proceeding, it is useful to define "decentralization." We follow Faguet and Sánchez (2013) and Manor (1999) in defining decentralization as the devolution by central (i.e. national) government of specific functions—with all of the administrative, political, and economic attributes that these entail—to regional and local (i.e. state/provincial and municipal) governments that are independent of the center within given geographic and functional domains.

The rest of this chapter is organized not according to the sections mentioned above, but rather by the substantive, integrated conclusions that emerge from the analysis therein. We first analyze why governments decentralize. Using examples from several sections of this volume, we show that decentralization reforms are largely driven by motivations of political survival and consolidation of power. This, as well as the fact that decentralization reforms often need to be negotiated against opposing political demands, leads us to the second conclusion: decentralization may fail to enhance development because it never actually happens. Instead, partial and "cynical" decentralizations are widespread in which, for instance, spending responsibilities are devolved without decision-making autonomy, or opposition forces are merely divided into various powerless entities to facilitate continued rule by the center.

In section 1.4 we show that the design of decentralization is more important than the decision to decentralize or not. In several countries analyzed in this book, serious fiscal and political problems that followed decentralization were the result of flaws in the design of reform—but these were successfully corrected through subsequent policy revisions that changed the incentives of subnational officials, and hence performance throughout the system. We also discuss other examples of how different decentralization designs can achieve divergent goals in developing countries.

Finally, we summarize evidence from this volume showing *how* decentralization can enhance development in four important ways: by (1) improving governance, (2) creating competition among subnational governments, (3) reducing clientelism, and (4) strengthening the state. We map positive and negative outcomes in each of these areas to particular elements of the decentralizations implemented. We argue in particular that the dynamic of decentralized government provides strong incentives for social learning—for long-term strengthening of the organizational effectiveness of civil society, and consequent increases in government accountability.

1.2 Why Do Governments Decentralize?

Let us begin with the most basic question about decentralization. Why would any national leader do it? In order for decentralization to happen, central government leaders—who by definition hold large aggregates of power and resources in their hands—must decide to devolve non-trivial shares to lower-level politicians with independent mandates and sources of authority, whom they cannot control. Why would any president, having spent a career achieving the pinnacle of power, willingly do this? This is the black hole at the heart of the decentralization debate that few address and none have satisfyingly answered (Faguet, 2012).

At the simplest level, the urge to decentralize is irrational in those who must do it. Are presidents motivated by normative arguments about state effectiveness? Is decentralization politically convenient? Can politicians be altruistic? These questions are not just interesting in their own right; they are also important because they point to the common incentives that leaders must face in cases of sincere reform. Such incentives surely shape the character of sincere decentralizations, and distinguish them from decentralizations that fail, or are never actually implemented.

One way to analyze this paradox is via close empirical examination of a case of reforming success. This is the work of Faguet and Sánchez de Lozada in Chapter 2, which plumbs the political, institutional, and personal circumstances of the reformers who decentralized Bolivia, as related by President Gonzalo "Goni" Sánchez de Lozada, the man who presided over it all. Sánchez de Lozada's account not only benefits from an intimate knowledge of the situations and relationships out of which the reform emerged, but is also strongly rooted in Bolivia's long-term historical trajectory, which created its rich, complicated social and political tapestry.

In Goni's case, the main factor driving his decision was the need to overcome his image as a foreign, upper-class interloper who bankrolled his own campaigns and was distant from the lives and problems of ordinary Bolivian voters. He felt respected by Bolivians in the sense of professional competence, but was equally sure that voters could not relate to him. "So I decided to do something that ended up being very wise. I got in a car with a driver and visited almost every town in Bolivia. I said 'Goni's listening'. Instead of giving speeches, I would listen. I would bring people together and they would tell me their problems."

This brought him into prolonged contact with living conditions strikingly different from urban Bolivia, and taught him that all over the country, especially amongst the rural, poorer, more deprived majority, people's highest priorities were improved health and education. These were the problems that most affected their lives on a daily basis. Therein also lay the main solutions to the real poverty they faced—the only kind of income redistribution in which they were willing to believe.

And in the doing, he came to the realization that "the people who know the best solutions are the people who have the problems, not the people who don't have the problems," and hence, "an idiot close to a problem is better than a genius a thousand miles away." In order to enact these solutions, it was necessary to redistribute power in the Bolivian polity; not just to delegate actions or devolve responsibility for government performance, but to hand down real authority to Bolivia's most deprived citizens. This was a radical vision for any centralized, unitary state—and much more so for a large, diverse country haunted since independence by the specter of disintegration.

This radical vision also promised to solve a second crucial problem that a possible Sánchez de Lozada presidency would certainly face: Bolivia's strong, militant, regional interests. As the Minister of Planning who defeated hyperinflation, Goni had himself done battle with the centrifugal forces that extracted resources and concessions from the center by threatening to break the country apart. These were wielded by regional business elites, most prominently in Santa Cruz and Tarija, where leaders were particularly adept at mobilizing broader movements behind them. In essence they were hangovers from Bolivia's military regimes: self-appointed regional bodies representing the strongest local interests in the name of the entire region. They demanded a federal Bolivia that would increase their ability to capture natural resource rents, under threat of secession or joining Brazil. Goni realized he could undermine them and cleave off their supporters by going directly to the grass roots and creating local governments instead.

Contrast this with decentralization in Pakistan, described by Cheema, Khan, and Myerson in Chapter 3, which differs from the Bolivian case in almost every possible way. Here, decentralization has been a tool of military regimes to legitimize themselves and strengthen their control over the state, and to try to peel popular support off the main, deposed political parties. Since independence, military regimes have sought on three occasions to build an alternative base of political support by creating and then patronizing a new class of locally elected politicians. Established political parties were consistently excluded from participating in local elections or even endorsing candidates. Such rules could be selectively applied against opponents of the regime, without limiting the generals' favored candidates. As a result, non-partisan local governments became tarnished in the popular imagination—and especially amongst the main political parties—as an instrument of military regimes for creating a class of political collaborators who displace parties at the local level.

Thus we have, in Bolivia, decentralization as a democratizing riposte to the agitation and demands of authoritarian regional movements that threatened repeatedly to fracture the country. And in Pakistan we have decentralization as an authoritarian strategy to undermine established political parties and legitimize military rule. It is not surprising that Bolivia's political parties—both established and new—took to local politics with relish, organizing territorially throughout the length and breadth of the country, while Pakistan's parties treated decentralization like a pox on the body politic, which vitiated it and closed down local governments upon their return to power. Reforms born out of different imperatives were designed in different ways and led to different consequences, resulting ultimately in very different fates for each: in Bolivia a strengthening and deepening of decentralization fifteen years later; and its abolition in Pakistan.

In Chapter 6, Faguet, Fox, and Pöschl provide examples of other motivations to decentralize. In many cases, decentralization processes were embarked upon for sheer political survival; in other cases for the consolidation of power, for example in the face of serious threats to the integrity of a country's borders by secessionist movements or a (violent) opposition. In Canada and Spain, decentralization helped appease fractious groups and hold these nations together. Reform has also been introduced as a power-sharing instrument to defend against conflict from warring factions, as in

Afghanistan and Iraq. Central governments may use it as a means to fragment the opposition and remain in power (Sabatini, 2003). In Ethiopia, decentralization was used by the central government to diffuse a menacing political opposition, allowing the ruler to remain in power while opposition parties competed against one another at the subnational level (Green, 2011). As discussed in the next section, the design and outcomes of decentralization—and their effect on development—are very much determined by the motives of those who wield power.

1.3 Political Obstacles to Reform and Partial Decentralizations

That national leaders may have strong reasons to decentralize does not, however, imply that national governments will proceed to do so. Admittedly, a military hierarchy like Pakistan's in the early 2000s may require little more than the agreement of a few commanders to ensure that reform proceeds. But in a democratic regime such as Bolivia's, even a president driven by a clear vision must convince his political coalition to approve such a reform, and then his by definition centralized bureaucracy to implement it. And neither is likely to want to for the reasons outlined above: to devolve authority and resources to significantly independent local officials with their own mandates and sources of legitimacy is to willingly give away the basic currencies of power to others—including potential rivals—whom they may influence but cannot control. Sincere decentralization requires those who implement it to change what they do in a way that reduces their own power, status, and sources of patronage for the benefit of others. It obliges those who must carry it out to diminish themselves professionally. The self-interested agents of positive political science are not expected to act in this way, and in practice real bureaucrats tend not to.

Pakistan faced comparatively miniscule obstacles to reform, but its long-term prospects were similarly small in a society where the sponsoring coalition was tiny and the largest political organizations were bitterly opposed. In Bolivia, by contrast, the main party of government—the MNR, also the most extensively organized party in the country—quickly saw that it would capture the larger share of local governments and resources, and hence reform was in their interest. Other parties experienced regional demands as internal conflict, and so also stood to benefit. And business leaders, who feared rising populist parties based in peri-urban slums, liked a reform that shifted power to the countryside, where such parties were largely absent. With a broad and multi-faceted base of support, it is not surprising that Bolivia's proved by far the more sustainable reform.

Politics thus plays a crucial role in determining the degree and kind of decentralization implemented, and the success or failure of those reforms (Montero and Samuels, 2004). Even sincere reformers are faced with many varied political obstacles, big and small, subtle and crass, along the way to implementing decentralization reforms. And many reforming governments are not sincere (Faguet, 2012). In fact, one of the most common failures of decentralization reform is that it often does not really happen (Faguet, 2004 and 2012; Faguet and Shami, 2008). Good intentions—or, in their absence, the letter of the law—are undermined by a central government that does not actually intend to hand power and resources down to legally distinct subnational governments with independent political and legal authority. Powers are thus often decentralized half-heartedly, or in exchange for others, and the structures that result may diverge widely from the original plan, let alone any theoretical ideal. In practice, political motives can easily highjack the incentives that reformed fiscal systems aim to create. Intergovernmental power relations and political motives thus merit close attention in any decentralization reform strategy.

For example, in Chapter 4 Mani Shankar Aiyar contends that decentralization to rural villages in India has been incomplete because of the central bureaucracy's reluctance to give up power. Rather than allowing village communities to decide their own issues, the bureaucracy imposed centralized decisions. This has led to a duplication of efforts and perverse outcomes, as various ministries fail to communicate with one another, providing overlapping services in the same areas without allowing space to the village communities to identify their own specific needs. In this way, local knowledge about local needs remains mostly unexploited while administrative overlap and inefficiencies prevail. The key benefit from decentralizing governance—that those who know best about the specific needs of people in each locality are empowered to make decisions—is undermined.

How can we tell where decentralization is sincere and where it is not? Can such efforts be measured empirically? Bossert attacked this question in a pioneering 1998 article that introduced the concept of "decision space," which he defined as the local discretion allowed by central government for functions and sub-functions about financing, service delivery, human resources, and governance. Carefully operationalized for empirical analysis, measures of decision space allow us to investigate the extent to which local authorities have policy discretion, or central authorities effectively circumscribe local choice through rules and incentives that promote central objectives.

As Bossert points out, the decision space approach has several advantages. It puts the focus squarely on the extent to which authority over public choices is shifted from central to local authorities. And it stresses that the choices in question are not simple and monolithic, but rather involve a range of discretion over different functions and types of decisions. Therefore we should expect a given decentralization reform to permit more local choice over budgets and financing in some areas (e.g. primary education), and hiring and firing in others (e.g. public infrastructure). This is a more realistic way of analyzing the complexity of real-world experience than the simple decentralized–centralized dichotomies that dominate the literature, concealing more than they reveal. Bossert proposes specific definitions of the range and levels of choices in question, using health sector functions as an example, with the goal of testing whether greater decision space at the local level results in better health system performance.

In Chapter 12, Bossert updates his 1998 findings with evidence from a broad range of countries across Africa, Asia, and Latin America. Interestingly, he finds that even in countries with reputations for decentralization, many functions remained highly centralized (i.e. local officials have "narrow" decision space). There is considerable variation in decision space among different countries, and within countries decision space varies significantly among different functions.

Bossert finds evidence for strong positive correlations among what he terms the different dimensions of decentralization: local decision space, local capacities, and local accountability for given functions in specific services and sectors. Hence municipalities reporting high levels of decision space in a specific function also reported high levels of capacities and accountability for that function. For example, districts with high decision space for strategic and operational planning also had high decision space for organization and delivery of a given service (e.g. vaccinations, primary education). Capacities and accountability also show consistent synergies amongst the three dimensions in three different country contexts (Pakistan, India, and Vietnam), and similar weaknesses of accountability and limitations on human resources decisions.

1.4 Design Matters

How should expenditures and revenues be assigned across levels of government? The theory of fiscal federalism holds that public services whose benefits are locally specific should be financed by local taxes on those residents. But where benefits spill over into a wider population, it is often appropriate for them to be partly financed by transfers from higher levels of government (Bird and Smart, 2010). Higher-level governments are better at redistribution and stabilization and hence should levy broader-based taxes. But lower-level governments are better at eliciting preference and time-and-place information (Ostrom et al., 1993), and hence should have significant expenditure responsibility. The resulting vertical imbalances can be corrected by intergovernmental transfers. These must be large enough to sustain local services, but not so large that local governments become "transfer dependent." Subnational governments' budget constraints should remain hard (Rao and Bird, 2011).

In Chapter 8, Brosio and Jiménez turn this issue on its head, seeking to understand why decentralization reforms that might be expected to lead to greater local taxation often result instead in increased tax *centralization*, alongside greater expenditure *decentralization*, in many countries. They analyze these issues as a negotiation between central and local governments, focusing on the expenditure side of the budget. Decisions about tax (de)centralization are related to decisions about how such revenues are likely to be used. Using evidence from Argentina, Canada, and Italy, they find that systems featuring decentralized expenditures and centralized taxation can result when taxes are more efficiently administered from the center, but electoral accountability for public services operates more efficiently at the local level.

These broad, well-established insights nonetheless leave open many important questions in the design of fiscal systems. Pöschl and Weingast turn to these in Chapter 7, analyzing how the distribution of tax powers, responsibilities, and resources vitally shapes not only subnational government institutions but also policy choices and economic performance. The design of transfer formulas can, for example, provide incentives to subnational leaders to collect taxes by tying central government transfers to tax effort. The motivation to collect taxes can, in turn, incentivize local officials to growth-promoting policies and investments, greater sensitivity to residents' needs, and better fiscal discipline (Moore 2007). By contrast, a dependence on central transfers can achieve opposite outcomes on each count.

As several of the chapters in this volume show, there are many varieties of intergovernmental spending and revenue systems in existence. They, and the various institutions that surround them, have different and powerful effects on outcomes. In Chapter 5, Grazzi and Jaramillo show that decentralization in Argentina and Brazil in the 1990s was expected to improve public accounts through efficiency gains. What occurred instead was "an explosion of decentralized expenditure and a deterioration of fiscal outcomes." A lack of clarity in the division of responsibilities between central and subnational governments and periodic bailouts created "tragedy of the commons" problems and moral hazards, leading to fiscal debts and severe macroeconomic complications. But since then, decentralization programs have been adjusted to mitigate these problems. Fiscal responsibility laws in Argentina and Brazil have curbed subnational debts by setting limits on subnational spending and borrowing. More stringent accounting rules have increased transparency and control of accounts. And an increase of subnational autonomy to raise own revenues appears to have created incentives for more fiscally responsible behavior.

Much of the decentralization and fiscal federalism literature lays out normative ideals of how intergovernmental tax and transfer systems should be designed in order to bring about the benefits of improved resource allocation, deeper democracy, and increased accountability. But views on what constitute optimal fiscal arrangements, and on which formulae will achieve these goals, differ markedly. Any particular design faces sharp trade-offs, and is bound to generate different sets of winners and losers. There is no consensus about ideal intergovernmental distributions of power and competencies, and there is enormous empirical variation across countries in these arrangements. But this, we hold, is as it should be. There should be no common model. Fiscal arrangements should be carefully tailored to each country's fiscal, political, and economic characteristics, and should be expected to differ as much as the countries do themselves. Research can help by laying out the trade-offs clearly, and analyzing how reformers chose between them in real episodes of reform, and what the consequences were.

1.5 How Does Decentralization Affect Development?

1.5.1 *Decentralization and Governance*

The most common claim made in favor of decentralization, and doubtless the most frequent normative aspiration of reformers, is that it can improve the quality of a nation's governance by taking government "closer to the people." The latter—more a slogan or rubric—can be broken down into three analytical arguments in decentralization's favor. The smaller scale of local government should permit: (1) better information about citizens' needs and wants; (2) greater participation of citizens in selecting, planning, and executing public projects that respond to these needs and wants; and (3) greater accountability of public officials to citizens for their decisions and use of resources. Taken together, these three advantages of decentralized government should lead to a democratic deepening that produces better-quality public goods and more effective government (Faguet, 2014c; Faguet and Wietzke, 2006).

These claims can be tested at two distinct levels: Have government *processes* changed in the ways described above, and are government *outputs* or *outcomes* more efficient or better matched to local needs? This book provides detailed evidence on changes at both levels.

Under which conditions can decentralization improve governance processes? Bossert's empirical evidence leads to specific recommendations for fine-tuning decentralized service provision systems. Evidence from Guatemala and Ghana suggests that better performance could be achieved if inventory control and logistics information systems were centralized, while planning and budgeting was decentralized. Both suggestions have a strong logical base.

Allowing variation in technically rigid functions like inventory control and information system formats is likely to result in poor quality logistics, while local knowledge of needs and finances would strengthen planning and budgeting. Ultimately, Bossert concludes, decision space studies support the idea that it is not so much *whether* policymakers choose to design and implement decentralization, but *how* they do so that matters. Where decision space over particular services was effectively decentralized to local authorities, local capacity and accountability for these services tended to be high. And where all three of these criteria held, health system performance was better than in more centralized cases.

Bardhan et al. report complementary findings in Chapter 13, albeit in a very different research context, from their study of local governments in West Bengal, India. The governance processes they focus on are political participation and awareness by ordinary citizens in rural areas, many of whom are relatively poor. Their objective is to investigate how participation and awareness vary with socioeconomic status, and how this in turn affects the poverty targeting of public services. They find high average levels of political participation in elections, political campaigns, and village meetings, as well as high awareness of programs administered by *gram panchayats* (GPs), the lowest level of local government.[2] They find no evidence of any significant variation in participation rates or awareness with regard to either land ownership or the caste status of households. In particular, neither landless nor low-caste households participate significantly less than others. The main determinants of participation are education, immigrant status, and gender, rather than land or caste.

What effects does the introduction of these decentralized governance processes have on public sector outputs and outcomes? For the health sector, Bossert finds clear and surprising evidence that decentralization has led to increased equity of allocations. Since decentralization, the gaps between the wealthiest municipalities and the poorest in Chile and Colombia have been reduced significantly. This is true both for intergovernmental transfers from the center, and for locally generated tax revenues. Before decentralization, intergovernmental transfers in Colombia favored the wealthiest fifth of municipalities, with six times higher per capita allocations than the mean before decentralization. After decentralization, the application of a population-based formula for allocations resulted in almost equal allocations from central government. While good news, this is less surprising given the Colombian government's stated goals. The real surprise is that the gap in own-source revenues for health also shrank between rich and poor municipalities, from a difference of almost 42 times higher per capita expenditures in the

[2] Each GP has a jurisdiction typically covering 10–15 villages, each of which elects a representative to the GP governing council.

wealthiest municipalities to only 12 times higher. Decentralization seems to have encouraged poorer localities to increase health expenditures, and wealthier localities did not keep pace.

With respect to service outputs, Bossert finds that stronger institutional capacities and broader decision space were associated with both improvements in health coverage and better administration of the health system. These are amongst the few findings that show how capacity-building interventions to improve decentralization at the district level may contribute to improved decision-making abilities, and improved health system performance.

Likewise for the targeting of public benefits, Bardhan et al. find little evidence that public services are distributed in a biased way on the basis of agricultural land ownership, caste, gender, education, or immigrant status within villages in West Bengal. They find no bias in favor of those voting for the majority party, nor for those actively involved in political campaigns. This sums to no evidence that local governments at the lowest level discriminated on the basis of caste, education, political partisanship, or wealth in allocating benefits within villages.

Across villages, however, the story is different. Bardhan et al. find large biases against villages with many landless households, which received fewer benefits from upper-level governments. Villages with greater land inequality allocated significantly lower shares of benefits to households from scheduled castes (SC) and scheduled tribes (ST). These results suggest greater accountability at the lowest level of local governments (GPs), compared with higher-level block or district governments.

The authors also find a tendency to allocate more resources to GPs where the Left Front political coalition was solidly entrenched (i.e., with a two-thirds majority or higher), compared to electorally more competitive GPs. They interpret this as evidence of partisanship in inter-village, as opposed to intra-village, allocations. Lastly, they find that villages with greater levels of *gram sabha*[3] (GS) participation delivered more benefits to landless and SC/ST households; and villages with fewer ST and landless households exhibited higher GS participation. This is consistent with the view that village meetings form a channel of accountability of GPs to poor and low-caste groups.

1.5.2 *Competition Amongst Municipalities*

How can we explain the sorts of changes in governance processes and outputs that Bossert and Bardhan et al. chronicle? Theorists claim that decentralization can improve governance through a variety of channels, some of the most

[3] Broadly, these are town-hall-style village meetings where elected officials must answer questions and account for GP activities to local citizens.

powerful of which are: better information on local needs, greater accountability to citizens (both mentioned above), and competition amongst municipalities for the prestige that attaches to better outcomes (Faguet, 2000, and 2014b; Treisman, 2007; Channa and Faguet, 2012). The former two channels have been researched far more extensively in the literature than the third (Besley and Case, 1995a and 1995b). This book adds to the evidence on municipal competition, both "yardstick competition" and area-based competitions and awards, with careful empirical studies of China and the Philippines.

Many developing country governments suffer weak mechanisms of public accountability. In such a context, can decentralization improve the delivery of public services through yardstick competition? In Chapter 10, Capuno et al. investigate whether a local government's expenditures or revenues from local sources are influenced by the fiscal behavior of its neighboring localities ("yardstick competition"), controlling for the mayor's term limit status. They find some evidence that yardstick competition in the Philippines has the predicted impact.

As in many developing countries, decentralization seems to have entrenched elites in control of local governments in the Philippines. Members of political clans continue to occupy elected local office despite improvements in electoral institutions (e.g. computerized ballot counting) and the institutionalization of a recall system by which officials who have lost voters' confidence can be removed from office. A local government's provision of a range of services, they find, is positively influenced by the mean expenditures on the same services of neighboring municipalities within the province. But this effect is present only when the incumbent mayor is not term-limited. This supports the hypothesis that electoral pressures make local officials responsive to constituents' needs. It also suggests that collecting and publishing standardized, comparable information on the performance of all local governments can influence how voters assess their own local government, through comparisons with others nearby. Interestingly, even members of the Philippines' powerful political clans appear to respond to yardstick-induced electoral pressures. This suggests that political dynasties persist in developing countries because they are substitutes for missing strong parties (de Dios, 2007).

But competition need not be subtle, indirect, or implied. In some countries, competitions amongst municipalities are overt and explicit, and may be more successful in promoting municipal effectiveness and particular policy goals. The Chinese government, for example, has extensive experience with area-based competitions (ABCs) and awards as motivating tools to improve municipal performance and local service provision. They are not alone. As Li and Zhang point out in Chapter 11, such competitions are also common in the UK, the EU, Singapore, and in the regular worldwide competitions to host the Olympic Games and World Cup. Their chapter analyzes the potential of ABCs to motivate local governments to invest in and provide public services, both theoretically and also empirically via the case of Xining City in Qinghai Province, China.

How do ABCs work? Local governments or service providers in different areas compete for prizes offered by regulators or higher authorities. The competitive dynamic transforms the local service provider into a "representative" of the area. Properly crafted, such competitions can boost popular support when the local identification of people living in a certain area increases. Motivation schemes of this kind can potentially reconcile alienated service providers and users, turning users into principals who actively monitor performance and work with providers to achieve shared goals. In this way, the interests of all three parties—the center, local authorities/service providers, and users—are brought into line with one another. ABCs can be focused on a single policy goal, such as GDP growth or educational targets, or a complex menu of goals and targets across different sectors. Li and Zhang examine one of the largest and longest-running ABCs in China: the Hygienic City program—a multidimensional competition that seeks to improve standards in the environment, service sector hygiene, and pest control.

For the case of Xining, they find that local governments, including provincial, city, and district authorities, were all keen for Xining to perform well in the campaign. All prioritized the campaign and spent significant resources on it. There was a striking increase in the number of volunteers from all sectors of society who joined Xining's Hygienic City campaign. This transformed the relationship between citizens and government. Instead of treating the campaign like another government project, the public began to see themselves and their government as members of a single team, and were willing to dedicate time and energy to support the campaign. Because user voice and participation can be the margin between winning and losing competitions, local authorities are more willing than usual to listen to suggestions, and are more open to innovative ideas that can help the city gain advantage. Indeed, ABCs may be an important source of innovation in local government.

But not all was rosy in Xining. In a city that has been almost entirely rebuilt since the 1980s, much of the city's campaign revolved around the demolition of older but functional houses in favor of building brand-new ones. This was done in the name of "city beautification," a concept never well defined by the competition. The danger of such vagueness in the design of a campaign is that beautifying a city can take up resources that could be better spent improving basic services. For a city that is already under-resourced, the costs of a competition such as this can be exceptionally high. Also, the massive increase in the number of competitions across China has placed exhausting burdens on local governments and citizens, meaning they can ultimately become counterproductive. Recognizing this fact, the Chinese central government carried out large-scale crackdowns on ABCs in 1996, and again in 2006 and 2007. In 2007, 1,705 national competitions were cancelled, as well as 90 per cent of competitions organized locally. But since 2007, the number of competitions has crept back up. Li and Zhang conclude that, as predicted by theory, participation in ABCs promotes a great deal of local learning by doing, and hence the educational effects of competitions are very strong.

1.5.3 *Clientelism vs. Development*

Clientelism is a political phenomenon[4] that argues against decentralization through its capacity to distort local government performance. Clientelism is "characterized by the combination of particularistic targeting and contingency-based exchange"[5] in electoral and non-electoral political markets. This is as opposed to political programs based on public investments and policies that promote public goods, universal access, and broad-based development. In some countries and regions clientelism fades away with economic development, but in others it adapts and persists (Hicken, 2011). The threat of clientelism has received much attention in the decentralization literature. But most of the empirical treatment has been qualitative, based on case studies and stylized facts. Amongst the few researchers who have attempted to explore the issue with quantitative data are Bardhan and Mookherjee in a series of studies on the political economy of decentralization (some examples are 1998, 1999, and 2006). In their chapter for this book, they are joined by Sandip Mitra and Abhirup Sarkar in an empirical study that plunges still further into the topic by examining household data from West Bengal.

Their findings are nuanced and detailed, yet provocative. The likelihood of voting for the Left Front coalition is correlated with the benefits received under previous Left Front-dominated local governments. But rather than infrastructure improvements or one-off benefits, it is recurring short-term benefits that affect voting patterns. Improvements in agricultural land ownership mattered, while improvements in income or housing did not. Emergency help provided by Left Front *gram panchayats* (GPs) in the past—classic symptoms of clientelism—were significant determinants of voting in favor of the Left Front. Controlling for these factors and other personal characteristics, poorer and SC/ST groups within a village were more inclined to vote in favor of the Left Front. Left Front support was also greater in areas with more agricultural workers.

These findings support the hypothesis that the continued Left Front domination of local governments in West Bengal over five successive electoral cycles is partly due to the dispensation of recurring short-term benefits

[4] Related to, but analytically distinct from, elite capture.
[5] Hicken, p. 289.

(e.g. subsidized credit, agricultural minikits, employment, and relief programs) by Left-dominated GPs to poorer voters. Personalized, short-term benefits of this type had a stronger effect on voter support than infrastructure improvements or more substantial one-off benefits, such as registering a tenancy contract or receiving a land title. Interestingly, this also explains why the Left Front's fortunes in local elections have been declining in recent years. Agricultural land ownership and occupations are in long-term decline due to rising population pressure, stagnation in agricultural yields, and increasing urbanization. At the same time, the awareness and aspirations of citizens have been raised through improving education and living standards, reducing their vulnerability to personal shocks and their subsequent dependence on local governments for emergency help.

This implies that, in the short term, clientelistic appeals based on targeted benefits are electorally more effective than universalistic, long-term development investments and policies. Such a dynamic can slow down a society's long-term development by restraining a certain class of public policy and public goods production. But the evidence from West Bengal also implies that it is unlikely to stop it entirely. In the long term, deeper development trends, including improvements in human development indicators related to improving education and health, will tend to undermine a clientelistic party's electoral support. In this sense, it may be important that there is no evidence that supporters of rival parties were excluded from benefits, nor of favoritism towards active political campaigners.

1.5.4 *Strengthening the State*

Perhaps the greatest fear about decentralization is that it will weaken the state and promote separatism in a diverse country, undermining national identity and making it more likely to break apart. The key question in this debate, Faguet, Fox, and Pöschl stress, is: Will decentralization stoke centripetal or centrifugal forces? Will reform empower those who seek secession, giving them a podium and a chance to demonstrate competence? Or will it peel away more moderate layers of support that can be assuaged with autonomy-type reforms like local control of primary services, minority language rights, etc., so isolating the hard secessionist core from their previous constituency?

Analyzing this question empirically is difficult, as the variables in question are not easy to see. In practice a more indirect analysis may in any event be more useful, as the determining factors are likely to be the regional specificity of elite interests. If coherent regional elites (1) exist in a particular country, and (2) have more to gain from secession (i.e. greater control over resources at the cost of lost markets and lost influence) than autonomy (i.e. partial control over resources, continued access to national markets and policy-making), then national disintegration is far more likely. The authors' question thus morphs into: When will regional elites have incentives to invest in candidates, parties, and social movements, infrastructure, and programs that promote either national breakup or national unity? Examples of the former include politicians who campaign on regionalist pride and secession, and exclusive local language and culture programs. Examples of the latter include improving transport and communication links to the rest of the country, and national educational and cultural programs built on shared elements of history and identity.

Answers to these questions will vary as according to countries' historic, demographic, and other characteristics. Very little systematic advice can be given on this score beyond stressing that reformers must take careful account of these factors before designing or attempting decentralization in any particular place. Shifting power and resources downward by definition implies a shock to the power balance between interstate actors and institutions. It may disrupt existing political settlements between elites; it may decide the demise or survival of a political party in power at the center; or alter the power of separatist groups threatening to dissolve a country. And it will inevitably create winners and losers in the population, including between regions and between different levels of government. These are the risks that reformers face when they decentralize, and hence reforms that promise one kind of shift of power and resources often accomplish a different kind of shift, or none.

But where the design of reform is concerned, such risks can be built into a reform program in a way that tends to hold fractious groups together rather than promoting secession; and this leads to much more general policy advice. Reforms tending to exacerbate regional tensions are those that limit themselves to the spatial confines of those tensions—i.e. decentralizations to administrative units that coincide with a country's major ethnic, linguistic, or other fractures.

Reforms that transcend these boundaries and ways of thinking, on the other hand, underpin unity. By decentralizing power and authority to a level beneath that of a country's major cleavage—e.g. to municipalities rather than provinces—empowered subnational units will tend not to be identified with group identity or privilege. Local government will become identified with issues of efficiency and service provision instead of divisive tensions. Reformers can go further, too, with complementary reforms that promote a single market for goods and services nationwide, thus helping prevent the development of elites with regionally specific economic interests who might gain from secession. This implies binding a country together "from the bottom up" through improved infrastructure and transport links, which will additionally tend to promote economic growth. Faguet, Fox, and Pöschl provide examples from Ethiopia, Canada, Spain, Bolivia, Afghanistan, and Iraq.

Another version of this debate contrasts the presumed strength of purpose and reach of a centralized state with the smaller reach and greater chance of contradiction when policy is made by many decentralized units. Against these claims, proponents of decentralization counter that a decentralized state will be more sensitive and responsive to local needs and conditions, leading to more appropriate, better quality public goods and services. This debate has for years stagnated at a theoretical level, with anecdotal or partial empirical evidence supporting one or another claim without general effect. Faguet, Fox, and Pöschl cut through this impasse in Chapter 6 by pointing out that, in fact, both claims are true. It is wrong to view decentralization as a simplistic choice between "strong" centralized government vs. "weak" decentralized government. The correct dichotomy contrasts: (a) a centralized command structure that is simpler and cleaner, but ultimately more brittle in the sense of being susceptible to failure in any of its parts, which will tend to lead to government failure, on one hand, with (b) a system that is more complex and based on more actors with independent sources of overlapping authority, where coordination and cooperation are far more important than command and control for the system as a whole to operate well.

A starker way of conceptualizing these issues is in politically personal terms, as a trade-off between the strength of a national leader and the strength of the state as institution. Under centralization, the leader has more discretion, her power is greater, and she can effect more, faster changes to public policy and organizations. The leader is stronger at the expense of the state. But where her discretion is circumscribed by rules, procedure, and the need to agree decisions with other independent actors before proceeding, then the state is stronger and more stable at the expense of the leader. By empowering subnational leaders and requiring a measure of consensus between them and the center for policy-making to proceed, decentralization sacrifices central leaders' authority and autonomy in the interests of increasing the institutional strength of the state as a whole.

A separate aspect of this argument that lacks theoretical subtlety, but in practice is quite important, concerns the extension of government in its local form to large areas of a developing country that previously lacked it. In centralized states, local government structures are often non-existent. The central administration is far away, and ordinary citizens have little experience of elections, accountable public authorities, or public decision-taking of any form. Exposure to new local governments can strengthen the state by expanding its presence, thereby improving the perception of state responsiveness and enhancing the legitimacy of national governments.

Another dimension of the state strengthening/weakening debate concerns decentralization's effects on political party systems. Ruling parties may use reform as a means to fragment the opposition and keep authoritarian parties in power (Sabatini, 2003). But the more important effects of reform, Cheema, Khan, and Myerson point out, are likely to go in the opposite direction, strengthening parties and the party system. In Pakistan, for example, President Musharraf's 2001 reform increased the number of popularly elected representatives by nearly 80,000—mostly at union council level, the lowest tier of government—and provided many more reserved seats for peasants and women. In a competitive party system where local candidates represent local chapters of national political parties, the election of such local leaders should contribute to the strength of the parties and the strength of the democratic system. But this effect is lost when national parties are disconnected from local government, as happened in Pakistan, where parties were banned from local politics. There, democratic competition to improve local government was weakened, and barriers to entry in provincial and federal politics were raised. It would be much more difficult for a future military ruler to displace elected politicians, Cheema, Khan, and Myerson observe, if their political organizations extended into local politics.

This is because what decentralization really does, as Faguet, Fox, and Pöschl argue, is to transform politics from an arena that is by definition national, top-down, and hence subject to oligopolization by a socio-economic elite based in a few powerful cities, to a "meta-arena" embracing many specific regional and local arenas, where pressing local concerns are taken up and addressed, or not, by local politicians and the parties they choose to join. Countries as diverse as Bolivia, Colombia, India, and the UK offer clear examples of political-systemic transformations along these lines following decentralization reforms. What can appear as a fragmentation of political forms in the short run should instead be viewed as the integration of constituencies and interests from the grass roots upwards in the long run.

But what about the threat of elite capture? The possibility that powerful individuals or interests will weaken the state by capturing local governments and distorting policy is one of the longest-standing, most theoretically robust arguments against decentralization. It is also a real threat, observed in regional and local governments across the world (Bardhan and Mookherjee, 1999; Treisman, 2007). Indeed, some decentralizations appear designed to facilitate political capture—by central authorities. In Chapter 9, Khemani offers a theoretical model of how this can work, plus some empirical examples. She argues that by dividing jurisdictions and creating small local governments that are highly dependent on central government grants (through expenditure decentralization without corresponding tax decentralization), the central government exerts power and control and keeps its party in power. When subnational governments depend on its grants, the central government can decide where funds are targeted. And it can target them for benefits to specific groups in exchange for political power (through patronage, vote-buying, and pork barrel projects) at the expense of broader public goods. Such a system goes beyond the "partial decentralization" described above, and might be termed "cynical decentralization."

Without doubt, arguments about capture have much merit. But by focusing on capture of local governments, which completely dominates this literature, its advocates underplay the comparative threat that elite capture poses at the *national* level. Hacker and Pierson (2011) show that the much greater rewards from distorting central policy-making lead the richest interest groups to invest enormous sums in capturing national government, with potentially deleterious effects for an entire nation, not least because the distortions introduced by local capture may still be attenuated or overturned by national government institutions and policies. But what combination of subnational governments will counteract a central government that is captured? Elite capture is a real threat. But it is a threat for all kinds and levels of government. It is a threat neither specific to nor more dangerous for decentralized government.

We come last to the issue of social learning. "Social learning" refers to the collective acquisition of knowledge, norms and practices, and trust that occurs amongst groups of voters organized by geography or issue areas of their concern. It is social because it necessarily concerns shared values, beliefs, and behaviors; the knowledge in question concerns cooperation and group-wise maximization, as opposed to individual maximization.

Social learning is intrinsically a learning-by-doing phenomenon, Faguet, Fox, and Pöschl argue, and hence relies on direct interactions amongst citizens. Unlike central government, local government provides ordinary citizens with real access to repeated interactions on matters of public policy and resources, both directly with local government per se, and indirectly through civic organizations that debate positions and compete with firms, other interests, and each other to influence policy. Either individually or through their civic organizations, the small scale of local politics allows citizens to become political actors themselves. Decentralized government accelerates social learning over time in a way that centralized government does not and, for the most part, cannot.

The key issue is scale. Scale is determinant and its effects are non-linear. The large scale of central government demands disproportionately greater resources and levels of organization than local government does for effective engagement. Therefore the experience of participation and engagement with public decision-making abounds in government in its decentralized, but not centralized, form. And so experience accrues and learning occurs amongst individual voters and their small-scale collectives (e.g. civic groups, local lobbies) in local government, as opposed to think tanks, professional lobby firms, and peak associations in central government. Participation in local government leads naturally to collective learning around narrow questions of effectiveness, but also higher-order issues like fellow citizens' needs, resource constraints, and the multiplicative effects of public as opposed to private action for certain classes of problems.

Local governments can thus promote political legitimacy and long-term state-building from the grass roots upward in a way that centralized government cannot. According to Faguet, Fox, and Pöschl, decentralization can make the state more "democratically supple," in the sense of the greater degree of organization that decentralization catalyzes in society, by providing strong incentives for group formation and for organizational effectiveness.

1.6 Conclusion

The academic and policy literatures on decentralization and local government abound in studies of decentralization. Initially based mainly on qualitative evidence and case study, this research has become more quantitative and formal over the past two decades. But as sample sizes have multiplied and methods become more technical, the focus of research has narrowed ever further to decentralization's effects on any number of policy variables, X_1, X_2, X_3, etc., leaving aside issues of crucial importance to policy makers contemplating real reforms, such as: How can decentralization be made politically feasible? Does decentralization improve governance? Do municipalities compete amongst themselves and what effects might this have on public policy and services? Will reform promote clientelism or broad-based development? How can decentralization be used to strengthen or weaken the state? Real-world reformers need to know the answers to some, if not all, of these questions before estimating the efficiency gains that decentralization might provide in specific policy areas. A reform that undermines a president's political party, or is likely to lead to national break-up, is stillborn regardless of the efficiency gains it may promise.

This book seeks to return attention to such large, nuanced, complex questions that rank among policy makers' firsts concerns, but are methodologically difficult to answer. We do this by marrying the views, insights, and experience of very senior policy makers involved in driving decentralization forward at the highest levels with academics working at the forefront of the field in economics, politics, and development and policy studies. The insights gathered here are the product of a five-year collaboration that began with a conference sponsored by the Initiative for Policy Dialogue at Columbia University, and culminates in this book.

Before addressing feasibility or governance we must answer a more basic question: Why does anyone decentralize? If we take the tenets of modern social science seriously, then we must admit that giving away power and resources to people you cannot control, some of whom are likely to be your opponents, is an absurd thing to do. And yet reform appears to be happening all over the world. What are we to make of this? Why does reform happen anywhere? In Bolivia, a much-cited example of radical reform, the answer is the confluence of an urgent short-term political problem that decentralization was able to solve, with a deeper conviction that the country's many failings and challenges required a fundamental redistribution of power in the Bolivian polity, from the heights of La Paz down to the people in the towns and villages where they lived.

Are both these elements necessary and sufficient to push through sincere reform? We cannot tell from a single case study. But the tactical difficulties—and sheer improbability—of devolving power anywhere suggest that both are required. A comparison with Pakistan strengthens the argument. Here, decentralization solved the short-term problem of legitimizing military rule by undermining established political parties. But this came at the cost of poisoning decentralization in the eyes of those parties, and in the absence of any longer-term vision of governance and development in Pakistan. Hence, whereas Bolivia's successive governments deepened and strengthened reform, Pakistan's return to democracy saw parties close down local governments and recentralize power.

Was the Bolivian President right to try to improve governance through decentralization? This book provides new, empirically rich, nuanced evidence that sheds light on this question. Across a range of countries in Africa, Asia, and Latin America, Bossert shows that the dimensions of "decision space"—essentially local discretion over resources and actions—tend to go together. Where decision space over, say, health services was effectively decentralized to local authorities, local accountability and capacity for health tended to be high. Where all three of these criteria held, health system performance was higher than in more centralized cases. Along broadly similar lines, Bardhan et al. examine the political participation of rural dwellers in West Bengal, and find high mobilization in political campaigns, elections, and village meetings, as well as high awareness of programs administered by low-level GP administrations.

Focusing on Latin America, Grazzi and Jaramillo show that decentralization initially led to a sharp deterioration of fiscal deficits via an explosion of subnational expenditure. Since then, however, fiscal accountability laws, more stringent accounting rules, and greater subnational tax-raising powers have changed subnational officials' incentives, leading to much more fiscally responsible behavior across the region. Pöschl and Weingast provide a more general analysis of how the design of tax and transfer formulas can provide incentives for subnational leaders to collect taxes, in turn incentivizing local officials to improve fiscal discipline, increase engagement with citizens, and improve accountability.

Changing governance processes can change incentives, and thus behaviors, up and down the system, with powerful effects on fiscal outcomes. But does this change substantive outcomes as well? Across a large range of countries and regions, Bossert says yes. In one of the first studies of its kind, he finds that broader decision space and stronger institutional capacities led to improvements in health coverage and better health system administration. In a similar vein, Bardhan et al. find that high levels of political participation led to greater accountability at the lowest level of government, with little evidence of discrimination based on caste, education, political partisanship, or wealth, in the allocation of public benefits. It is striking that this does not hold *across* villages, however, suggesting that the benefits of mobilization and participation were locally specific, and higher levels of policy-making suffered some sort of distortion or capture.

All of these results underline the fundamental point that it is not *whether* a country decentralizes, but *how* it decentralizes that matters. Shifting power and resources downwards implies a shock to the power balance between interests, actors, and institutions. It is likely to upset political and economic equilibria amongst elites that may be long-standing or hard-fought; it is likely to weaken or kill off particular parties, and end the careers of specific politicians who thrived under the previous dispensation; and it may fuel movements or groups who seek to break up the country. For good reason, politicians fear change of this nature, implying that such reforms, even once approved, will be continuously revised and renegotiated as they are implemented. Hence reforms designed according to one set of criteria often achieve very different objectives, or simply fizzle out. The many cases of partial decentralization across the world noted by Devarajan et al. (2009) are probably explained by such dynamics.

The larger lesson that reformers should take away is that the benefits of decentralization are achievable but never guaranteed. To succeed, decentralization must be implemented as sincerely as possible, and subsequently modified and recalibrated based on initial results, once the new incentives created by changes in rules and structures have played themselves out in practice. The ultimate effects of any multidimensional, complex institutional reform are impossible to predict with any accuracy, and this is especially true of decentralization. Decentralization is not a panacea. It is a process, and usually a long and detailed one, that requires sustained attention to get right.

If decentralization is associated with local-level learning-by-doing in China, improving fiscal governance in Latin America, fiscal stability and growth in China, and improved health system performance across three continents, how are we to understand the continued domination of local governments over five successive electoral cycles by the Left Front in West Bengal? This seems at odds with an emerging picture of reform that can improve citizen participation and learning, and systemic stability, across many countries. Bardhan et al. find the answer in the dispensation of personalized, recurring, short-term benefits by Left-dominated local governments to poorer voters. Clientelistic benefits of this type proved electorally more potent than longer-term public investments, such as infrastructure, or more substantial one-off benefits that were highly personalized.

Clientelism is bad news for those who hope decentralization can improve governance and lead to better development outcomes. But Bardhan et al.'s findings also highlight the continued decline of the Left Front in these same districts due to longer-term trends such as urbanization, the decline of the agricultural sector, and improving health and education standards, all of which conspire to reduce the susceptibility of the poor to electoral appeals based on small, personalized transfers. So while decentralized clientelism can restrain public investment in the sorts of public goods that promote development over the medium term, longer-term changes in many developing societies will naturally limit its electoral appeal, and hence its practice.

Perhaps the biggest question reformers face is: Will decentralization undermine national unity and promote separatism, or can it be used to further integrate the sorts of diverse societies and economies typical of so many developing countries? The question is best framed this way: Will decentralization promote stability and national integration by peeling moderate layers of political support away from secessionist movements with reforms like minority language rights and control over local education and health care, etc? Or will it add fuel to the separatist fire by providing firebrands with a platform and opportunity to show competence?

In practice the issue morphs into a question of the incentives and behaviors of regional elites. Where regional elites have incentives to invest in candidates, infrastructure, parties and social movements, and programs that promote national break-up, reform can interact with national fissures in a dangerous way. But where regional elites tend to invest in further integration, decentralization can actually strengthen the state by strengthening legitimacy and improving public sector outputs at both the center and periphery simultaneously. The key consideration, not surprisingly, is the type of decentralization implemented. Reforms, the architecture of which closely follows a country's main cleavages (e.g. to regions dominated by different ethnic groups), make break-up more likely by exacerbating its deepest tensions. By contrast, reforms that transcend these cleavages underpin unity instead. Consider the Bolivian example. By decentralizing power and authority to a level beneath that of the country's major cleavage—to municipalities rather than departments, reform undercut the divisive power of regional elites. The local governments so empowered became identified not with group identity or privilege, but rather with issues of efficiency and service provision. This helped to steer political competition away from zero-sum conflicts over the distribution of fiscal resources, towards positive-sum negotiations about public investment and service provision. In so doing, it helped bind the country together "from the bottom up" through improved infrastructure and faster economic growth.

Decentralization should not be viewed as a one-dimensional choice between a multi-tiered system of government that is "weak" vs. a unitary hierarchy that is "strong." A more accurate, analytically grounded dichotomy instead contrasts: (a) a more complex system based on independent actors with overlapping authority and separate information flows, where coordination and cooperation displace command and control as key operating modes, with (b) a simple, clean, centralized command structure that is ultimately brittle in that it lacks internal complementarities and redundancies, and so is susceptible to failure in any of its parts. While the latter is likely to take faster decisions, the former is likely to take better-informed, more accountable ones.

A starker way of conceptualizing of these issues is as a trade-off between the strength of political leaders versus the institutional strength of the state. Under centralization, the leader is strong at the expense of the state. Under decentralization, her discretion is circumscribed by procedure, rules, and the need to agree decisions with other independent actors. The state is stronger and more stable at the expense of the leader.

One important way in which sincere decentralization does this is by transforming politics from a top-down activity subject to oligopolization by a socio-economic elite, to a bottom-up system of representation where pressing local concerns are taken up and addressed by local politicians and parties. This changes the nature of political competition in a country, and very likely the nature of political organizations most likely to prosper. Parties structured to win in a narrow, oligopolized national politics are likely to be ill-suited to the broader, bottom-up politics of decentralization.

Many reforming politicians and parties seem not to understand this point. Others, however, probably do, and so design "cynical decentralizations" that create small local governments dependent on the center for resources. This facilitates continued central control over decision-making via the capture of local administrations not by local elites, but by the center.

The final way in which decentralization can strengthen the state is subtle but powerful, especially over the longer term. We call this "social learning"—the accretion of collective knowledge, norms, practices, and trust by groups of voters. Because social learning is intrinsically a learning-by-doing phenomenon, direct interaction amongst citizens is required for it to happen. The small scale of local politics encourages participation and allows citizens to become political actors either individually or through civic organizations. Local governments thus catalyze social learning in a way that centralized government not only does not, but, to a great extent, cannot.

Over time the dynamic of decentralized government provides strong incentives for group formation and for organizational effectiveness in civil society. It does so indirectly for the state as well, as the state is forced to respond to increasingly mobilized civic groups. The state thus becomes more "democratically supple" as the number of intermediating organizations and the density of their social interactions increase, in the sense of becoming more legitimate through greater responsiveness to society's needs. Social learning can also play a role in the deeper transformation of clientelistic politics into broad-based pro-development politics. Clientelism is a kind of divide-and-conquer strategy on the part of parties against voters' collective public interests. By making citizens see their common interests from the grass roots upwards, and teaching them to organize and cooperate, social learning can help transform clientelistic politics into policies and actions that drive development forward.

References

Bardhan, P. and D. Mookherjee (eds.), 2006. *Decentralization and Local Governance in Developing Countries: A Comparative Perspective*. Cambridge, Mass.: MIT Press.

Bardhan, P. and D. Mookherjee, 1998. "Expenditure Decentralization and the Delivery of Public Services in Developing Countries." Working Paper No. C98-104. Berkeley: Center for International and Development Economics Research.

Bardhan, P. and D. Mookherjee, 1999. "Relative Capture of Local and Central Governments: An Essay in the Political Economy of Decentralization." Berkeley: Manuscript.

Besley, T. and A. Case, 1995a. "Does Electoral Accountability Affect Economic Policy Choices? Evidence from Gubernatorial Term Limits." *Quarterly Journal of Economics*, 110: 769–98.

Besley, T. and A. Case, 1995b. "Incumbent Behavior: Vote-Seeking, Tax-Setting, and Yardstick Competition." *American Economic Review*, 85: 25–45.

Bird, R. M. and M. Smart, 2010. "Assigning State Taxes in a Federal Country: The Case of Australia," in Melbourne Institute, *Australia's Future Tax and Transfer Policy Conference* (Melbourne: Melbourne Institute of Applied Economic and Social Research, 2010), 72–94.

Channa, A. and J.P. Faguet, 2012. "Decentralization of Health and Education in Developing Countries: A Quality-Adjusted Review of the Empirical Literature." LSE/STICERD Working Paper No. EOPP 38.

De Dios, E. S., 2007. 'Local Politics and Local Economy', in: Balisacan, A.M., and Hill, H. (eds.), *The Dynamics of Regional Development: The Philippines in East Asia*. Cheltenham: Edward Elgar, 157–203.

Devarajan, S., S. Shah, and S. Khemani, 2009. "The Politics of Partial Decentralization." In E. Ahmad and G. Brosio (eds.), *Does Decentralization Enhance Service Delivery and Poverty Reduction?* Cheltenham: Edward Elgar.

Faguet, J. P. (ed.), 2014a. "Decentralization and Governance." Special issue of *World Development*, 53: 1–112.

Faguet, J.P., 2014b. "Can Sub-National Autonomy Strengthen Democracy in Bolivia?" *Publius: The Journal of Federalism*, 44(1): 51–81. doi: 10.1093/publius/pjt020.

Faguet, J.P., 2014c. "Decentralization and Governance." *World Development*, 53: 2–13.

Faguet, J.P., 2012. *Decentralization and Popular Democracy: Governance from Below in Bolivia*. Ann Arbor: University of Michigan Press.

Faguet, J.P., 2004. "Why So Much Centralization? A Model of Primitive Centripetal Accumulation." STICERD DEDPS No.43, London School of Economics.

Faguet, J.P., 2000. "Decentralization and Local Government Performance: Improving Public Service Provision in Bolivia," *Revista de Economía del Rosario*, 3(1): 127–76.

Faguet, J.P. and F. Sánchez, 2013. "Decentralization and Access to Social Services in Colombia." *Public Choice*. DOI 10.1007/s11127-013-0077-7.

Faguet, J.P. and M. Shami, 2008. "Fiscal Policy and Spatial Inequality in Latin America and Beyond." World Bank Policy Research Working Paper.

Faguet, J.P. and F.B. Wietzke, 2006. "Social Funds and Decentralization: Optimal Institutional Design." *Public Administration and Development*, 26(4): 303–15.

Green, E., 2011. "Decentralization and political opposition in contemporary Africa: evidence from Sudan and Ethiopia." *Democratization*, 18:5, 1087–105.

Hacker, J.S. and P. Pierson, 2011. *Winner-Take-All Politics: How Washington Made the Rich Richer—and Turned Its Back on the Middle Class*. New York: Simon & Schuster.

Hicken, A., 2011. "Clientelism." *Annual Review of Political Science*, 14: 289–310. DOI: 10.1146/annurev.polisci.031908.220508.

Manor, J., 1999. *The Political Economy of Democratic Decentralization*. Washington, DC: The World Bank.

Montero, A. P. and Samuels, D. J., (eds.). 2004. *Decentralization and Democracy in Latin America*. Notre Dame, Ind.: University of Notre Dame Press.

Moore, M., 2007. "How Does Taxation Affect the Quality of Governance?" IDS Working Paper 280. Brighton: Institute of Development Studies.

Ostrom, E., L. Schroeder, and S. Wynne, 1993. *Institutional Incentives and Sustainable Development: Infrastructure Policies in Perspective*. Boulder: Westview Press.

Rao, M. G. and R. M. Bird, 2011. "Coping with Change: The Need to Restructure Urban Governance and Finance in India." IMFG Paper No. 4, University of Toronto.

Sabatini, C., (2003). "Decentralization and Political Parties." *Journal of Democracy*, 14(2): 138–50.

Treisman, D., 2007. *The Architecture of Government: Rethinking Political Decentralization*. New York: Cambridge University Press.

Part I

Decentralization, Stability, and the Strengthening of the State

2

"Why I Decentralized Bolivia"

Gonzalo Sánchez de Lozada and Jean-Paul Faguet

2.1 Introduction

Why would any president, having spent a career achieving the pinnacle of power, willingly hand it over to others he cannot control?[1] This is the black hole at the heart of the decentralization debate that few address and none have satisfyingly answered (Faguet, 2004; Faguet, 2012). Strictly speaking, the urge to decentralize is irrational in those who must, by definition, do it. Are presidents motivated by normative arguments about state effectiveness? Is decentralization politically convenient? Can politicians be altruistic? Are there really philosopher kings?

This chapter attempts to answer these questions for the case of Bolivia, one of the most radical and well-known of decentralization reforming countries (Faguet, 2000). Our attempt takes the form of an extended interview between an academic researcher and the former President of Bolivia whose government designed and implemented reform. We begin with Bolivia's long-term historical trajectory, which created its rich, complicated social and political tapestry, and then home in on the formative experiences and political transformation of Gonzalo Sánchez de Lozada, the man who decentralized Bolivia.

The arid *altiplano* highlands of western Bolivia have long been home to ancient civilizations. Prior to the Inca conquest of the fifteenth century, the most important of these was probably the Tiahuanaco culture, centered on a small town of the same name just south of Lake Titicaca. From about 100 AD

[1] Based on interviews conducted on 31 March–1 April 2011 in Washington, DC. The authors are very grateful to Mauricio Balcázar for making the interviews possible, and to Drucilla Daley-Nelson and Susan Redgrave for interview transcriptions.

onwards, Tiahuanaco developed a strong religious, artistic, and agro-economic presence whose influence spread throughout the entire southern *altiplano* (Klein, 2003). Its distinctive pottery, religious artifacts, and important agricultural innovations, such as mountain terracing, complex irrigation, and the characteristic *suka kollus* (flooded-raised field) agriculture, which insulated crops from the cold and dramatically increased yields, spread far north and south to what are modern-day Peru, Chile, and Argentina.

A marked fall in precipitation around 1000 AD, and possibly a severe drought, appear to have led to the collapse of Tiahuanaco. By the mid-fifteenth century, Incas entering the region from the north recorded only remnants of Tiahuanaco amongst the wealthy, warlike, Aymara-speaking kingdoms of the *altiplano*. The Incas were a Quechua-speaking power centered on Cuzco (now Peru), who absorbed disparate peoples, cultures, and religions into a heterogeneous empire governed by a sophisticated administrative apparatus. They were an absolute monarchy and a vast empire, spanning most of South America's Pacific coast. But civil war, the resentment of many of the conquered, and the devastating effects of European diseases weakened the empire to the point where, in 1532, fewer than two hundred Spaniards fighting with firearms, cannon, and a few dozen horses were able to defeat a vast empire and an army numbering in the tens of thousands.

Spanish colonists came to Bolivia to exploit its enormous mineral wealth, and—in smaller numbers—to convert its indigenous peoples to Christianity. Many colonizers were rapacious, and the two-tiered society that grew out of conquest featured extreme levels of oppression, inequality, and exploitation. Spaniards and their descendants inhabited the towns and cities, and owned the mines and large landed estates. Indigenous peasants lived in villages and were forced to pay tribute and work the land and mines of their foreign overlords. This social and economic order was largely inherited by the republic after independence in 1825. It broadly endured for a further 125 years, with mining wealth becoming more and more concentrated in fewer and fewer hands. By 1950, Bolivia was a backward country mired in poverty, and presided over by a "typical racist state in which the non-Spanish-speaking indigenous peasantry was controlled by a small, Spanish-speaking white elite, [their power] based ultimately on violence more than consensus or any social pact" (Klein, 1993). The persistence of extreme poverty and inequality is striking. Bolivia's GDP per capita of only $119 in 1952 (Dunkerley, 1984) was highly unevenly distributed; most Bolivians lived in poor agricultural communities, while a tiny proportion of mining and landowning families controlled vast wealth. Only 8 per cent of Bolivia's population had finished secondary school, and only 31 per cent could read. Nearly one-third of all children died before their first birthday, and most who survived died well before 50 (Dunkerley, 1984).

The 1952–3 revolution set out to change all this. The middle-class revolutionaries of the *Movimiento Nacionalista Revolucionario* (National Revolutionary Movement, MNR) raided army weapons stores, armed workers and peasants, and led a popular uprising against the oligarchical regime and its *superestado minero* (mining superstate). They won a crushing victory, and then mounted a concerted effort to reorganize the country's economic and social relations. Their preferred instrument was a highly centralized, interventionist state. They destroyed the *superestado minero* by nationalizing the mines and other strategic sectors, and attacked the broader oligarchy by seizing its lands and redistributing them to the peasantry. Once the "commanding heights" of the economy were in its control, the MNR launched Bolivia on a state-led modernization strategy that used public corporations and regional governments to break down provincial fiefdoms, transform social relations, and create a modern, industrial, more egalitarian society. To this end the President directly named prefects, who in turn appointed entire regional governments and their various local dependencies, forming a cascading chain of authority that emanated from the capital.

The many coups and political uprisings that intervened between 1953 and my arrival in Bolivia in 1991 did little to change this defining characteristic of centralized, top-down rule. When I arrived in August of that year, Bolivia had some 100 legally incorporated municipalities, of which maybe 30 existed in any operational sense. The rest had perhaps an honorary mayor who presided over the town's annual festival and occasionally inaugurated a new school, but enjoyed no salary, budget, offices, or staff. Local decisions of any consequence were taken by central government in La Paz, or its representatives in one of Bolivia's nine departmental capitals. The few officials who resided beyond the regional capitals were implementing agents with small budgets and little discretion. Even minor decisions concerning local schools and clinics were the responsibility of central education and health officers, to whom local residents appealed from a distance, if at all.

Hence decentralization via the Law of Popular Participation (1994) was an unexpected shock that almost no one at first understood. The core of the law consisted of four points (Secretaría Nacional de Participación Popular, 1994):

1. *Resource Allocation*. Revenue sharing to municipalities[2] doubled to 20 per cent of all national tax revenue. Crucially, allocation switched from unsystematic, highly political criteria to a strict per capita basis.

[2] Strictly speaking, to "provincial municipal sections," which are territorial subdivisions of provinces that unite various municipalities having geographical and historical ties, such as "counties" in the US and "*comarcas*" in Spain.

2. *Responsibility for Public Services*. Ownership of local infrastructure in education, health, irrigation, roads, sports and culture, and water and sanitation was transferred to municipalities, along with the responsibility to maintain and extend these networks. Staffing and salary issues remained central responsibilities.
3. *Oversight Committees* (OCs; *Comités de Vigilancia*) were established to oversee municipal activities. Composed of representatives from grassroots groups, OCs propose projects and provide a parallel channel of representation in local policy-making. Their ability to have central transfers suspended gives them real power.
4. *Municipalization*. 198 dormant municipalities (out of 311 in total) were reactivated, and the borders of existing municipalities were expanded to include suburbs and rural catchment areas.

The change in local affairs produced by these measures was immense. Before reform, most Bolivians, and the vast majority of Bolivian territory, had no local government of any description, and the broader state was present—if at all—in the form of a health post, schoolhouse, or military garrison, each reporting to its respective ministry. After reform, elected local governments sprang up throughout the land.

As Faguet (2012) has shown, the effects on public investment and public services were dramatic. Decentralization shifted public investment from infrastructure and economic production (e.g. hydrocarbons, transportation, energy) into primary social services and human capital accumulation (e.g. education, health, water and sanitation). Smaller, poorer, rural municipalities—largely ignored since Bolivian independence—gained significant resources, producing a much more equitable distribution of resources across Bolivia's territory. Lastly and most impressively, decentralization made public investment much more responsive to objective local needs than it had been before, under centralized government. Whereas central government had invested more in education and health in wealthier cities where indicators of need were lower, local governments invested resources where they were needed more. Hence municipalities with lower literacy began to get more education investment, and those with worse access to sanitation received more investment in water and sewerage. This marked a reversal of central government's previous practices, which was to concentrate investments in districts already better off. The largest beneficiaries were Bolivia's smaller, poorer, more rural districts. The trends described are strong and hold across the universe of Bolivian municipalities.[3]

[3] Such trends hold across a broad range of countries as well. See Channa and Faguet (2012) for a survey of international effects on education and health; Faguet and Shami (2008) analyze decentralization's effects on spatial inequality.

Who is the man who pushed through these reforms? In many ways Gonzalo Sánchez de Lozada is a highly improbable politician and statesman. The son of political exiles, he was educated in the United States, studying philosophy at the University of Chicago. To this day he speaks Spanish with an obvious American accent, which he deploys to comic effect. His acid wit won him friends and enemies in equal measure throughout his career. His rivals admit that he is an intelligent, creative politician, as bold as he is stubborn. He is also a highly successful entrepreneur who, with his brother, built up one of the country's largest private mining companies and became one of Bolivia's richest men.

He came to prominence as the Minister of Planning and Coordination who mapped out Bolivia's return from hyperinflation and the brink of economic disaster in 1985–6, with the help of Jeffrey Sachs, then of Harvard University. Sánchez de Lozada went on to head the MNR ticket in the 1989 election and won a plurality of the popular vote. But he was denied the presidency by an alliance of the second- and third-place finishers, General Hugo Banzer of the ADN (*Acción Democrática Nacionalista,* Nationalist Democratic Action), and Jaime Paz Zamora of the MIR (*Movimiento de Izquierda Revolucionaria,* Leftist Revolutionary Movement). This alliance of the left- and right-most of the major parties was made further improbable by the fact that Gen. Banzer's dictatorship had persecuted and killed many MIR activists in the 1970s. "A river of blood divides the MIR from the ADN," Paz Zamora had famously declared. But when Sánchez de Lozada won the election, the ex-dictator and the ex-Marxist found a way to work together, and Paz Zamora became president.

Four years later Sánchez de Lozada ran again, won more votes, and this time his opponents could not stop him. In alliance with the populist UCS (*Unión Cívica de Solidaridad,* Civic Solidarity Union) and the intellectual left-wing MBL (*Movimiento Bolivia Libre,* Free Bolivia Movement), amongst others, he set about implementing his *Plan de Todos* (Plan for All), a strikingly ambitious set of reforms that had five major planks: privatization of state-owned enterprises via "capitalization" (i.e. sales proceeds were reinvested in 50/50 joint ventures with strategic private partners, as opposed to reverting to the general budget, as in most countries); decentralization via the Law of Popular Participation; education reform; pension fund reform; and reform of the executive branch and constitutional reform. In this way he hoped to increase economic investment, accelerate economic growth, deepen democracy, and make the state more effective and efficient. And the MNR hoped to reverse the steady inroads that the UCS and Condepa (*Consciencia de Patria,* Conscience of the Homeland), another populist party led by a popular television personality, were making into the MNR's core vote.

Sánchez de Lozada ended his term with strong economic growth and popular participation and executive/constitutional reform well under way, but capitalization only barely completed. He handed power over to Gen. Banzer, who had finally achieved the electoral victory he craved. After a period out of office as required by the constitution, Sánchez de Lozada ran and won again, but this time with a margin of less than two per cent over Evo Morales and Manfred Reyes Villa, who essentially tied for second place. With the vote continuing to splinter amongst more and more non-traditional political parties, Sánchez de Lozada returned to the Presidency at the head of a large and unwieldy coalition. Economic growth was poor and the fiscal deficit was large and growing. A cycle of popular protests abetted by Morales and his new political movement, the MAS (*Movimiento al Socialismo,* Movement to Socialism), whose principal support came from coca growers' unions, gained force when it was alleged that the government planned to export Bolivian gas to the USA via a Chilean port. Protest turned into a popular blockade of La Paz. Sánchez de Lozada ordered the army and police to intervene to allow essential supplies to reach the capital, and 59 civilians died in the ensuing violence. Amid much rancor and a fog of rumor and misinformation from all sides, Sánchez de Lozada resigned the Presidency and left the country.

The period that followed was one of deep political uncertainty as the old political party system centered on the MNR, ADN, and MIR collapsed, and a new politics struggled to emerge. The old certainties of left vs. right and labor vs. capital were swept away in the upheaval. Political parties and movements espousing a huge array of causes, many of them remarkably local, sprouted in their hundreds across the land. Into this vacuum stepped Evo Morales with a discourse of ethnic grievance, vindication, and recovery, filling the void that Sánchez de Lozada's resignation had left. Morales won the presidential election of 2005, and has since filled the Bolivian national stage to the exclusion of all else. The MAS now occupies the center of Bolivian politics, with other parties defining themselves against it and reacting to it, but none showing any ability thus far to make more than temporary inroads into its huge base of support. Whether the MAS, and the new Bolivian politics of identity, can outlive its dominant leader is for now impossible to tell.

2.2 Interview

2.2.1 *The Experience of Government under Victor Paz Estenssoro*

JEAN-PAUL FAGUET: The reforms your first administration introduced in the mid-1990s were breathtaking in their ambition. What made you think you could attempt so much? What made you think they would work?

GONZALO SÁNCHEZ DE LOZADA: I had had experience, thanks to the fact that I was Victor Paz Estenssoro's quasi-Prime Minister. I had been Minister of Planning and Co-ordination in his last government, when we tamed inflation. Because of how government was organized, the Minister of Planning presided over CONEPLAN,[4] which was the council where all the social and economic ministries sat, and where all kinds of important decisions were taken. We were all ministers, and we reviewed and agreed on policy matters. But I was the one who took these recommendations to the President and explained them to him. And then I took his decisions back down to CONEPLAN and explained again. Victor Paz very wisely held on to what is the essence of power: the ministries of foreign affairs, defense, homeland security, information, and other critical political ministries. He ran those directly. I didn't have delegative authority there. But I did have a lot of power over the other areas of government, although he always had the last word.

This was a very wise system. Take the stabilization plan. We rolled that out in three weeks, after discussing shock therapy vs. gradualism for one week, stabilization vs. indexing along Brazilian lines for another week, and, in a third week, writing the Supreme Decree (executive order). It was intensely discussed at cabinet level, and it made important political actors buy into the ideas.

JPF: Being in government with Dr Paz Estenssoro was clearly a very powerful experience for you, as I'm sure for everyone involved. Can you tell me a little more about that?

GSL: One thing about Dr Paz is that he called in very young people compared to him. He was already in his 80s, and a very famous, revered national figure.

Once I went to him—he had immense confidence in me after we stopped inflation, and I was a sort of a teacher's pet—and I said "President, I know it's not my business, but I'm worried because I understand that this commander of the army you appointed is very tied to Banzer. Aren't you a little worried about this?" He replied, "Goni, I really respect you. But your advice is not welcome in this area. I'm running foreign affairs, homeland security, defense, information—all the political ministries." And the last thing he wanted was a meddling guy who had lots of power but not much political experience. In spite of the fact that I was part of the inner circle, Victor Paz understood very well where my place was. I was invited not to express any further opinions. "You are logical," he said, "and I have a great deal of respect for your opinion. You may sway me, but I need to do this myself. I need to talk to the ministers that have line responsibility and make these decisions."

The economy and social affairs were a different story. I always defended the introduction of market economics to the MNR and the country as something that should have been done in the revolution, because we were not communists. From the start, we should have gone to a market economy and not a command economy. When we were pushing through the stabilization plan, we called it the New Economic Policy (NEP), just like the early Bolsheviks, because ours was a populist party and they would accept that. They *liked* the sound of that. An important component was the Emergency Social Fund, which

[4] Consejo Nacional de Economía y Planificación [National Council for Planning and the Economy].

was based on an idea of Victor Paz. He understood the need for it, as a cushion for the economic shock that was coming. I was very happy because I thought a market economy had to be regulated to be stable, because you know I never believed in free markets. It's like sports—imagine football without rules, without impartial referees. In markets, the minute you don't have rules and an appeals process, you don't have a market. A market is about competition. To compete, you need rules and umpires, otherwise it becomes monopolies. I believe in markets like the Chinese believe in markets—the cat's only good if it catches mice.

2.2.2 *A "Stolen" Election and Goni's Political Transformation*

JPF: How did you go from there to your first Presidential election?

GSL: I was conscious of the fact that I'd played a key role in stopping hyperinflation and achieving economic stability. Victor Paz was impeded by the constitution, and also by his age, from running again. And to everyone's surprise, including my own, I became the most viable candidate my party had. For electoral reasons, the number 2 man in the party started attacking the economic model that had permitted us to re-achieve growth and stop hyperinflation. I obviously realized it was a politician trying to win votes, but I was identified with the stabilization program so I started to defend it. And then I joined the primaries and lost them all, except for Cochabamba, the department I represented in Congress. I didn't really have political ambition then. I felt that my background—having been brought up in the USA, my accented Spanish, and being a successful mining entrepreneur—made me politically unviable. So I got into the elections for the best of reasons—to defend what we'd achieved. Being a modern man, I brought in modern technologies, like advertising and polling, and won the election by 1 per cent. The second round is decided in Congress between the top three candidates. And these two guys, Banzer to the right and Jaime Paz to the left, hated me because I'd come up through the middle and had very sharp elbows. I was able to unite Congress, but, unfortunately, against me! They didn't have the congressional representation to elect one or the other between them, so they played around with the electoral courts, and they were able to take away our majority in the Senate. Through very unfortunate interpretations of the law, and also through corruption, they were able to eliminate representatives in the Chamber of Deputies of smaller left and center parties. So these two parties who hated each other got together and formed a government and froze me out.

I wasn't aided by my sense of humor. I said, "You know, if Jaime Paz had known Banzer was persecuting him all those years in order to give him the presidency, he wouldn't have run so fast!" That didn't make me very popular with them.

But when I realized that there was a general acceptance that I'd been cheated, that the rules of the game had been violated, I set about using Jaime Paz's four years of government to get an impartial electoral court. "How can you play football if the umpires can be paid off?" I would say. I made adverts, gave speeches, and made the intellectual case. It weighed heavily on my mind. They could see it was going to be very difficult to get me next time, because you can play around with the electoral process if the difference is marginal—like the USA, where the presidency was decided by a political vote in the Supreme Court—but not if the difference is large. I had a lot of moral authority as people knew I had been cheated. So instead of attacking the government, I kept saying, "Let's get an impartial electoral court." I realized that if I was going to run again, I needed a level playing field.

I also needed to overcome the fact that I was seen as foreign, upper-class, and distant. The polling and focus groups showed that I was respected in the sense of competence, but people couldn't relate to me. So I decided to do something that ended up being very smart. I got in a car with a driver and visited almost every town in Bolivia. I said "Goni's listening." Instead of giving speeches, I would listen. I would bring people together and they would tell me their problems, and I would say to them something that I believe. I said, "You know, my wife and I are parents, and we've lived life, and have experienced the things our children do, the mistakes they're making. We know what they're doing, their mistakes, and at the same time we're intelligent enough and love them enough to know that the only solutions are the ones they find themselves, because they're the ones who have the problems. We're a generation away, and though we may be blessed by experience, wisdom, and affection, all you can do is support them because you really can't solve their problems. That's the basis of good family relations." So I went out and said, "I've come to hear your problems and hear your solutions, because the people who know the solutions are the people who have the problems, not the people who don't have the problems." There's a famous French saying, "Nothing is more bearable than other people's problems." What I had decided to do was listen to other people's problems.

This was extremely effective because if you listen and don't talk, people think you're intelligent. And they think you care about them. And that was my political problem. I had a very clear diagnosis of how people saw me—they saw me as honest, they saw me as capable, but they saw me as very distant from their lives and their problems. This was an eye-opener. I would say, "I want to know about your problems." The motto was "Goni escucha."[5] As you know, Victor Paz was always known as *El doctor Victor Paz Estenssoro*. Given all these difficulties, if I went out there as Gonzalo Sánchez de Lozada y Sánchez de Bustamante (my mother's name), I wasn't going to get very far. It would just confirm the image: totally upper class, totally distant from their lives, totally uncaring. So my associates and I took the wise decision to be "Goni" (my childhood nickname in the USA, where no one could pronounce "Gonzalo").

The problem was that if I wanted to be president I had to win by a landslide. Nobody really wanted me. The right hated me—they considered me a radical leftist—and the left considered me a neoliberal heartless capitalist. So if I wanted

[5] "Goni is listening."

to be able to win an election I had to be closer to regular people. I didn't realize it at first, but I learned two big lessons in this process. One, that what's important to people vis-à-vis the state is solutions to the problems that affect their lives on a daily basis—basically, education, health, and community development like sports and culture. I was very influenced by a woman who said to me: "You know, Goni, our problems are so great that nobody can solve them. But at least you've come to listen to what our problems are, although we know you can't solve them. And also we really appreciate that you're not promising anything. You're just listening." I realized that people are very conscious of what their problems are and they're convinced that their problems probably have no solution. But what they really resent is politicians who arrive at election time to make outrageous promises that they know they can't fulfill. So I ended up looking intelligent, sensitive, *and modest*, which is, of course, very desirable.

Secondly, I started learning about what people really want. I was the guy who had slain inflation, but I still didn't understand that. They know that the only solutions to poverty are two things—health and education. That's the only kind of income redistribution that they really believe in. They get suspicious if you promise anything else. They know those are key, and they tell you, "We're never going to get out of this poverty if we don't have health and education." And I also realized that the things that really affect peoples' lives are the things they can achieve through consensus, and that was the secret of stable democracies like the American, with its town hall traditions, the Scandinavian and some other European democracies.

By going out into the countryside and the neighborhoods and listening to their problems, I had a sort of conversion. By talking to these people and really listening, which in the beginning was done to improve my image, I started to learn from them. I went down and listened and found that they were 100 per cent right. It was very successful from a political point of view. But also, I became a believer not only in decentralization, but in a deeper social dimension, which was popular participation. That's a very nice phrase, but it reflected something different and deeper. People talk about decentralization like corporate entities delegating power and resources. I became a real believer in something that was intrinsic to the experience of the town hall meeting—of people discussing their problems and coming up with solutions. When people talk about decentralization they usually think of handing off responsibility but not authority. We wanted to hand down *authority*.

But if we did this, we'd be left with lots of poor municipalities. People's local problems might be solved, but what about the other great problem of today: the cost of government? Because the other big issue is that there's no way you can afford all the levels of government. If you have a central government, and then you have a state government, and then you have a county government, and then you have a municipal government, then you're dead.

JPF: Because it's too expensive?

GSL: Too expensive! You can't support it all. So what people want from government is what's really important to them. But if you try to run it all from the center the resources will never make it down, and you can't afford to run all the levels of government and all the services. But then I realized that could be solved too—hence "popular participation." Much of what was needed could be done on a volunteer basis. The tradition that the Spanish took up from the Inca empire is that people provided labor free as an obligation to the community, a bit like military conscription. You either went and worked, for example on the roads for a number of days, or you paid a tax and were freed of the responsibility. Usually the upper class paid the tax and the lower classes did the work. Since local government, especially rural local government, was so underfinanced, everything was made for the upper and middle classes. That's the absurd thing about public subsidies—they usually don't benefit the people who need them.

So in Bolivia the big cities had better services and poor villages had almost nothing. But we could revive and transform that tradition through popular participation, with citizens contributing to their own services, especially in rural areas where they're much more willing to volunteer. Secondly, people had to be able to hold politicians responsible. And that's where my idea for decentralization started. Both things were possible with popular participation. Without it, neither is.

So the experience of that campaign ended up being crucial, because I realized two things: (1) only the people who have the problems have the solutions, and (2) an idiot close to a problem is better than a genius a thousand miles away. Whoever's feeling the pain will know the solution better than anyone. So I went into this radical effort to decentralize power in Bolivia.

2.2.3 *"Why I Decentralized Bolivia"*

JPF: That's very compelling and idealistic and high-minded. And also . . . with the greatest respect . . . not entirely credible. At least not on its own. Are Presidents really motivated by philosophy?

GSL: I had to stop this fight for a federalist system which came from the regions. I realized that the "regions" are really local elites who wanted to capture rents from our natural resource wealth, and managed to mobilize broader movements behind them. I kept saying to them: "What you guys really want is not to have to come to La Paz to steal. You want to be able to steal at home, so you want to have a devolution of resources—you want power without responsibility." I was totally against these groups of rent-seekers.

JPF: These were the people pushing for decentralization then [before 1994]?

GSL: Yes! Landowners in Santa Cruz, growing soya, cotton, corn—people who had benefitted enormously from national policies and investments. For example, roads built all over the eastern lowlands. When Victor Paz nationalized the mines he fixed the exchange rate, which decapitalized the mines. They tried hard to diversify the economy, because Bolivia was dependent on imported food. And almost all of the capital they invested went to Santa Cruz and the other lowlands departments. From being a very backward place, Santa Cruz progressed rapidly, and became powerful and wealthy. And these people became unruly. They seemed to think they deserved it, or they had achieved it by themselves.

JPF: Was it a political project? I remember when I arrived in Bolivia in 1991, it would occasionally appear in the newspaper that certain organizations—the *Comité Pro-Santa Cruz,* for example—were agitating in favor of decentralization. And as you say, it was always regional decentralization. Was it just the elites, or did this have any sort of popular echo?

GSL: It had an echo because everybody identifies with the region they're born in. Especially in a country that's ethnically and geographically divided into isolated areas: the *altiplano* speaks Aymara, the valleys speak Quechua, and the lowlands speak Guaraní. They're very different—their religion and beliefs, culture, folk music. Those identities are strong in Bolivia. So here was a country with a strong tendency towards federalism—granting it would have led to a continual struggle for the rents that raw materials produce.

I really believed that unless there's a deep reason for federalism—like in the United States with all the states big and small, which were basically founded for reasons of religious liberty—it's not advisable. When you really study it, what the US has is a religious geography: Puritans, Quakers, Baptists, Mormons. The basis of the Union was a desire for religious liberty independent of the state. That's why they didn't want to be in a system where the greater populations of states like New York, Massachusetts, or Pennsylvania could dominate the rest. And that's why everybody pushed for this crazy idea of Washington, DC, which is not in any state. Because, you know, the capital of the United States should have been Philadelphia.

Bolivia's characteristics were different. There the main divides are geographic and ethnic, and that makes Bolivia very heterogeneous. I was very worried by this. Bolivia was historically dominated by where the wealth came from. The capital was Sucre. Why? Because it was close to the silver mines [of Potosí]. Then we had a civil war at the turn of the century, and the government was taken to La Paz, the center of production of non-ferrous minerals. But, in one of those compromise solutions, the capital stayed officially in Sucre, where the judicial branch [i.e. the Supreme Court] physically remained, but the executive and legislative branches were sent to La Paz. And if I had been a better politician and a lesser statesman, what I would have done is move the government to Santa Cruz, where it had to be because of the gas, oil, soya, iron ore, and everything else. That would have been another step in a logical progression. But I was very worried because there was an immense amount of pressure, especially from the most favored departments. There were even threats of secession as they demanded a bigger and bigger piece of the pie, even though they were highly privileged by public investment.

As a solution to this political problem I decided that you had to go to the roots, you had to create local government. You could only have a unitarian state if it was decentralized, because Bolivia—like so many countries—was a tree without roots. The state wasn't being nourished; no nutrients were going up.

I realized we could decentralize the things that really matter about government to people—health, education, local development, agriculture, local roads, sports. And it became very clear to me that instead of fighting and trying to repress these regional movements that were so powerful, there was another solution.

That solution allowed me to undermine the elites. I was able to pull the rug out from under this movement by not going to the regions, but instead going down beneath them. I pulled the rug out from under these dominant elites and their attempts to control public funds.

I was very interested to find that in municipal elections, only half the population could vote. The towns were like the medieval, walled towns where the people, the *vecinos*, lived who owned the land, which the Indians, the *campesinos*, worked. Indians couldn't vote, so municipal elections were held amongst townspeople only. We got a group of people together—sociologists, economists, agricultural experts, historians, and politicians—and we found that in the colony, what was called the *cantón* was basically the Indian community, and the *provincias* were provinces, a concept inherited from France. After spending more than 300 hours in meetings, and many drafts of the law, we found that the provincial municipal sections had fallen into disuse, and we decided to revive them as a basis for the Law of Popular Participation.

To sum it up: why did I do it? I did it because the struggle between the regions and the central government, which was ironically most vigorous in those areas that the central government had most helped to develop, threatened to undermine political stability.

JPF: So you were really worried about centrifugal forces that might break the country up . . .

GSL: I was; I had seen it in Victor Paz's government. Elites were continuously fighting land taxes; people agitating on behalf of regional universities' budgets; the regional *Comités*—all of that was a leftover from the military regimes. They were really regional de facto governments that just wanted more public resources. It got so bad that these regional interests would decide where the state oil company should drill its wells. It was just a mess. Many of these reforms—not just decentralization but also education and others—were born out of the fact that I had to beat this force that was going to destroy the country. These privileged persons are the worst. The people who are the best off fight the hardest. You never have a problem when you raise taxes on the poor. You have terrible problems when you raise them on the rich, because they control the newspapers, and they go out screaming and yelling that jobs will be lost. So my problem was that I was fighting this regional battle which is a battle that cannot be won.

JPF: Was that the basic reason why you decided to carry out popular participation?

GSL: No.

JPF: That, plus the visits to people who knew their own solutions . . .

GSL: Those were the two intrinsic reasons. I became an advocate—I was converted. And then a third reason: I realized that strong democracies are decentralized because by decentralizing, you push the problems that are really important to people down to their level, where they can do something about them, if you're willing to give them the resources. If you keep power centralized, you suffer the risk that the discontents and frustrations of their daily lives put the stability of the state in jeopardy.

I wanted to build roots for Bolivian democracy. I saw that you could use OTBs [*Organizaciones Territoriales de Base,* local Grass-Roots Organizations]—which are basically Indian communities or neighborhood associations, and which are intrinsic to Bolivian society—as building blocks. They would become the *Comités de Vigilancia* [Oversight Committees], which would have control over the budgeting process and the execution of investment. It would be based on local groups, which would have different natures in different parts of the country. And then you would graft onto it the European system—decentralized municipal government. Of course the minute you did that, you took all the steam out of the regional elites.

So my decision to decentralize was intellectual. And it was political. And finally it was highly personal. I really believed then and believe now that you can't have a tree that doesn't have roots.

JPF: So that's why you decentralized.

GSL: Yes. But not only that. It was because I'd won in a landslide.

JPF: Aha! This is the black hole question. You won and you won big, and you finally held national power in your hands. And you turned around and gave it away? Are you kidding?

GSL: That's the only time you can give it up!

JPF: When you have it. Yes. The self-interested actor of political science might see that this is the right thing to do, might see that you have an opportunity because you've won with a big electoral majority, but would nonetheless not do it because as between having power or giving it away, you prefer to have it. After all, what were you fighting for in all those elections?

GSL: The big point is this. Why was I attacked by the right and left and so weakened in my second government? Because when they saw the reforms I'd pushed through, including popular participation, they realized that my party would govern Bolivia for a very long time.

2.2.4 *Political Equality*

GSL: Let's go to the next stage which I think is very important—the big discussion of how to distribute rents. I learned something. There are societies like the Japanese and maybe the Chinese where the culture promotes sacrifice in favor of others. Compare that to my own childhood. My father was a professor in political exile, and we were living on a very tight budget. Back then you ate what was in season. So when it was cherry season, you were lucky and you got cherries. And I learned that you cannot convince children that your brother needs more or your sister deserves more because they'd done something good or were growing or whatever. No. The kids would count all the cherries and we wouldn't forgive anyone who got one more. So I became convinced that on a human level people intrinsically like democracy because of equality.

Now, I had some very sophisticated people telling me we had to have a poverty index to give more money to poorer areas and less to the rich . . . all this bullshit. Intelligent bullshit. So finally we came up with two solutions. The definition of the unit of government was a mixture of rural communities and urban municipalities, because Bolivian municipalities were basically medieval structures from feudal times. Many more have recently included suburbs. But to decentralize to them, you had to expand and make flexible the definition of municipalities to include surrounding rural areas. And we realized that the only way this can be tolerated is if resources are divided per person. No formulas, no poverty indices, just the same amount of money for everyone everywhere.

But there's more. First you transfer responsibilities. Then you transfer funds, and you know in advance that the funds you're giving them are much smaller than the responsibility they're taking on. The only way they can make it work is if the community volunteers a lot. Let's say retired people, older people, groups that volunteer to work for the community. And the only way you can make that work for services they need is if they're working for themselves, and seeing the benefit of it. So all of these things came together: (1) We had to get away from what would have been hell for my government, which was fighting with the regions; (2) it enabled me to be a statesman; and (3) I had a deep personal commitment related to my own family experience and to what I'd learned travelling around Bolivia. And, finally, it had to be simple—and we had to actually do it.

JPF: The per capita criterion was bold and powerful in its simplicity. I've studied decentralization in many countries, and Bolivia stands out for having this simple mechanism, and for its profound effects on making decentralization work. Many times in my research I saw groups of *campesinos* demanding a school or clinic for their community. They'd accost the mayor and say, "We know there are 50 families living in our village. That's 250 or 300 people. That adds up to Bs. 46,000. *So where's our school?*"

GSL: Of course! If we'd put a formula in there, the mayors would've told the peasants, "Sorry, the formula says you don't get a school this year." And the peasants would have turned around and gone home. Or actually they wouldn't have travelled to see the mayor in the first place. Because it was always like that; the peasants were always getting cheated for some reason they couldn't understand. This reform they *could* understand. And once they understood it, they made it work for them.

We did something else they'll never pardon me for. We reformed education to teach in local people's languages. We said to them, "You don't want to speak only Quechua and Aymara. You want to speak Spanish. But the only way you can do that properly"—this was the most important part—"is to learn reading, writing, and arithmetic in your mother tongue. Once you've learned that, you can go to Sanskrit, Mandarin, English—it will open doors for you. But you can't start learning *in* Spanish if you don't speak Spanish. You have to start learning in your tongue, and then you can learn Spanish." And I would say to them, "If you're not careful, your children will start speaking like me!" And this started getting to them, that you have to respect your culture.

But the teachers who spoke Aymara, Quechua, and Guaraní didn't want it because they had struggled to become superior to the people they were teaching. They could speak those languages, but felt it was denigrating to do so. This refusal to do something they obviously could do made them "superior" to the *campesinos*, and made the *campesino* schoolchildren dumber. So bilingual education in indigenous languages was a major equalizing reform in both senses.

But equality isn't the only thing, and in Bolivia it gets taken too far. Education is a good example. It was my grandfather who first introduced the concept of university autonomy in Bolivia, which means no political interference in public higher education. So it was funny to go to universities and be told that I was against their autonomy. I would tell students, "You know, I've got bad news for you. You're here because you don't know and you hope that the people who are teaching you do know. How can you be equal? You're not equal. We in democracy are equal." The people would say "Why are we all equal? Why are you the same as I am?" They would look at me and go "We're not the same, we're poor. Why are you the same?" And I would say, "Because we're all gonna die. That's the basis of equality, that's why your vote is as good as my vote. That is the primary reason of God-given equality." And people would say, "Yes, you're right." That's why a beggar or poor man has one vote and we have one vote. And the rich or genius or visionary or saint has one vote—because we're all gonna die. That's the basis of the equality of man. That's the basis of democracy. But at a lower level, you can't have full equality everywhere because in education there's an inherent inequality. A student doesn't know, otherwise why is he there?

So I believe in equality, fraternity, and liberty. And the most important of the three is equality. When we talk about popular participation, we mean radical decentralization with grass-roots participation. That's why we have oversight committees, which are grass-roots, volunteer committees that participate in picking projects and controlling expenses. It's based on this notion of equality.

2.2.5 *Bolivia's Historical Context*

JPF: These are powerful ideas. Where do they fit in Bolivia's broader history?

GSL: Look at the leaders Bolivia has had in the past and think of the economic booms and busts. We are condemned because of our incredible natural wealth. The interesting thing is that historically you see swings between *presidentes bárbaros y presidentes letrados* (barbarian vs. educated presidents). The history of Bolivia has been a generational swing between very educated, clear-thinking, and honest statesmen like Victor Paz and—in spite of my failures—I'd like to think, myself, vs. Gen. Montenegro, Gen. Melgarejo, Evo Morales, and other *bárbaros*. That's been the swing, and it's usually around very powerful booms in raw material prices.

Ask yourself: Why did Chile take over Bolivia's sea coast in the nineteenth century? The one thing Chile didn't need is more coast. Why did they do it? That little piece of land has been 40 per cent of Chile's GNP for 120 years because that's where all the copper and nitrate and guano are. And we can go further. There are two countries in Latin America that are only half their original size. One is Bolivia and the other is Mexico. We lost big blocks of land and it's always around raw materials. We had a war with Brazil, who set up *La República del Acre* because when the rubber boom came [in the nineteenth century], the most valuable area belonged to Bolivia. And they learned from the Americans and set up a republic which they later absorbed. We had to go all the way down to the jungle and have a war; we were able to stop it, but we lost a lot. They signed a treaty that they would compensate for lost territory by building railroads, which they never did. So you have two countries that are twice their original size: Brazil and the United States. And two countries that are half their original size: Mexico and Bolivia. And in all of these wars with our neighbors, our problem has always been the immense wealth we had, which they wanted.

All of this was mirrored inside the country, too, when powerful regional elites tried and often succeeded in monopolizing some resource and holding the country to ransom. For most of Bolivia's history from colonial times, our natural wealth has been a source of autocracy, dictatorship, and tremendous inequality. The first people who tried to break with that were Victor Paz Estenssoro and the MNR revolutionaries of 1952, who nationalized the mines and redistributed the land.

My father was a member of the MNR and always admired the pre-Columbian community system, the *ayllus*, which were territorial areas made up of forty-eight agrarian communities, twenty-four called upper communities and twenty-four called lower communities. Marriage was only permitted between members of upper communities with members of the lower communities or vice versa to avoid inbreeding. Interestingly enough, the areas occupied by the *ayllus* were basically the provincial municipal sections. During the republican period, many of the communities became *haciendas*, where peasant farmers would work three days for the land owner, three days on their own plots, and one day, Sunday, for the Church. My father rather romantically wanted the land reform done in such a way that peasants would become owners of their original plots of land, and then work the *hacienda* lands collectively as a community. The MNR preferred to divide the land and give it to peasants, and leave in place the Napoleonic code that permitted inheritance amongst offspring. This resulted in the creation of *minifundios* (small landholdings), and as the transfer and sale of land was prohibited, productivity in the highlands and valleys plummeted. An interesting experience is the story of the nanny who brought up my two children. Her family did not divide the land through inheritance; they get together during the winter among all the descendants of legal age to decide through lottery who works their land the following year. It's interesting to note that the Spanish system of *mayorazgo,* meaning inheritance by the oldest male of the landholdings with the obligation to compensate other heirs, was abolished at the beginning of the nineteenth century, and *hacienda* holdings subdivided, which weakened landholdings even before land reform.

Because of their material dialectic formation, the MNR also believed that the *Revolución Nacional* required the fusion of the two races, Indians and whites, into the New Bolivian Man. Along those lines, in my first term in office I was accompanied by Victor Hugo Cárdenas, an indigenous intellectual who was not a member of the party but had his own indigenous party, as the country's first indigenous Vice President. I introduced the concept of unity in diversity, which Evo Morales is now doing all he can to break down, leaving a racist fight between white people and brown people.

2.2.6 *Was Decentralization a World Bank Imposition?*

JPF: Let's come back to decentralization. Many decry it as an imposition of the World Bank and other aid agencies on developing countries. As an academic, I've often heard claims, and occasionally even reviewed papers asserting, that decentralization was imposed on Bolivia by the Bank. But I was working for the World Bank at the time, and this doesn't seem right to me.

GSL: Oh, they didn't have the slightest idea!

JPF: I remember my colleagues in the La Paz office asking, "What is this?" None of us knew. Colleagues from Washington called wanting to know what was going on. I was the officer in charge of health, education, and rural development. If I didn't know, then neither did anyone else. "So they want to legislate participation?," we mocked, unfunnily. Eventually, I went and read the law, and that's how we all found out.

GSL: But it took you a while. You guys were clueless.

2.2.7 *Design of the Law of Popular Participation*

JPF: When you were campaigning for the presidency in the early 1990s, what did you diagnose as Bolivia's major challenges?

GSL: Well, the country was economically stable. Jaime Paz's government hadn't destabilized too much. The country still had many structural problems that had to be attended to. In his last term, Victor Paz had said, "Look, I dismantled all I did in the Revolution. I'll stop at privatization. When you become President, you can do that if you want." Jaime Paz was too scared, so that sort of thing was left to us. And we did it. We had to make an electoral offer, so we came up with a comprehensive plan, which was called the *Plan de Todos*, which was our governing agenda. The name was great. And it was serious. A lot of the things we ended up doing were in that plan. We worked with a good team of people, and it was an important step in re-imagining what the new Bolivia should be.

JPF: When you became President and you had this idea of popular participation—who was in favor and who was against it then?

GSL: Our governing coalition included a populist, Max Fernandez [leader of the UCS]. Max owned Bolivia's most important brewery, and his only real interest was to make sure we didn't increase sin taxes, which are a very good source of revenue. He supported us, but basically because he didn't want us to become too energetic in collecting taxes by changing inspectors all the time. Then we had to give it a progressive tinge. We had the MBL [*Movimiento Bolivia Libre*], a sort of radicalized Christian Democrat bunch led by Antonio Araníbar, who had broken with Jaime Paz because they considered him corrupt and willing to do deals with ex-dictator Hugo Banzer and the ADN. We called people in from those two parties, and of course from our party. We set up a multidisciplinary group of people who were interested in this concept of progressive social and income policies. These were very much intellectual, left-wing people. But it was awkward because the MBL supported the reforms and helped write the laws, but then voted against them in Congress!

We realized it was extremely important that people in the coalition be part of this. We had people from Santa Cruz who were important regional figures, but also willing to break with the quasi-feudal organizations that defended elite interests there. You have to understand that during twenty years of military rule there hadn't been any sort of democratic participation. In that context, self-appointed groups of landowners, businessmen, even workers grew up and prospered. They weren't elected by anybody, and had a lot of power. They were "civic organizations" of a kind favored by the fascists. Opposing them was popular.

JPF: In terms of interest groups within the economy, or within society, were there organized interests groups pushing for it? Or was this a discussion amongst a small group of technocrats?

GSL: A small group of people, thirty or forty in total I guess. The relevant interest groups were pro-regional elites, and they were all going to be against it. Our response was, first of all, to make sure there was a lot of participation by high quality people from the parties in the coalition. And then by a lot of people who were lawyers, sociologists, technical finance experts, etc., looking at popular participation in a holistic way. We had to make sure that it wasn't just my project or the group's project. It had influential people from every party, and from wings of every party, who would guarantee us breadth of support. But it was selective—we looked for people who were interested and sensitive to this. This was not a cake that had already been baked. We really went for this inclusive process of working out the idea. In its design, too, it was a *Plan de Todos*.

JPF: What did you rationally expect popular participation would achieve?

GSL: We knew what we wanted. We wanted local governments that could be held accountable for their actions, and not just demand money from the central government. We wanted to make it something that the people owned—that's why it was so important. We had a concept of participative government where people who participated and accepted responsibility took over. We had a general idea, but of course the devil's in the detail and that's what we had to work on. But we also had a good name: popular participation—people being involved. It was a kind of unity of the pre-Columbian village institutions that had been overlaid by European and French Revolution ideas like the prefectures and departments.

We knew we had something but we didn't know quite what it was—that had to be worked out. I think we went through close to a hundred different versions of the law. There was a great deal of platonic dialogue. We would talk about it and explore different ideas, and at the end I would kick it to pieces and we'd go back to zero. We would go on for hours. It didn't take very long for me to learn that meetings shouldn't go on for more than three hours because you just don't maintain any focus. We were running long meetings with hundreds and hundreds of hours. And just when we thought we'd made a breakthrough, I would start discussing it and—like a good platonic dialogue—you end up kicking it to pieces again.

It was an extremely progressive experiment of reform. It was anti-feudal, because it went against all those interests groups. The country was very feudalized—you had the COB [*Central Obrera Boliviana*—the national workers' union], the *Comités Cívicos,* and others. They elected themselves and were never accountable to anyone else, like many NGOs are. They had great influence nationwide. We wanted to change that.

That was a great time. We were trying really hard to do something good, to think things through carefully. All things considered, it was a very honest and idealistic type of government, my first government.

JPF: Did you think it was necessary to keep discussion of the various versions of the law away from the public eye?

GSL: No. The real issue is that for a long time we didn't really have anything to put forward. We needed something concrete before opening it up to a broader discussion. I felt that you had to have a clear proposal, and that proposal first had to be intensely discussed—intensely criticized and argued against. I remember many times I found to my surprise that some of the criticisms that seemed worst or least fair turned out to be right. Somebody would walk into the room and say, "I'm a historian. The problem of how to govern a country of this size from points so distant with poor communication is not new . . ." So it was really a process of discovery and innovation.

We were never able to get a high level of consensus with the hard opposition—Banzer and those people—or with Jaime Paz. The military believe in the central government; that's the way they're organized, that's the way they think. The LPP (law of popular participation) was an affront to the authoritarian way of thinking. We were looking for something that could be tolerated by the opposition and still be acceptable to the government. This was very important. We really went and discussed it with everyone, and people came back to us and we made changes. We kept working and finally got to a point where the opposition wasn't so offended that they would walk out on us in the middle of the night. They weren't happy, they wouldn't support it, but they tolerated it. And it's funny—the MBL voted against all the popular reforms. I don't know why but they just voted against it. But some of those congressmen had been working with us on the draft law, and they voted in favor. So we split the parties.

We tried to explain it as part of the popular nature of the National Revolution. We considered it an extension of the Revolution in areas that it had forgotten, but shouldn't have.

JPF: What was opposition to the reform like?

GSL: The big attack on the LPP had to do with the structure of the MNR. Our party was organized around *comandos* [village or neighborhood party organizations] that were almost like cells. It was a revolutionary party, but also a quasi-fascist right-wing party when it started out. Then it evolved into a left-wing party highly influenced by the communists. We had a tradition of looking after the people, and the party wanted to nurture that. So we worked hard to keep that kind of support. Much of the criticism came from sectors within the MNR, but also from other parties—from people worried that the grass-roots organizations [*OTBs* in Spanish] we were organizing to oversee municipal performance would turn into some system of thought control, like the commissars in the USSR. And they screamed and yelled about that.

I think one of my big failures was that I didn't make decentralization political. I tried to keep it depoliticized. I think I did my party a great deal of harm because rural municipalities had so little money to work with up to then, and this was a huge windfall. The MNR could have benefitted hugely from that, but I chose not to play it that way. And so I think the biggest mistake I made was not to make it political. I should have said, "This is our invention – we are giving you both economic and political power!" People saw it as a big play to consolidate power and build a powerful organization to serve the party. Unfortunately it wasn't that. I didn't want that, and I felt it was intellectually dishonest to sell it even to my own party as something it was not. I think I made it so technocratic that it lost its charisma and its sex appeal. I tried to make it apolitical, which was a big mistake.

JPF: How would you have politicized the LPP to help the MNR?

GSL: Well, we would have said, "The MNR gave you the land and the vote, and now we're giving you power." But with the transfer of funds we felt that would be a big mistake. We felt the LPP was of national interest, and that it would be accepted better if it wasn't identified too much with the party, although the party was tickled pink. These municipalities had so little money because they had been deprived of the land tax, which had been the basis of municipal financing. They started hating departmental capitals as much as the central government, because everything went to them and stopped there. They were left with crumbs in the countryside. So I think I made a big mistake. If I'd said, "This is something like land reform, like the universal vote. This is something that the party will be identified with," I think it would have been much better. I tried to show this as a national interest, and people attacked it anyway as a political move to win votes for the MNR.

Actually it was a way to decentralize authority and resources, based on very simple, non-discussable facts. Many wanted to distribute resources according to poverty measures, but instead we tried to make it very concessional and create something along the lines of the Emergency Social Fund. What we really did was to create these municipal entities and put World Bank money in to help the poor. Poorer municipalities only had to put up 20 per cent of the cost of a project, but also had to have the approval of central government institutions. Richer municipalities had to put up 50 per cent. It meant they had to use transferred resources to co-finance public investments with the central government, because no project would work without local input. Many of these payback schedules were obviously subsidized. If you got a loan and you put up 20 per cent of the project cost, theoretically you were borrowing 80 per cent. But they got that back out of future transfers. So you almost had a lien on that money.

There was also the issue of what to do with the poorest populations. We wanted to say everyone was equal, but of course in certain places you had to have subsidies and investments and grants. For the poorest it was grants and concessional loans, often based on what we were getting from international aid agencies, including the World Bank.

2.2.8 *Political Feasibility and Passage into Law*

JPF: How did you make this technocratic reform politically feasible?

GSL: I tried to get my political allies to commit. I pushed the most able people who were political leaders and bought into this project to go out and try to sell it to the country. In the discussions that followed we often surprised people by making big changes to the reform. "This guy is a pig," opponents cried. "All he wants is to grab resources. He doesn't really care about the poor." They were just waiting for us to run out of steam. But many more times than I care to remember, even when they criticized in bad faith, they turned out to be right. So we modified the law, and everybody thought we were negotiating. But we weren't negotiating—we were trying to get a serious dialogue going, trying to make it better. You reached a point when the opposition wasn't that violently opposed. They hadn't bought into it, but we had backed off from our more extreme positions. At that point you took it to Congress, and it went through like a steamroller. The way it happened was, as you went through the law article by article, in meetings that lasted twenty to twenty-five hours, the opposition would get up and go home. They didn't want to support you, so they would leave and make big speeches saying "This guy is an idiot!" "This is against the interests of my department!" They would walk out and slam the door. But they didn't leave angry because what they were really doing was agreeing to respect the majority.

We could instead have rammed it through Congress with our majority. But then you lose the respect of the minority, and the minute you offend the minority you have some really tough guys to contend with.

JPF: Did it go through Congress rapidly?

GSL: Yes. These were very complicated laws—you couldn't play around with them. If people started making changes, they were likely to end up vetoed. Under the Bolivian system you have ten or fifteen days to send a letter to Congress saying "I veto the stand the two houses made." It's not like the committee system in the USA. If there isn't a two-thirds majority in Congress, they have to accept the changes you want. If they do have the two-thirds, they can impose their changes, but this was rare in Bolivian politics.

That's why the regional thing can be very bad for you. Because people say, "This affects my department," which trumps party loyalty, and they defect from your side. The big problem was always really the city of Santa Cruz, not the department. In our travels, rural Bolivians criticized departmental capitals because the capitals kept all the money they received and never sent it to the provinces. With popular participation, towns and villages realized the money would be deposited directly in their accounts, and that made a big difference.

2.2.9 *How did you carry the MNR?*

JPF: The most important question left is: How did you carry your own party? I buy your story about the process of becoming President—your big victory—it's very compelling. But the MNR—like any political party, and more so because it was the most successful political party in Bolivia—must have had a lot of self-interested politicians who, when you proposed to give away money and power to people in the municipalities, would have said: "No don't do that, because we're going to lose jobs, we're going to lose influence."

GSL: But the MNR was a national party, so they had people who felt they could win anywhere and everywhere and get jobs in the municipalities.

JPF: I was in Bolivia at the beginning of your presidency. I remember local *comandos* of the MNR taking out full-page ads in the newspapers that said, "The *comando* XYZ demands jobs for party members!" They must have been against decentralization. After all, you could have simply handed down jobs and resources to lots of people in your party. Instead, now they were going to have to compete in municipal elections themselves. Why had they worked so hard to help you win?

GSL: The party realized that this would be electorally powerful and would create jobs locally. When the 1964 coup[6] brought in Barrientos and Obando, people asked Victor Paz, "Why has this happened?" And he said, "Because we had 300,000 party members and only 250,000 jobs!" Basically it was a spoils system, but there weren't enough jobs in a centralized, unitarian government. So the party was quite unhappy. I think one of the biggest failures was not to sell this as something like the universal vote or land reform—as more power to the people.

[6] When a military coup overthrew an MNR government led by Victor Paz.

JPF: I take that point. I think it's quite right. Nonetheless, your party voted in favor in Congress, so it must be the case that at some level they were convinced.

GSL: They *were* convinced. The MNR might have been a lower-middle-class party, but they were also a party that understood populism. Remember that our area of greatest power was always the countryside. They saw that the level of enthusiasm for popular participation was very high in the countryside.

JPF: But it was more than just a good idea, no? I have a theory that even though you didn't present it politically, the MNR thought this would capture the vote, especially of rural Bolivians, for them for another generation—like land reform.

GSL: I didn't think of that. I wanted to be all-inclusive, unity in diversity, this phrase that justified Victor Hugo Cárdenas and others joining us; that concept of a diverse society where people lived together, not this racist concept we have now. I felt it was best to make it a national policy, and I undersold it. Maybe I should have put it in the party's hands, because later it went from *La Ley Maldita* to *La Ley Bendita* [from "the accursed law" to "the blessed law"]. And here I was saying it belongs to everybody. "It's really not about the party. We're serving the country!" A reform like this had to be used! It was a transfer of power, of real power to decide, and of money to do things, and maybe we should have taken advantage of that. But if we had politicized it, the resistance of the opposition might have been much greater, and we could have had a deadlock in Congress.

JPF: I remember all those people marching in the streets of La Paz calling it "*La Ley Maldita*." What happened to that?

GSL: When the radical left wing was told they were getting the money, and that real transfers had begun, their opposition evaporated. I had to overcome a lot of resistance on our side to make that happen. "Don't send out checks," demanded Miguel Urioste [a key MBL reformer]. But I said, "No – we're sending them out. Otherwise we won't have done anything. There'll be no decentralization." And then Carlos Hugo Molina [Secretary for Popular Participation] opposed changes to university funding that the reform implied. "Don't touch my alma mater!" The thing is, change is *very* hard. Everyone is afraid of it.

All the people from Banzer's party, who were very close to this concept of devolution, and Jaime Paz's party—they were the children of privilege. They wanted what *they* called decentralization; not giving power away to people. So they continued to oppose it, but more quietly after a while.

A lot of the positions around popular participation were of a political nature. Some of the people who resisted popular participation were the unions! Why? Because if you had to report to a community, you lost your power to negotiate. You went from speaking *for* them to answering *to* them. If you gave the community the power to hire and fire, you would break the back of the *inamovilidad*—the tenure system—in education, where promotion depends on years of service and not performance. Instead, you would have a community to respond to. When I travelled around, I realized that rural teachers who claimed, "We sacrifice ourselves for the country," actually lived in the cities. They spent three days a week in the community and imposed very long school days on poor students, so they could squeeze six days of lessons into three.

Lots of people talk about decentralization, but no one actually wants to do it. In the 1899 Civil War, La Paz flew the flag of federalism, promising to make Bolivia a federal country, against Sucre and the unitary state. They mobilized indigenous forces to fight alongside them, promising them land and better lives. But when they won and gained control of the government, they suddenly changed their minds. They found themselves happy to preside over a unitary state, and went back to repressing indigenous people. That's the dynamic—people never want to give up power.

JPF: Let's talk more about the Bolivian decentralization debate before 1994. What was it like? Who was pushing for decentralization and who was pushing against?

GSL: Well, there was and there wasn't such a debate. What they called decentralization was devolution to *regional* governments—to elected prefects (as governors) representing the departments, whose income derived from royalties on extractive industries: gas, petroleum, mining, forestry, etc. What they were really talking about was a federal system, which is not the same.

The regions and the capitals, mainly Santa Cruz and Tarija, were in favor. It was those two departments because they had petroleum. They wanted to control the income they produced. They wanted their own elected departmental congresses and prefects.

JPF: But who were "they"? Basically business leaders and landowners?

GSL: First of all, it was an elite—business groups and different social movements and civic organizations that were created for that end.

JPF: Why did the push for that kind of regional decentralization—what the *cruceños* and *tarijeños* [inhabitants of the departments of Santa Cruz and Tarija] wanted—never succeed before the LPP?

GSL: Because the parties didn't want it. We had internal problems because both the parties and government coalitions of the time were torn between their political and regional loyalties. Which pressures to obey? The pressure could become fierce. I was Minister of Planning and Co-ordination for the famous stabilization law, 21060. We cut a lot of things, and I was declared persona non grata in all the departments of Bolivia except one, which I was wise enough not to visit. In Cochabamba, my own district, I was declared persona non-grata twice.

JPF: Why specifically did the parties resist?

GSL: Because of conflict with the regions, which fought fiercely for their interests. It was a continual fight about resources. They wanted control of more and more of the national budget, not just royalties from their oil and gas. We were being pressured terribly by the teachers' unions, universities, and regional organizations. The parties were all suffering. Many felt it was expedient to be more loyal to regional groups and interest groups like teacher and health-worker unions from those areas. They demanded more and more without ever looking at where the money came from. Party discipline was a big problem because politicians feared the regions.

But the private sector was in agreement because they were scared of populist movements like Condepa and the UCS. Highland regions were also scared of so-called decentralization to regional governments, who would have had large incomes from raw materials. Regional elites were very well organized and vocal, and regularly made unreasonable budgetary demands. So really what I was doing was co-opting people by going down to a much more popular level.

JPF: That's interesting. So you put together a coalition of highland interests, private sector interests, and others who could see that this was going to solve a number of problems?

GSL: Yes. I didn't know exactly how those problems would be solved, but I had something that was very important: high credibility from having been with Victor Paz Estenssoro, and stopping hyperinflation, and also being able to communicate well.

JPF: I remember this period vividly. The MNR had been out of power and it was obviously a painful experience for them. No party likes being out of power, and the MNR—who made the National Revolution—always felt that it was the natural party of government.

GSL: They also had good political instincts. They weren't ideologically blocked. They weren't like the communists, or the fascists, blocked into a rigid way of thinking.

JPF: How did you convince the MNR to support popular participation?

GSL: Because it appealed to the MNR by its very name and substance—giving power back to the people. Also, as a national party the MNR was built of local and regional *comandos*. That's why we were so good in elections, because we had a political structure all over the country at all levels. We had the *comandos departamentales, comandos provinciales, comandos municipales* . . . and we had people who could see that this was a transfer of power and money. They had a good intuition and could see the political benefit.

But I tried to make it something very intellectual and that was a big mistake. "*No lo politizaremos* [Let's not exploit this politically]," I insisted. Instead perhaps I should have made speeches saying, "We gave you the land, we gave you the vote, and now we're going to give you power so you can participate in local decisions about the things that really affect your daily life." We were attacked for politicizing it anyway—*La Ley Maldita,* and everyone who said "These guys are going to use it politically." But they didn't realize it was going to be a true restructuring of political power and development.

But the MNR understood it immediately. They supported it, they applauded it, and they won local elections. They were very happy because instead of fighting for jobs they could win the local election. They went and sold it to the people, "We're going to have this and that," and the MNR just took over local power. We had landslides in the first municipal elections. We wiped everybody out because we had party members in all the regions, and we were a party that identified with the countryside. I had broken the glass ceiling of being able to win the cities for the MNR. I can't tell you the results we had in those first months.

2.2.10 *Popular Participation in Action*

JPF: So now the law's been promulgated. What happens next?

GSL: Before, no one ran for local government because the municipalities had no money. A few women ran and won. When popular participation came, and money with it, the men were indignant. They began throwing the women out of office. They'd say, "In the next election we've got to get rid of all these women, who only became candidates because there was no money."

So lots more men came in. But many women remained—many more than in national government. And I really learned. I really listened and I saw the wisdom of it. I saw, of course, that local government is women's government—and they're fifty per cent of the population and the mother of the other fifty per cent. So I think it's all about the power of women.

JPF: So this is unlocking women's power in some sense?

GSL: I belonged to a society where my mother was the one who taught us how to swim. My father was very affectionate. He was a great intellect and a very wise man, but my mother had the balls.

JPF: Then what happened?

GSL: Then the people had to decide what to do. So the first thing they do is fix the plaza, and then they fix the football field. "These idiots, they should be spending on education," said the critics. But these were the things that meant a lot to people. It was their right, their local identity. Of course, they later got around to education and health, which were vital. And what popular participation did was public investment. Before, the World Bank and other donors financed many wonderful hospitals and filled them full of equipment. But nobody had money for maintenance. The central government paid salaries, but the hospital had no band aids, they had no alcohol, they had nothing to operate with.

With participation, local people had the money to make sure these things actually ran. As they put up the money, they made sure the work got done and the money wasn't stolen. That's when it went from *Ley Maldita* to *Ley Bendita*—it was very sudden. And that's when everybody who was in politics started hating us. "These people gave everybody the vote together with land reform," they said, "and we won't be able to get rid of them for generations. Now they are going to stay forever!"

We tried to reintroduce land taxes, but we weren't successful. We did reintroduce land taxes on large plots of land, though.

JPF: When were land taxes abolished? In the Revolution?

GSL: When they gave out the land they abolished the tax. Which was idiotic because it was a firm principle of ownership since colonial times—if you pay a tax on it, it belongs to you. That created a big problem because with urbanization people who wanted to build couldn't get title to the land. "How are we going to know who owns it?" they kept saying. It's very simple, you just walk along and if a dog starts barking at you, that's the beginning of someone's property. Dogs know where the property is. You can't do it with aerial photography or GPS. But you can with a dog—a dog is trained to know what belongs to his master.

The World Bank wanted very sophisticated answers on how we were going to implement these measures. And of course all this "give all the power to the Soviets" stuff, they didn't like that very much. Nobody likes it because what everyone wants is to control other people. But popular participation worked because if communities didn't put money in, they didn't get money out. This was based on the Emergency Social Fund, which was Victor Paz' great idea. I was a technocrat; I wanted to talk about inflation. He said, "Goni, you can't do it if you don't take care of the people. You've got to create jobs." He was a good politician.

JPF: Looking back on it now, do you think that the LPP did what you set out to achieve?

GSL: I think it did in part. It was attacked violently from the left and the right. But it worked. I'm always very proud of the fact that when I went into government, 75 per cent of public investment was managed from La Paz and 25 per cent in the regions, and when I left government 25 per cent was managed from La Paz and 75 per cent in the regions. It increased funding for education and health all over the country. It was a fabulous reform.

JPF: Were there any outcomes from decentralization that you didn't expect?

GSL: I didn't expect a high level of corruption.

JPF: You didn't? Really?

GSL: No, I felt people would run things well. When the Catholic Church said corruption would increase, I always had a very good reply. I'd say, "At least we'll have achieved a true democracy in corruption. Usually only the guys on top steal, and that's not fair. Now everybody steals!" But the church was right—they had a more realistic view.

But, you know, as time went by people started to pay the price for corruption. My grandmother used to say, "There are two things you can't hide. One is money and the other is love." And money in a small community is hard to hide. You can't put it in Switzerland. People would look and say, "Where the hell did that truck come from?"

2.2.11 *Goni's Political Legacy*

JPF: Let's move on to the end of your presidency.

GSL: I left government in 1997 because I had to comply with the Constitution. But many people said that I had a constitutional method of staying in power for another term. A clause in the constitutional reform increasing the presidential term from four to five years would have permitted re-election once, with a two-thirds vote in Congress. But I knew I had a conflict of interest so I didn't take the re-election, and I'll tell you why. To get the two-thirds vote I needed to do a deal with either Banzer or Jaime Paz. Jaime Paz approached me and said, "The Americans are persecuting me because they say I used drug money for my campaigns." They'd taken away his visa and were pressuring me to apply the anti-drug law to throw him in jail. So Jaime Paz said to me, "I'm willing to vote for your re-election." "And benefit from a deal with the accused?" I said. "You don't have to do a deal with me. I won't persecute you. I've told the Americans that if they have proof of what they're alleging, they should apply for your extradition instead of taking away your visa and degrading your reputation." I promised unconditionally not to do it, even without his support.

The cynical American ambassador said to me, "You know, the proof we have wouldn't be permitted in a US court." They wanted me to do their dirty work for them. So I didn't take that deal, and everybody's criticized me because I didn't have enough time to see my reforms through. Maybe I did the right thing, maybe I didn't. But that's the way I did it.

JPF: You could have traded for it?

GSL: Yes, because he came in thinking that I was a good politician, which obviously I wasn't.

In fact, it was the wrong thing. When I was out of government, Banzer and Jaime Paz worked very hard over five years destroying everything we did. The biggest mistake I made was not making that deal with Jaime Paz to get another term. Because with his party we had the two-thirds I needed to run again. My party didn't help me either because they didn't want me to stay. Everybody wants to replace you. I felt bad about it on ethical grounds, but it was a terrible mistake. I could easily have won an even bigger re-election. They would have asked, "Why do you need five more years?" and I would have answered, "Trees need time to produce fruit. It took a year and a half to put these reforms in place, now let me finish." And the people would have said, "Let him finish. Let's see if it works." With five more years we would have seen the reforms bear fruit, and then Banzer and Jaime Paz wouldn't have been able to cut those trees down.

Indeed, that's why we moved to a five-year term. I learned that traveling around the countryside. Reform is like a fruit tree—you have to wait years to get the fruit. In the third year you start getting some fruit, and then more in the fourth year, and in the fifth year you finally see full production. So if you reform, a fifth year gives you a chance of seeing results before your party goes through another election.

All of these reforms could be dismantled. I felt the changes we'd made were so fundamental they couldn't be reversed. But they were.

JPF: Where do you fit in Bolivia's political history? Where is your place?

GSL: When I was elected, there were primaries and Guillermo Bedregal (the party's no. 2) won most of them. But then the party chose me, because the people in the party knew they couldn't win an election with him but they could with me. First, because I was more credible, and second—I had money! So they and the technocrats said, "This is the man who can do it."

But politicians are so self-centered. Although Victor Paz helped me, he was really upset because he wanted to finish his career with all of us, like Hindu wives, burnt on the pyre of his retirement. He was very upset with me when I became the candidate, although he did help me to obtain the nomination. He was upset because he was worried about his future. He was going into history and he had had some bad scrapes, but was able to return to power each time. His was the best government—his first and last governments—the last was a great government. I gave a speech and said that a politician is a man who looks at the next election, and a statesman is a man who looks at the next generation. So when I went to visit Victor Paz to present my resignation [as Minister], he said to me, "Goni, I've seen a lot of people over my career, and among the few that I think could be statesmen is you. But please explain to me, how the hell are you going to win this coming election?!?"

JPF: You think he was worried about being overshadowed by you?

GSL: No. I think, first of all, he couldn't leave it to a guy with a mining background; second, to a guy who had taken all the brunt of stabilization and all that brutal criticism; and third, to a guy who had this accent so far removed from peoples' lives. This was my first election, which I won and they stole from me. He couldn't believe that I had any chance. He preferred me to leave the scene, and for him to outlive his party. He wanted the party buried because he had founded it; he made the big revolution, and then the big counter-revolution—in this way Victor Paz is what Mao always dreamed of being. But Mao didn't have the experience, and he didn't have the people who would listen to him like Victor Paz did, by following him out and then following him back again. He had this wonderful reputation and he really deserved it.

I wish I hadn't been so intellectually arrogant. But you know you have to be an egomaniac to be a politician. The cost–benefit is so bad that you can't think you're human. My wife and my daughter—real people—were never in agreement that I should stay in politics because they had lived the ups and downs of political service. My wife's grandfather—a very good judge who happened to be the president of an interim government that called elections after the revolution that brought down the *ancien regime*—he was exiled by the MNR. The MNR got into power and of course threw him out. My wife and daughter saw how he suffered, an honest man and all the rest. So nobody wanted me to be in it. But I obviously had it in my genes. When democracy came to Bolivia, my father said, "Goni I don't think you really want to be the richest man in South America's poorest country. Now you have to go into public service." So of course I went to help the MNR and ended up in Parliament. That's a long story. A lot of it was luck, and a lot of it was instinct and something that I wanted.

JPF: Did you think that your first presidency would be a second revolution? And that you would be a second historic figure for Bolivia?

GSL: Yes. Whitehead said, "Progress is change with order and order with change." We were making a revolution in democracy. What is the definition of a revolution? It's irreversible change. But that's where I made a dramatic mistake. I didn't realize that in four years, the time it took me to get these concepts clarified and go through the dialectic, not only would it take so long to prepare, but once we presented the law we needed to go through hours and hours of meetings at community level with the unions and with parties, and we would even hold a great deal of meetings at town halls. People would come and Victor Hugo Cardenas [Bolivia's first indigenous Vice President, from 1993to 1997] and I would answer questions about popular participation. All these interest groups, like the teachers, and all the party members were against this, saying,

"How can you give power to ignorant people? How can they vote if they don't know how to read or write? How can they run their own affairs if they're illiterate?" And I said, "The majority of Bolivians are illiterate, but they all know how to count. Go down to the market and see if you can get a good deal out of these *cholas* [indigenous women in traditional bowler hats]. They know better than anybody what to do!"

JPF: In 1997 you handed over the Presidential sash to Gen. Hugo Banzer. But you chose to stay in politics. Why?

GSL: I always said the best job I ever had was in Congress. I loved being part of Congress. I liked negotiating in the halls, and all the horse trading. I always said, any job where you go to committee meetings after 10 a.m., and you don't have to go to work until after 3 p.m., is a good job. And every idiotic thing you say is recorded for posterity.

There are three things that people struggle for in politics. First money, but I already had that. I don't think honesty is a virtue, I think honesty is a habit. My family has had generations of people who didn't steal. Secondly you want women, and I'd had enough of that. I would have loved to be like Gaddafi and Berlusconi, but I'm too timid. I'm dominated by my wife! And thirdly, you do it for social position, and I had social position. That was my weakness—I had confidence, I was educated. So when you have those things, why are you in politics? You have a mix of, let's say, a desire for public service and you want to effect change. You want that change to be irreversible, but it's not. Or at least it wasn't.

Public service, wanting to serve your country—I think it's the ultimate arrogance. It's Greek hubris to think you can leave a mark in history. You can't. I think you plant a seed and maybe a tree grows, but you can't guarantee what it grows into. I wasn't able to—probably due to factors beyond my control. I think part of it is that you can't be a politician if you're not willing to bend with the wind. If you think you can be perfectly ethical and be in politics, you don't understand what you're doing! It's like thinking you can ride a horse without a bridle. So I think it was just absolute hubris. I felt I could do it and have all these things without dirtying my name. And now, of course, I'm accused of genocide.

2.2.12 *Changes in Bolivian Politics Since 1994*

JPF: It's self-evident that Bolivian politics have changed a lot in the last decade. Around the time when you were winning elections in the 1990s and early 2000s, we had a stable equilibrium of political parties that varied in terms of composition and ideology. But there was broadly a left–right spectrum, pro-labor vs. pro-business, with the MNR roughly in the middle, straddling that divide. How have Bolivian politics changed since then?[7]

[7] For interested readers, Faguet (2013) discusses the broad changes in governance that decentralization can be expected to bring about.

GSL: Of the so-called "traditional parties," the MNR had the strongest position because the changes it made were long-lasting. Land reform gave the MNR great strength in the countryside. Village elders told the young how life had been before land reform, and the peasantry voted for the MNR again and again. But over time people migrated to the city, farming and land became less important, and the elders started dying out. And the countryside began to lose that memory, and that gratitude.

Also, the ADN and the MIR worked very hard to discredit what we achieved. I gave Banzer five years in power,[8] but he didn't know what to do with it. All he wanted was to return to the Presidential Palace via the ballot box. He didn't actually have a platform—no idea what to do with the power he'd finally won legitimately. So he set about destroying many of the things I'd done, like the *Bonosol*. [The *Bonosol* paid elderly Bolivians a pension that raised many above the poverty line, out of the dividends from the capitalization of the big state-owned enterprises.] It was a beautiful idea. But they destroyed it.

JPF: Why do you think they did this?

GSL: Because they were worried that with these reforms the MNR would be in power forever. They had to undercut the basis of our popularity.

Since then everything has changed. Evo Morales came in and sold the idea of *lucha de razas* [racial warfare] to Bolivians.

Another big change has to do with drugs. I underestimated the problem of drugs. Since the 1950s, with land reform, coca was a symbol of colonial humiliation. People looked down on it. But the US decision to make it illegal had terrible effects on Bolivia. Prices and profitability shot up, and people started producing it like crazy. But we don't even capture much of the profit. Only 15 per cent of the street value of cocaine stays in Bolivia. The other 85 per cent goes to foreign traffickers.

Some of this drug money started flowing into politics. That's what the Jaime Paz deal was all about. Bolivian politics was already very corrupt—corruption was tied up with coalitions and agreements between parties over legislation and policy. People ran for office because of the corruption opportunities available to the winners. It was always going to be hard to eradicate. But then the drug money came in and turbo-charged the whole thing.

JPF: How were parties structured internally prior to 1994? Were they elitist? Verticalist? Or horizontal with strong grass-roots support?

GSL: The ADN were people who benefitted from Banzer's dictatorship. The MIR were a bunch of leftists who sold out for money. Both parties were vehicles for their respective leaders, Hugo Banzer and Jaime Paz, with everyone else basically riding their coat-tails. Neither survived the demise of the leader.

All the parties were run from the top down. All of them had lost touch with their grass-roots supporters. This was a worse problem for the ADN and MIR, which lacked the strong structure of the MNR's local and regional *comandos*.

[8] Goni's reform of the executive branch lengthened the presidential term from four to five years.

And that was made worse when Banzer's government began destroying my more popular reforms. People could see through that; it wasn't smart.

JPF: Did decentralization contribute to the downfall of the traditional parties?

GSL: The parties were already in trouble, and then, with popular participation, you could no longer use the political hacks you had before—they would lose local elections. You had to find people who were popular locally. We did this, but it was hard. The MNR had a structure that should have made it easier, but we weren't used to operating that way. And the other parties had worse traditions and no structure, so they were totally out of touch.

In the MNR, we just couldn't get used to it. The problem of women in politics is one example. Before the reform, local government was powerless and moneyless, and women dominated it. After reform, the men realized what was going on and went and kicked all the women out of their local offices. A lot of those were MNR men kicking out the women. It didn't help us win elections.

More broadly, the system of the second round in Congress [which traditionally decided most Bolivian elections] began to break down, because the way you held coalitions together was through patronage and corruption. With popular participation, patronage and corruption spread throughout the country. At the national level it got harder and more expensive to hold governments together. That was part of the political collapse. That is the story of my second term.

2.3 Afterword: Bolivia's Recent Political History

The changes alluded to above undermined the Bolivian political party system, although happily not its democracy.[9] Following on from decentralization by about a decade, a political tidal wave swept Goni from power and drowned all of the traditional political parties, and with them the political party system that had run the country for fifty years.

Since the 1952 Revolution, Bolivian politics had been centered on the MNR, accompanied by various opponents and offshoots to both left and right that alternated in power in a broadly stable, left–right, pro-labor vs. pro-business equilibrium that survived numerous coups and dramatic economic shocks. In 2003, political protests against Goni's second MNR-led government morphed into a popular uprising that led to his resignation and exile in the USA. With fewer congressmen than before, Goni depended on a larger number of more diverse parties for his congressional majority. As his position weakened in 2002–3, he drew more parties into the alliance. When civilians were killed by security forces and protest turned into full-scale revolt, not only the President was implicated, but most of the political system. When Goni fell, all of the traditional parties fell with him.

[9] As of this writing.

The old regime collapsed, leaving a yawning political vacuum. Into this stepped Evo Morales and his *Movimiento al Socialismo* (MAS). Bolivia's new politics is amorphous and still developing; its key competitive dimension since around 2005 has been ethnic and regional identity, although there is no guarantee that this will persist. The MAS itself is a comparatively loose political movement, much less organized or institutionalized than the MNR was before, its appeal largely centered on Morales himself. How it is likely to develop within a new Bolivian politics is impossible to say. But we can already conclude that the rise of the MAS was predicated on decentralization, which was crucial to the political transformation that swept the country.

To see this, consider these stylized facts. Until the 1990s, Congress was dominated by Bolivia's landed, business, and professional elite. More than 90 per cent of its members were educated upper-middle- and upper-class people with European surnames, private educations, and residences in its largest cities' best neighborhoods. They were typically men who developed careers in the private sector before penetrating national politics horizontally, via a party. Today, over half of Bolivia's Congress, and over four-fifths of its Constitutional Convention, comes from small towns and villages. They tend to be browner than their forebears, with indigenous surnames like Quispe, Callisaya, or Mamani, fewer diplomas, and backgrounds as carpenters, truck drivers, and farmers (as distinct from landowners). As Zuazo (2009) notes, they overwhelmingly got their political start in local government, as mayors, leaders of grass-roots organizations, and municipal councillors. Decentralization served as both platform and training ground, allowing them to ascend to higher levels of politics through successive elections. In simple terms, it provided a ladder up for budding politicians in Bolivia's villages and poor neighborhoods where previously none existed. Although they joined established parties for the first few elections, they soon turned their backs on such parties and overthrew them in favor of their own amorphous movement.

If the future of this new politics is hard to predict, the future of decentralization is not. Bolivia's current rulers were formed in the crucible of local politics. They see it as both natural and "theirs." They want more of it, as do voters. Hence one of Morales' major reforms has been a dramatic deepening of decentralization via the 2009 Constitution and the 2010 Law of Autonomies and Decentralization (Faguet, 2014). Major innovations include the introduction of indigenous and rural autonomous governments for "nations and peoples who share a cultural identity, language, historical traditions, institutions, territory, and world view" (Government of Bolivia, 2010, Art. 30(1)). The law allows such communities to govern themselves and organize their economies according to their own principles, practices, and forms of organization. Within such areas, traditional institutions and practices supersede the legal forms of the state (e.g. elected mayors and municipal councils). These are key elements in the construction of what the MAS calls the new, diverse, "pluri-national" Bolivia.

This leaves us with a final, potent irony: Morales, the MAS, and the "new Bolivia" want badly to stand for the deliberate, systematic rejection of a "neoliberal" past—the most potent symbol of which is Gonzalo Sánchez de Lozada. But all are, in the deepest sense, his own creation.

Bibliography and Further Reading

Albó, Xavier, 1990. *Los Guaraní-Chiriguano: La Comunidad Hoy*. La Paz: CIPCA.

Albó, Xavier, Armando Godínez, Kitula Libermann, and Francisco Pifarré, 1990. *Para Comprender Las Culturas Rurales en Bolivia*. 2nd edn. La Paz: MEC/CIPCA/UNICEF.

Albó, Xavier and Victor Quispe, 2004. *¿Quiénes son los indígenas en los gobiernos municipales?* La Paz: CIPCA.

Ardaya, Rubén, 1996. *La Construcción Municipal de Bolivia*. La Paz: Editora Ateneo.

Blanes, José, 2000. *Mallkus y Alcades: La Ley de Participación Popular en comunidades rurales del Altiplano paceño*. La Paz: PIEB.

Boone, Peter and Jean-Paul Faguet, 1998. "Multilateral Aid, Politics and Poverty: Past Failures and Future Challenges," chapter 2 in Richard Grant and Jan Nijman (eds.). *The Global Crisis in Foreign Aid*, Syracuse, N.Y.: Syracuse University Press.

Cabrera, Juan E., 2011. "La construcción del territorio plurinacional. Bolivia de 1960 a 2010." *Territorios*, 24: 13–58.

Campbell, Timothy, 2001. *The Quiet Revolution: The Rise Of Political Participation and Leading Cities with Decentralization in Latin America and the Caribbean*. Pittsburgh: University of Pittsburgh Press.

Channa, Anila and Jean-Paul Faguet, 2012. "Decentralization of Health and Education in Developing Countries: A Quality-Adjusted Review of the Empirical Literature." LSE/STICERD Working Paper No. EOPP 38.

Dunkerley, James, 1984. *Rebellion in the Veins: Political Struggle in Bolivia 1952–82*. London: Verso.

Faguet, Jean-Paul, 2014. "Can Sub-National Autonomy Strengthen Democracy in Bolivia?" *Publius: The Journal of Federalism*, 44(1): 51–81; doi: 10.1093/publius/pjt020.

Faguet, Jean-Paul (ed.), 2013. "Decentralization and Governance." Special Issue of *World Development*. <http://dx.doi.org/10.1016/j.worlddev.2013.01.002>.

Faguet, Jean-Paul, 2012. *Decentralization and Popular Democracy: Governance from Below in Bolivia*. Ann Arbor: University of Michigan Press.

Faguet, Jean-Paul, 2004. "Why So Much Centralization? A Model of Primitive Centripetal Accumulation." LSE-STICERD Development Economics Discussion Paper No.43, London School of Economics and Political Science.

Faguet, Jean-Paul, 2000. "Decentralization and Local Government Performance: Improving Public Service Provision in Bolivia," *Revista de Economía del Rosario*, 3(1): 127–76.

Faguet, Jean-Paul and Zulfiqar Ali, 2009. "Making Reform Work: Institutions, Dispositions and the Improving Health of Bangladesh." *World Development*. 37: 208–18.

Faguet, Jean-Paul and Fabio Sánchez, 2013. "Decentralization and Access to Social Services in Colombia." *Public Choice*. Winner of the Corporación Andina de Fomento International Research Paper Prize. DOI 10.1007/s11127-013-0077-7.

Faguet, Jean-Paul and Mahvish Shami, 2008. "Fiscal Policy and Spatial Inequality in Latin America and Beyond." World Bank Policy Research Working Paper.

Faguet, Jean-Paul and Frank-Borge Wietzke, 2006. "Social Funds and Decentralization: Optimal Institutional Design." *Public Administration and Development*, 26(4): 303–15.

Government of Bolivia, 2010. Ley Marco de Autonomías y Descentralización "Andrés Ibáñez." La Paz: Ministry of Autonomy.

Klein, Herbert, 1993. *Historia de Bolivia.* La Paz: Libreria-Editorial Juventud.

Klein, Herbert S. 2003. *A Concise History of Bolivia.* Cambridge: Cambridge University Press.

Madison, James, Alexander Hamilton, and John Jay, 1961. *The Federalist Papers.* New York: New American Library.

Manor, James, 1999. *The Political Economy of Democratic Decentralization* Washington, DC: World Bank.

Quiroga, Giancarla de, 1999. "Gobernabilidad y participación ciudadana." *Revista Cidob d'Afers Internacionals*, 47: pp. 169–74.

Oxhorn, Philip, 2001. "La construcción del Estado por la sociedad civil: La ley de Participación Popular de Bolivia y el desafío de la democracia local." BID Serie de Documentos de Trabajo I-20 CAN. Washington, DC: Banco Interamericano de Desarrollo.

Regalsky, Pablo, 2010. "Political Processes and the Reconfiguration of the State in Bolivia." *Latin American Perspectives*, 37: 35–50.

Rodden, Jonathan A., Gunnar S. Eskeland, and Jennie Litvack, 2003. *Fiscal Decentralization and the Challenge of Hard Budget Constraints*. Cambridge, Mass.: MIT Press.

Rondinelli, Dennis A., John R. Nellis, and G. Shabbir Cheema, 1983. "Decentralization in Developing Countries: A Review of Recent Experience." Staff Working Paper 581, Washington, DC: World Bank.

Secretaría Nacional de Participación Popular, Ministerio de Desarrollo Sostenible y Medio Ambiente, 1994. *Ley de Participación Popular, Reglamento de las Organizaciones Territoriales de Base*. La Paz.

Shah, Anwar, Theresa M. Thompson, and Heng-Fu Zou, 2004. "The impact of decentralization on service delivery, corruption, fiscal management and growth in developing and emerging market economies: A synthesis of empirical evidence." CESifo DICE Report, 1/2004: 10–14.

Smoke, Paul. 2001. Fiscal Decentralization in Developing Countries: A Review of Current Concepts and Practice. Democracy, Governance and Human Rights Program Paper No. 2, UNRISD, Geneva.

Treisman, Daniel, 2007. *The Architecture of Government: Rethinking Political Decentralization.* New York: Cambridge University Press.

Urioste, Miguel, 2001. *Bolivia: Descentralización municipal y Participación Popular.* La Paz: Tierra.

Weingast, Barry, 2013. "Second Generation Fiscal Federalism: Political Aspects of Decentralization and Economic Development ." *World Development*, vol 53, pp 14–25.

Zuazo, Moira, 2009. *Cómo nació el MAS. La ruralización de la política en Bolivia.* La Paz: FES.

Zuazo, Moira, Jean-Paul Faguet, and Gustavo Bonifaz (eds.), 2012. *Descentralización y democratización en Bolivia: La historia del Estado débil, la sociedad rebelde y el anhelo de democracia*. La Paz: Friedrich Ebert Stiftung.

3

Breaking the Countercyclical Pattern of Local Democracy in Pakistan

Ali Cheema, Adnan Q. Khan, and Roger B. Myerson

3.1 Introduction

The history of Pakistan shows a paradoxically countercyclical pattern for local democracy. Three times in the country's history, elected institutions of local democracy have been created by military regimes, and each time the subsequent civilian governments have either failed to revive elected local governments or replaced them with unelected administrators. In the most recent transition from military to civilian democratic rule, elected local governments were created by General Pervez Musharraf's military regime, but the revived civilian provincial governments completed their five-year term in office without holding local government elections and again placed these governments under the authority of unelected administrators.[1] Thus, although incumbent political parties have promised local democracy in their election manifestos and have finally reenacted local government legislation after six years in office,[2] the institutionalization of empowered democratic local governments in Pakistan remains in doubt.

Supporters of democracy in Pakistan must understand this countercyclical pattern of local democracy to seek ways of escaping from it. Successful democracy depends on a vital relationship between democratic politics at the local and national levels.[3] A commitment by civilian democratic regimes to functional elected local governments would strengthen the foundations of federal

[1] This is true as of August 2014, when this paper was last updated.
[2] The legislation was finally passed after considerable pressure from the Courts.
[3] Giuliano and Nunn (2013) provide preliminary evidence on the association between a tradition of democracy at the local level with contemporary democracy and democratic attitudes.

democracy in Pakistan. The democratic parties' disconnection from local government has created local political vacuums that have been repeatedly exploited by nondemocratic forces to undermine the national system of civilian governance.

This detachment from local politics has had particularly disastrous consequences in the Federally Administered Tribal Areas (FATA), where the regular court system does not function, arbitrary colonial era laws remain in force, and until recently political parties were not allowed to operate. In these tribal areas, local democracy has never been introduced and colonial modes of governance continue. The long neglect of democratic and legal rights in the tribal areas set the stage for militant insurgency, which has had profound national and regional consequences and prompted some demand for military action. However, such military action could only be successful if combined with the building of responsible local government in these areas, which could hardly take place at a time when local democracy is being suspended in the rest of the country.

In this chapter, we consider how this disconnection between political parties and local democracy evolved, and how the foundations of democracy in Pakistan could be strengthened by healing this rift.

3.2 Non-Representative Regimes have Championed Local Government Reforms

In 1959, General Ayub Khan's Basic Democracies Ordinance established local councils that included both elected members and members appointed by the government, with administrative supervision by an appointed civil servant. Zulfikar Ali Bhutto's civilian government did not establish elected local governments during its tenure from 1971 to 1977. Elected local governments were revived in 1979, under General Zia ul-Haq's military regime, and this time all council members were locally elected. After the restoration of civilian constitutional government in 1988, however, tensions between elected provincial and local tiers over who controls and dominates local patronage resulted in the suspension of elected local bodies and their replacement for the most part with unelected administrators.

Elected local governments were again established in 2001 by the Local Government Ordinances of General Pervez Musharraf's military regime. Under General Musharraf's reforms, local administrators reported to the locally elected government, instead of supervising it. However, since the revival of democratic governments at the federal and provincial levels, true to the countercyclical pattern, the incumbent political parties have continuously delayed holding local government elections, and each of the four civilian provincial governments have run local governments through unelected administrators. Although new local government legislation has been passed by provincial legislators in all four provinces—six years after the latest transition to democracy after considerable pressure from the Courts—there seems to be no urgency to hold local government elections and institutionalize an empowered democratic local government system in the near future.

3.3 Why has Local Democracy been Associated Only with Military Regimes?

Elected local governments have helped military regimes to legitimize and strengthen their control over the state. To counter the popular support of democratic political parties, military regimes built an alternative base of political support by patronizing a class of new locally elected politicians. Elected local officials could offer the non-representative central government a vital political connection to local constituencies throughout the nation (Cheema et al. 2006). Local officials could communicate local concerns to the non-representative center as they helped it extend its influence in local politics. As later military rulers confronted a more developed system of party politics at higher levels of government, elected local officials were given progressively greater authority over local administration under the later rounds of military-sponsored local government reforms.

In all these local government reforms, however, political parties have been consistently excluded from any role in sponsoring candidates for local elections. Rules against partisan politics could be selectively applied by the military regime to restrict its opponents without limiting its own favored candidates. As a result of this rule, mainstream political parties have historically seen non-partisan local governments as an instrument of military regimes for creating a class of collaborative politicians to displace the parties' organization at the local level.

In a democratic regime, it is very difficult to institutionalize an empowered democratic local government system when the political parties' representatives in the national and provincial assemblies see elected officials at the local level as competitors for power and patronage. Parties and their legislators might promise to reform local democracy and even pass legislation, but the governments in power would find it more convenient to keep delaying the transfer of power to elected local governments on different pretexts. Thus, it is not surprising that institutions of elected local democracy have been kept weak and withered, while civilian democratic governments have been restored at the provincial and federal levels.

3.4 The Disconnection from Local Democracy has weakened National Democracy

A simple count of the number of elected officials illustrates the potential importance of local government in strengthening the national democratic system. General Musharraf's 2001 reform increased the number of popularly elected representatives by almost 80,000 members at the lowest tier of elected governments, the union councils. It also resulted in a significant increase in the number of elected positions reserved for peasants and women, with a total one-third reserved seats, as compared to 5 and 10 per cent in district councils previously. These elected local councilors represent a large pool of potential political talent, compared with about 1,100 elected members of national and provincial assemblies who form the basis of constitutional government today.

These local political leaders should be contributing to the strength of the whole democratic system, but their contribution is lost when political parties are disconnected from local government.[4] In a strong democratic system, outstanding achievements in local government should open a path for local leaders to advance to higher political offices, but such paths are closed when mainstream parties are separated from local government.[5] When local government is nonpartisan, political parties cannot enhance their reputations by sponsoring better local governance. Thus, democratic competition to improve local government is weakened, and barriers to entry are raised in provincial and federal politics.

The structure of political parties has been affected by their disjunction from democratic local government. Political parties in Pakistan are highly centralized, and their national and provincial leadership retains considerable control with regard to the nominations of legislative candidates and strategic decision-making. Their organizational structure does not reach broadly down to the local grass-roots level. According to Duke University's cross-country Democratic Accountability Survey, in comparative terms, Pakistani parties exhibit fairly high levels of organizational centralization combined with

[4] National political parties have played an important role in the sustainable introduction of local democracy in a number of successful transitions to decentralization in Latin America and South Asia, such as Bolivia (Faguet 2012 and 2014), Bangladesh (Faguet and Ali 2009), Brazil (Heller 2001), Kerala (Heller 2001), and West Bengal (Bardhan et al. 2009). In fact, the earliest and most sustainable transitions to local democracy in post-Independence India have happened in states where national political parties have taken ownership of the decentralization agenda. Crook and Manor (1998), Enikolopov and Zhuravskaya (2007), and Ponce-Rodriquez et al. (2012) find cross-national evidence that the benefits of political decentralization can depend on strong competitive political parties at the national level. In fact, the evidence of Ponce-Rodriquez et al. (2012) provides support for the hypothesis that the combination of democratic decentralization (popularly elected subnational governments) and party centralization (national political parties playing a role in local candidate selection) produces the best outcomes for public service delivery.

[5] Myerson (2014) elaborates the theoretical reasoning underlying this argument.

average levels of organizational extensiveness (Kitschelt and Palmer 2009). Interestingly, the survey data found that experts' assessments of these measures had little variation across the different Pakistani parties.

A consequence of the barriers to entry in provincial and federal politics resulting from the disconnect between local governments and political parties is the much higher incidence of dynastic dominance in Pakistani politics compared with other polities. A recent study finds that the incidence of dynastic politics among Pakistan's elected representatives is nearly double the incidence found in India and five times the incidence found in the USA during the Civil War period (Cheema, Javid, and Naseer 2013). It finds that between 1985 and 2008 approximately two-thirds of the elected legislators and around half of the top three contestants in the national assembly elections in Punjab were dynastic,, and the incidence of dynasticism has remained remarkably stable over this period. The lack of a strong competitive presence of mainstream parties in local politics has been exploited three times already by military rulers to consolidate their regime after a coup. It would be much more difficult for a future military ruler to displace the democratic political parties if their base of support extended into local politics.

The weakness of local democracy has been particularly problematic in the Federally Administered Tribal Areas (FATA). Under Article 247 of the Constitution, the regular court system does not function in FATA. Local government laws have never been applied in these areas. Denying legal and democratic rights in tribal areas fostered a narrow tribal leadership that was vulnerable to Taliban insurgency. This local political vacuum has thus served the interests of militants and has worked against moderate political parties, which have been barred from organizing political activities in these areas.

To restore government authority in these areas, military operations against insurgents can only be a first step, and they must be followed by a political process of building effective local government. The legitimacy and durability of governance in tribal areas would be strengthened by the involvement of a broadly representative group of elected local leaders, who would become stakeholders in the political system. The introduction of local democracy in the tribal areas could be a vital step toward restoring government authority there in a form that can win greater support from the local population. But the extension of local democracy to tribal areas seems unlikely while local democracy is being suspended in other parts of the nation.

When we recognize the vital importance of local democracy, we can begin to ask what forms of local democracy can contribute most to the strength of the national democratic system. This question requires us to consider the structures of local government in some detail, as seemingly minor details in the rules of the political game can sometimes have major consequences for the nature of political competition.

3.5 Local Government Reforms have been Designed to Fit the Purposes of Military Regimes

The 2001 reforms reduced the significance of union councils by giving executive authority to mayors (nazims) who were elected separately, instead of allowing the local councils to elect their leaders and hold them responsible as in a parliamentary system. The union council is the lowest tier and it is the only tier where the councilors and mayors were directly elected by the people. By elevating the mayor above the union council, the reforms narrowed the effective base of local democratic leadership in the tier of government closest to the citizenry (Cheema and Mohmand 2004).

General Musharraf's local government system required the deputy mayors and mayors of all union administrations located within the jurisdiction of the relevant tehsil (sub-district) and district to serve as the councilors of the two higher tiers of local government; the tehsil and district respectively. This system of constituting district governments from union governments may have advantages for encouraging cooperation between the different levels of local governments. However, the cooperative connection between different tiers was weakened by the fact that union mayors and deputy mayors were made higher-tier councilors in their personal capacity and not as representatives elected by their union councils.

Under the 2001 system, the district and tehsil mayors were not subject to direct popular election but were indirectly elected by a large electoral college that included all members of the union councils in the district and tehsil respectively. Once elected, however, the district mayors were responsible only to a smaller council of local union mayors. Having members of the union councils elect district mayors and tehsil mayors over whom they had no subsequent power encouraged corrupt manipulation and vote-selling excesses, beyond the forms of coalition-building that are normal in parliamentary systems where the executive is answerable to the same group that elects it.

An important feature of this system is that local union councils were popularly elected by a voting rule called single non-transferable vote (SNTV) (Keefer et al. 2006; Cheema et al. 2006). SNTV is a kind of multi-seat proportional representation system, but without any party lists. In SNTV, each voter must cast a ballot that endorses just one individual candidate among the many candidates who are competing to fill many available seats. In the local elections of 2001, a voter could cast one vote for a candidate to fill the eight general unreserved seats on the council, plus separate votes for several other categories of reserved seats for women, minorities, and disadvantaged groups.

Historically, SNTV was introduced in Japan in 1900 by oligarchic rulers who had an interest in keeping democracy weak (Ramseyer and Rosenbluth 1998). When SNTV was used in Afghanistan's 2005 parliamentary election without political parties to coordinate voting blocs, the result was that losing candidates split large majorities of the votes in each province. In the long run, because of such coordination problems, SNTV tends to favor factions that have supporters who will obey their leaders' coordinating directives about how to vote.[6] Thus, SNTV tends to reinforce the power of corporate or tribal leaders who exercise authority in patron–client relationships.[7]

The exclusion of parties from local elections, the concentration of power in separately or indirectly elected mayors, and the use of SNTV in council elections may have made sense if the goal was to reduce the non-representative central government's costs of managing the local political system. However, these provisions seem less well designed for the goals of strengthening broad democratic representation and accountability in government.

3.6 Well-Designed Local Government Reforms can Strengthen Pakistan's Federal Democracy

A reformed local government system that strengthens Pakistan's federal democracy must engage the mainstream political parties and give them a stake in supporting local democracy. Most importantly, by engaging the provincial and national parties, local democratic institutions should help the parties to develop a broader political base of active local supporters, whose energies would strengthen their party at all levels. The strength of a democratic political party must ultimately depend on the quality of its candidates. Well-designed local governments should serve as a primary source of candidates who can advance democratically to higher offices after first proving their ability to earn popular approval at the local level.

In the following, we offer examples of how local institutions could be better designed to meet these criteria.

A vital role for parties in local elections can be assured by electing local councils according to a list system of proportional representation, in which voters choose among competing party lists. Any party that has at least some minimal representation in the provincial or national assembly should be able to nominate a list of candidates for local elections throughout the province. Local council seats would then be allocated to each party list in proportion to the number of local voters who choose this party on their ballots.

[6] Cheema and Mohmand (2008) provide evidence that under Pakistan's 2001 local government system traditional rural elites were much more successful at coordinating electoral voting factions than the leadership of low-income, poor, and marginalized households.

[7] The coordination problems under SNTV become more severe when the number of seats being allocated is larger. So the problems of SNTV may have contributed to the decision in 2005 to decrease the size of the local union councils from 21 to 13 (See Myerson 2009).

But if voters only choose among party lists that were formed by party leaders, then local elections will do nothing to promote the political advancement of individual candidates who achieve greater popular approval. In a well-designed local government, local elections should help each party to measure the popular support that its local candidates have helped it to earn in each community. To achieve this function, voters' ballots in local elections should also include some indications of approval or disapproval for individual candidates. Such votes for individual candidates can be incorporated into a party-list system of proportional representation by using what is called an "open list." For example, each voter who supports a party could be asked on the ballot to indicate an approval rating for each candidate in the party's list. Then the seats that the party wins on the local council would be awarded to its candidates who get positive approval ratings from the largest numbers of the party's supporters in the election. Such an approval-voting open-list proportional representation system would give each party a clear indication of who among its candidates has earned the broadest support from local voters.

The recent local government legislation passed by the provinces in 2013 has institutionalized partisan elections, which will give parties a stake in supporting local democracy. This is an important first step towards building effective democracy in Pakistan. However, initial indications[8] suggest that the selection of local electoral candidates is likely to be the preserve of the provincial party leadership. This is likely to strengthen the control of federal and provincial dynastic politicians in parties and their clients, which will perpetuate barriers to entry into politics. By denying a formal role to the voice of voters in candidate selection this local electoral system may weaken the ability of the local government system to act as an effective nursery for the selection and advancement of talented politicians. This will strengthen political oligarchies as political advancement is likely to depend on loyalty to the party leadership rather than on an independent reputation for public service.[9]

Letting local councils at each level elect their own executive mayor or nazim would give effective responsibility for local government to a broadly representative group of local leaders, which would be consistent with the systems of parliamentary responsibility that are already constitutionally mandated in government at the provincial and national levels in Pakistan. This reform should be initiated at the level of the lowest tier, the union council, and followed through the higher tiers.

The past system of including local union mayors in the councils of larger districts may be a good way of encouraging higher levels of local government

[8] This was clearly the norm during the election campaign in Punjab's local government elections that were scheduled to be held in January 2014 but were suspended one month before the date of polling.

[9] On this centralizing tendency, referred to as the Iron Law of Oligarchy, see Michels (1915).

to cooperate effectively with lower levels. Enacting parliamentary democracy at the union council level will ensure that union mayors and deputy mayors become higher-tier councilors in their capacity as representatives of their respective union councils, and so will strengthen the links of cooperation between different tiers of government. But to provide a way of identifying popular local leaders in larger districts, a district council should also include some representatives who are elected at large by the voters of the entire district, using the approval-voting open-list system as suggested above. It would be natural to suggest that the district mayor should be chosen by the council from among these at-large representatives. Then the position of district representative at large could become an important step in the ladder of democratic advancement (between local union councils and provincial assemblies) for politicians who earn the trust of voters in the district.

Established leaders in the national and provincial governments might naturally have concerns about elected local officials becoming future competitors for power. Any reform that enhances democratic competition is bound to raise such concerns. But these concerns would likely be substantially assuaged when candidates for local elections are nominated by the parties that have representation in the national and provincial assemblies. Giving district councils the power to replace their mayors would also be likely to help reduce concerns about local political dominance by a too-powerful district mayor. Under open-list proportional representation, district councilors at large would get votes from only a fraction of their party's supporters, but assembly representatives are elected in single-member districts and so would regularly get votes from all their party's supporters. So an assembly representative could generally expect to get more votes in his electoral district than any councilor of local government.

The political benefits of local democracy depend on voters having the right to entrust their local governments to local leaders who are entrusted with adequate political, administrative, and budgetary authority to deliver and who may later become rivals for higher offices on the basis of their reputation for better governance at the local level. Therefore it is important that political, administrative, and budgetary authority for local governments should be defined and protected by law. Historically, local governments in Pakistan have not been granted sufficient authority to demonstrate better governance. Nearly all resources for local governments have flowed from the province with only negligible levels of local revenue generation (Keefer et al 2006).[10] Local governments had historically been assigned limited municipal and

[10] This is also true for provincial governments which receive more than 80 per cent of their revenues from federal transfers despite most expenditures being assigned to the provinces, especially after the passage of the 18th Amendment to the Constitution. However, unlike local governments, provincial governments hold the required political, budgetary, and administrative authority under the Constitution to effectively deliver public goods and services.

development functions. Although General Musharraf's 2001 reforms devolved major functions to the local governments, with finances, staffing, and salaries still controlled by the province the devolved governments under the 2013 legislation would continue to have severely curtailed administrative and budgetary authority (Cheema et al 2006; Manning et al 2003).

Institutionalizing effective local democracy will require giving local governments control over the planning and provision of all local public goods and services, control over their administrative staff, and rights to predictable and effective finances. The current legislation in the country's two major provinces has recentralized key functions such as education, health, and urban planning and assigned them to provincial authorities.[11] The recentralization of these functions will disempower local governments and local politicians and weaken the foundations of democracy.

Credible commitment to effective local democracy will require protection for local governments against selective politically motivated interference in their domain by higher tiers of government. There is always a risk that provincial and national politicians may be tempted to use the power of the higher tiers of government to undermine local leaders who are seen as potential political rivals. So it may be important to provide some constitutional protection for local governments or independent judicial review of such actions against them. While the current legislation has placed some time limitations on the provincial governments' power to suspend local governments, it needs to provide much more clarity about the ambit of independent judicial review.

3.7 Local Government Reforms have Vital Importance for Pakistan and the World

People value democracy because the welfare of any community depends on how its leaders are chosen. We have focused here on the detailed rules of local government because the way that local leaders are chosen can have fundamental consequences for the successful development of democracy at all levels of government. Successful democracy requires a flexible system of strong political parties and a plentiful supply of candidates who have good reputations for responsible public service. Local democracy greatly increases this supply of political talent and thus provides the broadest foundation for building a strong, successful democracy.

[11] See the recently enacted 2013 Local Government Acts of Punjab and Sindh. See Channa and Faguet (2012) for a review of international evidence on the effects of decentralization on education and health in developing countries.

Democracy in Pakistan faces formidable challenges. Intervals of military rule, which retarded the development of connections between mainstream political parties and local democracy, have ended at last with a recognition that effective, stable government must be based on civilian political organizations that are widely trusted by the voters. At present, several areas of Pakistan are threatened by violent guerrilla forces, and such insurgencies can be defeated only by effective cooperation between national political leadership, military forces, and local political leaders who are trusted by their communities. To overcome these challenges, Pakistan's mainstream political parties need to develop broader networks of local leaders who have earned the trust of voters throughout the nation.

In particular, Pakistan's political forces and military should be working together now to build popularly supported local government in the tribal areas, where the long neglect of local democratic rights has had such disastrous consequences. Involvement of elected local leaders from these areas in political, economic, and administrative decision-making would provide greater legitimacy to counter-insurgency efforts and would provide a broad representative base of stakeholders for a stronger system of local government.

At this critical time, the continued hesitation about institutionalizing empowered elected local governments must be seen a serious step in the wrong direction. Current decisions about re-establishing empowered democratic local government in Pakistan, and reforming its political institutions to enable these governments to become effective nurseries, able to ensure the selection and advancement of talented politicians, should be recognized as having vital importance for the people of Pakistan, and for all those throughout the world who care about the prospects for Pakistan's constitutional democracy.

Bibliography

Bardhan, P., S. Mitra, D. Mookherjee, and A. Sarkar, 2009. "Local Democracy and Clientelism: Implications for Political Stability in West Bengal," *Economic and Political Weekly* Vol. XLIV No. 9: 46–58.

Channa, A. and J.P. Faguet, 2012. "Decentralization of Health and Education in Developing Countries: A Quality-Adjusted Review of the Empirical Literature." LSE/STICERD Working Paper No. EOPP 38.

Cheema, A., H. Javid, and M. F. Naseer, 2013. "Dynastic Politics in Punjab: Facts, Myths and their Implications," Institute of Development and Economic Alternatives Working Paper No. 01–13.

Cheema, A., A. I. Khwaja, and A. Qadir, 2006. "Local government reform in Pakistan: Context, Content, and Causes," in Bardhan, P. and D. Mookherjee (eds.) *Decentralization and Local Governance in Developing Countries*. Cambridge, Massachusetts: The MIT Press, pp. 257–84.

Cheema, A. and S.K. Mohmand, 2008. "Decentralization and Inequality in Pakistan: Bridging the Gap that Divides," in S. M. Ali and M.A. Saqib (eds.) *Devolution and Governance Reforms in Pakistan*. Karachi: Oxford University Press.

Cheema, A. and S.K. Mohmand, 2004. "Provision Responses to Devolved Service Delivery: Case Evidence from Jaranwala Tehsil." LUMS-McGill Social Enterprise Development Centre.

Crook, R.C. and J. Manor, 1998. *Democracy and Decentralization in South Asia and West Africa*. Cambridge: Cambridge University Press.

Enikolopov, R. and E. Zhuravskaya, 2007. "Decentralization and Political Institutions," *Journal of Public Economics* 91: 2261–90.

Faguet, J.P., 2014. "Can Sub-National Autonomy Strengthen Democracy in Bolivia?" *Publius: The Journal of Federalism*, 44(1): 51–81; doi: 10.1093/publius/pjt020.

Faguet, J. P., 2012. *Decentralization and Popular Democracy: Governance from below in Bolivia*. Ann Arbor, Michigan: University of Michigan Press.

Faguet, J.P. and Z. Ali, 2009. "Making Reform Work: Institutions, Dispositions and the Improving Health of Bangladesh." *World Development*. 37: 208–18.

Giuliano, P. and N. Nunn, 2013. "The Transmission of Democracy: From the Village to the Nation-State," *American Economic Review* 103(3): 86–92.

Heller, P., 2001. "Moving the State: The Politics of Democratic Decentralization in Kerela, South Africa and Porto Alegre," *Politics & Society* 29: 131–63.

Keefer, P.E., A. Narayan, and T. Vishwanath, 2006. "Decentralization in Pakistan: Are Local Governments likely to be more Accountable than the Central Government?" in Bardhan, P. and D. Mookherjee (eds.) *Decentralization and Local Governance in Developing Countries*. Cambridge, Massachusetts: MIT, pp. 285–303.

Kitschelt, H. and D. Palmer, 2009. "Expert Survey on Citizen-Politician Linkages Initial Findings for Pakistan in Comparative Context," mimeo, Duke University.

Manning, N., D. Porter, J. Charlton, M. Cyan, and Z. Hasnain, 2003. "Devolution in Pakistan—Preparing for Service Delivery Improvements," A working paper prepared for the Forum on Intergovernmental Relations and Service Delivery in Pakistan 27–9 June 2003.

Michels, R., 1915. *Political Parties: A Sociological Study of Oligarchic Tendencies in Modern Democracy*. New York: Hearst's International Library Company.

Myerson, R. B., 2014. "Democratic Decentralization and Economic Development," mimeo, University of Chicago.

Myerson, R. B., 2009. "Local foundations for strong democracy in Pakistan," *Social Science and Policy Bulletin* 1(2):2–20 (Lahore University of Management Sciences).

Ponce-Rodriguez, R.A., C. A. Hankla, J. Martinez-Vazquez, and E. Heredia-Ortiz, 2012. "Rethinking the Political Economy of Decentralization: How Elections and Parties Shape the Provision of Local Public Goods," International Center for Public Policy, Andrew Young School, Georgia State University, Working Paper 12–32.

Ramseyer, J.M. and F. M. Rosenbluth, 1998. *The Politics of Oligarchy: Institutional Choice in Imperial Japan*. Cambridge: Cambridge University Press.

4

Inclusive Governance for Inclusive Development

The History, Politics, and Economics of *Panchayat Raj*

Mani Shankar Aiyar

> I shall work for an India in which the poorest shall feel that it is their country, in whose making they have an effective voice.
>
> Mahatma Gandhi

4.1 Introduction

From the time Mahatma Gandhi led the struggle for Independence to the present day, there has been extensive recognition in India that *panchayat raj*[1] (local self-government) is imperative for both deepening India's democracy and making its development processes "inclusive." That is, *panchayat raj* is crucial for ensuring that the people at large, and especially the poor, tangibly benefit from the growth process.[2] The aim was to involve the people in the running of their own affairs in their respective neighborhood communities. "Institutions of local self-government" (note: not merely self-governance but

[1] In common parlance, rural local self-government is referred to as Panchayati Raj or Governance *of* the Panchayats; purists insist, however, that grammatically the correct expression should be Panchayat Raj or Governance *by* the Panchayats. I have here followed the grammarians' injunction.

[2] This view is strongly supported by an extensive international literature on the potential decentralization has to strengthen democracy and improve the provision of essential services. See, e.g., Faguet (2000, 2008, and 2014) and Channa and Faguet (2012).

self-government, the expression expressly used in the Constitution) comprising their own elected representatives, responsible to their own community electorate, would be more likely than a distant bureaucracy to respond to the felt and articulated needs and demands of the neighborhood communities.

However, the actual progress in securing this goal has been fitful, uncertain, and unsustained. There are now nearly 300,000 institutions of democratically constituted units of local self-government, to which some 3.2 million representatives have been elected, 1.2 million of whom are women.[3] However, instead of empowering an army of democratically elected community and neighborhood leaders to deliver public goods and services to the intended beneficiaries, state governments and union territory (UT) administrations continue relying on the bureaucracy and their partners in civil society to do so. In consequence, as this chapter attempts to show, outcomes are nowhere near commensurate with outlays.[4]

There are two main reasons for this. First, there is insufficient clarity and conviction regarding the indispensability of *panchayat raj* for inclusive development. Second, there is considerable resistance to the systemic revolution entailed in effective *panchayat raj* on the part of the polity and the bureaucracy, who stand to lose their powers of patronage and influence if there is indeed a genuine overhaul of the development process.

In the meantime, while GDP grew at over 8 per cent per annum on average from 2006–11, poverty alleviation languished at under 0.8 per cent per annum (Planning Commission 2011). Four hundred and sixty-four police station jurisdictions spread across 95 districts in 11 States are in the grip of the Maoist/Naxalite insurgency. Moreover, the lower-to-middle "middle class," who are often proudly presented as the principal beneficiaries of accelerated growth, are expressing their profound resentment at the glass ceiling they have hit as they peer through it at soaring income and wealth inequalities, which are the inescapable concomitant of the growth pattern that has been adopted. This chapter apprehends that in view of the patent failure to secure inclusive growth, both democracy and development—the twin key

[3] Initially, the constitutional amendment provided for 33 per cent reservation for women. Starting with Bihar, several states have since amended this provision to provide for up to 50 per cent reservation. As these amendments in state laws come into effect, both the number and share of women in Panchayats is likely to substantially increase to over half as women may also contest general seats—and several have already done so successfully.

[4] Subsequent to the submission of this chapter, the author was appointed chairman of a government-sponsored Expert Committee on the leveraging of panchayat raj institutions (PRIs) for the more effective delivery of public goods and services. The Report was submitted on National Panchayat Raj day, 24 April 2013, and may be seen at <http://www.panchayat.gov.in/report-of-expert-committee>. The Report details the measures by which Panchayats might be administratively and otherwise empowered to be initiators and participants in the planning and implementation of schemes designed to provide public goods and services to rural India. Many of the suggestions made would apply *pari passu* to the urban institutions of local self-government.

achievements of independent India—are being seriously endangered in twenty-first century India. When a fair share of economic growth is denied to a substantial majority of the population in the short term, and when development leads to deprivation rather than immediate benefit, as in tribal India, development is considered not desirable but disruptive, and democracy itself is discredited.

This chapter argues that it is the incentivization of effective devolution through *panchayat raj* institutions (PRIs) across the length and breadth of the country alone that can end the paradox that India is prospering but Indians are not. It also argues that inclusive governance in tribal areas, as provided for in the Provisions of The Panchayats (Extension to Scheduled Areas) Act, 1996 (PESA), holds the key to preventing democracy from being destabilized and development from being disrupted by Maoist or Naxalite violence.

Panchayat raj is crucial to bringing free or affordable public goods and services to the doorstep of the poor and the vulnerable. At present, the delivery of these public goods and services is through well over a hundred Centrally Sponsored Schemes (CSS) directed at the same set of beneficiaries—the poor and the vulnerable—by an equal number of mutually insulated administrative silos. These silos not only absorb a disturbingly high proportion of total outlays on administrative expenses but also stand in the way of effective convergence at the receiving end. In consequence, notwithstanding an eighteen-fold increase in central budgetary expenditure on social sector and poverty alleviation schemes over recent years (1994–2012), India's relative position on the United Nations Human Development Index stagnates at the same position it held in 1994.

If the delivery of these schemes is converted into self-delivery through PRIs rather than bureaucratic delivery—which was the central purpose of the constitutional amendments—then rural India, accounting for nearly two-thirds of the population, would experience such an increase in welfare and growth benefits as to more than offset the adverse impact on democracy and development of income and wealth inequality.[5] Steps also urgently need to be taken for similar measures for urban India—but that is beyond the scope of the present chapter.[6]

The rest of this chapter is structured as follows. Section 4.2 provides an overview of the history, philosophy, and politics of *panchayat raj*. It introduces the intellectual debate between the Gandhians and the "Ambedkarites," and

[5] Faguet and Shami (2008) explore the effects of decentralization on inequality across a range of countries.

[6] For decentralization and inclusive governance in India's fast-growing cities, see Rao and Bird (2011), Rao and Raghunandan (2011), Ahluwalia, Kanbur, and Mohanty (2014), and also Bahl, Linn, and Wetzel (2013). For a broader view of the political economy of urban (non-)development in Africa, see Fox (2014).

their competing views on (local) democracy in India. It describes the political compromises that brought about apparent but not true decentralization in India. Section 4.3 shows how recent growth has not translated into inclusive growth. Section 4.4 then specifies the problems that need to be addressed and suggests a series of solutions.

4.2 The History, Philosophy, and Politics of *Panchayat Raj*

Under the leadership of Mahatma Gandhi, India's liberation movement was never limited to independence for the country. It extended to freedom for her people. While, therefore, the commitment to democracy was woven into the warp and the woof of the century of struggle that climaxed with independence on 15 August 1947, there never was consensus in the run-up to freedom on whether such democracy should be limited to Westminster-type institutions in New Delhi, and US-type state assemblies in state capitals,[7] or extended down to the grass roots—to institutions of local self-government.

The boldest initiative to make *panchayat raj* the very foundation of the Constitution was "*A Gandhian Constitution for Independent India*"[8] by Sriman Narain Agarwal, one of Gandhi's close associates, published in 1946 on the eve of independence with Mahatma Gandhi's endorsement. Gandhi was concerned with involving the mass of the people, and not just the higher echelons of society, in governance. He therefore pressed for village development as the priority and progressively moved beyond focusing on village sanitation and village industries to pressing for democracy at the grass roots.

He had in mind a modernized democratic version of the traditional 5,000-year-old Indian institution of "*panchayats*," which had weathered, over centuries, all kinds of central governments as well as the trauma of military conquest, political turbulence, and economic disruption that have pockmarked the millennial history of the country. However, as against the traditional practice of five elders constituting the *panchayat* (which literally means "the council of five"), Gandhi's idea was that the village council (or *panchayat*) would be constituted by democratically elected leaders on the basis of universal adult franchise and the one person, one vote principle.

His conception of *panchayat raj* rested on virtually self-sufficient "village republics" which would be autonomous in everything they did, including meeting the community's economic needs—but restricting these needs to a frugal standard of living (Tendulkar 1953(1990: 405)). Although Gandhi's use

[7] See Dr. B.R. Ambedkar's Memorandum to the Constituent Assembly of 15 March 1947, especially his proposals for "Protection Against Communal Executive."

[8] Published by Kitab Mahal, Allahabad, 1946.

of the expression "village republics" did cause considerable alarm, presaging the disintegration of one India into 700,000 self-governing units just as the country was preparing itself for the trauma of Partition (which led to the secession of Pakistan), Gandhi, far from seeking the Balkanization of India, was actually articulating the governance principle now called "subsidiarity" as the basis for participative governance.

However, these ideas brought an angry reaction from Dr. B.R. Ambedkar, the leader of the scheduled castes (or "untouchables," as they were called at the time, a term since rendered illegal, indeed criminal, by the law of the land in independent India). Dr. Ambedkar, a renowned jurist and a known political opponent of Mahatma Gandhi, was named the Law Minister in India's first cabinet, and in 1947 was entrusted with chairing the drafting of a constitution.

In his draft, Dr. Ambedkar deliberately excluded *panchayats*. Drawing sharply negative comments from the Gandhians in the constituent assembly, Ambedkar famously—or notoriously, depending on one's point of view—retorted that her villages were "the ruination of India," dismissing them as nothing "but a sink of localism, a den of ignorance and communalism" (Constituent Assembly Debates 1948). While Gandhi visualized village *panchayats* as the very foundation of an effective and participatory democracy, Ambedkar saw what in today's idiom would be characterized as "elite capture" in a society where discrimination against the lower castes was entrenched in a scripturally sanctioned social system that had survived for millennia and justified itself in terms of the ancient jurisprudential system known as the Laws of Manu, India's Hamurabi.

Ambedkar dismissed village self-governance as romanticism bereft of the recognition of the deeply embedded social inequalities in village India:

> The existing village system has the effect of making the Scheduled Castes in the village slaves of the caste Hindus . . . Under the village system the Scheduled Castes are not allowed to live inside the village. They have to live on the outskirts . . . They have no independent means of livelihood. They own no land . . . They have to do forced labour day in and day out on pain of being driven away from their quarters by the Hindu landlords . . . They have to live a life of degradation, dishonour, and ignominy from generation to generation. It is a state of eternal perdition (Thorat and Kumar 2008: 270–2).

The Ambedkarite skepticism caused a major divide that has haunted local self-government in India ever since.

Gandhi, on the other hand, in early January 1948, on the eve of his impending assassination, expressed concern at news of there being "no mention or direction about village *panchayats* or decentralization" in the Ambedkar draft, then under preparation. He considered it an omission "calling for immediate attention if our democracy is to reflect the people's voice." He added: "The greater the power of the Panchayats, the better for the people" (Harijan 1947).

Prime Minister Jawaharlal Nehru's views on the need for participatory democracy at the village level had been stated in his defining work, *The Discovery of India*, published on the eve of Indian independence:

> The village can no longer be a self-contained economic unit... but it can very well be a governmental and electoral unit, each unit functioning as a self-governing community within the larger political framework and looking after the essential needs of the village" (Signet Press 1946 (1989: 523)).

For the Nehruvian modernists, in an India emerging out of the trauma of Partition and the problems over the integration of the Princely States the key imperative was a strong centre to combat the fissiparous forces of Balkanization that independent India had to overcome. At the same time, a commitment to village self-government as a principle of good governance was accepted but with implementation left to the states. Perhaps the strongest factor affecting Nehru's outlook was his conviction that a civil service for independent India modeled on the colonial ICS (Indian Civil Service) would be as effective in delivering development as it had proved for land revenue collection and law and order for the British Raj. There was therefore no disagreement between the Gandhians and Nehruvians about the need for grass-roots democracy; the difference was limited to emphasis and priority.

Nehru, however, kept out of the Ambedkarite–Gandhian arguments in Parliament and in public. It might well be that Nehru thought this was a subject for the states to handle, and since his party was in power in all states there should be no difficulty in getting *panchayat raj* through the state route instead of being embroiled in doctrinal disputes on the subject in the constituent assembly. Certainly, he did not share Gandhi's somewhat romanticized view of the village, although he also did not go as far as Ambedkar in viscerally condemning rural India or regarding the discriminatory Hindu order as immutable.

Following considerable public debate and discussion in the constituent assembly in November 1948, a compromise was found between Dr. Ambedkar and the Gandhians. The principle of *panchayat raj* finally did find passing mention in the Constitution, but the responsibility for this was vested entirely in state legislatures and governments:

> Article 40. The State shall take steps to organize village panchayats and endow them with such powers and authority as may be necessary to enable them to function as units of self-government.

While the "shall" gave the impression that the constitution and empowerment of village *panchayats* was ineluctable, the incorporation of Article 40 in the Directive Principles, instead of in the mandatory provisions of the Constitution as in the case of democratic institutions at the center and state levels, rendered enforcement of "village *panchayats*" null and void. Further, the responsibility for *panchayat raj* passed exclusively to the jurisdiction of the states, without any mechanism for ensuring that they would in fact live up to the letter and spirit of Article 40.

At first there was no controversy about this because it seemed self-evident that village *panchayats* were indispensable to good governance. But as feudalism was progressively dismantled with the integration into the Union of India of nearly 600 "princely states," combined with substantial land reform and tenurial reform, republican democracy created and empowered a whole new class, principally of career politicians (most of them former freedom-fighters), professionals (particularly lawyers and teachers), and small businessmen who filled with enthusiasm the power vacuum caused by the political eclipse of the feudal class who till then had held sway in the colonial political dispensation. This newly empowered class slowly realized that the concentration of political patronage and governmental power in their hands was threatened by empowering institutions at sub-state level "with powers and authority to function as units of self-government" as provided for in Article 40 of the Constitution. Self-interest prevailed over good sense. Thus, a withering away of *panchayats* characterized grass-roots governance through the first decade of Independence (1947–57).

This, however, was emphatically not to the neglect of grass-roots development. Indeed, it was the defining decade of experimentation in a novel postcolonial form of district and sub-district administration. In the colonial period, such administration was concentrated on the twin tasks of revenue collection and the maintenance of "public order" and "law and order" through the "steel frame" of the Indian Civil Service (ICS). The ICS was initially a virtually exclusive preserve of officers recruited in and from the mother country, Britain, but increasingly "Indianized" as empire gave way to independence. While many argued that independent India should dismantle the colonial administrative structure, Nehru himself seems to have felt the need to retain the steel frame but re-orient it towards a wholly new set of duties aimed at prioritizing rural development (Brecher 1959: 40).

This was called "community development." At the bureaucratic level, the major innovation was that the colonial (indeed, precolonial) revenue unit of the Tehsil or Taluqa was complemented by the establishment of development blocks, the key administrative officer being the block development officer. His duties included listening to the voice of the grass roots and delivering development to the people through his large panoply of staff stretching into every village. The head of the administration remained the

"Collector"[9] who retained his revenue-collection, law-and-order, and magisterial duties but was also generally in charge of rural development. Thus a regiment of the "best and the brightest" was put in place to mobilize the development process at the village community level as part and parcel of "planned development." Such planned development was envisaged as the means of not only raising the rate of annual average GDP growth from the miserable colonial figure of around one per cent per annum but also of ensuring the equitable distribution of the fruits of growth to the village level through a well-organized bureaucratic system of public goods and services delivery.

The "Community Development Programme," as it was called, was community based but essentially promoted by the bureaucracy and, therefore, left the people as beneficiaries rather than participants in their own progress and development. Accordingly, a study group under the renowned Gandhian, Shri Balwantrai Mehta (later chief minister of Gujarat), was constituted to examine *panchayat raj*.

The Balwantrai Mehta Study Group Report was published in 1957 and saw Nehru moving decisively towards participatory, as distinct from bureaucratically delivered, development. The Community Development Programme was to be subsumed under a three-tier democratic system of elected rural representatives, at district, block, and village level, under whose general aegis and supervision the new development block-based bureaucracy would work for the people in their immediate neighborhood; a synthesis of the precolonial steel frame and the postcolonial democratic ethos.

Nehru formally inaugurated the modernized system of *panchayat raj* on 2 October 1959. He was by then a colossus—albeit a "Gentle Colossus" as Hiren Mukherjee, one of his communist opponents in Parliament, described him (Mukherjee 1964). Not only did his Congress Party have an overwhelming majority at the center; all states (with the notable exception of Kerala, which had voted Communist), were under the firm grip of the Congress Party and alert to respond to priorities indicated from New Delhi. It was, therefore, by simple fiat emanating from the Prime Minister himself that all state governments fell smartly into line with the directive that they make the appropriate legal provisions for *panchayat raj*. Without altering a comma in the Constitution, *panchayat raj* was thus decreed all over the country and evolved, even flourished, through the remaining years of Prime Minister Jawaharlal Nehru (who died on 27 May 1964) and into the initial years of the successor regimes.

[9] Variously called the District Magistrate or Deputy Commissioner in different parts of the country.

The general elections in early 1967 saw a dramatic transformation in the national polity with the emergence of non-Congress governments in large measure. These reverses also marked great instability within the leadership of the Indian National Congress under Prime Minister Indira Gandhi. Faced with centrifugal challenges both within the party and within the government, the Prime Minister consolidated her position within her party and the country at large by a process of concentration of political and administrative power that inevitably meant more centralization than decentralization.[10]

Hence, over the next two decades, *panchayat raj* in rural India went through a phase of desuetude. It was a phase that I would describe as "whimsical *panchayat raj*"—elections taking place or not taking place; elected local self-government administrations not being allowed to take office or being dismissed soon after they did so, as suited the political compulsions, biases, or preferences of the state government concerned. Similarly, powers were endowed, withdrawn, or ignored as best suited the higher political echelon.

Not until Rajiv Gandhi became Prime Minister in 1984 was there a revival of interest in *panchayat raj*. During the numerous tours that Rajiv Gandhi undertook to the remotest corners of rural and tribal India, he discovered that a systemic solution was required to secure a "responsive administration." He promptly started his quest for a "responsive administration" through "representative" and, therefore, "responsible" institutions of local self-government. (Gandhi, R., 1988: 156, 161).[11]

The essential innovation by Rajiv Gandhi was to make detailed provision for the third tier of governance not through municipal law, as in Nehru's time, but by providing constitutional sanction, sanctity, and safeguards to *panchayat raj* with a view to making it ineluctable, irremovable, and irreversible.

At noon on 15 May 1989, the historic 64th Amendment was tabled in the Lok Sabha, the lower House of Parliament, by Prime Minister Rajiv Gandhi. The rationale he set out for constitutionally mandated *panchayat raj* might be summed up as follows (Gandhi, R. 1989):

- guaranteed regular, timely elections to the *panchayats* at all levels
- ending arbitrary suspensions and dissolutions of local bodies by state governments
- increasing the number of elected representatives relative to the size of the electorate with a view to bridging the gap between the elected and the electors, now being filled by power brokers and vested interests

[10] A not uncommon phenomenon, as Faguet (2004) discusses.

[11] Rajiv Gandhi, *Selected Speeches and Writings*, 1988, Vol. IV, Publications Division, New Delhi, speech to District Magistrates at Jaipur, 30 April 1988, pp. 156 and 161.

- widening opportunities for the deployment of India's vast human resources in governance at the grass roots
- securing reservations for scheduled castes and tribes to meet Ambedkarite apprehensions about elite capture of PRIs
- securing reservations for women so as to fully involve them in the management of community affairs
- ensuring planning from below
- linking economic development to social justice, particularly with a view to meeting concerns of elite capture of PRIs in the interests of the better-off, upper-caste segments of the rural population
- detailing the responsibilities of PRIs
- setting an example with the first rural employment program to be entrusted to the PRIs, namely, the Jawahar Rozgar Yojana launched in 1989 soon after the 64th Amendment bill was tabled
- demonstration of faith in the people to manage their own affairs

Although Rajiv Gandhi failed by five votes to muster in the Upper House (Rajya Sabha) the required two-thirds majority to amend the Constitution, his draft[12] remained on the anvil and, with a few changes (three of which were particularly significant), was eventually passed virtually unanimously by Parliament (but, alas, after his assassination) in December 1992.

The three most significant alterations were the following.

- First, the 73rd Constitution Amendment Act, as passed, established *gram sabhas* (village assemblies), comprising the entire adult population of the *panchayat* entitled to vote, to whom the elected *panchayat* would be responsible.[13]
- Second, it provided that Parliament, rather than the governor of a state, would legislate the law on *panchayat raj* for the tribal areas covered by the Fifth Schedule to the Constitution.[14] This led to the establishment of the Dilip Bhuria Committee, whose report constituted the basis of the Provisions of The Panchayats (Extension to Scheduled Areas) Act, 1996,

[12] Two documents together became in 1988–9 the basis for the draft amendment to the Constitution that inaugurated the present era of panchayat raj. The first was the outline constitutional amendments suggested by a 1978 committee headed by the veteran socialist Asoka Mehta, and the second was a draft of a possible constitutional amendment prepared in 1986 by another renowned jurist, L.M. Singhvi, who was also a member of the Asoka Mehta committee.

[13] According to Article 243 A, Part IX of the Constitution of India, "A Gram sabha may exercise such powers and perform such functions at the village level as the Legislature of a Sate may, by law, provide."

[14] According to Article 243 M (4) (b):"Parliament may by law extend the provisions of this Part to the Scheduled areas and the tribal areas ... " referred to in Article 244, read with the fifth schedule of the Constitution.

(PESA)[15]—the principal legal instrument available to include tribal people in the development process and potentially to assist government in countering Naxalite violence born of tribal discontent with their exclusion from the development process.

- Third, instead of the district planning committee, a key component of the *panchayat raj* structure, being elected by all the urban municipalities and the rural *panchayats*, with the district *panchayat* president as the ex-officio chairperson, the district planning committee was to be elected by and from among only the elected members of the district *panchayats* and municipalities, and it would be left to the state legislatures to determine the mode of electing or nominating the chairperson.

While the first two significant changes detailed above were progressive improvements on the Rajiv Gandhi draft, the third was retrograde and has not contributed to making the planning process as inclusive as it might have been. At the same time, it must be recognized that there was such determined opposition to the district planning committee in both joint parliamentary committees constituted in 1991 that without these changes the concept itself was likely to have been dropped.

While the mandatory elements, relating essentially to the election and constitution of the PRIs and their urban counterparts, have been universally complied with,[16] the operational aims and objectives have been left to state legislatures and state governments (and the union home ministry in respect of the union territories) to decide on. It is this that has resulted in such great variation in the practice of *panchayat raj* in different parts of the country and over time.

The 64th Amendment (that is, Rajiv Gandhi's initial draft legislation) provides the basis on which *panchayat raj* has been made ineluctable, irremovable, and irreversible. At the same time, however, the uneven performance in empowerment has been written into the system because the principal responsibility for effective devolution vests in state legislatures and governments (Alok and Chaubey, 2010: 219):

> ...it would be for State Legislatures to lay down the legislative parameters of devolution and for the State Governments to give practical effect to these parameters. We recognise that the precise pattern of devolution might vary from State to State.

Nearly two decades have passed since the Constitution was amended. *panchayat raj* Institutions have now been established countrywide. Their establishment

[15] Passed unanimously by both Houses in December 1996 with little discussion, which perhaps accounts for its poor implementation.

[16] Alok and Chaubey (2010: 10, 11) furnishes the details of the "mandatory" provisions.

has coincided with the era of economic reforms. GDP growth rates have been driven up to unprecedented levels, but the self-delivery of public goods and services through PRIs, which was the very purpose of the constitutional amendments, remains most uneven and a distant prospect, even in states, like Kerala and Karnataka, most inclined towards effective *panchayat raj*. This has had the most deleterious consequences for inclusive growth.

Those currently in authority see it as a major stumbling block that the Constitution leaves the processes of devolution to state legislatures/governments (and the union ministry of home affairs in regard to the union territories) (Planning Commission, 2011). Faced with this constitutional imperative, the Center pleads that there is little it can do beyond urging state governments to do more to promote the larger aims and objectives of *panchayat raj* or the fulfillment in spirit (although there is substantial compliance with the letter) of the constitutional amendments in this direction.

The central argument of this chapter is that the current approach is not in accord with the Center's constitutional obligations or political realities or the history of the evolution of *panchayat raj* in the country. Therefore, if a determined political will were evinced to make inclusive governance through PRIs the centerpiece of the endeavors towards inclusive growth, both the economic model of accelerated growth and the political model of full-fledged democracy might yet be saved. It is in these terms that the future of *panchayat raj* needs to be viewed.

4.3 Explosive Growth with Little Poverty Reduction

The basic issues we will be examining in this section are, first, why India is prospering, but Indians are not and, second, whether through *panchayat raj* India can promote inclusive growth. We go on to argue that even if it is not possible to significantly raise percentile incomes in any reasonably short period of time for the vast majority of Indians, particularly those who are poor and vulnerable, it should be possible through inclusive governance, that is, through *panchayat raj*, to dramatically improve their standards of living by providing access to their basic entitlements of public goods and services, thereby ensuring inclusive development in the very near future (Rodriguez-Pose and Gill, 2003).

4.3.1 *GDP Growth and Consequent Growth in Government Revenues and Spending*

Over the first millennial decade, India soared from an annual average GDP growth rate of just under 6 per cent in the first decade of reform (1993 to

2002), which was only a whisker above the previous decadal growth rate, to one over the next five years (2003–8) of approximately 9 per cent. Although India weathered the global economic downturn rather more effectively than the developed world or even her more prosperous neighbors in South-East Asia, there was an estimated dip to 6.8 per cent in *anno horribilis* 2008–9, but growth rates in 2009–10 and 2010–11 rose to an estimated 8 per cent and 8.6 per cent respectively (Ministry of Finance 2011:2).[17]

Moreover, high growth combined with fiscal reforms have doubled treasury revenue receipts from Rs. 350 billion in 2005–6 to an estimated Rs. 680 billion in 2010–11, and capital receipts by nearly three times from Rs. 1.58 trillion to an estimated Rs. 4.26 trillion in 2010–11, allowing total central government expenditure to soar from Rs. 5.06 trillion in 2005–6 to an estimated Rs. 11.09 trillion in 2010–11 (Ministry of Finance, 2011:45).

This, in turn, has facilitated the very impressive rise in central budgetary outlays on social sector spending (including programs of direct assaults on extreme poverty) from about Rs.75 billion in 1994–5 to about Rs. 1.85 trillion provided for in fiscal 2011–12. This places India among the fastest-growing spenders on programs designed to target multi-dimensional poverty.

Notwithstanding this impressive fiscal performance both on the revenue and expenditure side of the budget and, specifically, the exponential increase in social sector and anti-poverty spending, the downside has been a disturbing increase in inequalities of income and wealth on one hand, and unsatisfactory performance on human development indicators on the other.

4.3.2 *Income Inequality*

The National Council of Applied Economic Research (NCAER) estimated that if India's economy grew at an average of 8.75 per cent per annum over the years 2010–15 (Shukla 2010), as projected by the Planning Commission,[18] then by the terminal year of the millennium development goals, 2015, the top 20 per cent would have increased their share of the country's national income from 51 per cent to 55 per cent, while the share of the bottom 20 per cent would have shrunk from 6.1 per cent to 5.5 per cent. In absolute terms, the bottom 20 per cent of India's population would have added about Rs. 2,000 per year to their annual income while the top 20 per cent in urban India would

[17] Since this chapter was initially submitted for publication, Indian growth rates have plunged to below 5 per cent, but this does not alter the substantive thrust of the argument being made. Indications are that some recovery is underway.

[18] The assumption of 8.5% growth has since been belied. The new government that took office on 26 May 2014 have announced that they would be winding up the Planning Commission. At the time of writing, it is not known what would replace it.

have added as much as Rs. 75,000 to their annual income—37 times more than the poorest 20 per cent.[19]

The other deeply disturbing NCAER finding is that the poorer an Indian is, the more entrapped in personal debt he is likely to be. Thus, the poorest 5 per cent, earning less than Rs. 8 a day, consume Rs. 3,590 a year against an income of Rs. 2,145 a year: their share of expenditure is 167 per cent of income. As one goes up the income scale, the share remains high and does not significantly taper off until we have reached three-quarters of the population. It is only the richest 5 per cent whose percentile savings at 37 per cent mimic the national net savings. It is this high level of personal indebtedness of the poor, combined with easy access to corporate debt for the rich, that necessitates our regarding not only the utterly destitute but also the vulnerable as poor.

Recalling the Banerjee-Piketty study of 2001 based on income tax returns, which estimated that over the 1990s "real incomes of the top 1% of income earners increased by roughly 50%" and that "among this one per cent, the richest one per cent increased their real incomes by more than three times," Rajesh Shukla and Ishan Bakshi of NCAER have concluded through comparing both the Theil Index and the Gini coefficient that, "the all-India figures clearly show that income inequality has increased at both the rural as well as the urban levels," and go on to say:

> The problem is not that the rich have got richer but that those at the bottom have not been provided the wherewithal to improve their earning capability... over time, the benefits of near double digit growth should have percolated to the economically disadvantaged sections of society, which has not happened"(*Financial Express*, 2011).

That there has been some improvement is undeniable. The poor have not become poorer. But the rich have become far richer. What Nobel Laureate Prof. Amartya Sen has described as the "extremely asymmetric development of the global economy" is also reflected in the extremely asymmetric development of the Indian economy. India's widening Gini coefficient is a matter of deep concern, as much to our consciences as to the stability and sustainability of the country's political system.

Under the national poverty line, only 26 per cent are considered "poor," although Prof. Suresh Tendulkar, chairman of the Prime Minister's Economic Advisory Council,[20] has done his bit to ask for the national poverty line to be redefined to bring 37 per cent under that line. Most recently, the planning

[19] See also Vol.1, Chapter I, paragraphs 2.10–2.20, pp 19–28, including Boxes 2A, 2B, and 2C, and Tables 2.1 and 2.2, for a more detailed exposition of growing regional and personal inequalities associated with higher growth rates.

[20] Dr. Tendulkar has since passed away. Yet another committee, under Dr. C. Rangarajan, has now reported on the "poverty line." The confusion continues.

commission, in an affidavit filed in the supreme court of India on 20 September 2011, defined the rural poverty line as consumption in the amount of Rs. 781 per capita per month and the urban poverty line at Rs. 965. This would work out to a below-poverty-line population of 407 million. There is widespread rejection of this "underestimate."

Indeed, even the concept of a single national poverty line is ethically, politically, and economically flawed. It does not recognize the various components of multiple, multidimensional deprivation—ranging from the sectoral to the geographic to the social to the intergenerational—or its "drivers," "maintainers," and "interrupters." Nor does it recognize the various categories of poverty, ranging from the "chronic poor" to the "severely poor" to the "moderately poor," or the "dynamic of poverty—movement into or out of poverty, or staying in it" (Mehta and Shepherd 2006). To these categories of poverty, I would add the "transient poor" (as distinct from the "perennial poor") by which I mean those thrown out of employment after years of holding a steady job who tend to become, as in Gujarat in 2002, the vanguard of the "angry proletariat" mobilized against a demonized minority. That is why a nuanced, graded, and multi-deprivational definition of "poverty" should be the starting point of any serious frontal assault on poverty (Alkire and Santos 2010).

In India, the National Commission for Enterprises in the Unorganised Sector, in its August 2007 Report on *Conditions of Work and Promotion of Livelihoods in the Unorganised Sector,* identified the following categories of "poor," each of which requires an individually tailored strategy for poverty alleviation and eventual eradication: "extremely poor"; "poor"; "marginally poor"; and "vulnerable." While the report estimated that the number of "extremely poor" and "poor" had decreased during the first decade of post-1991 economic reforms, in 2004–5 they still comprised 237 million people Meanwhile, the number of poor and vulnerable together numbered 836 million, or 77 per cent of the population. Notwithstanding the rise in middle- and high-income persons to a significant 253 million, those crying out for help constitute three to four times the number who succeeded in standing on their own feet (National Commission 2007:6).

Instead of comprehending these complexities of multiple, multidimensional poverty, the national poverty line divides the entire population into two comfortable categories—BPL (Below Poverty Line) and Above Poverty Line (APL). This is "comfortable" for two reasons. First, poverty alleviation can then be reduced to the entirely feasible proposition of shifting some upper BPL over the line into the APL category and calling it "poverty alleviation." Second, it eliminates the distinction between the marginal survivor and the obscenely rich: all are APL and all, therefore, beneficiaries, in some aggregated manner, of the growth process.

Fortunately, recent academic and even policy-making interest in multidimensional poverty, notably the Oxford Initiative on Multidimensional Poverty which has informed recent UN Human Development Indices, has emphasized that poverty manifests itself in several inter-related dimensions.

Does the answer then lie in exponentially increasing budgetary allocations for social sectors and anti-poverty programs, as India has in fact done over the period of economic reforms? Could a frontal assault on the many dimensions of poverty result in the convergence of inter-linkages causing a multiplier spin-off effect on multidimensional poverty alleviation? Can we trace a broad causal connection between outlays and outcomes?

The Indian experience appears to indicate that while financial resources constitute an essential component of poverty alleviation, financial resources alone without effective community participation result in outcomes not being anywhere near commensurate with outlays. As noted earlier, India's record on central budgetary outlays on social sector spending including programs directly targeting extreme poverty) has been most impressive, rising from about Rs. 75 billion in 1994–5 to over Rs. 1.85 trillion in fiscal year 2011–12.[21] This makes India among the fastest-growing spenders on programs designed to target multi-dimensional poverty.

Yet, while the UN Human Development Index placed India at position 134 in the league ranking when it was first published in 1994, the comparable 2009 index placed India at the exact same position: 134.[22]

The World Food Programme tells us that half the world's hungry live in India and the International Food Policy Research Institute's most recent report classifies India's food security index as "alarming" (*Times of India* 2011:11). Notwithstanding India's extraordinarily high growth rate, India remains a low-income, food deficit country in which as much as 35 per cent of the population consumes less than 80 per cent of its minimum human energy requirements, nine out of ten pregnant women suffer from malnutrition and anaemia, and, in consequence, 47 per cent of children under the age of 5 are moderately to severely undernourished (WFP 2008). The Food and Agricultural Organization (FAO) tells us that in the five years leading to the turn of the century, India added more newly hungry millions than the rest of the world put together (FAO 2012). Action Aid has confirmed this for more recent years.

Why is there such a mismatch between the halting, uncertain, sporadic, and unsustained amelioration in the condition of the vast majority of Indians, the growth in the booming service and manufacturing sectors of the Indian

[21] This figure has steadily increased in the three subsequent fiscals notwithstanding the fall in growth rates.
[22] Virtually no improvement in ranking since.

economy, and the income of the entrepreneurial and highly skilled classes? Why is India prospering but most Indians are not? Why are higher outlays impacting so relatively little on all that makes life more bearable for the poor? And why is political attention to the issues of poverty so muted in comparison to the hurrahs we hear over GDP growth rates? For, alas, the poverty of our politics is reflected in the politics of our poverty!

In consequence, while there is no argument that augmented resources of the kind generated by economic liberalization are the *necessary* condition for poverty alleviation, it is becoming increasingly evident that exponential augmentation of anti-poverty spending is not a *sufficient* condition even for poverty alleviation, let alone poverty eradication.

In short, what, over and above increased spending, is required for accelerated growth to translate into inclusive growth? Could the answer lie in inclusive governance, that is, *panchayat raj*?

4.4 Problems and Solutions

The latest devolution index issued by the Indian Institute of Public Administration (IIPA 2011)[23] which assesses the state of devolution to the *panchayats* comprises four elements:

- *Panchayat raj* framework, that is, conformity to the provisions of the constitution to provide an "enabling environment" for *panchayat raj*
- Devolution of functions
- Devolution of finances
- Devolution of functionaries

These are then aggregated, with appropriate weightage, into an overall devolution index.[24] The overall ranking puts Kerala on top at 70.01, with Karnataka and Sikkim in second and third place but a good 10 to 12 points behind Kerala.[25] There is then a bunching of five states in the 50s; eight states in the 40s; four in the 30s; three in the 20s; and two in the 10s.

Rankings on other indices of devolution do not, however, conform to the overall ranking. For example, West Bengal, Madhya Pradesh, and Tamil Nadu, which are the three highest on the framework index, are in third, seventh, and

[23] It was the "latest" when this chapter was first written. There have been two subsequent reports but the format remains as explained here.

[24] The methodology and mathematical formulae used can be seen at Appendix 4.5, p. 32 of the Report.

[25] In subsequent years, Maharashtra has risen to the top, with Tripura and Haryana, and also Himachal Pradesh, making significant gains, indicating that panchayat raj is getting more effective all the time but nowhere adequately so.

sixth place respectively in the overall ranking. Similarly, in the ranking on functional devolution Gujarat is second but only eighth in the overall ranking, while Karnataka, second overall, drops to fifth position on functional devolution.

A cursory comparison of the Oxford Poverty and Human Development Initiative's (OHPI) Multiple Deprivation (Mo) ranking of Indian states[26] with the devolution index (D) ranking by the IIPA would appear to bear out a positive correlation between effective devolution and lower multiple deprivation, especially if the income deprivation index is abstracted from the OPHI, that is, if one looks only at the dimensions of deprivation on public goods and services alone (which is what PRIs are concerned with).[27]

It must be emphasized, however, that there are no simple lessons to be learned from the rankings about the impact of devolution on outcomes. The path to devolution requires dovetailing the devolution of functions, finances, and functionaries within the framework of an effective, constitution-conforming "enabling environment." In other words, the more holistic the approach to implementing in letter and spirit all the related provisions of the Constitution, the more effective *panchayat raj* will be. It would, therefore, be hasty to pass judgment on *panchayat raj* in any given state without reference to the enabling environment and the extent of effective devolution.

This underlines the point made in the introduction: the sporadic, halting, and uneven progress of *panchayat raj* is due to a lack of clarity about the conceptual dimensions of this systemic revolution in responsive administration; this, of course, provides grist to the mill of the vested interests, principally the political–bureaucratic nexus, who stand to lose patronage, prestige, and power if devolution proceeds apace.

The rationale for *panchayat raj* expounded by Mahatma Gandhi, Jawaharlal Nehru, and Rajiv Gandhi, summarized in section 4.2 of this chapter, and the data on income disparities given in section 4.3, provide ground for advancing the proposition that participatory development is to be preferred to bureaucratic delivery mechanisms for inclusive governance to lead to inclusive growth.

In the absence of inclusive governance, the people at the grass roots, that is, the intended beneficiaries of poverty alleviation programs, are left abjectly dependent on a bureaucratic delivery mechanism over which they have no effective control. The alternative system would be participatory development, or *panchayat raj*, where the people themselves are enabled to build their own future through elected representatives answerable to the local community and, therefore, responsive to their needs.

[26] OHPI Working Paper No. 15, Appendix 6, pp. 44–7, attached to this paper, Attachment III.
[27] See also Vol 1, chapter I, paragraphs 2.28–2.29, pp. 32–3, of the Expert committee Report.

The Indian experience of the last six decades would appear to confirm that bureaucratic delivery mechanisms absorb a disproportionately high share of the earmarked expenditure: up to 85 paise in the rupee, said Rajiv Gandhi (based on one study commissioned by the planning commission of one program in Bihar state); perhaps 83 paise says Dr. Kirit Parekh, former member of the planning commission, in an evaluation of one key program, the Public Distribution System;[28] not quite so high, says the Prime Minister. We may thus approximate that between 75 per cent and 85 per cent of expenditure on poverty alleviation schemes is absorbed by the delivery mechanism itself. No wonder outcomes are so derisory.

Worse, over a hundred schemes are delivered to the same set of beneficiaries through mutually insulated administrative silos, set up by central government ministries intent on jealously guarding their respective fiefdoms. Convergence of schemes at the delivery point becomes virtually impossible, thus depriving beneficiaries of the multiplier effect that would operate if the beneficiaries themselves, through their locally elected leaders, were to have the authority to plan and implement the utilization of these resources in keeping with their own respective priorities.

The challenge being to convert accelerated growth into inclusive growth, the path favoured by government after government in India has been to exponentially increase spending on social sector and anti-poverty programs in the expectation that a critical mass of expenditure will somehow be reached for the money thrown at the poor to become the straw they can clutch at to rise out of their misery. The intention is sound but commentator after commentator rues the fact that this has not worked.

The critical systemic fault lies in the present practice of implementation. Over a hundred social sector and poverty-alleviation Centrally Sponsored Schemes (CSS)[29] are implemented by separate agencies. Each scheme, operating through parallel bodies set up by the central and state government bureaucracy in collaboration with civil society organizations, performs tasks that the Constitution specifies might best be entrusted to the PRIs. In consequence, the beneficiaries remain hapless recipients of government/NGO largesse instead of actively participating in designing the schemes, adapting them to local community priorities and being effectively in charge of supervision, guidance, and disciplinary action. The implementation agencies, therefore, look over their shoulder to those who entrusted the task to them instead of towards the beneficiaries for approval or course correction. In these circumstances, it is hardly surprising that *gram sabhas* (village assemblies of all

[28] *Sarvekshana*, Jan–March 1994, pp. 1–34.

[29] Also ACA—Additional Central Assistance—allocated at its discretion by the planning commission.

adult members, mandated in the Constitution) are reduced to mere spectators and rubber stamps instead of providing "advice and consent" to the elected *panchayat* executive as is the democratic requirement when the executive is held responsible to the people. This proposition may be illustrated by a few specific examples.

Primary education is a task proposed for elected local bodies. It is instead being run under a very well-funded CSS, the SSA—Sarva Siksha Abhiyan ("Education for All Movement")[30] through "parallel bodies": the registered societies established by state education departments and NGOs largely or entirely dependent on government funding. Physical achievements, such as the number of school buildings, are impressive; so are teacher recruitment, child coverage rates (including the coverage of girl students), and reduction of drop-out rates. But the highly respected Annual Survey of Education Report points out that a disturbingly high proportion of standard IV students cannot read the text books prescribed for standard II or even standard I (ASER Centre 2010).

If parent–teacher associations were established under the *panchayats* and made responsible to the entire community through regular meetings of the *gram sabhas*, such democratic people-based supervision and control of primary education, instead of the present quasi-statist model, would, in all probability, lead to higher levels of learning. For, after all, the end result sought is not so much the number of school buildings but better-educated children.[31]

Certainly, the experience of Kerala, where all education, including college education, has been put under the three-tier *panchayat* system, would appear to bear this out. Kerala leads the country in the education sector. There is also considerable recognition of the progress made in this direction by an economically backward state like Rajasthan. The much-lauded move towards effective *panchayat raj* by Bihar in recent times is yet another indicator that such community supervision and control is not only possible in an educationally advanced state; it can also be undertaken in states not renowned for their educational advancement. The contrary example is that of Uttar Pradesh, where poor levels of education are associated with poor performance in effective *panchayat raj*.

Similarly, SSA provides for school buildings but it is a separate ministry and a quite separate CSS—the Total Sanitation Campaign, now called Nirmal Bharat Abhiyan, run by the ministry of rural development—that has been

[30] This was made a statutory requirement through the amended Right to Education Act, 2013.

[31] The interested reader is referred to Chapter XII Vol. 2, read with the Activity Maps for SSA in Vol 4, of the Expert Group report for a detailed examination of the connection between effective learning outcomes and the involvement of PRIs in planning and implementing SSA at the school and community level.

assigned the responsibility for providing school toilets, without which girl students in rural India tend to be withdrawn on attaining puberty. By correcting such parallelism, not only would sanitation improve but valuable lessons in hygiene would be learned by socially and economically deprived children and their families and the drop-out rate for girls at puberty would decrease sharply.

The political and administrative authority—that is, the central ministry concerned, the state departments concerned, and the NGOs concerned—is unenthusiastic about involving the PRIs because it would reduce their rigid control over their respective programs, call into question their self-assessment of outcomes, and bring their actions under the supervision and disciplinary control of the local elected authority.

The World Bank-funded Integrated Child Development Scheme (ICDS) to provide supplemental nutrition and child care for rural children, for instance, is run without reference to the PRIs although the eleventh schedule of the Constitution specifically recommends at entry 25 that ICDS be placed under community supervision through the *panchayats*.[32]

They would point too to their accountability for expenditure to the Accountant General for Central Revenues (AGCR) and the Comptroller and Auditor General (CAG), a much-dreaded constitutional authority who reports directly to Parliament and is responsible only to Parliament's premier standing committee, the Public Accounts Committee, chaired by a leading light of the opposition. Until, says the bureaucracy, their answerability to this awesome authority is modified, they have to account for each rupee that goes through their hands and that is much better done with their brethren in the permanent bureaucracy than in association with hundreds of thousands of transient elected *panchayat* representatives. The suggestions made in this regard for a thorough revamping of local bodies' accounts by the AGCR itself and the Institute of Public Accountants (a body invariably headed by the immediate past CAG) (Sixth Round Table 2004), and a recent offer by the Indian Institute of Chartered Accountants to make their 500,000 members available for social audit have not carried much conviction, principally because it would be like asking turkeys to vote for Christmas.

Only a determined political will can overcome such objections. While some state governments have displayed the will, others have not. The leader of the pack over the last decade and more has been Kerala, with Karnataka running a close second, and some others—Maharashtra, West Bengal, Tripura, Sikkim, Madhya Pradesh, Tamil Nadu, Gujarat, Rajasthan, and Haryana—slowly catching up. But most others remain reluctant start-ups. Bihar is the dramatic

[32] See Vol.2 chapter XIII, paragraphs 13.46–13.49 at pp. 502–4, and 13.65–13.76 at pp. 510–15, read with Activity Maps for ICDS in Vol 4, for a detailed treatment of this issue.

exception: what Bihar has achieved in the last few years in promoting effective local self-government is the most encouraging development in *panchayat raj* (Alok and Chaubey 2010: 77).

In a briefing to members of parliament on the eve of the finalization of the Approach to the Twelfth Five-Year Plan (2012–17), the deputy chairman of the planning commission underlined the point that while the economy had performed spectacularly on GDP growth rates, the single biggest failure of the government's "eleventh plan" (2007–12) had been the failure to secure inclusive growth (PRS Briefing 2011). This notwithstanding the exponential increase in central government funds made available to States under some 139 CSS. He attributed the failure to translate dramatically augmented outlays into commensurate outcomes to "management failures" on the part of the states.

However, "management failure" is not an attribute of state governments alone; it is a general failure on the part of both the central and state governments to fashion an efficient and effective delivery system for public goods and services for those most desperately in need of inclusive growth. This notwithstanding the constitutional obligation to move from bureaucratic delivery to self-delivery through PRIs of programs of economic development and social welfare.[33]

Therefore, whatever the primary responsibility of the state governments in this regard, it essentially lies in the hands of the central government to rise to its constitutional responsibilities under Parts IX and IXA of the Constitution by modifying CSS guidelines in such a manner as to ensure the centrality of PRIs in the planning and implementation of CSS. For, of the CSS, the former Prime Minister, Dr. Manmohan Singh, had this to say in 2004, soon after assuming office:

> It is for us to honestly ask the question of whether we are making the best use of the money that we spend annually on the schemes being currently implemented? Do we have too many schemes, which are fragmented in concept, are rigidly designed and impose national parameters on highly differentiated local realities in terms of resource endowments or felt needs? Does the compartmentalization of our effort in multiple schemes in the Ministry or Ministries—both at the Centre and in the States—without a core vision make this investment sub-optimal? Before we set this right at the Centre we cannot be asking the States to do so (cited in Ministry of Panjayati Raj, 2006: 50).

Recognizing the fundamental need to systemically alter CSS guidelines, the cabinet secretary had, on the instructions of the Prime Minister, in November 2004, issued a circular to all central ministries asking them to modify their

[33] See Article 243G, read with Article 243ZD, and the Eleventh Schedule of the Constitution of India.

respective CSS guidelines "within three months" to ensure the centrality of the *panchayats* in "planning and implementation" as provided for in the Constitution (specifically Article 243G read with the Eleventh Schedule, as well as the corresponding Article 243W in part IX A read with the Twelfth Schedule, and both with the provisions for district planning in Article 243 ZD).

An exercise to modify CSS guidelines had been undertaken, in consultation with the departmental secretaries concerned, by a committee chaired by Renuka Vishwanathan, special secretary in the cabinet secretariat, but as there was no high-level endorsement of the Renuka Vishwanathan Committee Report, nor any follow-up by the economically more influential ministries and entities concerned (ministry of finance, planning commission, PMO etc.), the Report has withered on the vine.

Moreover, the National Development Council's Empowered Sub-Committee on *panchayat raj* issues, comprising several state ministers of *panchayat raj* and chaired by the author in his previous capacity as minister of *panchayat raj*, had in 2008 submitted a Report unanimously recommending a host of steps for promoting the centrality of PRIs, that is, inclusive governance for inclusive growth. Five years on, the planning commission was yet to submit the report for ratification to the National Development Council.[34]

It is not enough for the Planning Commission to simply attribute the failure of inclusive growth to "management failure" on the part of state governments. A pro-active role by the central government, especially in respect of CSS, could make a breathtaking difference to the more efficient and effective delivery of public goods and services to the poor and vulnerable to provide for a measure of equity in the face of the inescapable widening of inequalities in income and wealth promoted by the present high-growth model. It was precisely this that was recommended by the Expert Group (2013) but, despite a reiteration of the Prime Minister's directive on 6 August 2013, there has been virtually no progress. It is to be seen whether the new Government that took office in May 2014 will be any more effective (or wish to be more effective) in providing Activity Maps indicating the way forward to the devolution of functions, finances, and functionaries for each CSS, as recommended by the Expert Group.

Equity now, not in some distant future, is essential for democracy to survive and development to be sustained. This is not hyperbole but common sense: already close to one-third of the districts of India, particularly districts with a dominant tribal population, are convulsed in Maoist/Naxalite insurgencies

[34] The Planning Commission, now wound up, never submitted the Report to the National Development Council, thus showing itself as being the most recalcitrant element of governance in regard to *panchayat raj*; it should, in fact, have taken the lead in encouraging, incentivizing, and monitoring *panchayat raj*.

fuelled by displacement and deprivation (Ministry of Home Affairs 2011; Ministry of Panjayati Raj, 2011). Grass-roots development through grass-roots institutions of democracy, as provided for in PESA 1996, would do more to bring the tribal people back to the mainstream of democracy and development than any other single measure.[35]

The key lies in designing CSS on the basis of scientific activity mapping based on the principle of subsidiarity—which holds that anything that can be done at the lower level should be done at that level and no higher level. Such carefully and consensually structured activity maps, annexed to each set of CSS guidelines, might detail the *functions* to be devolved respectively to the village, intermediate, and district levels, and thus provide the basis on which the devolution of *finances* is to be patterned, matched by a parallel devolution of *functionaries* to each level of self-governance, in rural as much as in urban localities.[36]

Such empowerment will enable the local community to deploy the financial resources made available to them (and mobilized by them) to themselves plan and implement their own programs of grass-roots development and poverty eradication instead of depending on the grudging patronage of higher-level politicians, who have their own agenda, and an indifferent, self-serving local bureaucracy: grass-roots development through grass-roots democracy, as appears to be happening currently in Bangladesh (Faguet and Ali 2009).

The imperative of inclusive growth has been grasped, but the imperative of inclusive governance has barely been incorporated into the conception and implementation of the Eleventh Plan or even key flagship programs for inclusion, equity, and social justice, notwithstanding the Prime Minister's public endorsement of the centrality of inclusive governance to inclusive growth.

Provided the required political will is displayed, and there is political mobilization at the highest level to secure consensus, it should be possible to effect a systemic revolution in the delivery of basic goods and services. Nothing would more dramatically and immediately drive up human development indices. To this end, clarity in conception and sincerity in implementation are required on several points, particularly the following: *panchayat raj* is not a panacea for ending all ills, but a systemic alternative to replacing a bureaucratic delivery mechanism that has failed to rise to the challenge. To be effective, *panchayat raj* has to be conceived and implemented holistically. Where *panchayats* are elected but not empowered; where the local bureaucracy and technocracy is not made responsible to the elected authority; where the president of the *panchayat* does not function as a president-in-council, consulting and

[35] Speeches and articles by the author and others, notably the Bandyopadhaya Committee Report of 2008, expanding on this will be readily made available by the author, who can be contacted at manirsmp@gmail.com.

[36] Vol. 4 of the Expert Group Report provides detailed model Activity Maps for eight of the Government's principal Centrally Sponsored Schemes.

securing the approval of his/her fellow *panchayat* members; where functions (activities) are devolved on paper but are not accompanied by a devolution of finances and functionaries; where the district planning committee is either non-functional, dysfunctional, or dominated by non-PRI chairpersons nominated by the state or willfully ignored by the state and central planning authorities—in all such cases, *panchayat raj* will be sub-optimal or worse in its results. Securing the independence and strengthening of the state election authority to ensure free and fair elections must be a continuing challenge, calling for the adoption of best practices evolved in different states.

While the most effective counter to corruption in PRIs would be through social audit undertaken in close association with committed NGOs, formal audit of local bodies along the lines recommended by the CAG and the Institute of Public Accountants would diminish, if not eliminate, corrosive corruption at the local level. In any case, the burden of leakages through currently rampant bureaucratic corruption together with the high administrative costs would be lowered through a systemic change to participatory development.

Community participation cannot end with the vote; it must translate into regular, informed, and effective meetings of the *gram sabha*. To this end, the codification by legislation of the authority, powers, and duties of the *gram sabhas* would considerably augment their role and responsibility, the essential countervailance to the abuse of power by the elected office-bearers in the PRIs and the local bureaucracy. It stands to reason that the more effective the outcome of *gram sabha* meetings, the greater would be the effective empowerment of the local community and therefore the more enthusiastic and purposeful would be attendance at *gram sabha* meetings. An elected *panchayat* executive must function in a collegiate manner and be responsible to the *gram sabha*. In the absence of this, there would inevitably be abuse of power by those elected by the community but not responsible to it. This calls for reconsideration of the constitutional provision that constructs a fundamentally parliamentary system of *panchayat raj* but then superimposes a presidential authority by allowing for the direct election of village *panchayat* presidents who then do not feel the need to even consult with their *panchayat* members.

To render office-bearers in PRIs more accountable for their actions, the periodicity of reservations needs to be revisited. In most states/UTs, the period of reservations is limited to a single term, making re-election rare. This facilitates elite capture (Palanithurai 2010). Extending reservations to at least two and, preferably, three terms would lead to greater social equity as office-bearers would mature in office and would be compelled to accord greater attention to the more disadvantaged sections of the village population in order to secure re-election.

Apart from redesigning CSS/ACA to ensure the centrality of PRIs in planning and implementation, there is a pressing need on one hand to vastly augment the present scheme of incentivizing states to promote further effective devolution and, on the other, to incentivize PRIs to be more transparent in their transactions and more accountable for their actions.

Perhaps the most urgent requirement of all is to cap, reverse, and eliminate tribal unrest, insurgency, and insurrection by prioritizing the implementation of PESA 1996. It could be the last bulwark against a people's uprising in tribal areas which spread over nearly a third of the country, assessed by the Prime Minister, as the "most serious challenge" to India's internal security.

These are pointers to improvements in legislation or institutional design that would progressively ensure better and cleaner *panchayat raj*. Many of these and others are detailed in the elaborate roadmap prepared by the Ministry of Panchayat Raj (2011). These improvements are flagged to stopper the frequently heard cry of despair that points to flaws in *panchayat raj* and intends to end the experiment altogether. That would be to throw the baby out with the bathwater. To paraphrase a 1954 quote from the A.D. Gorwala Committee report on cooperatives[37] that enjoyed considerable renown in its day: "*Panchayat raj* has failed. *Panchayat raj* must succeed."

Acknowledgements

The author would like to acknowledge his profound debt to Prof. J.P. Faguet and Dr. Caroline Pöschl of the London School of Economics who summarized the long-winded original manuscript into a much tighter and more easy-to-read text; Dr. David Malone of the International Development Research Centre, Ottawa; and Dr. Shaandana Mohmand of the Institute of Development Studies, Brighton, and his daughter, Yamini Aiyar of Accountability Initiative, Centre for Policy Research, New Delhi, for their invaluable assistance in guiding this chapter to a measure of academic respectability from the idiom of polemical politics with which he is more familiar. Of course, responsibility for the end-product remains, warts and all, with the author. The author would also like to record his appreciation of the assistance in research rendered by Prof. V.N. Alok of the Indian Institute of Public Administration, New Delhi, and his colleague, Dr. P.K. Chaubey, as also Dr. (Prof.) Rajesh Shukla, formerly of the National Centre for Applied Economic Research, New Delhi, and now in the Institute for Human Development, New Delhi, the principal scholar in India of income and wealth distribution. He also wishes to sincerely thank Dr. Nupur Tiwari, his long-standing senior research consultant, for diligently putting together his various writings and speeches on the subject, searching out previous researches and references, and pointing him in the right direction when he went astray (as he frequently did), as well as helping immensely with the footnotes. So also are thanks due to his younger research assistants, Vandana Seth and Ramandeep Singh. Anirban Bandyopadhaya of Jawaharlal Nehru University was also of assistance.

[37] "Cooperatives have failed. Cooperatives must succeed."

Bibliography

Ahluwalia, I. J., R. Kanbur, and P.K. Mohanty, 2014. *Urbanisation in India*. New Delhi: Sage Publications India.

Aiyar, M. S., 2013. *Activity Maps For Functions, Functionaries, Finance (Volume 4). Towards Holistic Panchayat Raj: Twentieth Anniversary Report Of The Expert Committee On Leveraging Panchayats For Efficient Delivery Of Public Goods And Services*. New Delhi: Government of India.

Aiyar, M. S., 2013. *Annexes (Volume 3). Towards Holistic Panchayat Raj: Twentieth Anniversary Report Of The Expert Committee On Leveraging Panchayats For Efficient Delivery Of Public Goods And Services*. New Delhi: Government of India.

Aiyar, M. S., 2013. *Appendices (Volume 5). Towards Holistic Panchayat Raj: Twentieth Anniversary Report Of The Expert Committee On Leveraging Panchayats For Efficient Delivery Of Public Goods And Services*. New Delhi: Government of India.

Aiyar, M. S., 2013. *Policy Issues (Volume 1). Towards Holistic Panchayat Raj: Twentieth Anniversary Report Of The Expert Committee On Leveraging Panchayats For Efficient Delivery Of Public Goods And Services*. New Delhi: Government of India.

Aiyar, M. S., 2013. *Sectoral Schemes (Volume 2). Towards Holistic Panchayat Raj: Twentieth Anniversary Report Of The Expert Committee On Leveraging Panchayats For Efficient Delivery Of Public Goods And Services*. New Delhi: Government of India.

Alkire, S. and M. E. Santos, 2010. *Acute Multidimensional Poverty: A New Index for Developing Countries*, July, OPHI Working Paper No.38.

Alok, V. N., *Strengthening of Panchayats in India: Comparing Devolution Across States; Empirical Assessment—2012–13*. New Delhi: Ministry of Panchayati Raj, Government of India, 2012. Print.

Alok, V.N. and P.K. Chaubey, 2010. *Panchayats in India: Measuring Devolution by States*, Macmillan India, 2010.

ASER Centre, 2010. *Annual Status of Education Report (ASER)*, 14 January.

Bahl, R. W., J. F. Linn and D. L. Wetzel. 2013. Financing Metropolitan Governments in Developing Countries, Lincoln Institute of Land Policy.

Brecher, Michael, 1959. *Nehru—A Political Biography*. London: OUP.

Channa, A. and J.P. Faguet, 2012. "Decentralization of Health and Education in Developing Countries: A Quality-Adjusted Review of the Empirical Literature." LSE/STICERD Working Paper No. EOPP 38.

Constituent Assembly Debates, 1948. Constituent Assembly of India Debates (Proceedings), 4 November, 1948 available at http://parliamentofindia.nic.in/ls/debates/debates.htm.

Constituent Assembly Debates, 1947. Constitutional Assembly of India Debates, 15 March, 1947.

Expert Group on Leveraging Panchayat Raj Institutions for the More Effective Delivery of Public Goods and Services, 2013. in five volumes.

Faguet, J.P., 2014. "Can Sub-National Autonomy Strengthen Democracy in Bolivia?" *Publius: The Journal of Federalism*, 44(1): 51–81; doi: 10.1093/publius/pjt020.

Faguet, J.P., 2000. "Decentralization and Local Government Performance: Improving Public Service Provision in Bolivia," *Revista de Economía del Rosario*, 3(1): 127–76.

Faguet, J.P., 2008. "The Determinants of Central vs. Local Government Investment: Democracy and Development in Bolivia." Chapter 7 in Ghosh, S. and S.S. Mishra (eds.) *Decentralization and Development*, Hyderabad, India: Icfai University Press.

Faguet, J.P., 2004. "Why So Much Centralization? A Model of Primitive Centripetal Accumulation." STICERD DEDPS No.43, London School of Economics.

Faguet, J.P. and Z. Ali, 2009. "Making Reform Work: Institutions, Dispositions and the Improving Health of Bangladesh." *World Development*. 37: 208–18.

Faguet, J.P. and M. Shami, 2008. "Fiscal Policy and Spatial Inequality in Latin America and Beyond." World Bank Policy Research Working Paper.

Financial Express, 2011. Newspaper, 15 January.

Food and Agriculture Organization, 2012. Statistics, available at <http://faostat.fao.org>.

Fox, S., 2014. "The Political Economy of Slums: Theory and Evidence from Sub-Saharan Africa." *World Development*, 54: 191–203.

Gandhi, R., "Briefing the Bureaucracy." Workshop on Responsive Administration. Bhopal. 10 December 1987. In *Rajiv Gandhi: Selected Speeches and Writings (1987)*. New Delhi: Government of India, 1989, pp. 120–9.

Gandhi, R., "Panchayats Must Be Development-Oriented." 13th All India Panchayat Parishad. New Delhi. 22 September 1986. In *Rajiv Gandhi: Selected Speeches and Writings (1986)*. New Delhi: Government of India, 1989, pp. 45–54.

Gandhi, Rajiv, 1988. *Selected Speeches and Writings*, Vol. IV, Publications Division, New Delhi, speech to District Magistrates at Jaipur, 30 April.

Gandhi, Rajiv, 1989. *Selected Speeches and Writings*, Vol.V, pp.167–78, Publications Division, 1991.

Government of India (GoI). 2008. *Development Challenges in Extremist Affected Areas*. Report of an Expert Group to Planning Commission.

IIPA, 2011. *Empowerment of Panchayats by States through Devolution: An Empirical Assessment 2010–11*. (Research Team: VN Alok and PK Chaubey).

Jawaharlal Nehru, *The Discovery of India*, Signet Press.1946 (1989). Centenary edition, Calcutta: OUP.

Mehta, A.K. and A.Shepherd (eds), 2006. *Chronic Poverty in India: An Introduction*, New Delhi, Sage.

Ministry of Finance, 2011. *Economic Survey 2010–11*, Government of India, available at http://indiabudget.nic.in.

Ministry of Home Affairs, Government of India (Home Ministry), 2011. *Ministry of Home Affairs Annual Report 2010–11*. Available at <http://www.mha.nic.in/AnnualReports>.

Ministry of Panchayati Raj: *Elected Women Representatives—A Survey*, 2007. Findings written up by Prof Nirja Juyal Gopal.

Ministry of Panchayati Raj, 2011. *Roadmap for the Panchayati Raj: An All-India Perspective*, Ministry of Panchayat Raj website, <http://panchayat.gov.in>.

Ministry of Panchayati Raj, 2006. *The State of the Panchayats*. (Subsequent biannual surveys, with the same title, have been prepared independent of Government by the National Council of Applied Economic Research, the Institute of Rural Management Anand, and the Indian Institute of Public Administration).

Mukherjee, Hirendra Nath, 1964. *The Gentle Colossus: A Study of Jawaharlal Nehru*, Oxford University Press.

National Commission for Enterprises in the Unorganised Sector (National Commission), 2007. *Report on Conditions of Work and Promotion of Livelihoods in the Unorganised Sector*, New Delhi: Dolphin Printo Graphics.

Palanithurai, G., (2010) *Elite Capture in Local Rural Governance*, presentation at the Round Table organized in Bengaluru on 28 June 2010 by the National Council of Applied Economic Research (NCAER).

Planning Commission, 2011. *Faster, Sustainable and More Inclusive Growth: An Approach to the Twelfth Five Year Plan*, August, available at http://planningcommission.nic.in.

Provisions of The Panchayats (Extension to Scheduled Areas) Act (PESA), 1996. Available at <http://panchayat.gov.in>.

PRS Briefing, 2011. Legislative Branch briefing of Institute for Policy Research Studies (PRS) to Members of Parliament, 9 March, 2011.

Rao, M. Govinda and Richard M. Bird, 2011. "Coping with Change: The Need to Restructure Urban Governance and Finance in India." IMFG Papers 04, University of Toronto, Institute on Municipal Finance and Governance.

Rao, M. Govinda and T.R. Raghunandan, 2011. "Panchayats and Economic Development," National Institute of Public Finance and Policy, New Delhi, Working Paper No. 2011–86, March.

Rodriguez-Pose, Andres and Nicholas Gill, 2003. "Is there a global link between regional disparities and devolution?" Research Papers in Environmental and Spatial Analysis, No.79, Department of Geography and Environment, London School of Economics and Political Science, February.

Shukla, Rajes., 2010. *How India Earns, Spends and Saves*, New Delhi: Sage.

Sixth Round Table of Union and State Ministers of Panchayat Raj, Guwahati, November 2004.

Tendulkar, D.G., 1953 (1990). *Mahatma—Life of Mohandas Karamchand Gandhi*, Vol.VII, Publications Division, 1953, reprinted 1990.

Thorat, Sukhadeo, and Narender Kumar, 2008. *BR Ambedkar: Perspectives on Social Exclusion and Inclusive Policies*. New Delhi: Oxford University Press.

Times of India newspaper, 2011. "Food Security: India ranks lower than Rwanda, India 67th in Global Hunger Index Among 81 Countries With Worst Figures," 12 October, p. 11, "Times Nation" section.

World Food Programme, 2008. <http://www.wfp.org>.

5

Is Latin America on a Path to Sustainable Fiscal Decentralization?

Matteo Grazzi and Fidel Jaramillo

5.1 Introduction

Everywhere in the world an increasing share of total public expenditures is performed at the subnational level of government, both at intermediate and local levels. But, compared with other regions, the fiscal decentralization process started with considerable delay in Latin America. The Latin American centralist tradition dates from the colonialist period. Only in recent decades, accompanying a progressive return to democracy and a wave of subnational electoral reforms, has a sufficient political consensus been reached to decentralize some functions usually attributed to central government.

Once triggered, the decentralization process has moved quickly across the region. Subnational expenditure's unweighted average percentage of total public expenditure in Latin America rose from 13.1 per cent in 1985 to 19.3 per cent in 2004 (see Figure 5.1). Considering more recent years (see Figure 5.2) this trend has not slowed down and the average ratios of subnational revenues and expenditures to GDP in the region have grown respectively from 5.4 per cent and 5.6 per cent in 1998 to 7.6 per cent and 8.00 per cent in 2009. In 2008 was there a reversal of subnational fiscal revenues consistent with the fall of fiscal revenues all over the world due to the financial crisis, but in 2009 the positive trend returned.

The situation in the region is heterogeneous; not all the countries are at the same point on the decentralization path. Moreover, the pace of decentralization in recent years has not been uniform across countries. Looking at Figure 5.3,[1] it

[1] Some caution is necessary in evaluating the figures contained in Figure 5.3. In fact, the data refer to different levels of government depending on the country. For example, figures for

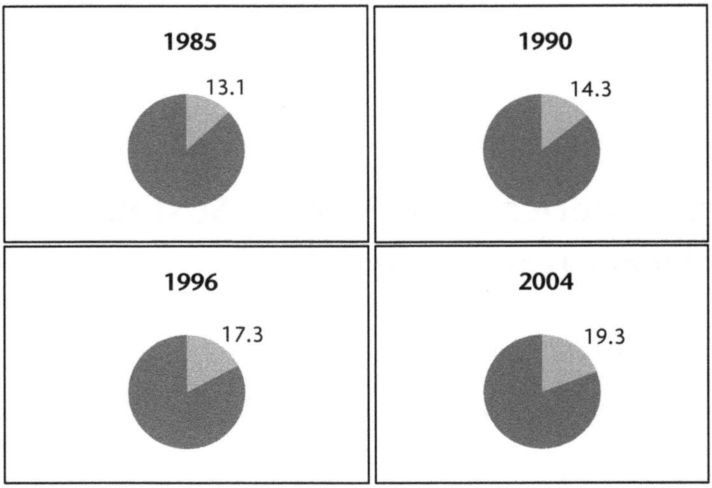

Figure 5.1. Subnational expenditure in Latin America (1985–2004) (percentages of total national expenditure).

Source: Authors' elaboration on data from Daughters and Harper (2007).

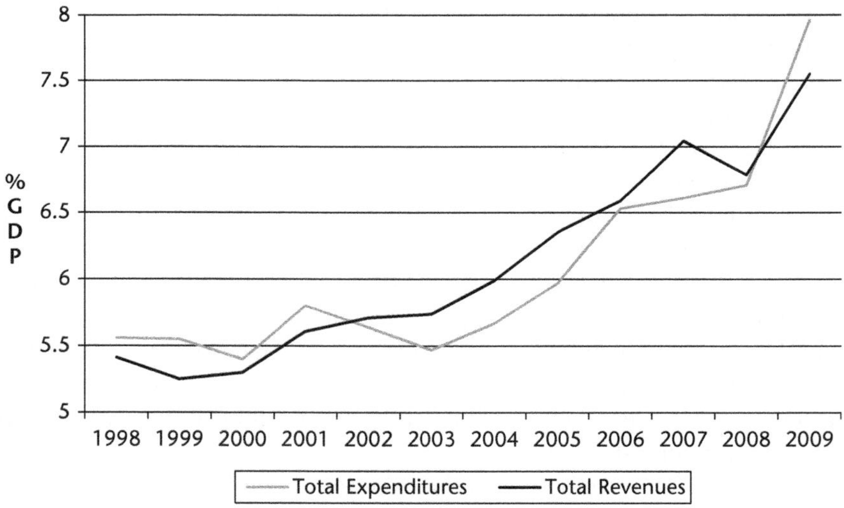

Figure 5.2. Subnational revenues and expenditure in Latin America (1998–2009) (percentages of GDP).

Note: Simple average of figures for available countries.

Source: Authors' elaboration on data from ECLAC (2007, 2011).

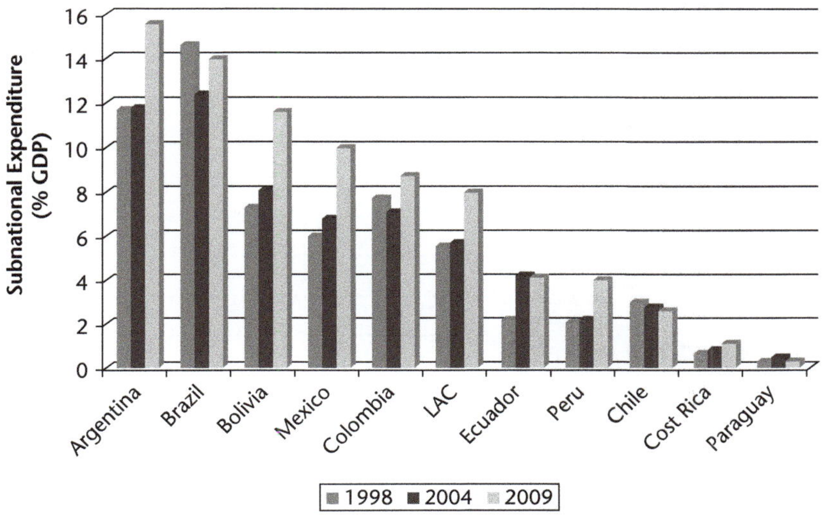

Figure 5.3. Subnational expenditure in selected Latin American Countries (1998–2009) (percentages of GDP).

Note: Figures for Paraguay are for 2008.
Source: Authors' elaboration on data from ECLAC (2007, 2011).

can be seen that the most fiscally decentralized countries—with subnational expenditures constituting over 14 per cent of their GDP in 2010—are Argentina and Brazil; both large countries with a long federal tradition. Bolivia, Colombia, and Mexico are also countries with significant expenditure decentralization, with subnational expenditures exceeding 8 per cent of GDP, and all three of these countries have increased their decentralized expenditure since 1998. Bolivia particularly shows a rise, from 7.3 per cent in 1998 to 11.6 per cent in 2009, reflecting a dynamic decentralization agenda.[2] Ecuador and Peru are still characterized by lower decentralization levels, but a significant rise in subnational expenditure has been registered since 1998. Finally, the remaining countries analyzed—Chile, Costa Rica, and Paraguay—show not only low levels of decentralized expenditure, but also a static situation. Figures for these countries have not significantly changed since 1998, and, in the case of Chile, the decentralized expenditure has even been reduced.

An important feature of the decentralization process is the progressive extension of subnational responsibility for key public service provision.

Argentina are related to provinces, while figures for Ecuador are related to town councils and municipalities.

[2] Faguet (2014) explores how Bolivian decentralization has changed and deepened significantly in recent years.

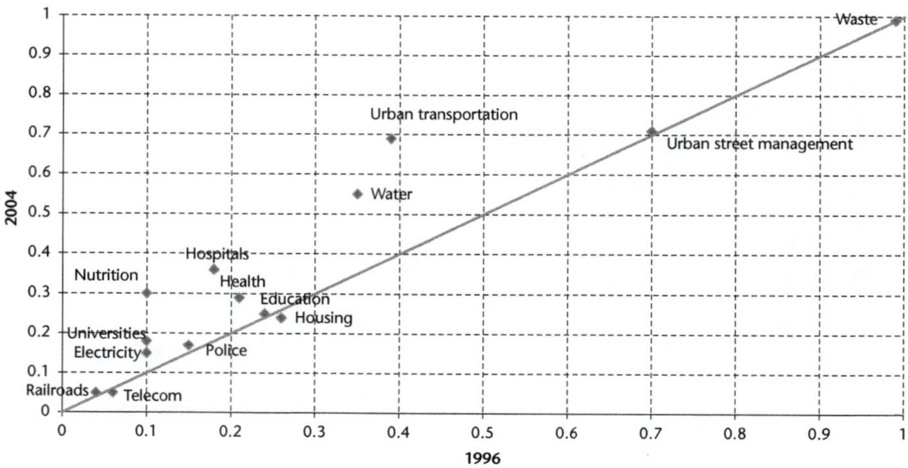

Figure 5.4. Activity Decentralization Index (ADI) in Latin America (1996–2004).
Source: Authors' elaboration on data from Daughters and Harper (2007).

Using the Activity Decentralization Index (ADI),[3] designed by the Inter-American Development Bank (IDB) to measure the degree of autonomy of subnational governments in the management of public services, it is clear that today subnational governments' responsibility is not limited to the traditional decentralized sectors of waste, urban transportation, and street management, but it is progressively extending to more and more sensitive sectors (e.g. water, health, and education). In Figure 5.4 ADI values for selected public service sectors in Latin America for 1996 are compared with those for 2004. Sectors on the left of the 45-degree line have increased their decentralization, while the opposite is true for the ones on the right.

The increasing share of public expenditures performed at subnational level in the region and the key role played by local administrations in the provision of sensitive public services call for a deeper look into subnational fiscal dynamics. In this study we analyze the performance of subnational finances in the region and we contribute to understanding the determinants of their fiscal outcomes.

The chapter is structured as follows. Section 5.2 contains a synthetic review of the economic literature on potential beneficial and adverse effects of fiscal decentralization. Section 5.3 presents the region's experience with "second-generation fiscal federalism"-type reforms, focusing on the design and

[3] The Activity Decentralization Index (ADI) is constructed considering the level of decentralization in four different areas of decision-making: amount, structure, execution, and supervision. For a detailed description of the ADI construction, see IDB (1997).

implementation of subnational fiscal rules. Section 5.4 analyzes the fiscal performance and debt sustainability of Latin American subnational entities, both at the regional level and also with a focus on the cases of Colombia and Peru. Finally, section 5.5 draws conclusions about the decentralization process in the region.

5.2 Fiscal Decentralization in the Economic Literature

Fiscal decentralization has traditionally been seen by the public finance literature as an important source of efficiency gains in the provision of public services. Oates (2006) identifies four basic elements to justify its economic rationale.

The first is the fact that subnational governments are in a closer and better position to adapt output of public services to the preferences of their constituency. This argument is based on the realization that many public goods do not have similar spatial characteristics and that different geographical areas could have different preferences in the provision of public goods. Central governments might lack information on such preferences, or might be unable to differentiate provision by geographical location. In these cases, decentralized entities are in a better position to supply the public good.[4] However, this efficiency argument holds true only under certain conditions; in the presence of interjurisdictional externalities or scale economies[5] in the provision of public goods and services, local governments will fail to internalize all costs and benefits and will produce an inefficient level of output.

Second, if individuals have perfect information and are free to move through different jurisdictions without cost, they can seek out the one that provides outputs better suited to their preferences (Tiebout, 1956). In this way,

[4] This argument has been formalized by Oates (1972) in his Decentralization Theorem, which states that "For a public good—the consumption of which is defined over geographical subsets of the total population, and for which the costs of providing each level of output of the good in each jurisdiction are the same for the central or the respective local government—it will always be more efficient (or at least as efficient) for local governments to provide the Pareto-efficient levels of output for their respective jurisdictions than for the central government to provide *any* specified and uniform level of output across all jurisdictions" (Ibid., p.35). Faguet and Sánchez (2014) test it empirically for Colombia, and Channa and Faguet (2012) survey international evidence for health and education.

[5] Prud'homme (1995) refers to studies which have found the existence of scale economies in the provision of some public services, but argues that the welfare losses implied by decentralization because of such economies of scale are minimal. Faguet (2004) explores the institutional implications of a bargaining game in the presence of scale economies and spatial heterogeneity/local knowledge.

preferences are revealed and aggregated by the individuals themselves and the result is a more efficient scenario.

Third, decentralized governments face competition from their homologous neighbors, receiving pressure for a more efficient provision of public services and constraining budgetary growth. The resulting competition increases the quality of delivery.

Fourth, decentralization can encourage experimentation and innovation, as individual jurisdictions are free to adopt new approaches to public policy. When a better way of providing a service is discovered by one jurisdiction, others will follow and an overall more efficient delivery is obtained. An additional, important argument in favor of decentralization is the basic principle that *accountability brings responsibility*, i.e. the view that when local officials are responsible for the provision of a public service, they are likely to have an incentive for better performance (Tanzi, 2000).

However, the decentralization process may also present some negative effects. In fact, an increasing shifting of responsibilities from central to local governments also means transferring power from central to local bureaucracies, which may significantly reduce the advantages of decentralization. Especially in developing countries, where qualified labor is scarce, a central administration can usually offer better opportunities than local entities, and consequently the quality of bureaucracy in local administrations is likely to be lower than in the central government (Prud'homme, 1995). Moreover, the close relation between local officials, citizenship, and interest groups, added to their discretionary decision-making, seems to cause higher corruption at the local level than at the national level (Prud'homme, 1995; Tanzi, 2000).

Beyond efficiency issues, decentralization also seems to have some worrisome implications for central macroeconomic management. First, the loss of control over an important part of public expenditure and revenues may introduce limitations and rigidities to the action of central government. Second, fiscal policies of subnational governments—which are usually procyclical—may undermine countercyclical stabilization policies of central government when needed. Third, the devolution of expenditure responsibilities to subnational entities without an adequate provision of own resources and a clear distinction of functions and responsibilities between government levels may have a negative effect on public accounts. If local expenditure is partly financed by common pool resources, local governments do not fully internalize the cost of their public programs (Stein, 1998) and decentralization could raise total expenditure and lead to unsustainable fiscal outcomes. And if local governors have free access to the credit market and fiscal bailouts from higher-level authorities are expected, there will be an incentive for the subnational entity to over-borrow and for lending institutions to over-lend, not properly discounting the risks associated with such lending (Daughters and Harper, 2007; Shah, 2004). In other words, in lacking a clear regulatory framework, subnational entities face a *soft budget constraint*: when there are no available resources *ex ante* to finance their desired level of expenditure, they obtain them from the central government *ex post*, after expenditures have been made or debt has been accumulated (Tanzi, 2000).

Considering these arguments, a possible outcome of the decentralization process is the deterioration of national fiscal accounts. To mitigate this effect and to control subnational finances, several approaches have been proposed. Ter-Minassian and Craig (1997) grouped them into four stylized categories: reliance on market discipline, cooperative arrangements between different levels of government, rule-based controls, and administrative controls. The effectiveness of market mechanisms depends on the presence of several necessary conditions, such as openness of financial market, good information on the borrower's repayment capacity, no perceived chance of bailout, and the presence of adequate institutions (Lane, 1993). Indeed, especially in developing countries, such stringent conditions are unlikely to be realized. Consequently, the most popular option in such countries has usually been the setting of fiscal rules, because they may be clear, transparent and relatively easy to monitor. These rules may take several forms, ranging from *ex ante* controls, such as setting limits on the level of debt and real expenditure growth, to *ex post* consequences, such as the prohibition of bailouts from the central government.[6]

However, the econometric evidence of the impact of such constraints on subnational fiscal discipline has been limited and mixed (Plekhanov and Singh, 2007) and there is still no consensus in the empirical literature on their actual effectiveness. Countries have been successful in fiscal consolidation both with and without rules in place, showing that they are not a necessary condition for fiscal adjustment. Moreover, the setting of a rule does not automatically imply its observance or enforcement. Webb (2004) therefore concludes that fiscal responsibility laws are neither necessary nor sufficient for fiscal prudence.

Over the years, several Latin American countries have designed fiscal responsibility laws containing rules aimed to improve subnational fiscal discipline. The experience of this region is thus particularly illustrative for evaluating the interaction between fiscal rules-setting and the effects of decentralization.

[6] For a complete discussion on different channels to control public deficits and debt, see Webb (2004).

5.3 Decentralization and Subnational Fiscal Rules: the Latin American Experience

When the decentralization process started in the region, the general thought was that at the macroeconomic level it could play a key role in contributing to the structural adjustment goals of many countries. Devolving expenditure responsibilities to local entities was seen as a way to reduce spending obligations of central governments and to improve their fiscal balances (Daughters and Harper, 2007). But as decentralization progressed, the devolution of expenditure power to subnational entities proved to be less beneficial for public accounts than had been imagined. This process was not accompanied by the strengthening of financial accounting and planning capacities of local governments, resulting in the mismanagement of the larger amount of resources. On the other hand, local governments became progressively more politically accountable for the provision of public services without being directly responsible for raising resources from their own constituents. This situation created an incentive for local entities to increase their expenditures without worrying about financial sustainability, and forced central governments to pay the price of subnational indiscipline through both expanded inter-governmental transfers to cover higher subnational deficits and periodic bailouts of over-indebted decentralized governments. Consequently, fiscal accounts of central governments actually worsened in the 1990s and early 2000s. The overall fiscal deficit reached 2.6 per cent of GDP in 2001, and total public sector expenditures in Latin America grew steadily as a percentage of GDP (See Figure 5.5).

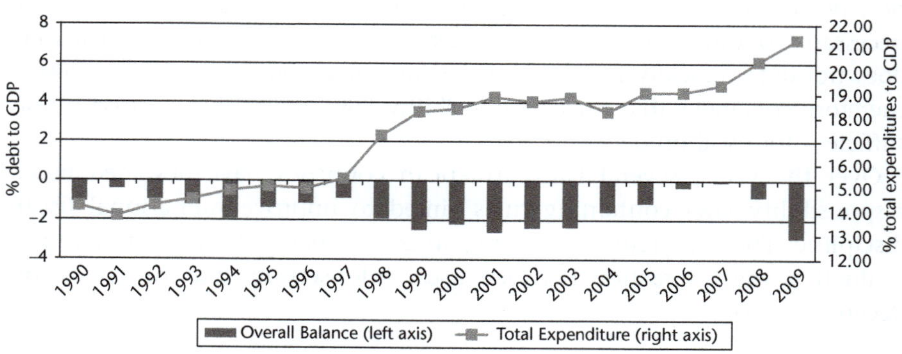

Figure 5.5. Public sector total expenditure and overall balance in Latin America (1990–2009, percentages of GDP).

Note: Simple average of available Latin American countries.
Source: Authors' elaboration on data from CEPALSTAT.

However, after a long period of deterioration, the situation of subnational fiscal accounts appears to have improved. On one hand, the autonomy of subnational governments in raising their own revenues has increased, reducing that vertical imbalance which has been identified by several authors as a major source of irresponsible fiscal behavior. On the other hand, most Latin American countries have recognized the necessity to control subnational accounts and have established institutional rules in order to contain subnational spending and borrowing. Furthermore, the regional empirical evidence suggests that those countries with more hierarchical and transparent budget processes and with a clear set of fiscal rules tend to present lower primary deficits (or higher primary surplus). Filc and Scartascini (2004) confirmed this relationship, by showing the positive correlation between a Fiscal Rules Index and Fiscal Performance—measured as the General Government Primary Result over GDP—in Latin America.

On average, regional subnational public debt decreased from a peak of 9.6 per cent of GDP in 2002 to 5.4 per cent in 2008, while the average overall balance has turned positive since 2003 and reached a record surplus of 0.6 per cent of GDP in 2005 (See Figure 5.6). Moreover, the ratio between decentralized debt and revenues has been stabilizing all over the region, returning to pre-2000 levels (See Figure 5.7).

Disaggregating by country, it can be seen that several countries have achieved a fiscal surplus at the subnational level and have reduced their

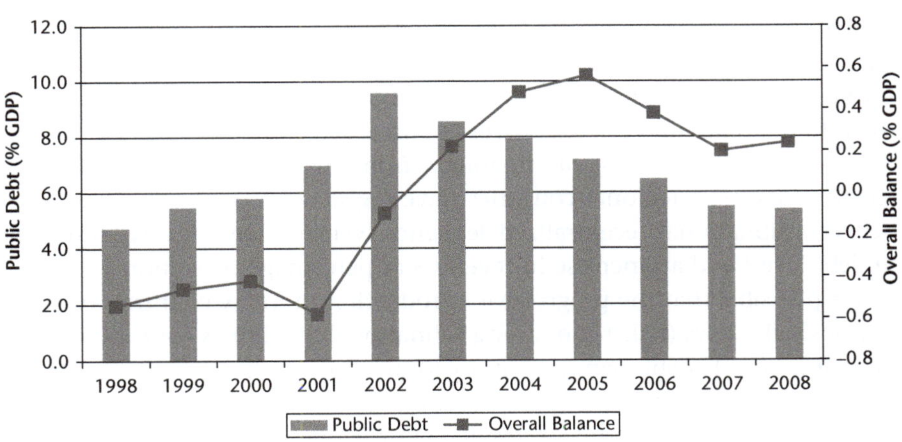

Figure 5.6. Subnational public debt and overall balance in Latin America (1998–2008) (percentages of GDP).

Note: Simple Average of figures for Latin American countries with available data (Argentina, Bolivia, Brazil, Colombia, Mexico).
Source: Authors' elaboration on data from ECLAC (2007, 2011).

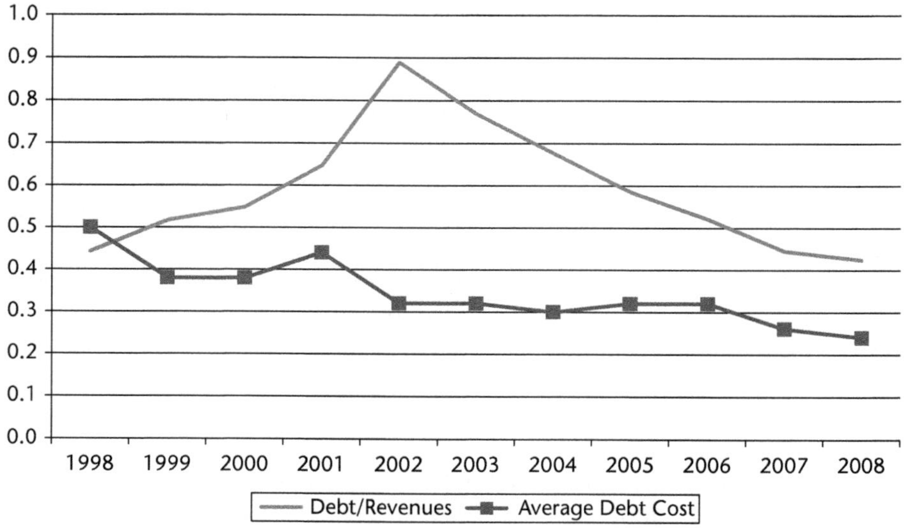

Figure 5.7. Subnational debt sustainability indicators in Latin America (1999–2008) (subnational debt/revenues & average real cost of debt).

Note: Simple Average of figures for Latin American countries with available data (Argentina, Bolivia, Brazil, Colombia, Mexico).
Source: Authors' elaboration on data from ECLAC (2007, 2011).

subnational debt (Figures 5.8 and 5.9). In particular, the debt levels of Argentina and Brazil decreased significantly from 2004 to 2009, while the countries which obtained the highest improvement in their overall subnational balances have been Brazil and Bolivia, which passed from a deficit in 1998 to a surplus exceeding 0.4 per cent of GDP in 2008, despite the adverse effects of the international financial crisis over the fiscal accounts.

As for subnational debt sustainability, from Figure 5.10 it is clear that in recent years most regional countries have registered a decrease in the ratio between subnational decentralized debt and revenues, due to both a reduction in debt levels and an increase in revenues as percentages of national GDP. It seems plausible that the progressive introduction in many countries of fiscal responsibility laws (FRLs) containing subnational fiscal rules contributed to a more responsible debt management by local administrations in several countries. However, such regulations have not been homogeneous across the region in motivation, forms, or results. On the one hand, the first countries to introduce FRLs were the more decentralized ones, attempting to mitigate a situation of deteriorated subnational finances. On the other hand, countries with centralist traditions accompanied the decentralization process with the drafting of corresponding regulation, in order to prevent uncontrolled subnational expenditures.

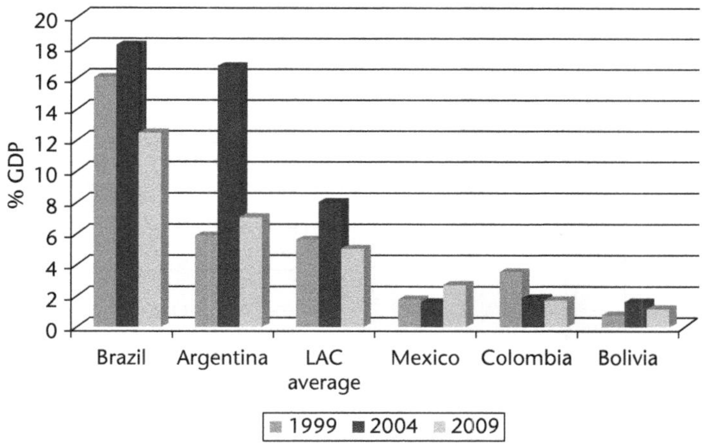

Figure 5.8. Subnational public debt in selected latin American countries (1999–2009) (percentages of GDP).

Source: Authors' elaboration on data from ECLAC (2007, 2011).

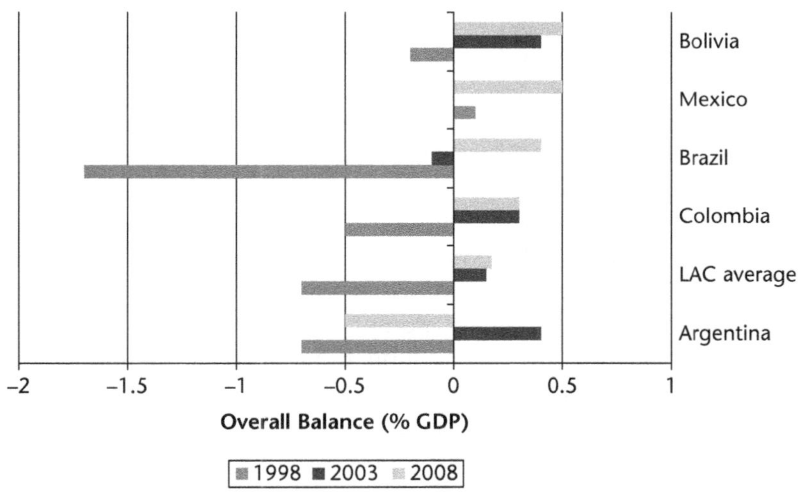

Figure 5.9. Subnational overall balance in selected Latin American countries (1998–2008) (percentages of GDP).

Source: Authors' elaboration on data from ECLAC (2007, 2011).

Among the former, Brazil approved in 2000 a comprehensive FRL which, bringing together different provisions contained in previous acts, consolidated and refined borrowing rules and fiscal efficiency standards for subnational entities. Similarly, in 2003 in Colombia, an FRL consolidated a process of "fiscal responsabilization," started in 1997 with the drafting of the Territorial

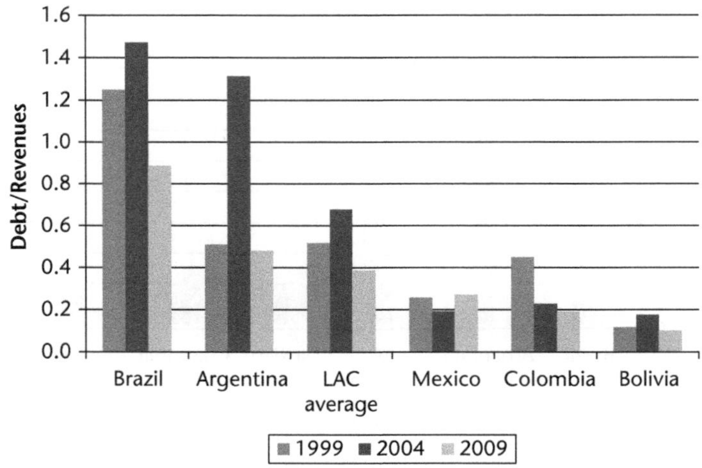

Figure 5.10. Subnational debt/revenues in selected Latin American countries (1999–2009).

Source: Authors' elaboration on data from ECLAC (2007, 2011).

Borrowing Law (better known as *Ley de Semáforos*)—an act which subjected borrowing by excessively indebted subnational governments to the prior approval of the Ministry of Finance—and continued in 2000 with Law 617, which defined a system of indicators and benchmarks to contain subnational public expenditure. However, not all the regional FRLs were successful and not all the regional experiences included FRLs. In 1999Argentina passed the National Fiscal Solvency Law which set a number of rules aimed at reaching fiscal balance at the central level no later than 2003. It included limits to the central government's fiscal deficit and expenditures, the adoption of multi-year budgeting, and the implementation of transparency measures. Although this law did not include rules at the subnational level, several provinces followed the national example and approved local fiscal rules. But in the presence of declining tax revenues, many provinces did not comply with their own commitments[7] and in 2001 the FRLs stopped working. A different approach to subnational debt management has been adopted in Mexico, where there is no national FRL and where a new borrowing framework based on the role of market forces in controlling subnational debt was introduced in 2000. The key elements of this reform were the elimination of discretionary transfers from the federal government, the setting of rules for the public disclosure of the debts and fiscal deficits of borrowing governments, and a tightening of the regulation of lending by private banks to states.

[7] In 2000, for example, only 5 out of 11 provinces which had imposed a hard budget constraint fulfilled it (Braun and Tommasi, 2003).

As for the countries that decentralized later, several governments drafted fiscal reforms aimed at controlling subnational finances following the example of Brazil and Colombia. For instance, Peru—a country with a clear centralist tradition where the decentralization process only actually started in 2002—approved in 2003 a regulatory framework with both *ex ante* constraints for subnational deficit and borrowings and *ex post* penalties for local governments violating the targets established by the law (Webb, 2004).[8] In particular, a set of ten different subnational fiscal rules[9] distributed in three different laws[10] was introduced, to ensure responsible debt management by regional and local governments. Nevertheless, the transfer cuts due to be enforced for rule-breaking were suspended, leaving the regulation somewhat incomplete.

5.4 Fiscal Performance and Debt Sustainability at the Subnational Level

In order to evaluate whether subnational fiscal balance has been historically consistent with the outstanding debt amount, we performed a debt sustainability exercise[11] for five Latin American countries (Argentina, Bolivia, Brazil, Colombia, and Mexico), the results of which are displayed in Figure 5.11.

The graph evaluates the sustainability dynamics of subnational finances in each country, by plotting the observed ratio of primary surplus on revenues (s) and the ratio required for fiscal sustainability[12] (s^*) in two different periods (1999–2002 and 2003–8). Each data point is labeled with a country, and shows the country's trajectory from the first period to the second[13] with an arrow from one point to another. When s is higher than s^*, e.g. the point lies to the right of the bisector, the corresponding country presents a sustainable subnational debt in that period.

The obtained results are consistent with the described stylized facts. In the first period only Mexico lies in the sustainable area, while Argentina, Bolivia, Brazil, and Colombia present unsustainable subnational fiscal accounts.

[8] In the case of violation of the law, the national government withholds some transfers so that the required debt payment is made.

[9] For the detailed list of rules, see Moron (2010).

[10] *Ley de Responsabilidad y Transparencia Fiscal*, *Ley de Descentralización Fiscal*, and *Ley Orgánica de Municipalidades*.

[11] For a description of the employed framework for fiscal sustainability analysis, see Appendix. The exercise is preliminary and it is limited by the scarcity and incompleteness of data.

[12] We define s^* as the surplus necessary to stabilize the debt-to-GDP ratio for a given real interest rate, growth rate of the economy, and initial stock of debt.

[13] The choice of these periods is justified by the fact that for the year 2003 all the countries considered in the sample already had a legal framework that included some type of control over subnational fiscal accounts.

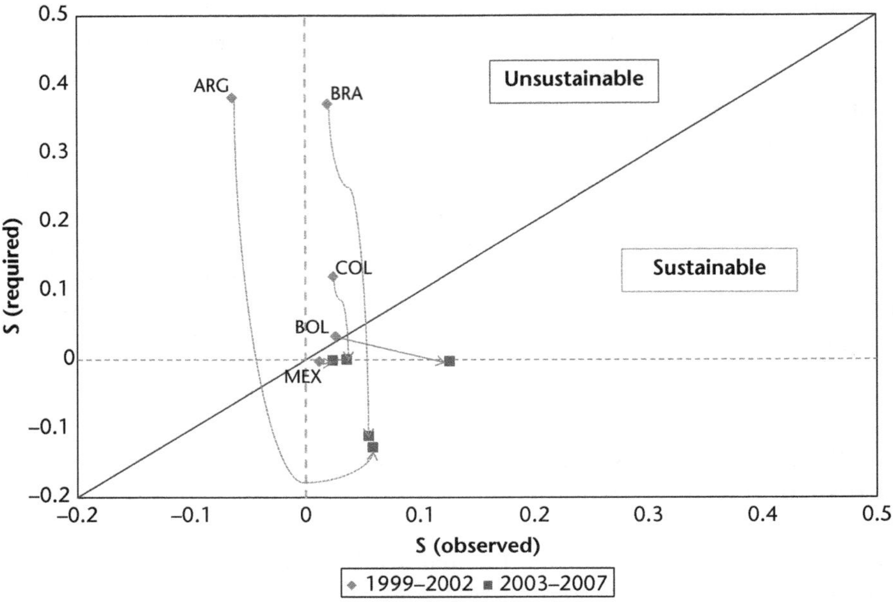

Figure 5.11. Subnational sustainability analysis (1999–2002 and 2003–8).
Source: Authors' elaboration on data from ECLAC (2009, 2010).

However, in the second period there is a generalized improvement and all the countries move to the right of the sustainability line.

Therefore, both descriptive figures and the sustainability analysis suggest that the introduction of second-generation fiscal reforms has contributed to stabilizing the subnational debt situation in the region. However, in order to confirm this hypothesis and to correctly assess the fiscal performance of subnational entities, it is necessary to set up a more formalized framework for statistical analysis. An IDB research project (Braun and Llach, 2010) proposes the application of a "true model" of subnational fiscal behavior which, in the absence of omitted variables, should provide a first approximation of the determinants of subnational fiscal performances in a country. It is a simple econometric model, where different measures of fiscal health depend on a large set of structural, macroeconomic, institutional, and political variables, as shown in the following equation:

$$\begin{aligned} \textit{Fiscal Performance} = f(&\textit{Structural Variables}, \textit{Macroeconomic Variables},\\ &\textit{Institutional Variables}, \textit{Political Variables}) \end{aligned} \quad (5.1)$$

As for the dependent variable, the authors identified in the literature seven possible indicators of *Fiscal Performance*, which account for different

Table 5.1. A "true model" of subnational fiscal performance—independent variables.

Category	Variable	Definition
Structural	GDP per capita	
	Population	
	Population density	
Macroeconomic	Regional economic cycle	GGP diversion from its trend
	Relative key prices	Wages, exchange rates, commodities associated to national or subnational revenues
	National fiscal surplus	
Institutional	Subnational fiscal rules	Classified between 0 (no rules) and 5 (very strict rules)
	Vertical unbalance	Transfer revenues as percentage of total revenues of the subnational entity
	Expenditure decentralization degree	Subnational public expenditure as percentage of total public expenditure
	Earmarking	Percentage of transfer revenues with specific destination
	Central government fiscal "goodness"	Transfers per capita to given subnational entity compared with transfers per capita to all other subnational entities
	Debt autonomy	Classification between 0 (prohibition) to 5 (full autonomy)
	Revenue autonomy	Classification between 0 (total centralization) to 5 (full autonomy)
	Expenditure autonomy	Classification between 0 (total centralization) to 5 (full autonomy)
	Bailout history	Number of bailouts
	Subnational representation in national government	Number of inhabitants in the subnational region for each Member of Parliament
Political	Subnational electoral cycle momentum	Dummy variable 1: electoral year; 0: no
	National electoral cycle momentum	Dummy variable 1: electoral year; 0: no
	Political color of subnational government	Matching with national government
	Ideology of subnational government	0: right or centre-right; 1 centre; 2: left or centre-left
	Electoral competition degree	Percentage of votes obtained by the government party in the three previous elections

Source: Adapted from Braun and Llach (2010).

dimensions of fiscal behavior of the subnational entity,[14] while, with regards to the right-hand side of the equation, they propose twenty-one possible variables across the four different categories (See Table 5.1).

Given the availability of sufficient information on the accounts of subnational entities in a country, the model should be estimated on a panel dataset over the highest possible number of years. However, a serious obstacle for this analysis may be constituted by the low accuracy of subnational accounts,

[14] The proposed measures of fiscal performance are: operative balance, primary balance, fiscal balance, operational balance, debt-to-GGP (Gross geographic product) ratio, debt stock to current revenues ratio, and debt interests to current revenues ratio.

especially at the municipal level. For example, Moron (2010) performed an evaluation of the available data in a sample of fifteen Peruvian municipalities, finding substantial problems of sub-recorded, unrecorded, or misclassified debt.

Keeping in mind this potential pitfall, the model proposed has been applied to the cases of Colombia and Peru in two IDB-funded studies, in order to identify the main drivers of subnational fiscal performance and the impact of fiscal rules implementation in each country. In the case of Colombia, Sánchez and Zenteno (2010) used instrumental variable (IV) regression on an original panel dataset with information on Colombian departments and municipalities from 1996 to 2007, to estimate determinants of subnational payment capacity (proxied by the ratio between debt stock and current revenues) and saving capacity (proxied by the ratio between primary surplus and total revenues or the ratio between current saving and total revenues (only in the case of municipalities)). The results show that variables such as population, wealth, and fiscal dependence on the central government have a significant positive effect on the payment capacity of a territorial entity. Likewise, vertical imbalance, wealth, and local election turnout rates significantly improve their saving capacity. As regards the effectiveness of fiscal rules, subnational entities that comply with the limits imposed by Law 617 are found to be positively correlated with both a better payment capacity and a better saving capacity.

Similarly, Moron (2010) evaluates the case of Peru, employing panel data from 1381 municipalities in the period 2003–8. Using IV estimation with the ratio between primary surplus and total revenues as the dependent variable, the author finds that in this case there is also empirical evidence that implementing fiscal rules improves subnational fiscal performance. On the other hand, differently from the case of Colombia, vertical imbalance has a negative and significant effect, showing evidence of *fiscal laziness*.[15]

This mixed evidence on the effect of vertical imbalance on subnational fiscal performance can be related to the different degree of discretion central governments have in the decisions related to the transfers system. In fact, the literature usually indicates that subnational governments manage finances more efficiently if transfers are distributed in a non-discretionary and transparent way and if amounts and sources of funding are predetermined. This allows subnational entities to have a more stable fiscal horizon, enabling better financial planning and reducing the soft-budget constraint problem.

Recently, many countries in Latin America, including Colombia and Peru,[16] have decreased discretionality in their transfer systems (Daughters and

[15] Meaning the higher the transfers a municipality receives from central government as a percentage of its total revenues, the less worried it will be about fiscal discipline.

[16] Since 1996, Peru, previously a very centralist country with a small, very discretionary transfer system, started to shift towards a more automatic system, based on formulas, to determine the

Harper, 2007). Considering the different time frames of the two studies (the data for Peru are considerably more recent than those for Colombia), it seems plausible that this reduction in transfer discretionality is a reasonable explanation for different results. Furthermore, the percentage of earmarked transfers is found to be linked to a positive impact on subnational fiscal performance, suggesting that local governments present better fiscal performance when there is higher central control on the use of inter-governmental transfers. From a theoretical point of view, earmarked transfers are often inefficient, as they can hinder subnational governments' ability to target programs to meet the demands of their constituents. Moreover, central governments often lack the ability to monitor the use of earmarked grants. This could degenerate into additional finance for a subnational government without the accountability that should be expected of local governments' spending from own-source revenues or untied transfers (Ahmad and Searle, 2006). However, especially in developing countries where local institutions are weaker, earmarked transfers can play a role in inducing enhanced management and reporting, if further transfers are conditioned to it. Evidence from Peru points in this direction.

5.5 Conclusions

The process of fiscal decentralization in Latin America has been the result of economic and political reforms which occurred in many countries in the region following democratic transition and constitutional reshaping. First-generation reforms essentially consisted of unconditional transfer of spending responsibilities from the central to the subnational level. The result was an explosion of decentralized expenditure and a deterioration of fiscal outcomes. Attempting to control subnational finances and to achieve fiscal sustainability, many countries designed a second generation of reforms which introduced fiscal responsibility laws with subnational fiscal rules, allowed higher autonomy in raising revenues, and contained a stronger intergovernmental regulatory framework.

The analyses at both continental and national levels suggest that the introduction of such reforms significantly helped the fiscal consolidation of subnational governments in Latin America. Nevertheless, the aggregate picture hides differences both between and within countries. Moreover, the registered improvements may be due not to fiscal policy reforms but to external factors. First, from 2002 Latin America grew at a yearly average rate of 5 per cent of

transfer distributions to subnational entities, together with the decentralization process (Daughters and Harper, 2007).

GDP; improved fiscal accounts could simply reflect this positive cycle. Second, the boom in commodity prices benefited many local governments directly, granting them unexpected extra revenues. Finally, the decline in domestic interest rates decreased the cost of the debt and allowed better access to financial markets.

In conclusion, second-generation fiscal federalist reforms seem to have played an important role in the improvement of fiscal performances across the region, but further empirical research at a more disaggregated level is needed in order to isolate external factors and to better understand the real determinants of subnational fiscal outcomes. In this sense, a first attempt is constituted by the methodology proposed by Braun and Llach (2010). Their "true model" of subnational fiscal behavior, applied to the cases of Colombia (Sánchez and Zenteno González, 2011) and Peru (Moron, 2010), provides some empirical evidence on the effectiveness of fiscal rules in improving subnational fiscal performance.

Appendix: Subnational Sustainability Analysis

National and subnational fiscal sustainability analysis are similar, but with some substantial differences. Consequently, the standard analysis framework should be properly modified (Ianchovichina, Liu, and Nagarajan, 2006). First, decentralized governments do not usually have any monetary policy power. Consequently, each single subnational government cannot influence the nominal interest rate, and seigniorage revenues (or change in the monetary base) do not enter in its budget constraint. Second, foreign exchange risk may not directly affect subnational finance, as subnational entities are usually not allowed to borrow in foreign currency without approval and guarantee from the central government. Finally, central government's behavior significantly influences subnational debt dynamics, not only because transfers from the centre are the most important source of local revenues, but also because market participants could tolerate unsustainable subnational fiscal policies if they expect bailouts from the central government.

Following Ianchovichina, Liu, and Nagarajan (2006), the inter-temporal financing constraint of a subnational entity can be written as:

$$B_t - B_{t-1} = n_t B_{t-1} - S_t \tag{5.2}$$

Where B_t is the amount of public debt at the end of the period t, S_t is the primary balance (revenues minus non-interest expenditures), and n_t is the nominal interest rate in period t.

The identity shows that the net issuance of debt is equal to the difference between interest payments and the primary surplus.

In order to facilitate the practical fiscal sustainability analysis, we represent the subnational budget constraint in percentages of revenues (Y_t). Dividing both sides by Y_t and rearranging, equation (5.2) is then transformed into:

$$b_t = \frac{1+r_t}{1+g_t} b_{t-1} - s_t \qquad (5.3)$$

Where r_t is the real interest rate; g_t is the annual growth rate of revenues; $b_t = B_t / Y_t$ and $s_t = S_t/Y_t$.

In equilibrium, the ratio of debt to revenues, the primary balance, the real interest rate, and the growth rate are all constant. Then the budget constraint becomes:

$$s(required) = \left(\frac{\bar{r}-\bar{g}}{1+\bar{g}}\right)\bar{b} \qquad (5.4)$$

So, to give an assessment of debt sustainability it would be sufficient to compare the observed *s* with *s(required)*.

Acknowledgements

The contents are sole responsibilities of the authors, and do not necessarily reflect the position of the Inter-American Development Bank. We thank Marielle del Valle for her significant contribution and Camilo Bohórquez and Drew D'Alelio for excellent research assistance.

References

Ahmad, E. and B. Searle, 2006. "On the implementation of transfers to subnational governments." In E. Ahmad and G.brosio (eds.) *Handbook of Fiscal Federalism*. Cheltenham, UK: Edward Elgar.

Braun, M. and L. Llach, 2010. "Estableciendo y Evaluando Resultados Fiscales: Una metodologia". Banco Inter-Americano de Desarrollo, Washington, DC.

Braun, M. and M. Tommasi, 2003. "Fiscal Rules for Subnational Governments: Some Organizing Principles and Latin American Experiences." In G. Kopits (ed.) *Rules and Practice in Intergovernmental Fiscal Relations*. IMF and World Bank, Washington, DC.

Channa, A. and J.P. Faguet, 2012. "Decentralization of Health and Education in Developing Countries: A Quality-Adjusted Review of the Empirical Literature." LSE/STICERD Working Paper No. EOPP 38.

Daughters, R. and L. Harper, 2007. "Fiscal and Political Decentralization Reforms." In E. Lora (ed.) *The State of State Reform in Latin America*. Washington, DC: Inter-American Development Bank.

ECLAC, 2007, 2009, 2010, 2011. "Economic Survey of Latin America and the Caribbean." ECLAC, Santiago de Chile.

Faguet, J.P., 2014. "Can Sub-National Autonomy Strengthen Democracy in Bolivia?" *Publius: The Journal of Federalism*, 44(1): 51–81; doi: 10.1093/publius/pjt020.

Faguet, J.P., 2004. "Why So Much Centralization? A Model of Primitive Centripetal Accumulation." STICERD DEDPS No.43, London School of Economics.

Faguet, J.P. and F. Sánchez, 2014. "Decentralization and Access to Social Services in Colombia." *Public Choice*, 160(1-2): 227–49. Doi: 10.1007/s11127-013-0077-7.

Filc, G. and C. Scartascini, 2004. "Budget Institutions and Fiscal Outcomes: Ten Years of Inquiry on Fiscal Matters at the Research Department." Paper prepared for the Research Department 10th Year Anniversary Conference, IDB, Washington, DC.

Ianchovichina, L., Liu, L., and Nagarajan, M., 2006. "Subnational Fiscal Sustainability Analysis: What can we learn from Tamil Nadu." World Bank Policy Research Working Paper No. 3947.

IDB (Inter-American Development Bank), 1997. "Latin America after a Decade of Reform: What Comes Next?" Economic and Social Progress in Latin America (IPES) Report. Washington, DC: Inter-American Development Bank.

Lane, T., 1993. "Market Discipline," *IMF Staff Papers*, Vol. 40 (March), 53–88.

Moron, E., 2010. "Descentralización y Desempeño Fiscal a Nivel Subnacional: El caso de Perú." Final Report, IDB.

Oates, W., 1972. *Fiscal Federalism*. Harcourt Brace Jovanovic, New York.

Oates, W., 2006. "On the Theory and Practice of Fiscal Decentralization." IFIR Working Paper No. 2006–05.

Plekhanov, A. and Singh, R., 2007. "How Should Subnational Government Borrowing Be Regulated?" Some Cross-Country Empirical Evidence." *IMF Staff Papers*, Vol. 53 (3), 426–52.

Prud'homme, R., 1995. "The Dangers of Decentralization." *The World Bank Research Observer*, Vol. 10, No. 2, 201–20.

Sánchez, F. and Gonzales, J. Z., 2011. "Descentralización y sostenibilidad fiscal subnacional: el caso de Colombia (No. 009241). Universidad de los Andes - CEDE.

Shah, A., 2004. "Fiscal Decentralization in Developing and Transition Economies: Progress, Problems, and the Promise." World Bank Policy Research Working Paper No. 3282.

Stein, E., 1998. "Fiscal Decentralization and Government Size in Latin America." IDB OCE Working Paper No. 368.

Tanzi, V., 2000. "Policies, Institutions and the Dark Side of Economics." Cheltenham, UK: Edward Elgar.

Ter-Minassian, T., and J. Craig, 1997. "Control of Sub-National Government Borrowing." In T. Ter-Minassian (ed.) *Fiscal Federalism in Theory and Practice*. Washington, DC: IMF.

Tiebout, C.M., 1956. "A Pure Theory of Local Expenditures." *Journal of Political Economy* 64 (October): 416–24.

Webb, S.B., 2004. "Fiscal Responsibility Laws for Subnational Discipline: The Latin American Experience." World Bank Policy Research Working Paper 3309.

6

Does Decentralization Strengthen or Weaken the State?

Authority and Social Learning in a Supple State

Jean-Paul Faguet, Ashley M. Fox, and Caroline Pöschl

6.1 Introduction

Many developing countries are caught in a vicious circle of poverty, weak institutions, corruption, low levels of legitimacy, and low economic growth rates. For decades, development specialists debated how international aid and other external interventions might spring countries from this trap (Boone and Faguet, 1998). In more recent years, attention has turned to home-grown solutions. Decentralization was widely advocated as an institutional solution from the 1960s onwards, and became exceedingly popular during the 1990s. It has been promoted as a means of strengthening the state for developing countries suffering from low organizational capacity, poor public service provision, and sectarian violence (Brancati, 2004). The policy response has been highly enthusiastic, with most of the world's countries experimenting with some form of decentralization over the past four decades (Manor, 1999; Faguet, 2012).

This is ironic, as a strong state has traditionally been equated with a centralized state. Strong states were understood as unitary rather than federal, with power concentrated in the executive branch. Such centralized states were generally considered to be better able to formulate policy independently and carry out specific goals without obtrusion. They were seen as exercising greater control over their populations, ensuring conformity in legal mandates and concentrating power at the top of the chain of command, giving them greater authority (Evans, Rueschemeyer, and Skocpol, 1985; Skocpol 1985).

But the appeal of the "strong state as centralized state" idea diminished during the 1990s, while at the same time decentralization was becoming the new consensus (Stepan, 2000). Proponents argued that decentralized governance structures may actually be more effective in strengthening the state. While centralized states are strong in some respects, they may be "brittle" in others (Faguet 2014a and 2014b). They may stoke tensions amongst fractious groups, leading to violence. They may be unresponsive, inefficient, or wasteful in the use of public resources. And they may facilitate tyranny over the majority or elite capture on a national scale.

Has decentralization strengthened the state? Or has reform instead weakened state institutions, giving voice to disparate and competing factions? Traditionally—and oddly—the literature has been unable to answer these large questions (Treisman, 2007; Faguet, 2012). But a surge of new evidence from diverse countries provides a basis for settling some of these disagreements, and also correcting some of the fundamental misunderstandings in the literature about what decentralization is and how it affects the state. This chapter uses such evidence to reconceptualize some of the key trade-offs regarding decentralization and state strength, and then offers practical guidance to assist development scholars and policy makers in navigating the potentials and pitfalls of reform. We review both the theoretical and empirical literature on the ways decentralization is believed to either strengthen or weaken the state, highlighting where theory is indeterminate, and focus on the underlying conditions that can cause the same reform to have very different outcomes. We suggest policy and structural factors that policy makers can use to design sincerely[1] decentralized institutions that strengthen the state and promote its legitimacy.

Just as the flexibility of an aircraft's wings increases the aircraft's resilience through their capacity to dissipate shocks, we argue that decentralizing a state may increase its strength by making it more "supple." By increasing the density of government structure in terms of elected local and regional representation, decentralization can generate more feedback loops and increase the overall level of accountability to which government is subject. This serves to both increase the state's sensitivity to local complaints and conditions, and increase its options for response through overlapping responsibility and multiple redundancy in the policy realm. Simply put, in a centralized system a citizen has one authority to appeal to. In a

[1] "Sincere" decentralization refers to authentic attempts to devolve power and resources to subnational levels of government, as opposed to declarations of intent, or even promulgated laws and decrees, that have little practical effect (Faguet, 2012).

decentralized system she has several, each with its own powers and independent incentives to listen. All else equal, she is more likely to get satisfaction for at least some of her concerns in the latter. And by bringing government "closer to the people," decentralization may increase participation in state-building processes from the ground up.

We make this argument piecemeal. We focus on some of the most important components of state strength identified in the literature, linking these to the principal challenges facing weak states in developing countries, and then analyze how decentralization can affect each challenge. The major arguments are summarized in Table 6.1. Section 6.2 discusses some of the most important conceptualizations of state strength in the literature and identifies four key dimensions that should be affected by the level of (de)centralization in a country's government. Section 6.3 examines how decentralization might affect a state's authority over its territory and people, and its ability to maintain peace and prevent conflict. Section 6.4 discusses whether decentralization increases or decreases the state's ability to formulate policy autonomously and uphold the law. In section 6.5 we consider whether decentralization can make public services more responsive and accountable to citizens. Section 6.6 delves into a potentially powerful effect that has received very little attention—social learning through democratic practice, and how decentralized government can achieve it in ways that centralized government cannot. We conclude with recommendations for specific policies and structural factors that can guide decentralization processes towards state-strengthening, and not state-weakening, outcomes.

6.2 Defining State Strength and Decentralization

What is a strong state? Though many scholars have considered the question, there is no agreed-upon understanding (see e.g., Kocher, 2010; Mkandawire, 2001). Numerous labels and analogous concepts have been used, including state capacity (Migdal, 2001), state autonomy (Geddes, 1996), state efficacy (Delacroix and Ragin, 1981), good governance (Kaufmann and Kraay, 2002), state weakness, failed states (Esty et al., 1997), fragile states, resilient states, and developmental states (Putzel and DiJohn, 2012; Johnson, 1982), among others. Most definitions of state strength tend to comprise a list of partly overlapping but sometimes contradictory components or characteristics (Kocher, 2010). Bräutigam et al. (2008), for example, define state capacity as the administrative, fiscal, and institutional capacity of governments to interact constructively with their societies and pursue public goals effectively. Kaufmann, Kraay, and Mastruzzi (2005) define state efficacy broadly in terms of the efficiency of the bureaucracy and public servants, roles and responsibilities of

Table 6.1. Summary arguments—does decentralization strengthen or weaken developing states?

Components of State Strength	Strengthen	Weaken
1. Authority over territory and people, maintaining peace, and preventing conflict		
Decentralization and the ability to hold together fractious groups	Decentralization and federalist institutions act as a pressure valve to alleviate ethnic tensions.	Can reinforce cultural or ethnic identities leading fractious groups to demand ever more autonomy, with the potential for secession.
Recommendations:	*1. Decentralize below the level of major groups, so that decentralized government is identified with service provision and not group identity or privilege. I.e. if ethnicities are concentrated in regions, decentralize down to the municipal level.* *2. Complementary reforms that promote a single internal market for goods and services.* *3. Improved infrastructure and transport links that help integrate people and the economy.*	
Decentralization and conflict	Decentralization reduces pressures for conflict by empowering and including local minority groups whose concerns are often ignored by the center, and makes the state more accountable to them.	Encourages separatism. Empowers chauvinist leaders to discriminate against local minorities.
Recommendations:	*Strengthen democratic local accountability in subnational units and implement strong central safeguards of minority rights to which individuals and groups can appeal, to protect against decentralized governments becoming minor tyrannies.*	
Decentralization as a power-sharing arrangement	Decentralization can end the winner-take-all problem by shifting power and resources to subnational governments that opposition political parties can win control of.	Can shift conflict to the local level rather than eliminating it.
Recommendation:	*Complementary reforms that promote open, competitive, local politics, especially electoral finance laws that support a level political playing field, can help turn conflict and violence into electoral contestation.*	
Decentralization as an institutional constraint on the regime	Decentralization can guard against the concentration of power of one group over other groups in the state.	Can cause political fragmentation of the opposition, which can be exploited by authoritarian rulers to remain in power.
Recommendation:	*Given open, competitive politics, a fragmentation of the opposition that strengthens the official party is a short-term dynamic at best. In the longer term, decentralization is likely to transform politics, and all parties, from a top-down into a bottom-up activity with strong local roots.*	
2. Formulating policy autonomously and compelling compliance with the law		
Decentralization and the command structure	Due to greater homogeneity of local preferences, local decision-making can avoid the policy deadlocks that occur among more heterogeneous preferences at the center.	Weakens centralized control mechanisms and the chain of command. Increases the chances of elite capture.
Correction and Recommendation:	*The question is not "strength" vs. "weakness," but rather concerns moving from a simpler, clearer but more brittle centralized system of command and control, to a more complex system of overlapping authority that demands coordination amongst multiple actors to operate well, but is more supple and robust to failure in any of its parts.* *Elite capture is always a threat for all kinds of government.* *Openness and competition are the best counter-measures.*	

Decentralization, policy stability, and a stable institutionalized bureaucracy	A greater number of actors in the decision-making process leads to greater policy stability, making dramatic policy switches harder to achieve.	1. Multiple interests at different levels weaken state autonomy and increase clientelism. 2. Policy implementation may be hampered if the preferences of local government conflict with the preferences of the center.
Corrections:	*1. A better way to view these issues is the strength of leaders vs. the strength of the state. Decentralization strengthens the state by strengthening subnational actors and the systems in which they operate. This comes at the expense of leaders' discretion.* *2. This is equivalent to arguing "Central government should decide without local input." The point of decentralization is to give local preferences some, as opposed to no, systemic weight.*	
3. Responsive, accountable public service delivery		
Decentralization and responsive, accountable public services	Local democratic decision-making is more responsive and accountable, and thus better matches local government outputs to local preferences.	Local governments may be more vulnerable to interest group capture of the local political process, and the distortions of political representation in small electoral environments. Economies of scale will be lost. Technical and human capacity is lower subnationally. Local fiscal laziness can undermine state stability.
Recommendations:	*Interest group capture is a threat to governance at all levels of the state. Open, free, and fair political competition and the presence of an active, free press are the best guarantees against capture by any single group or interest.* *Decentralize goods and services with low economies of scale; retain production with high economies of scale centrally.* *Decentralize taxation as well as expenditure, and prohibit bail-outs.*	
4. Social learning		
Decentralization and social learning in a dynamic context	By reducing the scale of government, decentralization makes it possible for citizens and their voluntary associations to participate directly in government. This in turn generates social learning at the individual and group level, which improves democracy substantively and strengthens its legitimacy in voters' eyes.	No such learning occurs, and so the additional costs of a decentralized administration are uncompensated by benefits.
Recommendation:	*Decentralize to local units small enough that individuals and voluntary groups can actively participate and regularly affect decision-making.* *Open, free, and fair political competition and the presence of an active, free press are key catalysts of the sorts of citizen engagement that lead to social learning.*	

local and regional governments (including the administrative and technical skills of government), effectiveness of policy and program formulation, governing capacity, and effective use of resources. Fukuyama (2004) distinguishes between two dimensions that have often been confused in definitions of state capacity—state strength versus state scope. He argues that the hallmark of "stateness" is its enforcement functions, rather than the scope of activities performed.

While each of the many terms and definitions encapsulate nuanced differences, several common components of state strength can be derived. Strong states are typically characterized as being able to establish authority over their territory and population. Several definitions draw from Max Weber's (1946) definition of a state as an entity that successfully has monopoly on the legitimate use of force over a territory. Often cited is the ability to maintain order, preventing large-scale violence, civil war, and secession. Many other authors measure a state's strength by the degree to which it is able to enforce the law, implement its policies, and react to external shocks. While some definitions list the ability of adopting decisions autonomously, independent of social groups, others emphasize the salience of organizational capacity and a stable professional bureaucracy. A third thread focuses on the degree to which a state can respond to the needs of its citizens and provide basic services such as water, sanitation, electricity, health, and education. Other scholars analyze the state's ability to extract resources, through taxation or otherwise. A last consideration, which few scholars address but which is potentially powerful, is the extent of social learning that occurs in a state, which can increase the effectiveness and legitimacy of its actions.

The sections that follow examine these key components of state strength or weakness as discussed in the literature, with specific bibliographical references, and discuss in detail how decentralization may impact upon them. In spite of much overlap across the components, they are put forward separately in the interest of clarity and presentational ease. Although the literature distinguishes several types of decentralization (Rondinelli et al., 1983; Faguet, 2000 and 2012), we focus on the variant that we consider to be analytically the most powerful and practically the most important. Decentralization is henceforth defined as a reform that establishes or increases the political power of subnational units via the devolution of power and resources to locally elected subnational officials. This is different from administrative deconcentration, where the central government delegates functions to local agents but retains decision-making control; from delegation, where managerial responsibility is transferred to organizations outside the regular bureaucratic structure; and from privatization, where state assets and responsibility for service delivery are transferred to the private sector.

6.3 Authority Over Territory and People, Maintaining Peace, and Preventing Conflict

One key component of state strength is the ability of the state to exert authority over a given territory and its population (e.g. Price-Smith, Tauber, and Bhat, 2004. Many developing states were born out of international agreements, often with arbitrarily defined borders based on colonial partition more than internal political factors, with little to hold them together beyond guarantees by the international system (e.g. Jackson and Rosberg, 1986; Englebert, 2000; Herbst, 2001). They exist *de jure* but, unlike European states in which power over a territory and its population generally came first and sovereignty and international recognition followed, many developing countries have not been able to consolidate power in order to achieve the internal consent or territorial reach necessary to exert authority over the entire state (Jackson and Rosberg, 1986). This is a fundamental problem facing many African leaders (Herbst, 2001; Englebert, 2000).

The state may instead be made up of different ethnic groups spread over sometimes vast geographic areas, each with its own customs, language, and culture. A consciousness of common nationality is often lacking. Citizens do not feel represented by the government and perceive that leaders cater mainly to people of their own tribe or region, rather than to all citizens equally. In addition, parallel or rival forms of authority (e.g. traditional chiefs, religious leaders, or drug lords) may supersede the authority of the state (Myrdal, 1968). The discussion that follows highlights the close interconnections between a state's authority over territory and people and its ability to maintain order and protect citizens from violence as different aspects of the same dimension of state strength (e.g. Esty et al., 1997; Homer-Dixon, 1999; Migdal, 2001; Price-Smith, Tauber, and Bhat, 2004).

6.3.1 *Decentralization, Self-Determination, and Secession*

How might decentralization address these challenges? First, decentralization may help mitigate them by bringing government "closer to the people." When small subnational governments with decision-making powers are created throughout a country, citizens can more easily raise concerns with public officials; the closer government authorities are to them, the more likely they are to work with them (Faguet, 2004 and 2012). Decentralization can thus give the state greater presence and reach, enabling citizens in every corner of the state to have their interests reflected in policy and public services.

Similarly, bringing locally elected subnational leaders from different segments of the country into government, and thus giving representation to people of different groups, may incite parts of the population that formerly felt excluded from the state to feel represented and included. Indeed, federal, decentralized institutions have long been recommended as a mechanism to hold together fractured, "multi-national states" (Lijphart, 1977; Stepan, 2001; Horowitz, 2003; Brancati, 2004). Where divisions are defined territorially, decentralization is said to promote the formation of multiple but complementary identities where citizens can simultaneously carry an ethnic identity and identify with the polity as a whole (Stepan, 2001). Decentralization can thereby act as a pressure valve for nationalist aspirations. In Canada and Spain, for example, decentralization has been deemed a success in keeping fractious provinces like Quebec and Catalunya from seceding. In the UK, the devolution of regional powers to the Northern Ireland Assembly was the critical element that made successful peace talks with the Irish Republican Army possible.

But there are also many opposing arguments. Some claim that decentralization will build a federalist mentality, undermining efforts to build national unity and identity. It may even deepen divides between groups and intensify conflict by reinforcing cultural or ethnic identities. Second, decentralization may lead fractious groups to want ever more autonomy. In this vein, former British Prime Minister John Major argued against devolving powers to Scotland, claiming it was "the Trojan horse to independence" that would lead to friction and eventually demands for full independence (Major, 1995, quoted in Brancati, 2009). Powers were devolved by the Labour government that followed and, as a result, a referendum for full Scottish independence took place in 2014. With more power and independence, decentralized areas may realize they can manage their affairs better on their own. Decentralization may give subnational leaders experience in governing. Several decentralized regions have seceded after first setting up their own decentralized institutions. South Sudan is one recent example.

The key theoretical issue concerns whether decentralization will stoke centripetal or centrifugal forces. Opponents of decentralization claim devolving power and resources will empower those who seek secession, and—if they prove reasonably competent—assuage citizens' ill-formed fear of the unknown by showing them local authorities who provide services and manage public budgets adequately. Proponents claim that the same stimulus—the devolution of power and resources to even secessionist politicians—will generate the opposite response. Like an onion, it will peel away the outer layers of support from such leaders and parties, stripping them of constituents whose demands can be satisfied by more limited measures of autonomy, such as local control over public services, minority language rights, and symbolic goods such as public art and celebration, so isolating from the mass of citizens the hard secessionist core that seeks full independence.

Which side of this argument is correct is not an issue of decentralization per se, but rather depends on the nature of the secessionist impulse and the source of such parties' and leaders' appeal. Where groups are distinct, geographically concentrated, and highly mobilized against one another through violence, it may be difficult to imagine continuing cohabitation within a single nation, barring the comprehensive defeat of one group. But where groups are harder to distinguish, or where they comingle, or where mobilizations are only partial, decentralization may offer the pressure valve required to satisfy those who actually demand autonomy, not full secession, and hold a nation together.

In practice, the more important factor is likely to be the regional specificity of elite interests. If coherent regional elites (1) exist, and (2) have more to gain from secession (greater control over resources at the cost of lost markets and lost influence) than autonomy (partial control over resources, continued access to national markets and policy-making), then national integrity is in much greater peril. Regional elites will have an incentive to invest in creating conditions propitious to national schism. Beyond funding political parties and campaigns, they may also support armed insurgencies and invest in the sorts of violence against civilians that peace talks cannot later reconcile. The recent history of the Balkans richly and sadly illustrates this dynamic.

On the other hand, the evident success of both developed and developing federations that have strong regional identities but much stronger national identities, such as the United States, Germany, India, and Brazil, demonstrates that decentralized government can stitch together diverse countries in ways that lead to neither subnational tyranny nor secession. One of the keys is regionally diverse elite interests. There are undoubtedly powerful elites in California, North Rhine-Westphalia, Uttar Pradesh, and São Paulo. Any of these would rank as a medium-sized to large independent country in both population and GDP. It would be a perfectly respectable country of important weight in the international system. And yet secession is not seriously debated in any of these places.

Why don't these states' elites agitate for secession? Because their political and economic interests span state boundaries. Business and political leaders in California and Uttar Pradesh have more to lose than to gain from splitting from the other forty-nine US or twenty-seven Indian states, despite the fact that all of them are smaller economies. Pulling up the drawbridges would leave elites in North Rhine-Westphalia and São Paulo unambiguously in control of a non-trivial country instead of a state. But from their leading positions in these states, elites in all four exert considerable influence over much larger and more important countries. And they have access to considerably larger internal markets, and can influence international treaties that give them better access to the world economy and a stronger voice in international affairs. They benefit from the unity of a nation they can expect to sway and perhaps even lead. They would lose from its break-up. So they invest in unity, not division.

Interestingly, Stepan (1999) argues that another deciding factor in the ability of federalist states to hold together fractious groups is the timing of elections. When elections are introduced in the subunits of a new federal polity prior to countrywide elections, and in the absence of countrywide parties, the potential for subsequent secession is high compared to when national elections are held first. National elections produce a sense of common nationality whereas subnational elections can generate fractious local parties. Of the nine states that once made up communist Europe, six were unitary and three were federal. Yugoslavia, the USSR, and Czechoslovakia are examples of countries that first held subnational elections prior to national elections, and subsequently broke up into twenty-two independent states.

Can decentralization be designed in ways that hold fractious groups together rather than promote secession? Yes—by decentralizing power and authority to a level *below* that of major ethnic, linguistic, or other identity groups. In this way, empowered subnational units will tend not to be identified with group identity or privilege. Rather than stoking divisive tensions, local government will instead become identified with issues of efficiency and service provision. In a country where an ethnic minority is concentrated in one region, decentralizing to the regional level is far more likely, all else equal, to reinforce ethnic divisions and place authority and resources in the hands of those with most to gain from national break-up. Decentralizing to the local level, by contrast, will create many units of any given ethnicity, and most likely others that are mixed. No level of government will be associated with any particular ethnicity, nor with ethnicity per se. Comparisons across local governments will tend to focus more on issues of competence in service provision than identity, revindication, or pride.

Complementary reforms that promote a single internal market for goods and services nationwide can also help by preventing the development of elites with regionally specific economic interests who might gain from national schism. These would instead be substituted by elites whose assets or historical bases might be in a particular region, but whose economic interests are multiregional, and who therefore have a strong interest in national integrity and growth. Specific measures such as improved infrastructure and transport links can help bring this about, in addition to facilitating the flow of people and ideas across an economy, so binding it together from the bottom up.

6.3.2 *Decentralization and Conflict*

The relationship between decentralization and conflict has long been a topic of debate (Green, 2008). Arguments overlap significantly with those on self-determination and secession, since the failure to integrate regions and minorities into the state is a key source of conflict. As argued above, decentralization can accommodate diversity by giving territorially concentrated groups the power to make their own decisions about issues that most interest them (Tsebelis, 2002; Lijphart, 1977).[2] This may diffuse social and political tensions and prevent conflict (Bardhan et al., 2008). Giving groups control may protect them against abuse or neglect from the center or from one another, which can cause conflict. For instance, if a group is experiencing economic disadvantage, it could be given the power to control its own resources and decide how to allocate them. If fear of social extinction is the cause of conflict, it could be granted control over issues such as education, religion, or culture in order to protect its language and customs (Brancati, 2009).

Others take the view that decentralization will instead lead to increased conflict among fractious groups. Roeder and Rothchild (2005), for example, contend that decentralization will give subnational leaders the resources and "institutional weapons" they need to mobilize the local population and demand more political power from the center, thereby raising tensions. Subnational leaders may gain prominence and followers, and subsequently threaten the power of national political elites, again causing conflict. Some note that decentralization has produced local leaders who discriminate against minorities in their own regions (Horowitz, 2003; Lijphart, 1977). Brancati (2009), for example, points out that allowing parts of northern Nigeria to adopt their own (Sharia) law has aggravated rather than defused tensions between Christians and Muslims, as the Christian minority was forced to comply. This underlines the importance of protecting minority rights, which theorists going back at least as far as Madison, Hamilton, and Jay in the *Federalist Papers* (1961 [1788]), and including most major contributions since (see e.g. Dahl, 1971 and 1989), have considered critical to the stability and sustainability of democracy as a form of government.

How can decentralization be implemented so as to dampen, and not promote, conflict? Decentralized governments that are responsive to national minorities will drain tensions from the polity. But local governments that become "minor tyrannies," ignoring or oppressing local minorities, will stoke tensions, threatening not just particular governments but the notion of democracy itself. Hence decentralization should be designed with strong local accountability mechanisms that align local leaders' incentives with the will of local citizens and allow voters to hold politicians responsible for their decisions. And central government should enact strong safeguards of minority rights nationwide, to which individuals and groups in any locality can appeal.

[2] As Brancati (2009) points out, this is less so for territorially dispersed ethnic or other groups.

6.3.3 *Decentralization as a Power-Sharing Arrangement*

In a post-conflict environment, decentralization can be a key component of a power-sharing arrangement that settles power struggles and ends violent conflict. This operates by creating or empowering subnational levels of government to which political power and responsibility, and resources, are devolved. In doing so it also creates new fora for political competition, and hence new prizes over which opposing parties can compete. This solves the winner-take-all problem inherent to centralization, where parties in government wield huge central government resources and reap huge rewards, and opposition parties are left to wither. In a federal system, by contrast, opposition parties can still win power over states and local governments (O'Neill, 2003), and hence claim enhanced voice in national debates and opportunities to display competence in government. The penalty of losing national elections is much less severe, and so the temptation to win at any cost is greatly lessened. This can help cement the peace in a post-conflict environment.

Decentralization, for instance, has recently been advocated for Iraq and Afghanistan with exactly this in mind (Brinkerhoff and Johnson, 2009; Barfield, 2011). Green (2011) explains how Ethiopia's decentralization process in the 1990s was part of a civil war settlement that successfully maintained the peace. The country was divided into eleven federal regions. This fragmented the political opposition, creating various new parties that competed against one another for power over the newly created regions, while preventing a return to conflict for power over central government. Peace was maintained and the government in power at the federal level remained free of coups (and electoral defeat). Such shifts in power arrangements can be used to diffuse power struggles at the top. But in other cases, decentralization may merely shift conflict downward rather than eliminating it altogether. Uganda's government under President Yoweri Museveni implemented a decentralization program in 1986 in order to reduce national-level conflict. While successful in this regard, Green (2008 and 2013) argues that the ultimate effect was to replace conflict at the top with conflict at the local level.

Can decentralization be designed in ways that promote power-sharing? A properly operating decentralized system should naturally lead to the sharing of powers that have been devolved to different subnational levels of government. Few additional reforms are required other than the avoidance of electoral and fiscal distortions. In countries where politics is closed or captured, measures that promote open, competitive, local politics will tend towards fairness and power-sharing, and away from capture and conflict. Electoral finance laws that support a level political playing field have particular importance in this regard, as one of the most powerful and prevalent ways in which democracy is distorted is through the flow of money into campaigns. Where political competition is open to new entrants and the playing field is level, elections will tend to be fought over issues of substance to local voters. In such places, political conflict and violence will tend to transform naturally into electoral contestation, which is less risky for participants.

6.3.4 *Decentralization as an Institutional Constraint on the Regime*

Decentralization may also guard against the concentration of power, with one group wielding it over other groups in the state (Leff, 1999). In Peru, following Fujimori's authoritarian regime, for example, a national consensus to decentralize crystallized around the desire to avoid a repeat of the abuses of overly powerful central government leaders through the safeguards and checks and balances that decentralization affords (de la Cruz, Pineda, and Pöschl, 2010).

But decentralization may also cause political fragmentation of the opposition, and this may help authoritarian rulers remain in power. Sabatini (2003) argues that decentralization has been used in Latin America to split opposition parties into numerous small, uncoordinated local parties as a method for remaining in power. But the experience of at least two countries in Sabatini's sample, Bolivia and Colombia, suggests that something deeper is at work. The rise of local political competition that necessarily accompanies democratic decentralization undermines pre-existing national parties with weak local roots, and can generate many new, locally based political parties with strong local roots. But the experience of both countries suggests that strengthening the official party and fracturing opposition parties is at best a short-term, transition dynamic. Over longer periods of time (e.g. two decades) some of these new local parties ally, federate, and otherwise morph into political organizations capable of contesting national elections. And official parties with weak local roots also do not survive expulsion from power (Faguet, 2012).

What decentralization really does is to transform politics from an arena that is by definition national, top-down, and subject to oligopolization by a socio-economic elite based in a few powerful cities, to a meta-arena embracing many specific, local arenas where pressing local concerns are taken up and addressed, or not, by local politicians and the parties they choose to join. This sort of bottom-up politics is characteristic of federal countries like the USA, Germany, and India, and is in many ways the opposite of politics in a unitary state. The transition from the latter to the former will be treacherous for many existing centralized political parties. That is an argument of interest, not of principle, against decentralization.

Decentralization has been a relatively successful tool for deterring conflict in some countries (such as Canada, Spain, Belgium, and India) but not others (Yugoslavia). What accounts for the differences? By empowering a new set of players, decentralization inherently shifts the intrastate balance of power.

Power shifts and disruptions in political settlements can cause conflict (Putzel and Di John, 2012). And conflict can be stoked with a view to shifting the balance of power, as discussed above. On the other hand, power shifts can also be used to diffuse conflict. The design of decentralization processes may play a role in their success or failure as conflict-mitigation tools, but this most likely depends on the specific power balance, and the political bargains and settlements of the players involved. Weingast (2013), North, Wallis, and Weingast (2009) and Stepan (1999 and 2001), amongst others, examine this question. It remains a complex, important area ripe for further research.

6.4 Formulating Policy Autonomously and Compelling Compliance with the Law

Further important components of a strong state are the ability to formulate policy goals autonomously from particular groups in society (Vogel, 1986; Evans, Rueschemeyer, and Skocpol, 1985; Evans 1992; Kohli, 2004) and the capability of compelling compliance with the law or policies while remaining autonomous from social influence or competing authority structures (Kay, 2003; Geddes, 1996). Some scholars add to this the ability to guide the economy (Johnson, 1982; Woo-Cummings, 1999; Mkandawire, 2001).

The inability to implement goals or to police effectively, and the subversion of policy objectives by government agents (agency loss), on the other hand, are considered characteristics of weak states (see e.g. Evans et al., 1985; Engelbert, 2000). Centralized states may have fewer players involved in the decision-making process, whereas decentralized countries with more than one level of government have more players involved (often a lower house) with veto powers. The command structure in centralized states has therefore been viewed as cleaner and decisions easier to execute, and execute quickly, than when certain decision-making powers are moved to other levels.

6.4.1 *Decentralization and the Command Structure*

In contrast with the view that a strong state is, by definition, a centralized state (Skocpol, 1985), a major promise of decentralization is that the more proximal command structure can produce better policy outputs by creating a closer match between local government outputs and local preferences (Faguet, 2004 and 2012). The greater homogeneity of preferences at the local as opposed to the national level allows local governments to tailor policy decisions and public goods more precisely to local needs and preferences than central governments typically manage.

On the other hand, decentralization may bring about a certain loss of control at the top and an inability to act quickly or in concert. It may weaken coherence between local endeavors and national-level issues (Sabatini, 2003; Treisman, 2007). For example, it may be more difficult for the central government to exert fiscal discipline if it has granted spending powers to subnational governments, leading to macroeconomic problems, as explained by Jaramillo and Grazzi in Chapter 5 and Ardanaz, Leiras, and Tommasi (2014).

In fact, both claims are true. Decentralization should not be viewed simplistically as a choice between "strong" centralized government and "weak" decentralized government. It is, rather, a move from a centralized command structure that is simpler and cleaner, but ultimately more brittle (in the sense of being susceptible to failure in any of its parts, which will tend to lead to government failure), to a system that is more complex and based on more actors with independent sources of overlapping authority, where coordination and cooperation are far more important than command and control for the system as a whole to operate well. This greater complexity is more difficult to manage, and coordination harder to achieve than command adherence. But it also implies greater suppleness in the sense of robustness to failure in any of its parts, which—unlike centralization—need not be terminal for public services in the affected area. Hence, in a centralized system, corruption or ineptitude amongst the officials responsible for local education will have serious consequences for education in that locality. In a decentralized system, by contrast, the same failings in local government officials can be attenuated or even overturned by the actions of regional and national authorities, who share responsibility for local education.

Local governments may be more vulnerable to interest group capture of the local political process, and the distortions of political representation in small electoral environments. Where these phenomena exist, interest groups can gain a decisive influence over local government, and decentralization will tend to favor these small local groups disproportionately. The logic is developed and tested empirically by Bardhan and Mookherjee (1999 and 2006), Blair (2000), Crook and Sverrisson (1999), Dreze and Sen (1996), Manor (1999), and Prud'homme (1995), and is as follows. Local elites are "large" compared to local civil society and local governments, which will often be too weak to oppose them and may even internalize elite priorities as their own. In such a context, decentralization can lead to weak local governments that are cowed and captured by local elites. One effective remedy is a centralized state that is comparatively wealthy and powerful—"large" compared to local elites. Decentralization will not lead to transparent, equitable local government because the local societies in which local governments operate are distorted by extreme inequalities of wealth and power. And thus reform will lessen the transparency, responsiveness, and accountability of the state.

While this argument has much merit, it underplays the comparative threat that elite capture poses at the national level. As Hacker and Pierson (2010) show, the much greater rewards from distorting national policy-making lead the richest interest groups to invest enormous sums in capturing national government. When successful, this gives such interest groups powers and privileges enormously greater than anything available through local capture, with potentially deleterious effects for an entire nation. Elite capture is a real threat. But it is a threat for all kinds and levels of government. It is not a special threat for decentralized government. As argued below, political openness and competition are the best antiseptics.

6.4.2 *Decentralization, Policy Stability, and a Stable, Institutionalized Bureaucracy*

Several scholars mention the existence of an autonomous institutionalized bureaucracy, as opposed to personal rule or neopatrimonialism and systemic privatization, as the characterizing feature of a strong state (Kocher, 2010). This is expected to achieve policy continuity, decisions that are more likely to be in the interest of society rather than based on personal relationships, stability of expectations, and an organized professional bureaucracy. States are considered weak when their political institutions—e.g. constitutions, electoral rules—are often altered and lack continuity or support. If the "rules of the game" change frequently, this is said to undermine confidence in the state and the state's ability to make "credible commitments." For instance, term limits may be regularly changed by incumbents, constitutions may be rewritten frequently, or life tenure for judges may be ignored in practice (Levitsky and Murillo, 2009). This instability and lack of institutionalization of rules and procedures undermines the ability of the state to generate shared behavioral expectations that shape and strengthen political structures.

States that are captured by special interests are argued to be less effective at formulating and carrying out social policy designed to meet the public good (Cox and McCubbins, 2001). Traditionally, centralized states have been viewed as more autonomous in their ability to formulate policy by diminishing the influence of particular groups in society (Vogel, 1986; Evans, Rueschemeyer, and Skocpol, 1985). By fracturing centralized power, such authors argue, decentralization reduces the autonomy of the state and makes it more susceptible to personalistic, clientelistic forces.

Proponents of decentralization contend that more players in the decision-making process may lead to greater policy stability, which in turn strengthens the state by making dramatic policy switches harder to achieve (Cox and McCubbins, 2001). In fact, it has been argued that decentralized systems are stronger precisely because by increasing the total number of actors in government required to approve rules, laws and policies cannot be as easily and frequently changed and greater stability is attained (Tsebelis, 2002; Treisman, 2007).

A better way of thinking about this is as a trade-off between the strength of the leader and the strength of the state as institution. To the extent that the leader has more discretion, her power increases and she can effect greater, faster changes to public policy and organizations. The leader is stronger at the expense of the state. But where her discretion is circumscribed by rules, procedure, and the need to agree decisions with other independent actors in order to proceed, then the state is stronger and more stable at the expense of the leader. By increasing the number of independent actors and requiring a measure of consensus amongst them for policy-making to proceed, decentralization weakens central leaders and creates or empowers subnational leaders, thus increasing the strength of the state by strengthening it institutionally.

The relative autonomy of a centralized state may also come at the expense of efficiency. Although centralized states may be more autonomous in their ability to formulate policy, due to their relative isolation during this planning phase they may face an uphill battle in implementing policies for which the participation and cooperation of other citizens and groups is necessary. As Grindle (1980) outlines, a common problem in implementation occurs when policies designed centrally are ill-suited to local conditions.[3] For example, local implementers may need to appease local elites, who may stand to lose from certain programs. Opposition from such elites, especially in a context of inflexible implementation rules, will lead to dynamic inefficiencies as the policy is rolled out. By granting opportunities for participation to regions and local governments in policy design, decentralized decision-making will respond more precisely and dynamically to diverse local conditions, will tend to be regarded as more legitimate, and is likely to gain greater compliance from civic actors. Decision-making may be slower, but the resulting decisions are more likely to "stick."

Furthermore, in many highly centralized states local government structures are simply non-existent. Exposure to new, vibrant local governments can strengthen the state by expanding its presence, providing citizens with more direct interactions with government and elections and thereby improving the perception of state responsiveness and enhancing the legitimacy of national governments. For instance, prior to decentralization most of the Bolivian countryside lacked any form of local administration that provided services or represented citizens. Following decentralization, elected local governments accountable to local voters sprang up throughout the land. In countless

[3] Birney (2014) analyzes the complex issue of discretion and accountability in the Chinese context.

interviews, poor rural citizens responded to the question "How has decentralization affected your life?" with assurances that they finally felt Bolivian, that decentralization had given citizenship meaning, and that at last there was evidence that they mattered and the state cared for them (Faguet, 2012). In Bolivia, the spread of local governments, a stable local bureaucracy, and the services they provide have clearly strengthened the legitimacy of the state in citizens' eyes.

6.5 Responsive, Accountable Public Service Delivery

Drawing again on Weber, another marker of a strong state is the ability to carry out policies in an efficient manner that is responsive to public needs (Bates, 2008). Providing basic services to the population is regarded as a basic function of the state, and the extent to which it achieves this may be regarded as a direct component of state strength. It may also indirectly contribute to state strength as success will likely enhance its legitimacy and authority.

One of the most frequently cited and powerful arguments in favor of decentralization is that it will have a positive impact on responsiveness to basic public needs. By allowing government to tailor decisions to the specific demands and needs of the local population, decentralization facilitates matching resources with citizen needs more precisely and cost-effectively. Additionally, competition between subnational governments for residents and investment may induce them to improve services (Tiebout, 1956; Hayek, 1939).

Decentralization is further expected to enhance public services by improving accountability and responsiveness of the government to citizens (see Green, 2013). By bringing decision-making power closer to the represented and creating popularly elected positions at the local level, incentives for accountability can be transformed (Faguet, 2012). Rather than local officials being accountable mainly to their superiors in government, they become accountable to their constituents as they become dependent on them for their votes and tax revenue. It is also generally easier for citizens to scrutinize, participate in, and make demands of nearby local administrations than of a distant central government in a far-off capital. In both Bolivia and Colombia, for example, such a shift in incentives and accountability relations has altered investment decisions and resulted in significant improvements in basic service delivery (Faguet and Wietzke, 2006; Faguet, 2012; Faguet and Sánchez, 2013). In Ethiopia, too, decentralization from the 1990s devolved spending powers to the regions, allowing funds to reach many previously neglected poorer local governments (*woredas*) for the first time. The shift in spending decisions that resulted improved health and education indicators markedly (Rajkumar and Garcia, 2008).

A related explanation of the benefits of decentralization for government performance rests on the ability of decentralized structures to leverage local social capital (Putnam, 1993). A high density of civic organizations that encourage people to work together and build trust fosters behavior that makes for better performance in local institutions. Where social trust and civic organization are present, local government will have a strong tendency to respond to local needs more precisely and effectively, and work with less waste and corruption, than would otherwise be the case.

However, while there is reason to believe that decentralization can foster local social capital by bringing governance closer to the people, proponents of social capital are skeptical that government policy can work to create this trust or build this capital. For instance, Putnam (1993) suggests that in Italy, areas which did not develop social capital in the Middle Ages are not likely to perform well in the twentieth century. Likewise, Fukuyama (2004) suggests that the success of certain public sector institutions in newly developed East Asian countries stems from their "mandarin bureaucratic tradition," which cannot be easily replicated. In fact, direct investment in civil society is seen as weakening the state by bypassing it.

Other arguments counter the view that decentralization will improve a government's ability to respond to basic needs and services. These include the loss of economies of scale (Wallis and Oates, 1988) and the possibility that decentralized funds may be more easily diverted or captured by local elites (Manor, 1999). Opponents of decentralization argue in particular that the devolution of responsibility only increases the discretion of local elites in the distribution of public goods, and can strengthen patron–client relationships (Bardhan et al., 2008). Also, subnational governments may not have the technical or human capacity to provide services with the same efficiency and quality as central government (Treisman, 2007). Studies of federal systems have tended to find that central governments are more effective at making equitable allocation decisions, especially for assisting the poor (Linz and Stepan, 2000). And politically induced interregional inequality can lead to conflict, weakening the state.

"Fiscal laziness" is another potential unintended consequence of decentralization, which can critically undermine state stability and strength (World Bank, 1994). State and local governments may have little incentive to match intergovernmental transfers through local taxation (Peterson, 1994). If the ability to tax is a marker of state strength and legitimacy as some have suggested (Levi and Sacks, 2009), this fiscal laziness could be consequential, laying the foundation for a less capable state. But it can also attack state strength directly, as happened in Argentina in 2001 (Ardanaz, Leiras, and

Tommasi, 2014). There, the governors of certain poorer provinces who preferred to under-tax their populations were able to force central government to repeatedly bail them out via the requirements of the national congressional coalition. This fed persistent unsustainable fiscal deficits, which ultimately led to the 2001 economic collapse.

These risks can be combatted by decentralizing not only expenditure but taxation too, and prohibiting either bail-outs, local deficits, or both. In such cases, local governments will have a strong incentive to tailor local policies and services to the priorities of those who pay (Faguet, 2012). And citizens will have a greater incentive to monitor the use of funds. Hence, fiscal laziness is a problem not of decentralization per se, but of badly designed decentralizations, and can be remedied in a technically straightforward fashion by altering the subnational incentive structure (Ardanaz et al., 2014). Likewise, the question of loss of economies of scale can be addressed through well-designed decentralization. A decentralization that loses important economies of scale is a badly designed decentralization. Any rational decentralized system will involve continuing co-production of public goods and services at the central, regional, and local levels (Faguet and Sánchez, 2013). Goods with large economies of scale should be produced centrally, and those with significant heterogeneity or local informational inputs should be produced locally.

Where elite or interest group capture is concerned, it is worth reiterating that this is not a problem particular to either local or regional government. Policymaking in central governments as rich, powerful, and professional as that of the United States can suffer from significant degrees of elite capture (Hacker and Pierson, 2010). Empirical evidence shows that the way to combat this in a decentralized system is through open, free, fair political competition in a broader context of civic organizations and economic interests that interact extensively through politics (Faguet, 2012). So long as there is transparency in politics and the playing field is level, economic interests and civic groups will have strong incentives to interact with one another as they compete through politics to obtain amenable outcomes, and this interaction itself will tend towards responsive, accountable government and away from capture and tyranny.

6.6 Social Learning

We have seen that well-designed decentralization can strengthen the state by averting secessionist tendencies and conflict, enhancing compliance with the law, and improving service delivery. We now turn to the final "meta-issue" or mechanism through which decentralization can serve to strengthen the state. Social learning has received far less attention in the literature. But the effects of decentralization on state strength via social learning, although second-order, may ultimately be the most powerful considered here, not least because it operates through each of the first three components discussed above, as well as in other ways.

The key to understanding social learning is that it occurs over time and thus requires dynamic analysis, unlike most of the literature which uses comparative static analysis to discuss decentralization's effects on both technocratic (e.g. education investment) and governance-related (e.g. compliance with the law) issues. Indeed, one of the overarching themes of this chapter is the need to analyze the effects of decentralization in a dynamic context, as decentralization is not a one-off change but rather a process that develops and matures over time. Our treatment builds on Faguet's (2012) analysis of the importance of interactions amongst social, private sector, and political actors in the local political economy as critical determinants of responsive and accountable government.

Decentralized government accelerates social learning over time in a way that centralized government does not and, for most people, cannot. This is because decentralized government operates at a community level that is susceptible to personal action and initiative, as opposed to regional and national governments that operate through elected or delegated representatives, where agency is exercised through higher-order collectives. The small scale of local politics allows citizens to become political actors either individually or through civic organizations. Such organizations are often informal, with small or non-existent budgets, and rely on volunteers to staff critical positions. They are ideal entry points for naïve citizens to first encounter politics, expose themselves to political debate and public decision-making, and become politically engaged.

Social learning is a learning-by-doing phenomenon, and hence relies on direct interactions amongst citizens. Local government provides ordinary citizens with real access to repeated interactions on matters of public policy and resources, both directly with the local government apparatus and indirectly through civic organizations that debate positions and compete with firms, other interests, and each other to influence government. It does so for the common citizen in a way that central government, with its high resource thresholds, professionalized organizations, formal and intricate rules and norms, and obscure jargon, cannot.

To better understand this, let us follow Faguet (2004) and consider some elemental tasks that are crucial to democracy, but which are commonly overlooked. For democracy to represent and then act on the will of its citizens in a way that is fair and responsive, it must be able to: (i) identify and articulate shared preferences and opinions, (ii) aggregate shared preferences, and (iii) enforce accountability. Preferences can be thought of as wants and needs, some of which are individual and hence private (e.g. my favorite sandwich, my favorite shirt), and others of which are shared in society and so the object of public action (preferred quality of schools, preferred level of taxation).

Consider how a new political idea arises in society. Only some of an individual's many needs and preferences are shared with others. For politicians to be elected, they must identify those needs shared by the most voters, articulate them in ways voters find convincing, and propose viable policy solutions. By making people realize certain demands are shared, politicians convert private into public preferences; they create political voice where before there was none.

Once the public has been convinced that certain policy ideas are important, society must weigh competing demands and the trade-offs they imply, and choose which options to pursue. In other words, social preferences must be aggregated. This is where political process and government come in, trading off the needs and demands of different groups, firms, and organizations in the search for something like a social optimum. This occurs most obviously through elections, where individuals vote for competing candidates offering different combinations of policies, and the most preferred wins. But in a well-functioning democracy it operates in many other ways, continuously, at all levels of society.

Once a polity has expressed its preferences, formed them into political options, and chosen which of these it wishes to pursue collectively, it requires mechanisms for holding politicians to account. In a democracy, citizens must have levers of influence over elected officials that allow them to ensure that: (a) socially preferred bundles of policies are implemented (b) with reasonable efficiency. Absent accountability, all the preceding is for naught—an illusion of democratic choice that confers little voice and no power to the people. Regular elections are the most obvious accountability mechanism by which voters can remove unsatisfactory officials from power. But, again, there are others.

Each of these processes—preference articulation, preference aggregation, and accountability—is necessary to democracy. All three operate continuously, relying on government–society and society–society interactions for their success. Civil society is conceived here as both individuals and the set of collectivities that aggregate their ideas and efforts, interacting amongst themselves and with the institutions of government. Such organizations develop their own norms of behavior and responsibility organically, and over time may build up stores of trust and credibility that enhance capacity, or not. Governance relies on these autonomous organizations to mediate—and ultimately empower—citizens' participation in the decision-making that governance implies.

Why does decentralization matter? Because scale is determinant and its effects are non-linear. The large scale of central government demands disproportionately greater resources and levels of organization for effective engagement than does local government. Hence, the autonomous organizations that populate the space between politicians and voters are open to citizen participation and agency at the local level, but closed to most citizens at the central level. The overwhelming majority of citizens who might become participants in local governance must remain as voters, onlookers, and perhaps dues-payers where central government is concerned.

So the experience of participation and engagement with public decision-making abounds in government in its decentralized, but not centralized, form. And so experience accrues and learning occurs amongst individual voters and their small-scale collectives (e.g. civic groups, local lobbies) in local government, as opposed to think tanks, professional lobby firms, and peak associations in central government. Participation in local government leads naturally to social learning around narrow questions of effectiveness, but also higher-order learning about fellow citizens' needs, resource constraints, and the multiplicative effects of public as opposed to private action for certain classes of problems. The experience of working together teaches people to work together better. A gradual convergence of individuals' perspectives around local needs and service standards ensues, generating greater political legitimacy. Initial impulses of conflict and contestation can be transformed into regularized interaction and cooperation, which induces stores of trust that can be drawn on when real conflict threatens. The workings of central government, by contrast, tend to reinforce the organizational, technical, and financial advantages of highly professionalized groups, thus deepening the chasm between policy-making and the ordinary citizen.

Decentralization and local government can thus promote political legitimacy and long-term state-building from the grass-roots upward in a way that centralized government cannot. This is the deeper meaning of the "democratically supple" state introduced above. But we see now that "suppleness" is far more than the linear concept of "more elected officials." It is, additionally, the greater degree of organization that decentralization catalyzes in a society by providing strong incentives for group formation and for organizational effectiveness. And it is the iterative experience at the level of individual citizens of interacting with others to define and solve collective problems that makes future such actions easier, more reliable, and more easily sustained—through the simple fact of having done them before. As a result, democracy as a method of choosing leaders and arriving at collective decisions is deepened, substantively improved, and made more legitimate in the eyes of voters who engage in it directly, locally.

The dynamic described above should operate naturally in a sincerely decentralized system; little is required additionally in terms of complementary reforms or institutions other than the absence of active distortions. Our main recommendation follows logically from the analysis: Reformers should decentralize to government units sufficiently small for individuals and their voluntary organizations to actively participate in decision-making and regularly affect outcomes. The degree of non-linearity of resource and organizational thresholds required for effectiveness will vary by country and level of development. But for a "typical" developing country, a local government in which citizen participation is viable might number in the tens of thousands of inhabitants, as opposed to hundreds of thousands or millions. It should also be sufficiently geographically compact that an ordinary citizen at one edge of a local government has some direct knowledge of how her counterpart at the other extreme lives.

This raises the difficult issue of metropolitan governance in a decentralized system. Urban giants such as Cairo, Mumbai, and São Paulo represent a large and increasing share of the population and economic output of the developing world; any one of these is larger in both dimensions than many small countries. They are natural political as well as economic units, but their scale dwarfs the idealized parameters outlined above. How can a decentralized system incorporate such behemoths? Unfortunately, this complex issue lies beyond our scope. We limit ourselves here to note that the government of large urban areas requires asymmetric approaches to decentralization, permitting different rules for different sizes and types of local governments. Large cities, for example, may require decentralization to the sub-municipal (e.g. district, ward) level in order for its full benefits to be captured. Further detailed treatment of this and related questions can be found in Bahl, Linn, and Wetzel (2013), Ahluwalia, Kanbur, and Mohanty (2014), Fox (2014), and Rao and Bird (2011).

6.7 Conclusion

The academic literature contains different definitions and conceptions of a strong state. We argue in favor of the following key identifiable, intellectually discrete components of "state strength": (i) authority over territory and conflict prevention; (ii) policy autonomy and the ability to uphold the law; (iii) responsive, accountable service provision; and (iv) social learning. Theory is indeterminate on the impact of decentralization on the first three components, and the fourth has been largely ignored. But a surge of evidence over the past two decades from real policy experiments provides a basis not only for settling theoretical disagreements, but for reconceptualizing decentralization's effects on the state in fundamental ways.

Where authority over territory, self-determination, and secession are concerned, the key question is whether decentralization will stoke centripetal or centrifugal forces. We argue that a well-designed reform that decentralizes power and resources to a level below that of major social or regional cleavages is most likely to identify local government with issues of efficiency and service provision, as opposed to social identity and grievance. Such a decentralization can undermine secessionist movements by peeling away layers of support from citizens whose demands can be satisfied by more limited measures of autonomy. In practice, a key factor will be the regional specificity of elite interests. To support national integrity, regional elites must be made to have more to lose than gain from national schism, so that they do not invest in politicians, parties, and events (including violent ones) that promote national break-up. Complementary reforms promoting a single internal market for goods and services, and improved infrastructure and transport links, can help convince elites that continued access to national markets and policy-making trumps dominance of local resources and power. Such reforms can also facilitate the flow of people and ideas across an economy, binding it together from the bottom up.

By reducing secessionist tensions, decentralization designed in this way should also reduce the threat of conflict in a society. Strong local accountability mechanisms combined with strong national safeguards of minority rights can help by aligning leaders' incentives with those of local citizens, preventing subnational governments from ignoring or oppressing local minorities. These should accompany electoral measures that support open, competitive local politics on a level playing field, and campaign finance regulations that support transparency and fairness, so promoting power-sharing and discouraging capture.

Interestingly, the literature is ambivalent about whether decentralization is likely to strengthen or weaken the central state. Some argue that it will fragment political opposition to authoritarian rulers, thereby strengthening their centralized control. Others argue that it will bring about a loss of control at the top by creating new centers of power and complicating a simpler, "cleaner" command-and-control system. We argue that both perspectives are wrong because they fundamentally misunderstand one of decentralization's central effects.

What decentralization really does is to transform politics from a top-down, national arena subject to oligopolization by a small urban elite, to a bottom-up meta-arena embracing many specific, local arenas where local politicians are pressed to address local concerns. It represents a move from a simpler command structure that is ultimately more brittle (in the sense of being susceptible to local failure, leading to government failure), to a system based on more actors with independent sources of overlapping authority, with complex complementarities amongst them, which as a whole is more robust to failure in any of its parts, and hence more supple. Decentralization strengthens the institutions of government, their accountability and legitimacy, at the expense of central leaders' discretion. We think this is a good trade-off.

But will politicians? It is probably safe to categorize national leaders into two groups: (i) those who are primarily self-interested, and (ii) those whose self-interest is tempered by a concern for the common good, or their place in history, which may be observationally similar. Leaders who are primarily self-interested will tend to keep power and resources in their own hands. If they decentralize, such reforms will tend to be "paper decentralizations" of form, not substance, or perhaps outright mistakes. As argued in Chapter 1, paper reforms probably account for a large share of the world's decentralizations. And mistakes are strictly irrational, perhaps the product of calculative failures, and so not a good subject of analysis.

Category (ii), by contrast, is far more interesting. Leaders with at least some concern for the collective good (or their place in history) may well decide that decentralizing power and resources is the superior alternative. As Faguet (2012) stresses, decentralization is not a switch that can be flipped, but rather a process that consolidates over time. A leader who announces decentralization at the start of her term is likely to see it fully implemented only towards the end of her term. Reform is likely to constrain her successors far more than herself. In many political contexts, this may in itself be an appealing prospect. And history will credit her, not her successors, for the initiative. Furthermore, as we saw in Chapter 2 for the case of Bolivia, if the leader's party has a strong subnational presence, then reform will tend to appeal to the larger number of party members who are regional or local—but not national—party figures.

This implies that the apparently deep paradox of self-interested politicians who devolve power to others may, at least sometimes, actually be a logical response to objective opportunities. Let us consider a leader with long-term horizons (i.e. "a place in history") who privately believes that decentralization can improve governance. What will she do? Real power and authority would drain much more from future leaders than from her. And where the party is well organized, her followers would be rewarded with the creation of many subnational offices that they will disproportionately win. These considerations transform reform from "paradoxical" to "attractive." Furthermore, her substantive belief and her concern for the future make it far more likely that the reform she pursues is sincere. Rather than an historical aberration, Goni Sánchez de Lozada is thus a good example of a class of rational leaders with a strong party and an eye on history.

Whether or not decentralization will increase the responsiveness and accountability of public services is another major cleavage. Proponents claim that taking government "closer to the people" will transform public incentives, from upward-looking to the bureaucracy to downward-looking to voters. Opponents counter that local governments are more susceptible to interest group capture, and suffer from lower economies of scale, lower technical and human capacities, and a tendency to fiscal laziness. We argue that these objections are not problems of decentralization per se, but rather of badly designed reform. They can be overcome in a technically straightforward way by decentralizing only activities with low economies of scale, devolving taxation, and prohibiting bail-outs and/or subnational debt.

Lastly, we develop the concept of social learning in a decentralized environment. The small scale of local politics allows citizens to become political actors either individually or through their civic organizations. It provides ordinary citizens with access to repeated interactions on matters of public policy and resources, both directly and indirectly through civic organizations that debate positions and compete with firms, other interests, and each other to influence government. In this learning-by-doing fashion, social learning makes citizens better at democracy across all stages of the formation and aggregation of public preferences, and the enforcement of accountability. It promotes political legitimacy, long-term state-building, and "democratic suppleness" from the grass-roots upwards in a way that centralized government, with its large scale, professional cadres, daunting resource requirements, bureaucratic forms and norms, and obscure jargon, cannot.

References

Ahluwalia, I. J., R. Kanbur, and P. K. Mohanty (eds.), 2014. *Urbanisation in India: Challenges, Opportunities and the Way Forward.* New Delhi: Sage.

Ardanaz, M., M. Leiras and M. Tommasi, 2014. "The Politics of Federalism in Argentina and its Implications for Governance and Accountability." *World Development,* 53: 26–45. <http://dx.doi.org/10.1016/j.worlddev.2013.01.004>.

Bahl, R., J. F. Linn, and D. L. Wetzel (eds.), 2013. *Financing Metropolitan Governments in Developing Countries.* Cambridge, MA: Lincoln Institute of Land Policy.

Bardhan, P. and D. Mookherjee, 1999. "Relative Capture of Local and Central Governments: An Essay in the Political Economy of Decentralization." Berkeley: Manuscript.

Bardhan, P. and D. Mookherjee (eds.), 2006. *Decentralization and Local Governance in Developing Countries: A Comparative Perspective,* Cambridge, MA: MIT Press.

Bardhan, P., Mitra, S., Mookerjee, D., Sarkar, A., 2008. "Political Participation, Clientelism, and Targeting of Local Government Programs: Analysis of survey results from rural West Bengal, India." The Institute for Economic Development Working Papers Series dp-171, Boston University—Department of Economics.

Barfield, T., 2011. "Afghanistan's Ethnic Puzzle: Decentralizing Power before the US Withdrawal." *Foreign Affairs*, Vol. 90, Issue 5, pp. 54–65.

Bates, R., 2008. "State Failure." Annual Review of Political Science, 11.

Birney, M., 2014. "Decentralization and Veiled Corruption under China's 'Rule of Mandates'." *World Development*: 53, 55–67. <http://dx.doi.org/10.1016/j.worlddev.2013.01.006>.

Blair, H., 2000. "Participation and Accountability at the Periphery: Democratic Local Governance in Six Countries." *World Development*, 28(1): 21–39.

Boone, P. and J.P. Faguet, 1998. "Multilateral Aid, Politics and Poverty: Past Failures and Future Challenges." Chapter 2 in R. Grant and J. Nijman (eds.) *The Global Crisis in Foreign Aid*, Syracuse: Syracuse University Press, 11–26.

Brancati, D., 2004. "Can Federalism Stabilize Iraq?" *The Washington Quarterly*, 27, 2, Spring, pp. 7–21.

Brancati, D., 2009. *Peace by Design: Managing Intrastate Conflict through Decentralization*. Oxford: Oxford University Press.

Bratton, M., 1994. *State Power & Social Forces: Domination and Transformation in the Third World*. Cambridge: Cambridge University Press.

Bräutigam, D., Fjeldstad, O.-H., & Moore, M., eds., 2008. *Taxation and State-building in Developing Countries: Capacity and Consent*. Cambridge: Cambridge University Press.

Brinkerhoff, D. and Johnson, R., 2009. "Decentralized local governance in fragile states: learning from Iraq." *International Review of Administrative Sciences* 75, no.4: 585–607.

Cox, G. and McCubbins, M., 2001. "The Institutional Determinants of Economic Policy Outcomes." In Haggard and McCubbins (eds.) *Presidents, Parliaments, and Policy*. Cambridge: Cambridge University Press.

Dahl, R., 1989. *Democracy and Its Critics*. New Haven: Yale University Press.

Dahl, R., 1971. *Polyarchy: Participation and Opposition*. New Haven: Yale University Press.

Delacroix, J., Ragin, C.C., 1981. "Structural Blockage: A Cross-National Study of Economic Dependency, State Efficacy, and Underdevelopment." *The American Journal of Sociology*, 86(6): 1311–47.

de la Cruz, R., C. Pineda, and C. Pöschl (eds.). 2010. *La alternativa local: Descentralización y desarrollo económico*, Washington, DC: Inter-American Development Bank.

Englebert, P., 2000. *State Legitimacy and Development in Africa*. Boulder: Lynne Rienner.

Esty, D. et al., 1997. "State Failure Task Force: Phase II Report." Washington, DC: Science Applications International Corporation.

Evans, P., 1992. "The State as Problem and Solution: Predation, Embedded Autonomy and Structural Change." In S. Haggard & R. Kaufman, *The Politics of Economic Adjustment*. pp. 143–81. Princeton, NJ: Princeton University Press.

Evans, P.B., Rueschemeyer, D., and Skocpol, T. (eds.), 1985. *Bringing the State Back In*. Cambridge: Cambridge University Press.

Faguet, J.P., 2014a. "Can Sub-National Autonomy Strengthen Democracy in Bolivia?" *Publius: The Journal of Federalism*, 44(1): 51–81. Doi: 10.1093/publius/pjt020.

Faguet, J.P., 2014b. "Decentralization and Governance." Lead paper of a special issue on Decentralization and Governance. *World Development*. <http://dx.doi.org/10.1016/j.worlddev.2013.01.002>.

Faguet, J.P., 2012. *Decentralization and Popular Democracy: Governance from Below in Bolivia*. Ann Arbor: University of Michigan Press.

Faguet, J.P., 2004. "Building Democracy in Quicksand: Altruism, Empire and the United States." *Challenge: The Magazine of Economic Affairs*, 47: 73–93.

Faguet, J.P., 2000. "Decentralization and Local Government Performance: Improving Public Service Provision in Bolivia." *Revista de Economía del Rosario*, 3(1): 127–76.

Faguet, J.P. and F. Sánchez, 2013. "Decentralization and Access to Social Services in Colombia." *Public Choice*. Doi 10.1007/s11127-013-0077-7.

Faguet, J.P. and F.B. Wietzke, 2006. "Social Funds and Decentralization: Optimal Institutional Design." *Public Administration and Development*, 26(4): 303–15.

Fox, S., 2014. "The Political Economy of Slums: Theory and Evidence from Sub-Saharan Africa." *World Development*, 54: 191–203.

Fukuyama, F., 2004. *State Building: Governance and World Order in the 21st Century*. Ithaca, NY: Cornell University Press.

Geddes, B., 1996. *Politician's Dilemma: Building state capacity in Latin America*, Berkeley, CA: University of California Press.

Green, E., 2008. "Decentralization and Conflict in Uganda." *Conflict, Security and Development*, 8 (4), pp. 427–50. ISSN 1478–1174.

Green, E., 2011. "Decentralization and political opposition in contemporary Africa: evidence from Sudan and Ethiopia." *Democratization*, 18:5, 1087–105.

Green, E., 2013. "The Rise and Fall of Decentralization in Contemporary Uganda." UNU WIDER Working Paper No. 2013/078.

Grindle, M., 2007. *Going Local: Decentralization, Democratization and the Promise of Good Governance*. Princeton, N.J.: Princeton University Press.

Grindle, M., 1980. "The Implementor: Political Constraints on Rural Development in Mexico." In *Politics and Policy Implementation in the Third World*, ed. Merilee Grindle, 197–223. Princeton, NJ: Princeton University Press.

Hacker, J. S. and P. Pierson, 2010. *Winner-Take-All Politics: How Washington Made the Rich Richer—and Turned Its Back on the Middle Class*. New York: Simon & Schuster.

Hayek, F., 1939. "The Economic Conditions of Interstate Federalism." *New Commonwealth Quarterly*, 5, 2, pp. 131–49, reprinted in Friedrich Hayek, *Individualism and Economic Order*. Chicago: University of Chicago Press: 1948, pp. 255–72.

Herbst, J., 2001. *States and Power in Africa: Comparative Lessons in Authority and Control*. Princeton. N.J.: Princeton University Press.

Homer-Dixon, T., 1999. *Environment, Scarcity and Violence*. Princeton: Princeton University Press.

Horowitz, D. L., 2003. "The Cracked Foundations of the Right to Secede." *Journal of Democracy*, 14(2): 5–17.

Jackson, R., Rosberg, C., 1986. "Sovereignty and Underdevelopment: Juridical Statehood and the African Crisis." *Journal of Modern African Studies*, 24(1): 1–31.

Johnson, Chalmers A., 1982. *MITI and the Japanese Miracle: The Growth of Industrial Policy, 1925–1975*. Stanford, CA: Stanford University Press.

Kay, Stephen J., 2003. "State Capacity and Pensions." Paper prepared for the LASA XXIV International Congress in Dallas, March 27–29.

Kocher, M.A., 2010. "State Capacity as a Conceptual Variable." *Yale Journal of International Affairs*, Spring/Summer: 137–45.

Kohli, A., 2004. *State-Directed Development: Political Power and Industrialization in the Global Periphery*. Cambridge: Cambridge University Press.

Leff, C.S., 1999. "Democratization and Disintegration in Multinational States: The Breakup of the Communist Federations." *World Politics*, 51(2): 205–35.

Levi, M., and A. Sacks, 2009. "Legitimating Beliefs: Concepts and Indicators." *Regulation and Governance*, 3 (4): 311–33.

Levitsky, S. and Murillo, M.V., 2009. "Variation in Institutional Strength." *Annual Review of Political Science*, 12: 115–33.

Lijphart, A., 1977. *Democracy in Plural Societies*. New Haven: Yale University Press.

Linz, J.J., Stepan, A., 2000. "Inequality Inducing and Inequality Reducing Federalism: With Special Reference to the 'Classic Outlier'— the U.S.A." Paper presented at the XVIII World Congress of the International Political Science Association, August 1–5, Quebec City, Canada.

Madison, J., A. Hamilton, and J. Jay, 1961 [1788]. *The Federalist Papers*. New York: New American Library.

Manor, J., 1999. *The Political Economy of Democratic Decentralization*. Washington, DC: The World Bank.

Migdal, J.S., 2001. *State in Society: Studying how States and Societies Transform and Constitute one Another*. Cambridge: Cambridge University Press.

Mkandawire, T., 2001. "Thinking about Developmental States in Africa." *Cambridge Journal of Economics*, 25: 289–313.

Myrdal, G., 1968. *Asian Drama: An Inquiry into the Poverty of Nations*. New York: Pantheon.

North, D.C., J.J. Wallis, and B.R. Weingast, 2009. *Violence and Social Orders: A Conceptual Framework for Interpreting Recorded Human History*. Cambridge: Cambridge University Press.

O'Neill, K., 2003. "Decentralization as an Electoral Strategy." *Comparative Political Studies*, 36(9): 1068–91.

Peterson, G.E., 1994. *Decentralization Experience in Latin America: An Overview of Lessons and Issues*. Washington DC: Urban Institute.

Price-Smith, A., Tauber, S., and Bhat, A., 2004. "State capacity and HIV incidence reduction in the developing world: Preliminary empirical evidence." *Seton Hall Journal of Diplomacy and International Relations*, 5: 149–60.

Prud'homme, R., 1995. "On the Dangers of Decentralization." *World Bank Research Observer*, 10:210–26.

Putnam, R., 1993. *Making Democracy Work: Civic Traditions in Modern Italy*. Princeton: Princeton University Press.

Putzel, J. & Di John, J., 2012. "Meeting the Challenges of Crisis States." Crisis States Research Centre Report, London School of Economics and Political Science, London, UK.

Rajkumar, A. S. & Garcia, M., 2008. *Achieving Better Services Delivery Through Decentralization in Ethiopia*. Washington DC: The World Bank.

Rao, M. G. and R. M. Bird, 2011. "Coping with Change: The Need to Restructure Urban Governance and Finance in India." IMFG Paper No. 4, University of Toronto.

Roeder, P.G. and D. Rothchild (eds.), 2005. *Sustainable Peace: Power and Democracy after Civil Wars*. Ithaca: Cornell University Press.

Rondinelli, D. A., G. S. Cheema, and J. Nellis, 1983. "Decentralization in Developing Countries: A Review of Recent Experience." World Bank Staff Working Paper No.581. Washington, DC: World Bank.

Rotberg, R., 2003. *State Failure and State Weakness in a Time of Terror*. Washington DC: Brookings Institute Press.

Sabatini, C., 2003. "Decentralization and Political Parties." *Journal of Democracy*, 14(2): 138–50.

Skocpol, T., 1985. "Bringing the State Back In: Strategies of Analysis in Current Research." Pp. 3–43 in Peter B. Evans, Dietrich Rueschemeyer, and Theda Skocpol (eds.), *Bringing the State Back In*. Cambridge: Cambridge University Press.

Stepan, A., 1999. "Federalism and Democracy: Beyond the U.S. Model." *Journal of Democracy* 10(4): 19–34.

Stepan, A., 2000. "Brazil's Decentralized Federalism: Bringing Government Closer to the Citizens?" *Daedalus*, 129 (Spring): 145–69.

Stepan, A., 2001. "Toward a New Comparative Politics of Federalism, (Multi)Nationalism, and Democracy: Beyond Rikerian Federalism." Pp. 315–61 in Alfred Stepan *Arguing Comparative Politics*. Oxford: Oxford University Press.

Tiebout, C. M., 1956. "A Pure Theory of Local Expenditures." *Journal of Political Economy*, 5: 416–24.

Treisman, D., 2007. *The Architecture of Government: Rethinking Political Decentralization*. New York, N.Y.: Cambridge University Press.

Tsebelis, G., 2002. *Veto Players: How Political Institutions Work*. Princeton, N.J.: Princeton University Press.

Vogel, D., 1986. *National Styles of Regulation: Environmental Policy in Great Britain and the United States*. Ithaca, N.Y.: Cornell University Press.

Wallis, J. J. and W. E. Oates, 1988. "Decentralization in the Public Sector: An Empirical Study of State and Local Government." In H.S. Rosen (ed.) *Fiscal Federalism: Quantitative Studies*. Chicago: University of Chicago Press.

Weber, M., 1946. "Politics as a Vocation." Pp. 26–45 in H.H. Garth and C. Wright Mills (eds.), *Essays in Sociology*. New York: Macmillian.

Weingast, B.R., 2013. "Second Generation Fiscal Federalism: Political Aspects of Decentralization and Economic Development." *World Development*. <http://dx.doi.org/10.1016/j.worlddev.2013.01.003>.

Woo-Cummings, M., 1999. *The Developmental State*. Ithaca: Cornell University Press.

World Bank, 1994. *Colombia: Toward Increased Efficiency and Equity in the Health Sector. Can Decentralization Help?* Washington DC: World Bank.

Part II

Designing Decentralization: Taxes, Transfers, and Expenditures

7

A Fiscal Interest Approach to Subnational Government Incentives

Implications for the Design of Tax and Transfer Systems

Caroline Pöschl and Barry R. Weingast

7.1 Introduction

How can subnational governments be motivated to promote the prosperity of residents in their jurisdictions? According to modern scholarship on fiscal federalism and decentralization, one way is through the design of the fiscal system (Faguet, 2012; Faguet and Sánchez, 2013; Weingast 2013). Recent advances in the field emphasize that the specific arrangement of tax and transfer systems affects the incentives of subnational political officials. In this chapter, we focus on the fiscal interest approach. Because systems of taxation affect the incentives of subnational governments, they affect these governments' policy choices and, consequently, the performance of their jurisdictions (Wallis, Sylla, and Legler, 1994; Weingast, 2009). The design of the fiscal system shapes institutions and influences whether subnational government officials strive to create growth and prosperity or let their localities stagnate, and whether they rule in the interest of the ruled.[1]

This chapter reviews the literature and discusses *how* different tax and transfer systems affect incentives in decentralized settings. In particular, it discusses how their design can influence whether subnational political

[1] The analysis in this chapter thus falls into the category of "second-generation fiscal federalism," which analyzes decisions by subnational government officials based on the incentives they face (Oates, 2005; Weingast, 2009, 2013).

officials choose policies that foster markets and serve as a helping hand to their population or instead choose predatory and distortionary policies. It looks first at the incentives created through reliance on different sources of revenue, comparing tax revenues with central government transfers. It then discusses specific taxes and different systems of intergovernmental transfers, assessing their effect in shaping subnational government policy-making.

7.2 Incentives of Taxes versus Transfers as a Source of Subnational Government Revenues

Scholars have long shown that different sources of revenues affect the incentives of governments differently (Moore, 2004 and 2007; Prichard, 2009). At the subnational level, too, researchers see an important difference between governments that depend largely on own revenues, such as taxes and fees, and those that depend predominantly on central government transfers. To be sure, taxes and transfers are not independent. How tax systems are assigned, designed, and collected influences how transfers are designed and vice versa (Ter-Minassian, 1997; Bird, 1999). Nonetheless, we argue that, ceteris paribus, subnational dependence on tax revenues affects their incentives in a different manner than subnational government reliance on transfers.

Subnational governments that depend on own revenues have incentives to be more accountable to citizens, to provide market-enhancing public goods, and to be less corrupt (Singh and Srinivasan, 2006; Rodden, 2003; Careaga and Weingast, 2003; Ambrosanio and Bordignon, 2006; Faguet, 2004 and 2014). While many of the arguments in support of these claims have been made with a view to the national level, they are applied to subnational governments as well. The arguments go as follows. Dependence on taxes is said to create several incentives. First, it is believed to motivate governments to show that they are accountable and govern in the interest of their residents because they want to ensure compliance with tax payments. Beblawi and Luciani (1987: 73), for instance, write that a state that is dependent on taxation "must give credibility to the notion that it represents the common good." As Levi (1988) explains, tax payments are quasi-voluntary and depend on compliance of the taxpayers. And, as Timmons (2005) illustrates statistically, at the local level voluntary compliance with taxes is higher when citizens receive public goods and services they value in exchange for taxes. Thus, to motivate greater compliance and greater government revenues, governments that depend on taxes have the incentive to govern in the interest of their constituents and provide the services they require.

Second, if a government is dependent on citizens and businesses for taxation, it has an incentive to increase productivity in its territory in order to secure or raise future earnings (Oates, 1972; Olson, 1993, 2000). This interest in turn provides the government with incentives to collect information about citizen needs and to respond to them—at least to the productive needs of those whom it sees as potential producers of taxable wealth. As Adam Smith (1776 [1904]: V.1.87) explains in *Wealth of Nations*, countries where

> the revenue of the sovereign arises almost altogether from a land-tax or land-rent, which rises or falls with the rise or fall of the annual produce of the land [. . .] the great interest of the sovereign [. . .] is in such countries necessarily and immediately connected with the cultivation of the land, with the greatness of its produce and with the value of its produce. But in order to render that produce both as great and as valuable as possible, it is necessary to procure to it as extensive a market as possible, and consequently the freest, the easiest and the least expensive communication between all the different parts of the country; which can be done only by means of the best roads and the best navigable canals.

Where this is not the case, "the sovereign does not feel himself so directly called upon to promote the increase, both in quantity and value, of the produce of the land, or, by maintaining good roads and canals, to provide the most extensive market for that produce" (ibid).

Shleifer and Vishny's (1998b) study of the differential local government support for the economy in Poland and Russia draws on this logic. Using survey techniques, they find that local governments in Poland are far more supportive of business than in Russia. Shleifer and Vishny attribute this difference to government officials' incentives. They explain that while local politicians have different electoral incentives in Russia than in Poland, their fiscal incentives also differ significantly. In Poland, local governments rely on local taxes and fees (particularly property taxes), so fostering local economic prosperity yields greater revenue. In Russia, by contrast, most local revenue comes from higher levels of government. What is more, the center reduces these transfers when cities increase their revenues. Studies of other countries reveal similar patterns (e.g., Díaz-Cayeros, 2006 on Mexico; Singh and Srinivasan, 2006 on India). While the first design provides incentives to foster local economic development as local governments are rewarded by this with the rise in revenues generated, the second has the opposite effect.

Third, governments are likely to be more prudent with their own income and more wasteful with "unearned" income or "other people's money," such as revenue transfers from the federal government. As Bird and Smart (2002) note, "So long as local governments are spending what they and their constituents view as 'other people's money,' they are unlikely to be under much local pressure to spend this money efficiently." Smith (1776 [1904]: V.1.76) deliberates that only when public services are directly paid for through user taxes is it possible to avoid wasteful spending: "A great bridge cannot be thrown over a river at a place where nobody passes, or merely to embellish the view from the windows of a neighboring palace: things which sometimes happen in countries where works of this kind are carried on by any other revenue than that which they [the users] themselves are capable of affording" (also cited in Skinner, 1995). Bahl and Linn (1992: 428), in their authoritative study of local fiscal federalism in developing countries, observe that "grants can make local governments less accountable for their fiscal decisions (they may now increase spending without increasing taxes); hence there will be less incentive to improve the efficiency of local government operations and develop innovative methods of delivering public services."

Taxation also creates incentives for the government indirectly by influencing residents' behavior. If citizens are made to pay taxes, they are relatively more inclined to watch over or scrutinize the government's activities, and to demand representation in government and influence in policy decisions. As Bird (2010: 20) posits, "local residents are more likely to hold officials accountable if local public services are financed to a significant extent from locally imposed taxes and charges as opposed to central government transfers." By contrast, as Ambrosanio and Bordignon (2006: 316) write, "If everything were financed with money coming from outside the jurisdiction, citizens living in that jurisdiction would have very little incentive to check how that money was spent."

The reasoning behind this argument is the following. First, as Bird (2010: 20) writes, "People care much more about how their 'own money' is spent than they do about the efficiency with which 'other people's money'—such as transfers—is used." Thus, if people entrust their local government with their own earnings that they have worked for, they will be more concerned about how the government utilizes it and may also demand more transparency and influence over policy decisions (Ross, 2001).

Second, taxation is intrinsically coercive and can be very burdensome on the taxpayers. This can lead to revolt, bargaining, or other forms of collective action by citizens in attempts to resist it or control it. In this way, taxation provokes citizen engagement with the state through protest and "provides an opportunity for the creation of consensual and representative government through 'revenue bargaining' between states and organized citizens" (Bräutigam, 2008: 3). Di John (2010: 111), for instance, claims that "taxation is the main nexus that binds state officials with interest groups and citizens. Not only can taxation enhance government accountability, it also provides a focal point around which interest groups (such as producers groups, labor unions and consumer groups) can mobilize to support, resist and even propose tax policies." Besides provoking collective action, a dependence of local governments on their citizens for taxes also gives citizens greater bargaining power to make demands. It may help to shift the balance of power in favor of residents.

The importance of taxation has also been expressed negatively in the literature on the "natural resource curse" and foreign aid. It has been frequently argued that poor governance and impeded development of resource-rich states derives from the fact that large alternative sources of income free politicians from the need to tax their citizens (Auty 2001; Auty and Gelb 2001). Referring to natural resource rents, Samuel Huntington (1991: 65), for instance, posits that because natural resource rents substitute for taxation, they "reduce the need for the government to solicit the acquiescence of its subjects to taxation," and hence reduce the incentives for and necessity of governments to be concerned with the interests of citizens. Bräutigam and Knack (2004) consider foreign aid, another "unearned" external source, to have an analogous effect and write that it takes away a government's need to tax its own citizens and thereby diminishes the citizens' bargaining power vis-à-vis their government in collective action problems.

Central government transfers have been regarded in the literature as a somewhat external source of revenue for subnational governments, which eliminates or reduces their need for taxation, and is also "unearned" or at least "less earned," much like natural resources and foreign aid at the national level. Gervasoni (2010), for instance, terms large central government transfers "fiscal federalism rents."

The connection between the source of subnational government revenue on one hand and the degree to which governance is representative and responsive or corrupt has been analyzed statistically. Gadenne (2013) examines public expenditure in Brazilian municipalities and shows that as the proportion of tax revenue to transfer revenue rises, governments spend more on public goods and less on private rents. Similarly, Brollo, Nannicini, Perotti, and Tabellini (2010) find that higher grants from the federal government lead to a rise in the incidence of corruption. In his analysis of Argentine provinces, Gervasoni (2010, 2011) uses both quantitative and qualitative evidence to show that central government transfers are negatively associated with levels of democracy. He argues that such rents allow the provinces to forgo taxation, and thus to restrict democratic contestation and weaken checks and balances.

7.3 Tax Systems

If local taxes are important, how best should they be collected? Do different types of taxes and different ways of collecting them affect higher-order goals, such as economic growth and political inclusion? The literature differentiates how the type of taxation affects whether government officials choose to foster thriving markets or manipulate them—the difference between Shleifer and

Vishny's (1998a) "grabbing hand" and a "helping hand." We discuss three ideas from the literature.

First, to provide the positive incentives outlined above, taxes require a relatively broad base of society. When government officials capture revenue based on broad taxes on economic activity, they have incentives to provide market-enhancing public goods and to create new market opportunities as a means of increasing the fiscal proceeds generated by markets. In contrast, a narrow tax base leads political officials to cater to the specific groups or sectors bearing the tax burden. For instance, when a jurisdiction raises revenue by selling monopoly rights, then officials will choose to restrict markets generating monopolies; further, officials have little fiscal incentive to foster competitive markets in other sectors (Wallis, Sylla, and Legler, 1994; Weingast, 2009).

Second, taxes need to be visible. If people see more clearly that they are being taxed by the subnational government, they are more likely to hold the government accountable for effective use of their tax money (Bird, 2010). According to Grabowski (2008), when taxes are visible to taxpayers, they will be more likely to resist them, either directly (through protest or revolt) or indirectly (through evasion). As the government cannot entirely suppress such resistance through punishment or violence, it must reciprocate and provide services in return. One of the frequently cited arguments for developing countries, in favor of replacing indirect taxes such as tariffs with more visible direct taxes—a widespread policy furthered by the international financial institutions throughout the 1990s and beyond—was that the direct taxes would enhance the accountability of the government (Mahon, 2009).[2]

Third, taxes should be tied to the growth or prosperity of residents, and subnational governments need to have the ability to affect that growth and prosperity. Tiebout (1956), as extended by Oates (1972), shows how property tax incentivizes local governments to improve public goods in its jurisdiction. Because the value of public goods is capitalized into the value of local property, dependence on property taxation leads city managers to choose public goods that maximize local property values. Moreover, city managers facing intense inter-jurisdictional competition have incentives to maximize property values as a means of inducing scarce capital and labor to locate and remain in their jurisdiction. These specific taxes thus provide incentives for subnational political officials to design policies that foster markets and attract capital and labor (Bahl and Linn, 1992; Fischel, 2001; Glaeser, 1996).

The theory that different types of taxes or tax systems affect government accountability, responsiveness, and representation differently has also been applied to explain differences in development trajectories more generally.

[2] Moore's (2001) distinction between earned and unearned income is closely related to the idea of visibility discussed here.

Grabowski (2008), for instance, argues that different taxes (resulting from different agricultural models) influenced a divergence in long-term development paths between Latin America and East Asia. "The way a ruling elite raises revenue influences how state institutions evolve over time" (2008: 31). In Japan, Taiwan, and Korea, the government relied on a broad-based, "earned," direct, and visible land tax that penetrated the countryside. The government repeatedly subdued resistance to tax rises by providing services in return for the tax revenue extracted. The government created, upheld, and enforced property rights. It also established a research and extension system to the agricultural sector, and provided access to more productive technologies. In Latin America, by contrast, governments have relied heavily on export taxes. This is a narrow tax that is easy to collect and does not involve the same effort or outreach to the broad population. These governments therefore had few fiscal incentives to provide investment, services, and property rights to the broad population in the Latin American countries examined. Grabowski further shows how counter examples (Costa Rica and the Philippines) in the respective regions equivalently fit the theory. Sokoloff and Zolt (2007) similarly argue that differences in inequality across the Americas can be traced back to tax systems (which in turn developed because of factor endowments and other pre-colonization conditions).

7.4 Transfer Systems

The scholarship generally views own revenues as superior to central government transfers as a source of revenues for subnational governments in terms of the incentives they create for growth and development. Yet the specific transfer design and how intergovernmental transfers relate to taxes is also important (Faguet and Wietzke, 2006; Weingast, 2009). Depending on their design, intergovernmental transfers to subnational governments can mitigate or magnify some of the incentive problems connected to transfers outlined above. They can encourage or destroy incentives for promoting growth directly and also indirectly by affecting incentives for tax collection.

7.4.1 *Effect on Promoting Growth and Development*

Transfers to subnational governments are typically set by a formula that comprises a series of weights for different criteria, including economic and demographic characteristics, such as income and population. However, the attempt to correct horizontal imbalances by allocating more transfers to poorer regions often means that these transfer systems exhibit poor responsiveness to localities that foster local economic growth, and sometimes can even produce completely perverse incentives. In Mexico, for instance, transfers have been tied to the poverty levels of subnational governments in an attempt to compensate poor regions. This has allegedly created perverse incentive for regional governments to keep poverty levels high in order to receive greater transfers (Diaz Cayeros, 1997).

More generally, transfer formulas that are negatively related or only weakly positively related to income growth also provide poor incentives for subnational governments to foster growth and development. For example, in India the Finance Commission's transfers of revenue to states reflect a series of weights for different criteria: around two-thirds is negatively related to a state's income, so that poorer states receive greater funds; 10 per cent is given on the basis of population; and the remainder is somewhat evenly divided among state area, an index of infrastructure, tax effort, and fiscal discipline.[3] This type of intergovernmental transfer system provides poor fiscal incentives for subnational jurisdictions to foster local economic growth: most of an increase in local revenue goes to the center (Singh and Srinivasan, 2006).

In some countries, formulas have been fixed with reference to a given year so that the center allocates revenue using the same proportions each year, with the only variable across years being the size of the revenue pool to be divided among subnational governments. If there are n provinces, then the average province receives $1/n$ of the total revenue pool, no matter how good or bad its policies. Careaga and Weingast (2003) called the poor incentives of these transfer systems "fiscal law of $1/n$."[4] In a country with even a modest number of states, this proportion is quite small. For instance, at times in Mexico revenue from all the states was put in a common pool and then divided by a sharing rule, which meant that for each newly generated peso in taxes, any one of its thirty-three states would receive only three *centavos* in return.[5] In contrast, fiscal systems that allow growing regions to capture a major portion of new revenue generated by economic growth provide far stronger incentives for local governments to foster local economic growth.

Zhuravskaya (2000) calculated the marginal revenue retention rate at only 10 per cent for Russian cities. For every increase in local revenue, the regional government within which the city is located extracts most of the value of the increase by *lowering* transfers. In contrast, provinces in post-reform China were allowed to retain a high proportion of revenue above a fixed threshold. Jin et al. (2005) calculate that during the high growth period following the

[3] These figures are for the 11th Finance Commission. See Rao and Singh (2005, ch 9, especially table 9.3) and Singh and Srinivasan (2006). The Planning Commission also transfers money to states based on different criteria.

[4] Following the results of Weingast et al. (1981) "law of $1/n$"; see also Inman (1988).

[5] The data presented in Shah (1998,136–44) suggest that the figures for Pakistan are less than a third. The data in Rao and Singh (2005, ch 9) suggest that the figures in India are similar.

initial reforms (1981–92), Chinese provinces on average retained a marginal rate of 89 per cent of additional tax revenue generated within the province, and that 68 per cent of all provinces faced a marginal retention rate of 100 per cent. According to Ahmad, Rydge, and Stern (2013: 2), this reform, together with a reduction in the taxation of profits from state-owned enterprises and collectives, "laid the foundations for a remarkable period of economic transformation and growth."

Courchene (1981) and McKinnon (1997) raise a related incentive problem with transfer schemes that are designed to provide substantial subsidies to the poorest regions in rich countries. McKinnon, for example, contrasts the huge subsidies by Canada to the Eastern Maritime Provinces and by Italy to the Mezzogiorno in southern Italy with the lack of subsidies by the United States to the American South. McKinnon suggests that the revenue transfers in Canada and Italy create dependency. Transfers allow these regions to finance ailing and inefficient enterprises, seeming to saddle southern Italy with highly capitalized, loss-making enterprises. The regional economy is far less likely to adapt to become more like the vibrant national economy. In contrast, southern states in America faced a hard budget constraint and no national subsidies. The poorest region in the United States from the Civil War through to the mid twentieth century, the southern states were able to grow rich by redesigning their economies with low regulatory burdens relative to the industrialized North and to take advantage of lower labor costs. This adaptation fostered the booming Sun Belt economy of the late twentieth century. While other factors, such as migration and political institutions, may have also influenced the differences between these development trajectories, McKinnon argues that the economic rise of the American South is unlikely to have occurred had it been subsidized in the manner of the Canadian Maritimes and the Italian *Mezzogiorno*. For this reason, Courchene (1981) argues that these types of regional transfers are self-perpetuating.

Krueger (2006) uses similar logic to explain the difference between the vibrant economy in Poland just east of the border with Germany and the lackluster economic performance of the former East Germany just west of the border: massive transfers from the German government have deterred economic development.

Transfer systems may exhibit other perverse fiscal incentives. The intergovernmental transfer system may result in soft budget constraints for subnational governments (Bordignon, 2006; Haggard and Webb, 2004; Wibbels, 2003; Rodden et al., 2001; Dillinger and Webb, 1999; McKinnon, 1997; Sanguinetti, 1994; Kornai, 1986). A soft budget constraint arises when subnational governments believe they will be able to externalize some of their fiscal burdens, such as through a bailout by the national government or borrowing. Subnational governments facing a soft budget constraint have reduced (or no) fiscal incentive to make prudent financial decisions. Some transfer systems are explicitly "gap-filling," meaning that provinces with larger deficits receive larger transfers. Because these systems subsidize spending beyond revenue, they provide subnational governments with incentives to spend imprudently and with profligacy.

Transfer systems may also provide poor incentives for subnational governments when they are not linked to clear responsibilities. Wiesner (2003: 23) argues that decentralization in Latin America often emphasizes subnational government entitlements to revenue rather than linking them to spending needs or growth: "These frameworks tend to neglect market-based mechanisms and make the capture of large unconditional transfers an easy ride for public sector rent-seeking." For example, Bolivia, Brazil, and Ecuador considerably increased the transfer of revenue without increasing the policy responsibility, allowing subnational governments to use these funds for patronage rather than local public goods (Wiesner 2003).[6]

7.4.2 *Effect on Tax Effort*

While fiscal transfers tend to enhance the centralized control (and possible manipulation) of subnational governments, own revenues grant subnational governments independence. McLure (1998: 1) observes that "Subnational governments that lack independent sources of revenue can never truly enjoy fiscal autonomy; they may be—and probably are—under the thumb of the central government." However, raising revenues through taxation is also associated with political costs for subnational governments. Besides creating administrative costs, imposing taxes is unpopular and may compromise (re)election. It may also drive out residents or business or discourage settlement in the specific jurisdiction (Tiebout, 1956; Salmon, 1986). As we argued above, these incentives require that subnational governments carefully devise policies and public goods provision so that taxpayers believe their taxes are worth paying. Between receiving transfers from the central government and raising taxes, subnational governments may thus prefer receiving transfers as a source of revenue. In receiving transfers, subnational governments draw from the common pool and can free ride on the tax effort of others.

Several authors have shown empirically how transfers "crowd out" taxation (Raich Portman, 2004; Cabrero Mendoza, 2006). Some transfer systems, however, include tax effort as a criterion in order to encourage subnational governments to maintain or increase tax revenues. That is, the more they increase

[6] The opposite phenomenon is equally problematic—the devolution of authority and responsibility without the fiscal resources to implement it.

their tax collection, the more transfers they will receive. These efforts may conflict with the equalization goals of transfers. Furthermore, subnational officials may still regard the political cost of collection higher than the economic cost of non-collection and simply leave potential government revenues uncollected. In Mexico, the central government collected vehicle tax from the 1960s until 2007. In 2008 this tax was reassigned to the states. However, despite being a desirable subnational government tax in most other aspects, many states chose not to make use of this tax power, preferring instead to receive their revenues in the form of transfers. In part they are afraid of the political competition effect (see Salmon, 1986, 2006): if neighboring states do not tax or choose a lower rate, people move or will register their vehicles elsewhere, but mainly they are concerned with the political and electoral consequences of collecting the tax.

7.5 Conclusion

As Schumpeter ([1918] 1978) noted in his famous essay "The Crisis of the Tax State," fiscal systems shape society and its institutions: "The spirit of a people, its cultural level, its social structure, the deeds its policy may prepare . . . all this and more is written in fiscal history." Modern scholarship on fiscal federalism and decentralization continues to recognize that the design of the fiscal system vitally shapes subnational government institutions and policies. Taxes and transfers are interlinked in complex ways. The devil is often in the details of design; for example, shared revenue bases complicate matters of fiscal design. In this chapter we have discussed some of the ways in which the design of the fiscal system affects subnational government policy-making and the development of local economies.

First, when subnational governments depend on their own revenue generation rather than relying on central government transfers, they become, ceteris paribus, more responsive to citizens and more willing to provide market-enhancing public goods. This responsiveness is enhanced when the central government assigns subnational governments the power to levy broad taxes on the general economy rather than rely on revenue sources with a narrow base, and when the taxes are tied to the growth or prosperity of residents. As students of fiscal federalism have long known, subnational government reliance on the property tax, for instance, can act as a powerful motivator to improve public services, attract markets, and protect property rights in order to see land values and property tax payments rise (Oates, 1972; Tiebout, 1956).

By giving subnational governments a stake in the economic development of their jurisdictions, decentralized taxation powers help ensure subnational governments' responsibility for their actions. In so many developing countries decentralization has expanded fiscal transfers and spending powers to subnational governments, yet has stopped short of transferring powers of taxation.

Increasing resource transfers to levels of government that are closer to the people, or to poorer regions within a country, may ostensibly appear an attractive option to alleviate poverty and to help lagging regions catch up. However, as abundant evidence in the literature suggests, this brings with it the risk of subnational governmental incentives that perpetuate poverty and dependence on the center. Reliance on such external, unearned resources robs subnational governments of the motivation to engage with their residents in order to find out how to help them produce wealth. Reliance on transfers also dampens the impulse to innovate, to pursue strategies that create growth from below, and to use resources more efficiently and effectively. Evidence shows that this reliance also creates complacent attitudes and disinterest amongst officials *and residents,* and leads to wasteful management of public finances and corruption. This reliance therefore has a detrimental effect on growth and development.

Second, the specific design of transfer systems is important. Transfer formulas in particular may either reward or punish efforts at promoting growth and prosperity in subnational governments' jurisdictions. They can encourage spending beyond means or promote prudent fiscal management. By, for instance, tying transfer formulas to revenue generation, or by allowing subnational governments to retain large portions of any new revenues they generate, transfer systems can serve as remarkable motivators for subnational governments to embark on wealth-enhancing policies, as evidenced by China in the 1980s and early 1990s. Designers of transfer systems should pay closer attention to the incentive effects inherent in transfer formulas, so that transfers do not subsidize free riding and stagnation but rather support the generation of wealth.

In decentralized settings, fiscal systems comprise a mixture of tax powers and transfers assigned to different levels of government. In designing these systems, central governments must balance various goals, such as protecting the poor, ensuring equity among regions, maximizing administrative efficiency of collection, and guaranteeing the provision of goods and services to all citizens. The fiscal incentives approach discussed in this chapter shows that different tax and transfer designs powerfully affect the incentives of subnational government officials and that these effects should not to be disregarded; they affect the policy choices of the government leaders that are closest to the people. Moreover, they are a strong predictor of whether subnational governments will tackle poverty and assist development and growth or choose not to.

References

Ahmad, Ehtisham, James Rydge, and Nicholas Stern, 2013. "Structural Change Drives Tax Reform Drives Structural Change." Paper prepared for China Development Forum, London School of Economics and Political Science, March 2013.

Ambrosanio, Maria Flavia and Bordignon, Massimo. 2006. "Normative versus Positive Theories of Revenue Assignments in Federations." In Ahmad and Brosio (eds.) *Handbook of Fiscal Federalism.* Cheltenham: Edward Elgar.

Auty, R. 2001. "The Political Economy of Resource Driven Growth." *European Economic Review* 45.4–6: 839–46.

Auty, R. and A. Gelb, 2001. "The Political Economy of Resource-Abundant States." In Auty (ed.) *Resource Abundance and Economic Development.* Oxford: Oxford University Press: 126–44.

Bahl, Roy W., Linn, Johannes, F., 1992. *Urban Public Finance in Developing Countries.* Oxford: Oxford University Press.

Beblawi, Hazem and Giacomo Luciani, 1987. *The Rentier State.* Croom Helm, Austrialia: Croom Helm Ltd.

Bird, Richard, 1999. *Rethinking Subnational Taxes—A New Look at Tax Assignment.* Washington, DC: International Monetary Fund.

Bird, Richard, 2010. "Subnational Taxation in Developing Countries: A Review of the Literature." *Journal of International Commerce, Economics and Policy* Vol. 2, No. 1 (2011) 139–61.

Bird, Richard and Michael Smart, 2002. "Transfers and Incentives in Intergovernmental Fiscal Relations." *World Development* Vol. 30, No. 6, pp. 899–921.

Bordignon, M., 2006. " 'Fiscal Decentralization : How to Harden the Budget Constraint' in E. F. Wierts, S. Deroose, and A. Turrini (eds.), *Fiscal Policy and Surveillance in Europe.* New York: Palgrave MacMillan, pp. 109–36.

Bräutigam, D., 2008. "Contingent Capacity: Export Taxation and State-Building in Mauritius" In: Bräutigam, Fjeldstad, and Moore (eds) Taxation *and State-Building in Developing Countries: Capacity and Consent.* Cambridge: Cambridge University Press.

Bräutigam, D. and S. Knack, 2004. "Foreign Aid, Institutions, and Governance in Sub-Saharan Africa," *Economic Development and Cultural Change,* 52, 255–85.

Brollo, Fernanda, Tommaso Nannicini, Roberto Perotti, and Guido Tabellini, "The Political Resource Curse." January 2010. IZA Discussion Papers, No. 4706.

Cabrero Mendoza, Enrique (2006) "Los Retos Institucionales de la descentralización fiscal en América Latina," CIDE, división de Administración Pública Documento de Trabajo, No 181.

Careaga, Maite, and Barry R. Weingast, 2003. "Fiscal Federalism, Good Governance, and Economic Growth in Mexico." In Dani Rodrik (ed.) *In Search of Prosperity: Analytic Narratives on Economic Growth.* Princeton: Princeton University Press.

Courchene, Thomas, 1981. "A Market Perspective On Regional Disparities." *Canadian Public Policy 7,* 506–18.

Díaz Cayeros, Alberto, 1997. "Asignación política de recursos en el federalismo mexicano: incentivos y limitaciones." *Perfiles Latinoamericanos* Vol. 6, no. 10 (June 1997).

Diaz-Cayeros, A., 2006. *Federalism, Fiscal Authority, and Centralization in Latin America*. Cambridge: Cambridge University Press.

Di John, Jonathan, 2010. "The Political Economy of Taxation and Resource Mobilization in Sub-Saharan Africa." In Padayachee, V. (ed.) *The Political Economy of Africa*. New York: Routledge.

Dillinger, William, and Webb, Steven B., 1999. "Fiscal Management in Federal Democracies: Argentina and Brazil." Working paper, World Bank.

Faguet, Jean-Paul, 2014. "Can Sub-National Autonomy Strengthen Democracy in Bolivia?" *Publius: The Journal of Federalism*, 44(1): 51–81; doi: 10.1093/publius/pjt020.

Faguet, Jean-Paul, 2012. *Decentralization and Popular Democracy: Governance from Below in Bolivia*. Ann Arbor: University of Michigan Press.

Faguet, Jean-Paul, 2004. "Why So Much Centralization? A Model of Primitive Centripetal Accumulation." STICERD DEDPS No.43, London School of Economics.

Faguet, Jean-Paul and Fabio Sánchez, 2013. "Decentralization and Access to Social Services in Colombia." Public Choice, 160 (1–2), 227–49.

Faguet, Jean-Paul and Frank-Borge Wietzke, 2006. "Social Funds and Decentralization: Optimal Institutional Design." *Public Administration and Development*, 26(4): 303–15.

Fischel, William A., 2001. *The Homevoter Hypothesis: How Home Values Influence Local Government Taxation, School Finance, and Land-Use Policies*. Cambridge, Mass.: Harvard University Press.

Gadenne, Lucie, 2013. "Tax Me but Spend Wisely: The Political Economy of Taxes. Theory and Evidence from Brazilian Local Governments." ULC Working Paper.

Gervasoni, Carlos, 2010. "Measuring Variance in Subnational Regimes: Results from an Expert-Based Operationalization of Democracy in the Argentine Provinces." In: *Journal of Politics in Latin America*, 2, 2, 13–52,online: <http://www.jpla.org>.

Gervasoni, Carlos, 2011. "A Rentier Theory of Subnational Regimes: Fiscal Federalism, Democracy, and Authoritarianism in the Argentine Provinces" *World Politics* 65, 302–40, April.

Glaeser, Edward L., 1996. "The Incentive Effects of Property Taxes on Local Governments." *Public Choice* 89, 93–111.

Grabowski, Richard, 2008. "Modes of Long-Run Development: Latin America and East Asia." *Journal of Institutional Economics*. 4: 1, 25–50.

Haggard, Stephan and Webb, Steven B., 2004. "Political Incentives and Intergovernmental Fiscal Relations: Argentina, Brazil, and Mexico Compared." In Montero, Alfred P. and Samuels, David J. (eds.) *Decentralization and Democracy in Latin America*. Notre Dame, IN: Notre Dame University Press.

Huntington, Samuel P., 1991. *The Third Wave: Democratization in the Late Twentieth Century*. Norman: University of Oklahoma Press, 14, 26.

Inman, Robert P., 1988. "Federal Assistance and Local Services in The United States: The Evolution of a New Federalist Fiscal Order." In Rosen, Harvey S. (ed.) *Fiscal Federalism: Quantitative Studies*. Chicago: University of Chicago Press.

Jin, Hehui, Qian, Yingyi, and Weingast, Barry R., 2005. "Regional Decentralization and Fiscal Incentives: Federalism, Chinese Style." *Journal of Public Economics* 89, 1719–42.

Kornai, Janos, 1986. "The Soft Budget Constraint." *Kyklos* 39 (1), 3–30.

Krueger, Anne, 2006. "The Role of Freedom, Openness and Individual Enterprise in Economic Development." Paper given at the Conference on "Freedom and Development," London School of Economics, May 25–26, 2006.

Levi, Margaret, 1988. *Of Rule and Revenue*. Berkeley: University of California Press.

Mahon, J., 2009. "Tax Reform and Income Distribution in Developing Countries." Latin American Studies Association.

McKinnon, Ronald I., 1997. "Market-Preserving Fiscal Federalism in the American Monetary Union." In: Blejer, Mario I. and Ter-Minassian, Teresa (eds.), *Macroeconomic Dimensions of Public Finance*. New York: Routledge, pp. 73–93.

McLure, Jr. Charles E., 1998. "Tax Assignment Problem: Conceptual Administrative Considerations in Achieving Subnational Fiscal Autonomy." Paper presented at the Intergovernmental Fiscal Relations and Local Financial Management Course, Vienna, 16–27 March 1998.

Moore, Mick, 2007. "How Does Taxation Affect the Quality of Governance?." IDS Working Paper 280. Brighton: Institute of Development Studies.

Moore, Mick, 2001. "Political Underdevelopment: What Causes 'Bad Governance'?" *Public Management Review*, Vol. 3 Issue 3, pp. 385–41.

Moore, Mick, 2004. "Revenues, State Formation and the Quality of Governance in Developing Countries." *International Political Science Review*, Vol. 25, No.3, 297–319.

Oates, Wallace, 1972. *Fiscal Federalism*. New York: Harcourt Brace Jovanovich.

Oates, Wallace E., 2005. "Toward a Second-Generation Theory of Fiscal Federalism," *International Tax and Public Finance* 12, 349–73.

Olson, M. 1993. "Dictatorship, Democracy, and Development." American Political Science Review 87(03): 567–76.

M. Olson and S. Kähköhnen (eds) *A Not-so-dismal Science: A Broader View of Economies and Societies*. Oxford: Oxford University Press.

Prichard, Wilson, 2009. "The Politics of Taxation and Implications for Accountability in Ghana 1981–2008." Institute of Development Studies. IDS Working Paper Volume 2009, No. 330.

Raich Portman, Uri, 2004. "Impacto de la descentralización del gasto en los municipios mexicanos." CIDE, División de Economía, Documento de trabajo No.281.

Rao, M. Govinda and Singh, Nirvikar, 2005. *Political Economy of Federalism in India*. New Delhi: Oxford University Press.

Rodden, Jonathan, 2003. "Reviving Leviathan." *International Organization* 57: 695–729.

Rodden, Jonathan, Eskeland, Gunnar, and Litvack, Jennie (eds.), 2001. *Decentralization and the Challenge of Hard Budget Constraints*. Cambridge, Mass.: MIT Press.

Ross, Michael, 2001. "Does Oil Hinder Democracy?" World Politics 53 (April): 297–322.

Salmon, Pierre, 1986. "Decentralization as an Incentive Scheme." *Oxford Review of Economic Policy* 3 (2), 24–43.

Salmon, Pierre, 2006. "Horizontal Competition Among Governments." In Ahmad and Brosio (eds), *Handbook of Fiscal Federalism*, Cheltenham: Edward Elgar, pp. 67–85.

Sanguinetti, Pablo J., 1994. "Intergovernmental Transfers and Public Sector Expenditures: A Game-Theoretic Approach." *Estudios de Economia* 21 (2), 179–212.

Schumpeter, Joseph, 1918. "Die Krise des Steuerstaates." Reproduced in: Hickel, J., 1978 (ed.), *Die Finanzkrise des Steuerstaates. Beiträge zur politischen Ökonomie der Staatsfinanzen*. Frankfurt/Main, pp. 329–79.

Shleifer, Andrei, and Robert W. Vishny, 1998a. *The Grabbing Hand: Government Pathologies and Their Cures*. Cambridge, MA: Harvard University Press.

Shleifer, Andrei, and Robert W. Vishny, 1998b. "Government in Transition," ch. 11 in Shleifer and Vishny (1998a).

Singh, Nirvikar, and T.N. Srinivasan, 2006. "Federalism and Economic Development in India: An Assessment." SCID Conference on the "Challenges of Economic Policy Reform in Asia," Stanford University, June 1–3.

Skinner, Andrew S., 1995. "Adam Smith and the Role of the State: Education as a Public Service." In Stephen Copley and Kathryn Sutherland (eds) *Adam Smith's Wealth of Nations: New Interpretive Essays*. Manchester: Manchester University Press.

Smith, Adam, 1776 [1904]. *An Inquiry into the Nature & Causes of the Wealth of Nations*. London: Methuen & co., Ltd. 5th Edition.

Sokoloff, Kenneth L. And Eric M. Zolt, 2007. "Inequality and the Evolution of Institutions of Taxation: Evidence from the History of the Americas." In Edwards, Esquivel, and Márquez, *The Decline of Latin American Economies: Growth, Institutions, and Crises*. NBER Books, National Bureau of Economic Research, Inc, number edwa04-1.

Ter-Minassian, Teresa (ed), 1997. *Fiscal Federalism in Theory in Practice*. Washington DC: International Monetary Fund.

Tiebout, Charles, 1956. "A Pure Theory of Local Expenditures." *Journal of Political Economy* 64, 416–24.

Timmons, Jeffrey F., 2005. "The Fiscal Contract: States, Taxes, and Public Services." *World Politics* (July) 57: 530–67.

Wallis, John Joseph, Sylla, Richard E., and Legler, John B., 1994. "The Interaction of Taxation and Regulation in Nineteenth Century U.S. Banking." In Goldin, Claudia and Libecap, Gary D. (eds.), *The Regulated Economy: A Historical Approach to Political Economy*. Chicago: University of Chicago Press.

Weingast, Barry R., 2009. "Second Generation Fiscal Federalism: the Implications of Fiscal Incentives." *Journal of Urban Economics* 65 (2009) 279–93.

Weingast, Barry R., 2013. "Second Generation Fiscal Federalism: Political Aspects of Decentralization and Economic Development." <http://dx.doi.org/10.1016/j.worlddev.2013.01.003>.Weingast, Barry R., Shepsle, Kenneth A., and Johnsen, Christopher, 1981. "The Political Economy of Benefits and Costs: A Neoclassical Approach to Distributive Politics." *Journal of Political Economy* 89, 642–64.

Wibbels, Erik, 2003. "Bailouts, Budget Constraints, nd Leviathans: Comparative Federalism and Lessons From the Early United States." *Comparative Political Studies* 36, 475–508.

Wiesner, Eduardo, 2003. "Fiscal Federalism in Latin America: From Entitlements to Markets." Inter-American Development Bank, Washington, DC.

Zhuravskaya, Ekaterina, 2000. "Incentives to Provide Local Public Goods: Fiscal Federalism Russian Style." Journal of Public Economics 76 (3).

8

Maintaining Taxes at the Centre Despite Decentralization

Interactions with National Reforms

Giorgio Brosio and Juan Pablo Jiménez

8.1 Introduction

Centralization of taxes is a clear feature of the long-term evolution of federal and decentralized systems, if this is taken to mean simply that present-day federal governments have taxing powers that are much larger than those reserved to them in their original constitutions. Also, transfers from federal to local governments were totally absent in the initial stages of all federations and unitary states, meaning that federal/central governments now have more tax resources than they need for their direct expenditure, while subnational governments now have lower tax resources compared to their expenditures (the so-called vertical fiscal imbalance). This long-term trend is compatible with extensive fluctuations of tax revenue over time and of the assignment of taxes between national and subnational governments.

There are immediate reasons for the appearance of subnational transfers, the most immediate of which is equalization. No present-day federal or decentralized system operates without some system of conditional or non-conditional equalization grants. What is less straightforward to explain is that even highly decentralized systems rely to a very large extent on transfers for the financing of basic subnational expenditure responsibilities, and that transfers play a predominant role in the financing of subnational governments in a large number of federations, such as most in Latin America. In general, one would expect that, during decentralization processes, the importance of local taxes should increase. This is, however, not always the case, as evidence for Italy shows. Decentralization of policies and expenditure responsibilities is often not accompanied by decentralization of tax assignments. This may happen because national tax reforms, which are concomitant with decentralization processes, can pre-empt the space for local taxes; or because reliance by subnational governments on transfers from the central government looks more attractive to local politicians.

While centralization of taxes can be fairly easily explained on the basis of a superior tax administration capacity in the central government, it is more difficult to explain why federal and decentralized systems are ready to accept, with tax centralization and the consequent demise of local tax administration capacity, a situation where they are at the mercy of the central government that could renege its commitment to finance subnational expenditure with its own grants.

This chapter analyzes this issue and tries to provide an explanation of the readiness of subnational governments to give up their power to tax. The chapter is divided into four sections plus the conclusions. The first section starts with the meaning of tax centralization and provides a review of the literature. The second presents the options available to the central and the subnational governments when they are negotiating ways of financing expenditure derived from the devolution of spending responsibilities. The third section deals with the commitment issue. Evidence is provided in the fourth section, and it is followed by the conclusions.

8.2 Centralization of Taxes in the Literature

Despite the fact that one of the main tenets of the literature on fiscal federalism prescribes that subnational governments should be financed as much as possible through local taxes and other sources of own revenue, the literature on the actual trends of tax (de)centralization and on their interpretation is not very large. The meaning of tax centralization and how to measure it is also not always well defined.

The literature on fiscal federalism makes a distinction between subnational governments' own local taxes (and fees) and other taxes. According to the scholarship, own taxes are those for which local governments have discretionary power in determining the burden they impose on their citizens. This discretionary power can be exerted with three different instruments (and their combination): (1) tax administration; (2) setting of tax rates; and (3) determination of the tax bases. Hence tax (de)centralization should refer to three instruments, and in doing so should also inform the measurement issue. One cannot infer simply from changes in the distribution of tax revenue between levels of government that tax (de)centralization has changed. For example, if transfers to local governments are replaced with shared tax revenue, no real decentralization of taxes has taken place if local governments have no discretionary power for determining the size of shared revenue.

Centralization of taxes being neither a necessity nor a continuous trend, we can observe extensive fluctuations over time in the assignment of tax bases between the national and the subnational governments. Even larger fluctuations can be observed in the apportionment of tax collections between the central and local governments. This is because, among other factors, tax collections do not depend only on assignment, but also on interdependent decisions about use of tax powers by distinct levels of government. For example, in the last seventy years the apportionment of the collection of personal income tax has varied widely in Canada, following agreements between the federal government and the Provinces about the use of their tax bases and the decision of the federal government to cede to the Provinces a number of tax points for personal income tax (see Chernick and Tennant (2010) and Winer (2000)).

There are various branches in the literature trying to explain or to make policy prescriptions about tax (de)centralization. The largest body of the literature is the normative, or prescriptive, theory of fiscal federalism (see Oates (1972), Inman and Rubinfeld (1997), and Ambrosanio and Bordignon (2006) for an excellent review). While initially (in the classical federal constitutions) the main criterion for assignment was avoidance of tax exportation (more precisely the minimization of tax impediments to the smooth working of the domestic market (thus tariff duties were assigned to the center, and sales taxes as well in most cases, such as in Canada)), the literature has later focused on the mobility of the tax base, more specifically on the elasticity of the tax base with respect to changes in tax rates.

Most of the normative literature stresses the efficiency advantages of centralization for the collection of all but a small number of taxes (such as the property tax). The prescriptions of the normative literature bear, however, only a pale resemblance with the real world.

Turning to positive theory, Breton (1996) presents a general explanation of the assignment of powers between levels of government. His analysis does not refer specifically to taxes, but rather to all government functions. Breton's argument is that assignment derives from competition among layers of government. In the case of taxation, economies of scale in administration and in collection would make the federal government the most likely winner, because it can better exploit these economies.[1] At the same time, other factors such as difficulty of coordination may constrain the bargaining power of

[1] Faguet (2014) and Faguet and Wietzke (2006) elaborate on this point.

central government. However, as for the other functions, Breton points out that there is no prevailing trend towards centralization or of backing away from it. This conclusion is also maintained in the positive literature.

This literature is mostly the work of political scientists (Riker, 1964; Filipov, Ordeshook, and Shvetsova, 2004; and more recently Diaz-Cayeros, 2006), addresses specific cases, and derives conclusions that in some instances do not go much beyond them. The authors stress the importance of the structure of political parties and of their capacity to make commitments for the striking of federal bargains concerning the allocation of taxing powers. In addition, political parties—more precisely the national structure of them—are essential for ensuring the benefits of tax decentralization (in addition to general decentralization). This is because with national parties, local officials have career incentives to take into account not only the benefits to their local constituency, but also the overspill of their decisions on other jurisdictions. This was the main argument developed by Riker (1964) for assessing the benefits of decentralization, and is a view particularly popular with Latin American scientists. O'Neill's (2003 and 2005) contributions to the analysis of decentralization are the main reference point of this literature and they establish a link between this process and the electoral incentives of political parties.

The political parties approach to centralization/decentralization has also been developed by Enikolopov and Zhuravskaya (2007). Filippov, Ordeshook, and Shvetsova (2004) are amongst the most widely quoted authors on the issue. However, their focus is on the design of stable federalism systems and on overall (de)centralizing trends in federations and not on (de)centralization of taxation per se. Clearly, proper tax arrangements contribute to stability and derive from proper institutions ensuring agreements among levels of governments. These include: (1) fundamental constitutional principles designing basic rules, such as the right to secession (their Level 1 constraints); (2) constitutional principles regarding the amendment of the constitution, the structure of the separation of powers, and the principles guiding the legislation process; and (3) political institutions that impact on the implementation of the rules and on the agreements reached through bargaining, such as electoral systems, and the structure of party systems and of political parties.

The centralizing role of national parties is questioned by Chhibber and Kollman (2004), who maintain that while one can surely argue that political parties are actually the instruments of centralization and decentralization, "evident trends toward centralization and decentralization are actually the consequences of larger forces that work mostly independently of the party system" (see Chapter 1 therein).

There is also a nascent political economy approach to the centralization of taxes. Or, better, it is possible, as Rodden (2004) shows, to develop some contributions to the political economy of decentralization in view of understanding the centralization of taxes. Rodden draws specifically on Bolton and Roland (1997) and sketches very briefly a model where centralization of taxes is promoted by a coalition of relatively underdeveloped jurisdictions that also keeps the cost of subsequent modifications high.

Levi (1988) provides a careful account of the process by which Australian States relinquished their substantial taxing powers and were left almost completely dependent on transfers from the federal government. There is no formal model of this process, but Levi stresses three factors: (a) the superior tax administration capacity of the federal government; (b) the capacity of the latter to keep commitments with the States due to strong national structure of political parties; and (c) the increasing unpopularity of widely diverging State tax systems. In other federal systems, wars and demand for social protection policies have facilitated the task of the federal government that Levi (1988: 150) views as essentially a revenue maximizer.

Winer (2000) compares the Australian and Canadian cases. In Australia the States have given up most of their taxing powers, accepting a centralization of intergovernmental relations that goes much further than the constitution prescribes. In Canada the evolution of fiscal assignment between the federal government and the Provinces is far from linear. Periods of intense centralization have been succeeded by periods of equally intense decentralization of taxes. In both cases, also, the constitutional discipline bears no resemblance with actual assignments in the various phases (see, especially, indirect taxation).

Diaz-Cayeros' work (2006) is focused primarily on Mexico and Latin America. He provides a stylized model of the bargaining process between the federal and state governments. Mexico is, possibly, the most tax-centralized federation. Centralization in Mexico is explained by Diaz-Cayero by the one-party (PRI) regime that prevailed for half a century and that allowed the federal government to make a credible commitment vis à vis the regional politicians concerning the payment of the transfers that replaced the taxes administered by the States. In the experience of other federations in the region (Argentina and Brazil), it is important to include the alternation in power between democratic and military governments as an element that helps in understanding the changes in tax authority between central and subnational governments.

In line with Brennan and Buchanan (1980), Blankart (2000) views tax centralization as the result of cartelization efforts between layers of government. By reaching an agreement on sharing the same tax base of personal income tax, for example, and on leaving the definition of the tax base and the administration of tax to the federal government, the federal and subnational government reduce the intensity of tax competition and can increase collections. Tax centralization is thus the obvious goal of greedy politicians, but it can be attenuated, if not eliminated, by proper institutions such as constitutional assignment of taxing powers, or by instruments of direct democracy such as referenda.

8.3 What is at Stake with Tax (De)Centralization: The Bargaining Framework

Building on the bargaining approach described by Díaz-Cayeros, let's consider the negotiation between a federal government and a region or a number of regions all of equal size and characteristics. The region is considering whether to take on a policy responsibility, namely education,[2] that is assigned in the constitution to the central government, but that may be assigned to regions if they request it. The new function obviously has to be financed. Hence the bargaining refers simultaneously to the expenditure and the revenue assignment. Introducing expenditure into the analysis allows us to focus on a typical decentralization process involving both sides of the budget.[3] We later relax the equality of regions by assuming that they differ by income conditions.)

To simplify the model, let's assume that there is only one earmarked tax for funding this function; the education tax. The tax base and the tax rates are determined in the constitution. Variations in the volume of tax collections depend only on the efficiency of administration. Skills and effort capacity can vary between levels of government. Since we are focusing on the negotiation between the central government and a single region, we will not consider possible scale economies. However, negotiation also could take place with other regions, since they have the same characteristics. In this case, scale economies in tax administration would be considered by the central government and would modify the bargaining process, making the perspective of tax centralization more attractive to it.

We are not considering variations in tax rates or in the tax bases that are, along with tax administration, the essential ingredients of subnational governments' own taxes. The main reason for this is to maintain simplicity: inserting tax rate variation would require the consideration of strategic choice if the tax base has some mobility. Moreover, getting or keeping tax administration is possibly more important in terms of subnational autonomy than setting of tax rates, since administration gives subnational government direct

[2] Education is one of the most important sectors of subnational expenditure across the world (Channa and Faguet, 2012).

[3] Diaz-Cayeros and other authors introduce a third, more radical, alternative. Regions can choose between tax decentralization, tax centralization, and secession. Their models stay, however, on the revenue side of the budget.

access to revenues without any intermediation and can also lead to different amounts of collections.

The assignment of education and of the administration of tax to either level of government are the objects of negotiation.

Let's start with the choice of the region. The choice is split into a two-stage process. Namely, the region has to decide if it wants to take on the new responsibility and how the new responsibility will be funded. There is no obvious hierarchical relation between the two stages of the decision process. The terms of negotiation are the following:

1. Centralization of tax administration will produce expected collections of C, accompanied by an expected transfer to regions of T, leaving revenue to the federal government equal to $C - T$.
2. Tax administration by the region will generate expected revenue L for the region.

The region will receive T with tax centralization and L with tax decentralization. Ceteris paribus, that is, if nothing other than revenue considerations enter into the decision-making process, the region will prefer tax centralization when $T > L$. It will prefer decentralization, by contrast, when $T < L$, that is, when the transfer it expects from the central government is lower than its own expected tax collections.

Let's turn to the devolution of expenditure. The region has to check whether its preferred choice for revenue—$R = \max(T,L)$—is enough to cover the expected new expenditure, E.

Summing up, in financial terms the region will ask for the assignment of the new function and will choose the transfer if: $T > L$ and $T \geq E$.

Let's turn now to the federal government. Again, it is faced with a double choice process. It has to decide whether to accept the devolution of education to the region and, second, the way it will be financed: either it will keep the administration of the tax for itself, or it will accept its devolution to the region.

The federal government will prefer tax centralization if the expected transfer it has to pay to the region is lower than the expected collections of the tax. Secondly, it will accept the devolution of the function if the grant is lower than, or at most equal to, the expenditure it is presently making for education. Otherwise, it will make no financial gain from the change. That is, the federal government will accept the whole package provided that: $C > T$ and $T \leq E$.

When we combine the four constraints we find that an agreement can be reached if: $C > L$, and $T = E$.

The agreement will be reached if tax centralization brings in higher revenue than decentralization, implying better administration with centralization, and if the size of the transfer is equal to the size of expenditures. The agreement means that there will be devolution of expenditure responsibilities only, with no devolution of tax administration responsibilities. Under the existing conditions, no level of government is going to gain in terms of revenue from the bargain. This is because the region will get exactly what is needed to fund the new expenditure and the central government will have to pay a transfer that is equal to the foregone expenditure.

There are, however, other possible financial reasons for the bargain and they derive from future actions by both levels of government. For example, the region might believe that it could spend with greater efficiency on education than the federal government, and so save part of the grant for other purposes. The central government, on the other hand, might believe that it could achieve larger efficiency gains in future administration of the tax. The gains could also accrue from centralizing deals reached with other regions. With the increase in the number of deals, national tax reforms also become more likely because the central government will reap larger benefits deriving from reform. This could explain the concomitance, frequently observed, between decentralization and tax reform.

The arguments developed in this section presume that governments are revenue (or power) maximizers. In a democratic setting, governments are constrained by voters, or more precisely by the extent and quality of political competition. This implies that governments have to maximize the difference between revenue, R, and expenditure, E, for the public services requested by citizens. The difference can be termed, as in the bureaucratic and managerial literature, as slack, and it can be spent for uses that give utility to Politicians, without necessarily implying corruption. What is more important to consider is that the amount of slack is reduced by the intensity of competition that forces politicians, if they want to stay in power, to use the expenditure according to the preference of citizens. In a truly competitive system—for example in the "consensual democracy" as defined by McGuire and Olson (1996) slack would disappear—$R - E = 0$—and all tax proceeds will be spent on the public goods desired; the politicians' choices are completely constrained by voters.

8.3.1 *Tax Centralization with Differences in Income and Fiscal Capacity between Regions*

Clearly, this is a more realistic case, but with less straightforward conclusions because redistribution comes to the fore and it is quite difficult to model. With tax decentralization, the revenue available to each region is related to its income and wealth conditions. Rich regions will have a larger tax base and larger potential revenue than poor regions: $L_r > L_n > L_p$, where the subscript distinguishes between rich and poor regions.

The choice between the tax and transfer will thus depend, prima facie, on the existing level of central government expenditure for education (centralization does not imply, de jure or de facto, homogeneity of levels of service provision across the country). If education expenditure is the same (per capita) across all the country, $L_r > T$ for the rich regions, and $L_p < T$ for the poor ones, making the former less inclined to accept the grant and to ask for devolution of expenditure responsibility, unless they fear they will have a weaker capacity in their tax administration or high expectations on their capacity to shrink expenditure.

If present levels of expenditure are higher in the rich regions than in the poor ones—this situation is actually observable for a range of services in many countries—the propensity of rich regions to choose transfer will increase, since its size will vary according to the income conditions, giving $T_r > T_p$.

Propensity for tax centralization can become stronger when we look at commitment issues, to which we come now.

8.4 Dependence on Transfers, and Commitment Problems

Intended future actions—savings on expenditure and higher tax administration effort—naturally introduce the commitment issue into the discussion.[4]

Like any other contract, intergovernmental long-term contracts are subject to this problem. Once the region has accepted the centralization of education tax and the compensating transfers, it is potentially at the mercy of central government. This government could in subsequent years renege on the agreement and reduce the size of the grant. One does not have to think of extreme situations where future transfers are set to zero to stress the importance of the commitment problem. Once the region has given up its taxing powers, taking them up again will take time—especially when they consist of tax administration—and even a modest reduction in value of the grant will do much harm to its finances.

Both the literature and observable experience provide more or less effective solutions to the commitment problem, depending on the context where they apply. There are broadly three solutions. The first is to increase the initial size of the transfer, to take care of the fact that the region applies a discount factor to transfers in future years. In other words, the central government posts a bond. This is an elegant analytical solution in a typical two-period time frame. The federal government will pay $T_1 = T(1+d)$ in the first period, where d is the

[4] Faguet (2004) in his bargaining model of decentralization also stresses the strategic importance of commitment in decentralization processes. Furthermore, when institutional conditions are insufficient for commitment, subnational governments should not relinquish strategic powers such as tax administration.

discount rate, to assuage the region's fear that the transfer will be reduced in the second period. This solution becomes more problematic in a more realistic multi-year time frame.

The second solution is to act with legal provisions. The commitment problem can be mitigated through the insertion in the constitution, using a law above the ordinary level when this kind of law exists, of a protection clause about the size of the transfer.

The third solution refers to the structure of political parties. This is the major argument advanced in political science literature on tax centralization. In essence, commitment is firmer when parties have a national structure at both levels of government and, especially, when the same party governs at both the federal and the subnational level. It is firmer still when the same party stays unchallenged in power for a lengthy period, as happened in Mexico with the PRI for seventy years (Diaz-Cayeros, 2006).

8.4.1 *Political Interactions between Levels of Government as a Major Source Of Commitment*

Political/electoral interactions are often a main player in ensuring commitment. The argument starts with considering that in (almost) every present-day intergovernmental system the various spheres of government are never completely separated, even in extremely decentralized systems. One implication of this missing separation is that the policies and services provided by subnational governments also impact on the popularity—and thus the probability of re-election—of the central government.

With the devolution of a function also inevitably comes the commitment to the transfers for that function if voters consider that this is also a central responsibility and hold the national government accountable for it. Coming back to our example, the region can clearly bet on this commitment, when it accepts funding through central government transfer. Furthermore, national government's dependence on regionally provided education could enhance the role of the federal government as an insurer against asymmetric shocks. This role is increasingly discussed and tested in the literature, although with no unanimous results (Hepp and Von Hagen, 2000; Rodden and Wibbels, 2010).

Summing up, comparative advantage in expenditure efficiency and in tax administration are crucial factors for explaining tax (de)centralization. Central government and a region can agree on devolution from the former to the latter of an expenditure responsibility and to finance it with transfers if the central government has (or is believed to have) better tax administration and the region has (or is believed to have) more efficiency and can make savings in the expenditure. However, the region has to ensure that the central government will not renege on the agreement and reduce the grant. Legal provision may help solve the commitment problem. At least as important is the fact that voters can hold central government partly responsible for delivery of the service, during and after the devolution taking place.

8.5 Evidence

We present selective evidence to corroborate our arguments. It refers to three countries—Italy, Argentina, and Canada—that have experienced substantial reshuffling of taxation powers between levels of government, either in the framework of large-scale tax reforms (Italy), after substantial devolution of expenditure responsibilities (Argentina), or in the wake of big societal events, such as a war, necessitating a substantial increase of tax revenue (Canada).

8.5.1 *Italy: The Tax Reform of 1970*

In 1970 a large-scale reform of the Italian tax system took place. It was based on the creation of a comprehensive personal income tax, a new corporate income tax aligned with the model prevailing in industrial countries, and the elimination of a number of nuisance taxes. VAT was also introduced to comply with European regulations and to modernize the taxation of consumption. This comprehensive national tax reform was enacted just before the regionalization of the country and it centralized all the taxes. All the existing municipal taxes (among them a simplified personal income tax and a octroi type sales tax) were abolished, while the regional governments were born without any taxing power and were financed (as were the municipalities) until the 1990s entirely through transfers from central government (and neither level of government complained). Hence, a major step towards the creation of a more decentralized system of government took place alongside the most complete centralization of taxes one could conceive.

The tax reform was conceived in the 1960s when the country found itself in a political mood very favorable to government intervention in the economy. Tax centralization rested primarily on the presumption of greater central government efficiency in the administration of taxes, which is difficult to test.

8.5.2 *Argentina: Creation of the Regime of Federal Co-participation Taxes in 1935*

In principle, or better de jure, Argentina is quite a decentralized federation. The present (1994) Constitution states that the Provinces retain all powers not delegated to the federal government. With regard to the financing side, the National Constitution (Article 75, paragraph 2) delimits tax powers of the central government and the Provinces by establishing that indirect taxes are concurrent between both levels, except in the case of import and export duties, which are the exclusive prerogative of the federal government (Article 4). In principle, direct taxes are exclusively provincial, but the federal government has the right to use them for a limited time if defense, common security, and general welfare require it. Hence in principle, Provinces have large access to taxing powers, but they make only partial use of them, preferring instead to rely on shared revenues collected by central government.[5]

The system of co-participation (revenue sharing) began in 1935, through laws 12139, 12143 and 12147, and was designed to increase resources collected by the federal government in order to face financial difficulties caused by the fall in revenue from foreign trade during the 1930s crisis. New taxes were introduced (on sales and profits), and the internal taxes at federal government level (excise taxes) were reordered and unified, eliminating those taxes that had the same characteristics as those collected at the subnational level.

In order to achieve the approval of these new taxes, two different mechanisms of distribution were established: on one hand, considering the concurrent character that the National Constitution had introduced for the new taxes (sales and profits), a compensatory revenue-sharing mechanism was stipulated for these taxes (a primary co-participation of 82.5 per cent for the Nation and 17.5 per cent for the fourteen existing Provinces and the Municipality of the City of Buenos Aires). In the case of internal taxes, their distribution was established in response to the derogation of similar taxes collected by the Provinces. Therefore, in lieu of the taxes abolished, each Province was guaranteed the same amount collected the previous year, plus a percentage increase. The commitment problem was mainly solved by three elements: the coexistence of authoritarian government with fragmented parliamentary power; the introduction and implementation of an automatic and daily system for disbursing the co-participation transfers by the Central Bank; and the granting of debt bail-out (law 12139) to several Provinces.

A further factor to remember is that tax centralization rested primarily on the presumption of greater central government efficiency in the administration of taxes.

8.5.3 *Argentina: The Decentralization of Education in 1991*

Still in Argentina, the experience in decentralizing education in 1991 and the subsequent shaping of the National Fund for Teacher's Incentive (*Fondo de*

[5] In fact, provincial taxes (there are four main ones, namely on real estate, motor vehicles, gross income, and also stamp duties) plus revenue from royalties represent some 40 per cent of total provincial revenues, the rest being supplement by the federal government through its transfer systems (Cetrángolo and Jiménez, 2004).

Incentivo Docente) in 1998 constitutes an interesting case that supports our argument.

In late 1991 the administration and financing of educational services, until then in the hands of the central government (mainly high schools), was decentralized to the Provinces. At the time this decentralization was decided, high school teachers employed by the central government had lower salaries than those employed by provincial governments. Therefore, the problem was to decide who would be in charge of leveling out the salary difference. This situation generated long negotiations and intense labor union conflicts. Finally, at the end of 1998, the federal government approved the National Fund for Teacher's Incentive, which would be financed with a provisional and federal tax on cars, reassuming, in part, the salary financing that was decentralized seven years before. In accordance with the decentralization index (Brosio, 2007), this means that this sector had a higher level of centralization than could be shown by a conventional indicator.

In 1999, facing a fiscal crisis, the authorities implemented a tax reform to improve public sector revenue. To get the additional revenues from this reform, the central government proposed to the provinces replacing the revenue-sharing mechanism with a fixed transfer amount. The commitment problem was solved with the implementation of the Program of Fiscal Adjustment and Financial Restructuring (Devoto and Jiménez, 2000), which included a restructuring of subnational debt, whichhad increased significantly in the previous decade, vis àvis a fiscal deficit reduction program.

8.5.4 *Italy: The 2001 Quasi-Federalization of the System of Intergovernmental Relations*

The bargaining model presented above is to some extent tailored to explain the recent decentralization process of Italy. The new Constitution extends the range of basic responsibilities assigned to regional governments to education, social protection, and a number of other areas. At the same time, there is no mention of subnational tax instruments, neither in the constitution, nor in the recent law (law 42 of 2009) that authorizes the government to issue the decrees that will define the new revenue system of regional (and local) governments.

Law 42 pays only lip service to regional tax autonomy, making a vague reference to the future introduction of regional and local taxes, whereas it addresses in detail the new system of equalization grants. The law explicitly mandates that IRAP, which is the most productive of regional own taxes (ensuring approximately 30 per cent of total regional current revenue and 70 per cent of own tax collections) will be eliminated as a soon as general conditions of public finances allow. The law also does not reverse the recent trend towards the shrinking of the base of the property tax, which is the main tax handle of municipalities.

This is somewhat surprising. Despite initial protestations in favor of tax autonomy, the richest regions and municipalities in the North seem to be happy to live with a system that will give them presumably very modest tax instruments. There are, however, reasons for the acceptance on behalf of all levels of government. The central government can believe that there are substantial possibilities of improving the tax administration process, or reforming taxes. Recent governments have all announced their intention to proceed with comprehensive tax reform. The likely strategy is that through tax reform they will be able to satisfy subnational governments' claims for resources while at the same time expanding central government control over the whole tax system.

On the other hand, subnational governments—including those of the rich areas that have huge own revenue potentials—may be happy with a financing system that makes them largely dependent on central government transfers. This is because it will be based on a generous transfer system for a set of basic local functions that accounts for 70 to 80 per cent of total subnational expenditure. These transfers will be based on the standard cost of provision according to nationally defined standards of service delivery. There are thus basically two guarantees for subnational governments concerning their (future) revenue. First, the central government has committed to covering the whole cost of service provision that corresponds to the standards. Second, the central government appears to be fully committed to the payment of adequate transfers in the future. This is because the introduction of nationally defined standards means that the policy responsibilities to which these standards refer are still, at least partially, centralized in Italy according to our previous definition of (de) centralization. That is, the introduction of standards implies that voters still consider the central government (partially) responsible for these services. This solves the commitment problem.

Obviously, these recent events are also compatible with a political economy approach to decentralization that stresses the costs for the rich regions to reverse a long time established trend in tax centralization that is supported by a large front of less rich regions.

8.5.5 *Canada: Moving Personal and Corporate Income Tax Up and Down*

Our model stressing the importance of efficiency in tax administration is supported by past Canadian experience with personal and corporate income tax. In 1941, the Provinces gave up their right to use personal and corporation income tax to help the federal government to finance the war effort. In 1947 *tax rental agreements* were signed between the federal government and the Provinces (with the exception of Ontario and Quebec) by which the latter gave up their right to administer the two taxes, getting in exchange a transfer equivalent to the lost revenue. They thus agreed to tax centralization. The tax rental agreements were replaced with the *tax collection agreements,* whereby the Provinces resumed their right to use both taxes by choosing their tax rates, which would have then been applied to a federally defined tax base. Both taxes remained under federal government administration. Hence, according to the prevailing index, Canada reduced its degree of tax centralization. Of course, centralization of the determination of the tax base and of tax administration can be viewed as clear evidence of government cartelization. At the same time it shows the importance of efficiency considerations with regard to tax administration.

8.6 Conclusion

This chapter has aimed to contribute to the literature on tax (de)centralization. It has presented a very simple bargaining model between the federal/central government and the regions to illustrate the main choices open to both levels of government in terms of revenue and expenditure assignments. The main results are that transfers will prevail over subnational taxes—that is, centralization of taxes will take place—when substantial efficiency gains are expected through the centralization of tax administration.

This chapter's main contribution lies, we believe, in the introduction of the expenditure side of the budget and its relevance for solving the commitment issue. When voters hold central government politically, or better, electorally, accountable for a devolved function, the latter must, after centralization of taxes, keep its commitment on the size of the transfer.

Selective evidence on Italy, Argentina, and Canada has been provided, yet our findings may be applied to a number of countries and systems.

References

Ambrosanio, M.F. and M. Bordignon, 2006. "Normative versus Positive Theories of Revenue Assignments in Federations." In Ahmad E. and G. Brosio (eds.), *Handbook of Fiscal Federalism*. Cheltenham, Edward Elgar.

Blankart, C., 2000. "The Process of Government Centralization: A Constitutional View." *Constitutional Political Economy*, Volume 11, Number 1, 27–39.

Bolton, P. and G. Roland. 1997. "The Breakup of Nations: A Political Economy Analysis." *Quarterly Journal of Economics* Vol. CXII Issue 4, November.

Brennan, G. and J. Buchanan, 1980. *The Power to Tax. Analytical Foundations of a Fiscal Constitution.* Cambridge, UK: Cambridge University Press.

Breton, A., 1996. *Competitive Governments. An Economic Theory of Politics and Public Finance.* Cambridge, UK: Cambridge University Press.

Brosio, G., 2007. "Cases for and Against Transparency/Obfuscation in Intergovernmental Relations." In Breton, A., G. Galeotti, P. Salmon, and R. Wintrobe (eds.) *The Economics of Transparency in Politics.* Aldershot, UK: Ashgate.

Cetrángolo, O. and J. P. Jiménez, 2004. "The Relations Between Different Levels of Government in Argentina." Cepal Review, 84, December.

Channa, A. and J.P. Faguet, 2012. "Decentralization of Health and Education in Developing Countries: A Quality-Adjusted Review of the Empirical Literature." LSE/STICERD Working Paper No. EOPP 38.

Chernick, H. and J. Tennant, 2010. "Federal-State Tax Interactions in the United States and Canada." *Publius: The Journal of Federalism,* 40(3), 508–33.

Chhibber, P. and K. Kollman, 2004. *The Formation of National Party Systems: Federalism and Party Competition in Canada, Great Britain, India, and the United States.* Princeton, NJ: Princeton University Press.

Devoto, F. and J.P. Jiménez, 2000. "Argentina: Coordination of subnational borrowing." In Ahmad, E., and Tanzi, V. (eds), *Managing Fiscal Decentralization.* London, UK: Routledge.

Diaz-Cayeros, A., 2006. *Federalism, Fiscal Authority, and Centralization in Latin America.* Cambridge, UK: Cambridge University Press.

Enikolopov, R. and E. Zhuravskaya, 2007. "Decentralization and Political Institutions." *Journal of Public Economics,* 91, pp. 2281–90.

Faguet, J.P., 2004. *Why So Much Centralization? A Model of Primitive Centripetal Accumulation.* STICERD—Development Economics Papers.

Faguet, J.P., 2014. "Can Sub-National Autonomy Strengthen Democracy in Bolivia?" *Publius: The Journal of Federalism,* 44(1): 51–81; doi: 10.1093/publius/pjt020.

Faguet, J.P. and F.B. Wietzke, 2006. "Social Funds and Decentralization: Optimal Institutional Design." *Public Administration and Development,* 26(4): 303–15.

Filippov, M., O. Shvetsova, and P. Ordeshook, 2004. *Designing Federalism: A Theory Of Self-Sustainable Federal Institutions.* Cambridge, UK: Cambridge University Press.

Hepp, R and J. Von Hagen, 2000. *Regional Risk-sharing and Redistribution in the German Federation.* Fordham Center for European Integration Studies (ZEI); Centre for Economic Policy Research, September.

Inman, R. P. and D. Rubinfeld, 1996. "Designing Tax Policy in Federalist Economies: An Overview." *Journal of Public Economics,* Volume 60, Issue 3, pp. 307–34.

Levi, M., 1988. *Of Rule and Revenue.* Berkeley: University of California Press.

McGuire, M. and M. Olson, 1996. "The Economics of Autocracy and Majority Rule: The Invisible Hand and the Use of Force." *Journal of Economic Literature,* 34 (1), 72–96.

Mueller, D. C., 1989. *Public Choice III.* Cambridge, UK: Cambridge University Press.

O'Neill, K., 2005. *Decentralizing the State: Elections, Parties, and Local Power in the Andes.* New York: Cambridge University Press.

Oates, W., 1972. *Fiscal Federalism.* New York: Harcourt Brace Jovanovich.

Riker, W., 1964. *Federalism: Origin, Operation, Significance.* Boston: Little Brown.

Rodden, J., 2004. "On the Migration of Fiscal Sovereignty." *PS: Political Science & Politics*, 37, 427–43.

Rodden, J. and E. Wibbels, 2010. "Fiscal Decentralization And The Business Cycle: An Empirical Study Of Seven Federations." *Economics and Politics*, vol. 22, March, pp. 37–67.

Winer, S., 2000. "On The Reassignment of Fiscal Powers in a Federal State." In G. Galeotti, P. Salmon, and R. Wintrobe (eds.) *The Political Economy of Collective Decisions*. Cambridge, UK: Cambridge University Press.

9

Political Capture of Decentralization

Vote Buying through Grants to Local Jurisdictions

Stuti Khemani

9.1 Introduction

Decentralization in the developing world has involved the political selection of the design of local jurisdictions by central and regional governments. In many countries, especially in the African and South Asian regions, and in poor provinces in Latin America, the governments' choice of decentralization instruments results in the creation of very local village-level governments, with low capacity, almost no access to own tax bases, and spending and decision-making powers restricted to the administering of higher-tier grants for local infrastructure and beneficiary selection of welfare schemes. In contrast, decentralization to municipalities or cities with revenue-raising potential has been stalled, with revenue powers being retained by central or regional governments.[1] Also, in the case of local public services such as village schools, even as some institutions for community participation are created, teacher management powers remain with central or regional governments. Devarajan et al. (2009) have characterized such decentralization as "partial," and have examined its implications for local service delivery.

This chapter addresses the question of why countries choose to decentralize partially. In one view, even grants-based decentralization to rural local

[1] In India, for example, decentralization has largely taken the form of charging locally elected village governments, the *gram panchayats*, with beneficiary selection of poverty alleviation schemes; while municipal governments with access to tax bases and user charges are denied the power to set these, and local revenue-raising power is retained by state governments (Mohanty et al., 2007).

governments is a significant institutional reform to address political agency problems in developing countries, particularly of government responsiveness to poor citizens (World Bank, various; Bardhan, 2002).[2] This chapter examines grants-financed decentralization from an alternative perspective, as a strategic political choice which enables the targeting of benefits to select constituents, at the expense of broad public goods. In this model, decentralization is subject to political capture, with local spending targeted to vote buying, patronage, or pork-barrel projects. The tension in the model is between clientelist politics (targeted transfers to buy votes) versus the broad public interest—clientelist transfers may indeed be targeted to the poor, but only to some of them or only in small amounts, at the expense of broad public goods for larger numbers.[3]

The chapter therefore explores a political economy explanation for cases where decentralization remains partial long after the initiation of reforms. It argues that partial decentralization is selected and maintained by politicians in the face of increasing participation by swing voters, because it enables them to win elections by dividing the strength of swing voters, and continue to provide targeted benefits to core supporters. Decentralization in this theory helps prolong clientelistic political competition at the expense of broad public goods platforms, even when elections become more broad-based and contested.

This risk of "political capture" of decentralization is to be distinguished from that of elite capture analyzed by Bardhan and Mookherjee (2000, 2005, 2007a). Under political capture, even when local spending is better targeted to poor citizens than centrally or provincially allocated spending, such local targeting enables central or regional political parties to buy votes and win elections even as they reduce general government allocations to broad public goods. Much of the evaluation of impact of moving from centralized to decentralized resource allocation has focused on whether the benefit incidence of decentralized spending is more likely to be on poorer households (Araujo et al., 2008; Bardhan and Mookherjee, 2007; Bardhan et al., 2007; Galasso and Ravallion, 2005; Mansuri and Rao, 2004). This chapter does not compare allocations by central and local agents, instead examining the

[2] Governments in developing countries pursuing decentralization reforms also describe these as designed to promote greater participation of poor citizens in public decision-making, and to strengthen citizen ability to exact accountability from their public agents. For example, these views were provided in publicly available conference papers by the initiator of Bolivia's *Ley de Participacion Popular* (Sanchez de Lozada, 2000), and the implementer of India's Panchayati Raj Act (Aiyer, 2009).

[3] Indeed, theoretical and empirical studies of "vote-buying" have concluded that such transfers are targeted to the poor (Harding, 2008; Stokes, 2005; Brusco et al., 2004).

political choice to decentralize and its implications for consolidated government tax and spending decisions.

The theoretical framework is derived from the literature on political determinants of fiscal policy, where political parties consist of organized interest groups that derive benefits from holding office and from club goods targeted to their group (Alesina and Perotti, 1995; Faguet, 2004; Persson and Tabellini, 2000; Persson et al., 2007). Within this political economy framework, it is difficult to find conditions under which any governing party would choose to decentralize. The typical conditions for decentralization in the technical literature, which would lead a benevolent planner to decentralize, revolve around heterogeneity of preferences across local settlements (Tiebout, 1956; Oates, 1972). In the presence of such heterogeneity, various models show that a benevolent planner would decentralize fiscal resources to be allocated at the discretion of local governments. However, when governments pursue political objectives, heterogeneity of preferences alone is not sufficient for a central incumbent to give up fiscal powers to jurisdictions where rival parties could be in power and thereby exercise control over the allocation of those revenues.

There are surprisingly few formal models of the political choice to decentralize powers and resources to lower-level jurisdictions. Available models of endogenous decentralization, to the best of the author's knowledge, are all consistent with the original insight of Oates (1972) that decentralization arises from regional heterogeneity of preferences. Oberholzer-Gee and Strumpf (2002) model state legislative decision-making for decentralization to districts within a state, and obtain as an equilibrium greater likelihood of decentralization in those states where there is greater heterogeneity of preferences across districts (on the policy issue being considered for decentralization, in this case liquor licensing in the USA). Cremer and Palfrey (1996), Lockwood (2004), and Redoano and Scharf (2004) examine the role of decision-making rules—national referenda versus legislative voting, majority and unanimity rules—in the selection of the degree of centralization, with preferences for decentralization distributed regionally.

Examinations of decentralization as a political strategy focus on incentives of national politicians to bypass regional governments that pose a political threat. Dickovick (2007) analyzes decentralization to municipalities in Peru, Brazil, and South Africa as a strategy adopted by national politicians to weaken intermediate levels of government. O'Neill (2003) argues that political parties devolve greater resources when support for them is more secure in local than in national elections, citing evidence from Bolivia, Colombia, Ecuador, Peru, and Venezuela. There are also several descriptions in the literature of decentralization as a political tool to accommodate ethnic or regional conflict within countries, the so-called "holding-together" decentralization (Panizza, 1999).

However, these works on politically motivated decentralization do not draw specific implications for the *design* of decentralization—which jurisdictions would be selected as key "local" or "subnational" jurisdictions? What fiscal powers and responsibilities would they be provided? The O'Neill (2003) argument seems to lend itself to decentralization of revenues, and local fiscal discretion, because political powers are more certain about being able to control these resources at local levels.

As indicated at the outset, this chapter is motivated by the observation of a specific form of decentralization in many countries—the selection of jurisdiction boundaries at sub-regional levels such as districts, towns, or villages, with minimal own revenue sources, overwhelming dependence on fiscal grants from higher tiers, and limited discretion in how to spend these. Large amounts of public resources for anti-poverty programs are being provided as grants to rural local governments who have the authority to select beneficiaries of local projects (Ravallion, 1999; Alderman, 2002; Mansuri and Rao, 2004; Bardhan and Mookherjee, 2005, 2000; Faguet and Wietzke, 2006). In several decentralized countries in Africa, Latin America, and South and East Asia, more than 90 per cent of local government expenditures is financed by grants from higher tiers (Chaudhuri, 2006; Faguet, 2000; World Bank, various).[4] Furthermore, this form of decentralization has also been accompanied by increasing fragmentation of jurisdictions into smaller and smaller units (Green, 2011).

Why are jurisdictions not selected to coincide with local economies that would allow some own revenue generation? For example, in some contexts, such as in India, why are urban centers not provided greater revenue-raising powers and discretion over their spending? In his case study of Uganda, Green (2011) argues that the particular form of decentralization there—the creation of new districts whose spending is financed by central grants—can be explained by patronage politics. In this chapter, I provide a general theoretical framework to examine when decentralization would be used for patronage purposes, and what implications this would have for the design of decentralization and incentives of local governments to deliver public goods.

Political incentives for decentralization in this framework depend upon whether mobilization of votes through local elections is cheaper than in national elections. When voters in national elections become increasingly "swing"—demanding broad public services or universal transfers—public resources need to be diverted away from political rents and towards winning their support. Decentralization can serve to divide the power of swing voters by identifying jurisdictions where votes can be mobilized through more

[4] Even this number, 90 per cent, masks the true extent of grants dependence of rural local governments which is closer to 99 per cent when some cities that do raise significant resources from own revenues are excluded from the calculation.

efficient targeting of benefits in exchange for political support. The particular design of decentralization that would be pursued is, therefore, to create jurisdictions where votes are cheaper to "buy" through targeted provision of benefits, with local spending and its financing being driven by patronage politics.

This framework yields implications for the design of decentralization that this chapter is motivated to explain: overwhelming or exclusive dependence on grants for local government spending and little or no devolution of revenue-raising authority; local government spending decisions characterized by welfare transfers to poor swing voters in exchange for their vote; and inter-jurisdiction grants distribution influenced by political affiliations of local incumbents. Decentralization policies are therefore determined in this model by politicians to facilitate vote mobilization for their political party to win office, akin to gerrymandering districts in electoral politics. Within this political economy framework, even if a "reform champion" emerges who pursues decentralization reforms to improve the quality of public goods, the implementation of those reforms would subsequently be subject to political capture.

Such a type of decentralization is therefore associated with another type of "swing voter's curse," in which greater demands by them for public goods are thwarted through greater decentralized vote-buying. When higher-tier political incumbents face more demanding "swing" voters, decentralized delivery of welfare programs may be used for more effective targeting of the "cheapest" swing votes, at lower levels of progressive taxes and public goods than in the absence of decentralized vote buying.

There is some available evidence, mostly anecdotal, from a range of countries, including Brazil, India, Nigeria, Pakistan, and the Philippines, on the salience of vote buying, patronage, and violence in local elections (Bardhan et al., 2007; Cheema and Mohmand, 2008). In the political capture model presented here, and in this anecdotal evidence, the capture of public resources for private benefits need not be restricted to the elite; even poor and traditionally disadvantaged voters may demand private goods from local politicians (such as jobs, subsidies, cash, and in-kind transfers) instead of broad public goods (such as quality health and education).

Indeed, the critical assumption required to derive the result of political capture of decentralization for greater clientelism at the expense of broad public goods is that the pivotal swing voters in local jurisdictions provide strictly greater vote returns when allocated private transfers instead of broad public goods. Lizzeri and Persico (2004) use completely opposite assumptions, of the increasing value of the public good to pivotal voters, to explain the extension of suffrage by English elites in the mid to late 1800s. They argue and provide some evidence that in England the increase in the value of urban public goods following the Industrial Revolution (public health infrastructure such as sewerage, waterworks, and paved roads), led to a majority of the franchised elite pushing for reforms to extend the suffrage so that political parties would have stronger incentives to deliver these public goods. They show that, following suffrage reforms, spending by municipal corporations on public health infrastructure increased substantially, while spending on welfare transfers to the poor was reduced. That is, a diametrically different conclusion than that provided here of local spending on targeted transfers. It has implications for innovation in current institutional interventions to improve accountability for public goods in developing countries by influencing the demands of pivotal voters.

The theory offered here of the political selection of jurisdiction boundaries has policy implications for international development assistance. Technical assistance and lending programs typically focus on addressing vertical and horizontal fiscal "imbalances," spring-boarding from the observation that new local governments are not devolved "sufficient" grants to fulfill the expenditure responsibilities assigned to them. This chapter suggests that when jurisdiction boundaries are deliberately chosen to keep them grants-dependent for political targeting, focusing policy largely on increasing grants on existing jurisdictions for greater local spending can exacerbate patronage politics. It can fuel people's evaluation of local governments on the basis of funding and projects that can be garnered from above, at the expense of inter- and intra-jurisdiction competition on the basis of competency to deliver broad public goods with scarce resources. Instead, the political analysis suggests strengthening other strategies that focus on identifying institutional and governance interventions to undercut patronage incentives and enable voters to mobilize to demand broad public services.

The next section provides a new theoretical framework for the choice of decentralization of public spending to local jurisdictions, financed by grants, to serve electoral objectives. Section 9.3 then discusses some evidence on decentralization experiences in select countries and regions that are consistent with the theory. Section 9.4 discusses the implications of the theory for international development assistance and explores the potential of local governance interventions to overcome local patronage politics. Section 9.5 concludes.

9.2 The Theoretical Framework

The key intuition of the framework proposed here is that, beginning with a standard workhorse model of partisan policy objectives in choosing fiscal policy, it is difficult to find conditions under which a ruling party would choose to decentralize revenue-raising authority. Decentralization would be consistent in these political economy models of fiscal policy only under assumptions of differential political support for parties in local versus central elections, or as grants-based decentralization driven by greater effectiveness of vote mobilization in local elections.[5]

There is a large literature on the political economy of fiscal policy choices (Alesina and Perotti, 1995; Persson and Tabellini, 2000; Persson et al., 2007). A basic premise in these models is that voters organize themselves into interest groups, represented by political parties, to influence public policy for their group's benefit. Khemani and Wane (2008) introduced into these models another type of voter; the poor and unorganized voter who only receives benefits from public spending programs (not from a party representing their interests being in power). The model is presented as an appendix to this chapter: it first adapts Khemani and Wane's (2008) centralized political decision-making model to the problem of choice between targeted transfers to buy votes versus allocating to the broad public good, and then examines its implications for the decision to decentralize. The intuition is that as swing voters become more demanding, requiring greater benefits from public spending to extend support to the incumbent party, the party has to forgo rents from public resources for its group members in order to remain in office through re-election.

The first critical assumption of this theoretical framework in order to derive results on vote-buying at the expense of public goods is that swing voters are cheaper to woo through targeted transfers than by increasing spending on the public good. As mentioned at the outset, Lizzeri and Persico (2004) use completely opposite assumptions, of the increasing value of the public good to pivotal voters in post-Industrial Revolution England, to explain how suffrage reforms led to substantial increases in spending by municipal corporations on public health and sanitation infrastructure. The micro evidence on voting behavior in poor countries, however, suggests that small private transfers provided within a *quid pro quo* arrangement may bring surer vote returns to parties than broad provision of public goods. This evidence depends upon social and political institutions that enable private benefits to be targeted to those who will respond by giving political support.

Finan and Schechter (2010) explore the role of social preferences such as reciprocity (the psychological pressure to return a favor received from someone) in shaping electoral strategies of vote-buying. Combining experimental

[5] Even with such local political differences, decentralization to locally elected governments might be trumped by other strategies of centralized targeting of local precincts of central electoral districts. Further details in the model are likely needed to explain the selection of decentralization.

games that measure the strength of reciprocal feelings among individuals with survey data on vote-buying offers made to individuals in the country of Paraguay, they find that political agents target vote-buying to individuals with greater feelings of reciprocity. A large literature on "get-out-the-vote" campaigns in the US finds that personal or direct contact with households is the most persuasive method in getting them to vote on election day, compared to other strategies that are more broadly targeted, such as distributing pamphlets (DellaVigna and Gentzkow, 2009).

This argument might logically extend to comparing the marginal vote returns from spending on broad public goods versus privately targeted transfers—broadly provided public goods might not generate the same strength of reciprocal feelings in individual voters as do private, one-to-one transfers. Even when an incumbent government provides broad public goods, voters that are targeted with private benefits from a rival party might still vote against the incumbent. Political studies of vote buying, largely concentrated in Latin America and in poorer constituencies in the US, have provided theoretical arguments as well as empirical evidence that low-income or poor voters are more likely to be targeted with vote-buying offers, and more likely to comply (Harding, 2008; Stokes, 2005; Brusco et al., 2004). Although the vote buying and clientelism literature has not made this explicit connection, the intuition is similar to models of price discrimination by monopsonists seeking suppliers that offer the lowest price.[6] Since incumbent governments in poor economies have access to state resources which challengers do not, they have some monopsony power over voters, enabling their use of vote buying as an efficient strategy to thwart contestation.

Recent work has uncovered direct evidence of a trade-off between vote buying and broadly delivered public services. Khemani (2013) finds that variation in vote buying across Philippine municipalities is significantly associated with variation in public health services—where vote buying practices are more widespread, public spending on health is lower, and children's health outcomes are poorer.[7]

Others have argued that in developing democracies where the median voters are the poor who live at or near subsistence levels they are more likely to reward with a vote even a small welfare transfer made directly to their household (Varshney, 2000; Acharya, 2004). Their private voting action may therefore be at odds with their publicly declared preferences for public goods, such as when they answer questions about priority problems for the village

[6] I am grateful to an anonymous referee for making this point. It is worthy of further exploration.

[7] This association is highly robust to multiple specifications, controlling in various ways for measures of poverty that might be independently associated with both vote buying and public health, driving a spurious correlation between the two.

where they invariably mention village infrastructure (Banerjee et al., 2007; 2010). Bardhan et al. (2007) included a secret ballot in their survey of rural households in West Bengal to examine the correlates of voting for the incumbent Left Front political parties. They find that an individual household's vote for the incumbent party is significantly correlated only with private and recurring benefits received, in the form of personal help in times of need or benefits from welfare schemes, and not with the availability of local infrastructure.

Hence, when faced with more demanding swing voters and a binding re-election constraint, the assumption discussed above yields the result that central political parties will try to divert resources from the club goods enjoyed by their members to buy votes from swing voters. In this setting, heterogeneity of preferences across local areas, the standard assumption behind the emergence of decentralization, has no influence on the central decision-maker since there is no assumption of benevolence, but rather of partisan incentives. The only conditions under which decentralization would be an attractive policy instrument pertain to when the central party gains some political advantage in local jurisdictions.

A second pivotal assumption in the theoretical framework here to explain the political selection of grants-dependent jurisdictions is that vote buying may be cheaper at local levels because of differences between local and national socio-political institutions that enable a reciprocal political exchange. The model in the appendix shows how this assumption yields the selection of decentralization of grants to local jurisdictions primarily for welfare programs such as the targeting of poverty alleviation transfers to beneficiaries. Decentralization of beneficiary selection is chosen by the central political incumbent if it is cheaper to buy votes from the poorest voters through the advantages of local-election vote mobilization than through centralized party machines.

Under such political capture of decentralization, it may well be that comparing central versus local targeting performance in the distribution of welfare programs shows that local targeting is more pro-poor; however, the cost of decentralization might lie in the ability of the political party to continue winning office with lower progressive taxation and investment in public goods than would have been possible in the face of the demands of swing voters. This framework therefore suggests a new type of "swing voter's curse" than is available in the literature (Robinson and Torvik, 2009; Feddersen and Pesendorfer, 1996). The more demanding swing voters become for broad public good, the less likely they are to receive their preferred levels because central politicians would use the means of vote buying in local elections to divide the strength of swing voters, targeting those that can be bought most cheaply, and win elections at lower levels of progressive taxes and public goods (than without well-targeted vote buying).

The framework may be extended to allow for heterogeneity in distribution of groups across localities, and to allow for other interest groups to emerge at local levels. This might lead to results on the fragmentation of jurisdictions. Depending on how groups are distributed geographically, the central politician might choose to further subdivide existing local jurisdictions into smaller units where votes are easier or cheaper to purchase.

9.3 Evidence on Characteristics of Local Jurisdictions

This section provides evidence from several countries around the world of characteristics of local jurisdictions that is consistent with the implications of a theory of political capture of decentralization explored above. The purpose here is to show that the proposed theory has empirical or practical relevance, rather than to formally test predictions.

Table 9.1 provides some data on characteristics of local jurisdictions in selected countries. These countries have been selected on the basis of available reports on the nature of decentralization to local jurisdictions. There is little systematic data available on fiscal characteristics of local jurisdictions such as villages, municipalities, and districts. The main source of comparable cross-country data employed in the literature on subnational finance is the Government Finance Statistics (GFS) database compiled by the International Monetary Fund (IMF); but although this provides reasonably reliable estimates of finances of states, regions, or provinces, it is widely acknowledged as not reliable for measuring finances of the lower level jurisdictions which are the focus of this chapter.

Table 9.1. Local government characteristics in selected countries.

	Local jurisdictions	Share of local own revenues in total revenues
India	~500 districts, ~6,000 blocks, >230,000 villages (rural local bodies)	3.7%[a]
Indonesia	440 districts and cities	8.8%[b]
Nigeria	>770 local government authorities	10%[c]
Peru	~1,700 district municipalities	27%[d]
The Philippines	~1,500 municipalities	14%[e]

[a] *Source:* Chaudhuri (2006).
[b] *Source:* World Bank (2008).
[c] *Source:* Author's own calculations from data provided by the Central Bank of Nigeria, 1999.
[d] *Source:* World Bank (2003), excluding the municipal area of the capital city, Lima.
[e] *Source:* Author's own calculations for municipalities from data provided by the Bureau of Local Government Finances, 2001–5.

For this chapter, detailed reports on local government finances were located for several large countries spread across four major regions of the world. There is clear evidence from three large countries, India, Indonesia, and Nigeria, where responsibility for public service delivery is being increasingly decentralized to local governments, that these local governments have negligible access to own-source revenues. The average share of own-source revenue in the total revenues managed by local jurisdictions in these three countries is less than or barely equal to 10 per cent. This average in fact masks even lower fiscal capacity among the majority of local jurisdictions in these countries. In Nigeria, for example, a detailed survey of local government finances in the rural state of Kogi finds that own revenues are only 1–2 per cent of total revenues managed by rural local governments (Khemani, 2006a). In another country included in Table 9.1, the Philippines, although the average share of own revenues is 14 per cent, the share in the median municipality is 10 per cent, and more than a quarter raise less than 5 per cent of their total income from local sources.

Municipalities in Peru, the country with the highest share of own revenues among those included in Table 9.1, have been characterized by some analysts as having no discretion over local rate setting and tax collection, and effectively being fully financed by central grants (Ahmad and Garcia-Escribano, 2006).[8] Even this relatively high share of own revenues, at 27 per cent, is comparable to the very lowest of such shares among OECD countries. Ambrosanio and Bordignon (2006) provide statistics on the share of grants in local government revenues in the 20 OECD countries, which shows that only three countries had a grants share greater than 55 per cent—Ireland at 76 per cent, and the Netherlands and the UK at 70 per cent. This OECD experience shows that even in the face of theoretical arguments in favor of grants-financed decentralization, in which taxes can be collected more efficiently at national levels and then distributed to subnationals as grants, grants dependence is not in the realm of 80 or 90 per cent of local revenues as in the countries listed in Table 9.1. Within the developing world, countries in the Latin American region appear to have a smaller share of municipal spending financed by grants, but even these are higher than in most OECD countries. In Brazil and Mexico grants constitute around 65 per cent of municipal revenues (Burki et al., 1999).

Grants dependence in these countries appears to go hand in hand with small size of local jurisdictions (in terms of population and area), and

[8] Some have argued that Peru should not be considered a decentralized country at all. Indeed, prior to 2002 spending by municipalities hardly accounted for a significant share of government spending. However, since 2002 the share of municipal spending has risen to 13 per cent and is expected to increase further. For the purposes of this chapter, the issue of interest is that even as the country moves towards greater decentralization of spending, it chooses national grants to finance it.

redrawing of jurisdiction boundaries or growth in number of jurisdictions over time. Although the average population size of local jurisdictions is higher in Latin America than in Europe, this average appears to be masking large disparities across jurisdictions. Burki et al. (1999) find that the vast majority of municipalities in the region have fewer than 15,000 residents. Burki et al. (1999) also report shrinking in jurisdiction size, with the number of *municipios* in Brazil increasing from 3,000 to nearly 5,000 in the fifteen years following the return to democracy in the country. In Venezuela, they report the number of *municipios* increasing from 202 to 330 within a decade. In a presidential address in Nigeria in 2003, then President Obasanjo indicated that state governments in the country were in the process of creating more than 500 new local governments, a 65 per cent increase over the existing 774 listed in the country's 1999 Constitution.[9]

In a review of international evidence on the distribution of grants across jurisdictions, Boex and Martinez-Vazquez (2005) find an inverse relation between jurisdiction size and per-capita grants; that is, smaller jurisdictions tend to receive larger grants per capita across a range of countries. This pattern is consistent with the theory of political capture of decentralization offered here, and resonates with recent lessons from field experience. Examples have been provided in the Philippines of redrawing of boundaries of municipalities and *barangays* (villages), or conversion of *barangays* into municipalities, to enable local political families to gain access to grants from higher tiers of government.[10] Burki et al. (1999) have also observed that demand for the creation of new jurisdictions is driven by the system of intergovernmental grants in many countries. Local requests for new jurisdictions typically have to be passed by the national or provincial legislatures, and the theory of political capture of decentralization is consistent with higher-tier authorities granting these requests to facilitate vote buying.

Although in many of the countries discussed thus far a large chunk of grants distribution across local jurisdictions is determined by criteria set out in national constitutions or a legal decree governing decentralization, there is evidence of significant political manipulation in targeting grants on the basis of local electoral characteristics. Reviews of international evidence are provided in Boex and Martinez-Vazquez (2005) and Khemani (2006b). Another striking feature in several countries is the provision of specific spending programs to local jurisdictions by higher-tier politicians, separate from and outside of the regular channels of intergovernmental grants. India, the

[9] Google search result on a national broadcast by President Olusegun Obasanjo in Abuja, Nigeria, on 18 June 2003, titled "On the Issue of the Review of the Structure of Governance in Nigeria."

[10] Descriptions provided to the author during field visits to municipalities in the Philippines in October 2008. No documentation of such changes has been accessible to date.

Philippines, and Kenya have recently launched programs that are generally termed "constituency development funds" (CDFs) which allow individual national or state legislators to provide funds for local public infrastructure investment.

Most, if not all, of the literature on inter-governmental fiscal and political relations in the Philippines emphasizes the importance of congressional, gubernatorial, and even presidential pork-barrel projects for city and municipal politics. De Dios (2007) and Rocamora (2004) argue that one of the two main pillars of local political contests in the Philippines is the generation of funds and projects from higher-tier governments.[11] In ongoing field work in the Philippines, in every municipality visited, respondents describe the importance of political affiliation of local mayors to provincial governors and national congressmen in attracting spending programs to their jurisdiction (Khemani, 2013).

In India, resources are transferred to local governments largely in the form of "schemes" for poverty alleviation, and the primary decentralized local responsibility is that of identifying beneficiaries. Such decentralization has been viewed in the literature as good policy design, in the face of solid evidence of informational advantages of local governments in appropriately identifying the poor or those that have faced particularly negative economic shocks (Alderman, 2002). However, the arguments in this chapter imply that such schemes-based decentralization might lead to clientelist local politics.

Analysis of perverse political incentives at local levels in India has focused overwhelmingly on the risk of "capture" of public resources by local elites for their own benefit, systematically excluding poor and disadvantaged people (Bardhan and Mookherjee, 2000, 2005; Baland and Platteau, 1999). The alternate hypothesis posited here is that even if such specified "elite capture" is not salient, and poor and disadvantaged groups are politically mobilized, their incentives are to demand short-term private benefits from local governments charged with beneficiary selection for poverty-alleviation schemes.

The existence of historical institutions of social inequality in India makes it a setting from which much evidence has been garnered on relative "capture" by local governments. We review this evidence here to argue that it is equally consistent with political mobilization of disadvantaged groups to demand private goods targeted to members of their "group," at the expense of broad public goods from which all group members would benefit.

Besley et al. (2004) focus on analyzing distribution of access to poverty alleviation schemes, a BPL (Below Poverty Line) card, by village governments (*panchayats*) in India. They find that legally identified disadvantaged groups, households belonging to the scheduled castes and tribes (SC/STs), are more

[11] The other being the control of illegal economic activity such as gambling and smuggling.

likely to receive a BPL card and/or targeted home improvement schemes (toilets, drinking water, electricity, repairs) when the elected position of head of the village government, the *Gram Pradhan*, is reserved for members of SC/ST groups.

They also find that a second institutional feature of decentralization in India—the requirement of village-wide meetings, the *gram sabhas*, to deliberate upon allocations of public funds reaching local governments—enables targeting of public benefits to disadvantaged groups. Specifically, they find that if a village is the kind of village that holds a *gram sabha*, then disadvantaged households are more likely to participate in it than are advantaged households, and they are simultaneously more likely to receive BPL cards.

It is important to note that the impact of political reservations and *gram sabhas* is *additional* to overall targeting of BPL cards to disadvantaged households. That is, in general, in all villages a household that is SC/ST, or landless, or poor along other measurable dimensions is more likely to receive a BPL card than upper-caste or richer households, and they are even more likely to be thus targeted when a village has political reservations and holds *gram sabhas*.

Besley et al. (2004) interpret this as evidence of appropriate targeting of disadvantaged groups when political decentralization is accompanied by institutional mechanism (political reservations, *gram sabhas*) to combat entrenched inequalities. However, the key question raised by the arguments in this chapter is whether such targeted provision comes at the expense of broad public goods. There is no evidence from their work, for example, that decentralized institutions improve the delivery of broad public services.

Other types of evidence suggest that broader public goods are simply not as salient in local politics as are targeted provision of narrow benefits. Bardhan et al. (2007) contribute evidence from the state of West Bengal in India that voters cite short-term private benefits received from their local governments as most important for their voting decision and support of incumbents, as opposed to longer-term policy initiatives taken by incumbents to promote general public goods. They also find little evidence of political marginalization or political exclusion of weaker socio-economic groups. This suggests that the critical issue is not elite capture per se, but political patronage—the delivery of narrow private benefits at the expense of broad public goods.[12]

Evidence on whether politicians representing disadvantaged groups have incentives to exert effort on broader public services is provided by Keefer and Khemani (2009) who examine a constituency development fund in India—the Member of Parliament Local Area Development Scheme. This scheme entitles every member of the national parliament, elected from single-member

[12] The only groups with low participation identified by Bardhan et al. (2007) are immigrants, women, and those with low education, not low-caste groups or low-income/-wealth groups.

constituencies, to substantial resources to spend on local public infrastructure in their districts. They find that dominant incumbents from districts that are reserved for SC/STs, that is, SC/ST politicians who have been elected for several consecutive terms, spend 14 percentage points *less* of their entitlement than other politicians. In short, dominant incumbents from reserved districts are not dominant because they exert great effort in providing public infrastructure to their constituents; their dominance likely comes from other kinds of private identity-based services, the mainstay of patronage politics.

Foster and Rosenzweig (2001) also provide evidence consistent with Bardhan et al.'s argument that voters place greater emphasis in local elections in India on short-term gains from public spending. They focus on three categories of public goods which together account for 73 per cent of the activities of village governments in their sample in India—roads, irrigation, and schools. They find that villages with democratically elected governments are more likely to provide more of all three public goods, but the largest effect is for irrigation, as calculated at the sample average, which is the service most likely to benefit the rural elite. However, in villages with a very high proportion of landless inhabitants (much above the sample average) public investment shifts from irrigation to road construction (rather than education, which is unaffected by the proportion of the landless), which suggests that capture by elites can be ameliorated when the numerical strength of the poor increases, but in a manner that might not be the most efficient for extending benefits to the poor. Roads built by village governments primarily benefit the poor, but largely by raising their (short-term) wages, as local road construction and improvement initiatives in India serve as employment programs for the landless poor. Education, which one expects to have the most profound effect on poverty over the medium and long term, seems least affected by decentralization. That is, political support from poor voters is easier to gain through targeted provision of private benefits, rather than through broad public goods.

Evidence from India specifically on decentralization of education services further illustrates this point (Banerjee et al., 2007). The study found that despite the existence of a local agency to improve village school performance, there was little public interest in improving the quality of public schools. The most salient issue raised by villagers was a government scholarship program intended to provide cash assistance to students from SC/ST groups. Following information and advocacy campaigns to encourage the community to improve the quality of education among their children, there was a dramatic impact on private efforts to improve the learning of lagging children, but no impact on the performance of public schools. This suggests that the lack of public action on education was not because people did not care about education, but rather that there was no political demand to improve it within the local public system.

9.4 Implications for International Development Assistance

Much of the reforms being pursued by donors in support of decentralization consist of providing greater revenues or transfers, and building capacity of local governments through training programs such as in public financial management. The arguments here suggest that these reforms on their own might not be efficient or effective in delivering improved public services for actual development outcomes, if the local jurisdictions being supported are politically captured. Greater funds devolved to local governments are more likely to go towards clientelist transfers rather than improvement of public goods. Capacity building can be a waste when local politicians have no incentives to develop technocratic skills for better service delivery.

One of the governance strategies being pursued in international development assistance to improve the impact of decentralization is termed community-driven development (CDD), in which communities are mobilized to identify their preferred projects and to participate in their implementation. The hypothesized governance impact of this strategy is greater social cohesion, and enhanced ability of citizens to demand and receive better public goods performance from their governments. Another strategy is conditional cash transfers (CCT), where households are mandated to access public health and/or education services in order to receive cash transfers. The governance impact of this strategy is hypothesized to be an increase in citizen demand for public health and education services which in turn strengthens political incentives to improve the quality of these broad public goods. Although there are several evaluations planned, underway, or completed on the impact of CDD and CCT programs on their directly targeted outcomes such as project quality and beneficiary household-level welfare outcomes, none are designed sufficiently rigorously to assess their impact on local public goods or local political incentives (to the best of the author's knowledge).[13] This is a serious gap in the policy research literature that should be addressed.

Another governance intervention that has not been widely experimented with may be used in concert with CDD and CCT interventions or alone. This is the promotion yardstick competition on service delivery performance by regularly and systematically providing independent, credible, and objective information to citizens and public officials about relative performance across jurisdictions. Part of the problem of clientelist local politics might be lack of

[13] Labonne and Chase (2008) make an attempt to assess impact of a CDD project on local governance in the Philippines, but do not appear to have useful governance outcome variables. The variable on which they do find impact—number of village meetings organized by local officials, and household participation in these meetings—is a requirement for a village to access the CDD project, and hence automatically expected to be higher in CDD villages because of the nature of program implementation.

independent data and expert analysis available to civil society to judge relative performance across local jurisdictions. New empirical methodologies can be used to fill this gap by measuring service delivery outcomes that are representative at the level of local jurisdictions in feasible and cost-effective ways. Once measured, the outcomes can be compiled as "municipal report cards" and disseminated to attempt to promote yardstick competition over performance improvements.

Brazil provides some examples of successful experiences with this type of governance intervention. Tendler (1997) describes how the politics of patronage in municipal governments in the state of Ceara in Brazil was tackled head-on through massive information campaigns by a state government that took office in 1987. The state government flooded radio airwaves with messages about how infant and child mortality could be drastically reduced through particular municipal government programs, thus bringing political pressure to bear upon the mayors to actually deliver basic health services. The state also created a new class of public health workers through a publicized recruitment effort that conveyed information to communities about the valuable role the workers could play in improving public health through community-wide effort. In only a few years coverage of measles and polio vaccination in Ceara tripled to 90 per cent of the child population, and infant deaths fell from 102 to 65 per thousand births. The campaigns' success has been credited with bringing a remarkable turnaround in the politics of the state—from clientelist and patronage-based to service-oriented (Tendler, 1997).

More recently, Brazil was the source of another innovative experiment in reducing local political rent-seeking by generating and providing credible information to citizens. In May 2003 the national government of Brazil launched an anti-corruption program based on the random auditing of municipal government expenditures by an independent public agency, and then publicly releasing audit findings on the internet and to media sources.[14] New evidence from more than 600 municipalities covered by the audit suggests that the disclosure of information significantly and substantially reduced the re-election rates of mayors who were found to be corrupt (Ferraz and Finan, 2008). Furthermore, this impact was significantly more pronounced in municipalities with greater access to radio stations.

More generally, there is a role for greater measurement and monitoring of citizen expectations and demands from government, and what policy issues they choose to organize for, to identify new ways in which collective action can be nudged towards broad public goods. More work is needed to identify

[14] In Portuguese, this program is called *Programa de Fiscalização a partir de Sorteios Públicos*, details of which are available from the following website: <http://www.presidencia.gov.br/cgu>.

innovative institutional design or conditions under which political capture is reduced and accountability for local public goods increases.

9.5 Conclusion

This chapter has examined a theory of decentralization as a political choice of national or provincial leaders to combat growing demands of swing voters for broad public goods, and to continue targeting private benefits to organized interest groups. Decentralization to new local jurisdictions may be subject to political capture, enabling politicians to buy votes from some swing voters while continuing to provide targeted benefits to their core constituents and to under-provide broad public goods. Local governments in the political capture model are financed entirely by grants, and spend it on targeted transfers to poor voters in exchange for their vote, at the expense of local public goods.

Examples are provided from several large countries of the developing world of decentralization to small local jurisdictions, financed almost entirely by grants or spending programs received from higher tiers of government, as evidence of the empirical relevance of the theory. Evidence of the importance of clientelism in local politics is also reviewed, in these same countries where grants finance small local jurisdictions, which further supports the conclusions derived under a theory of political capture of decentralization.

The aim of this analysis is to strike a note of caution for well-intentioned reformers who are attempting to implement participatory local government in political economy contexts that are inimical to organization of citizens for the broad public interest. By bringing to the fore the tension between citizen mobilization for private or group-targeted benefits versus the greater public interest, this work suggests the value of experimenting with other types of complementary governance interventions designed to overcome political constraints to broad public goods.

Appendix: The Model Underlying the Theoretical Framework in Section 9.2

Consider a population with three groups indexed by j. The welfare of group j's member is given by:

$$W^j(c, g) = c^j + H(g) \tag{9.1}$$

W is an increasing and concave function, c^j is private consumption, and g is a general public good such as village-wide infrastructure provision. Two of these groups are economic elites, controlling different economic resources, paying taxes, and organized into political interest groups (political parties) to gain private rents from office and public spending. The third group is poor, with income normalized to zero (and hence does not pay taxes), is not organized into a political group, and therefore votes solely on the basis of individual benefits received from government spending. Let the two elite groups organized into political parties be designated P_1, and P_2, and the third group of unorganized voters be designated as the swing voters S.[15] The size of each group is denoted by μ^j, for $j = P_1, P_2, S$.

For $j \notin S, c^j = y^j - \tau + r^j$. That is, the consumption of members of political parties consists of their disposable income, the difference between initial income y^j and the income tax τ, plus a private rent r^j targeted towards group members from public resources. For $j \in S$, $y^s \equiv 0$, and $W^s = f^s + H(g)$. That is, members of the unorganized swing group do not have any income, cannot be taxed, and receive welfare only from government spending on public goods and any welfare transfers f^s targeted to their group.

Raising taxes is costly for the government. It may need to allocate resources for enforcing the payment of taxes and prevent tax evasion, for instance. We assume that when the government imposes an amount τ in taxes it only collects $\theta(\tau)\tau$ i.e. the cost associated with this level of taxation is $(1-\theta(\tau))*\tau$. The inefficiency of the tax system is captured by $\theta(\tau)$ which has the following usual properties for an inverted-U Laffer curve for tax revenues: $0 \leq \theta(\tau) \leq 1, \theta'(\tau)<0$, and $\theta''(\tau)<0$ for $0 \leq \tau \leq y^j, \forall j$. The tax rate at which revenues are maximized is given by $\tau = \tau^{\max}$. Correspondingly, the maximum amount of public good that can be provided in this economy is given by $g^{\max} = \tau^{\max}$.

The general public good, g, the rents to political party members, r^j, and the private transfers to swing voters, f^s, are financed one-to-one with tax revenues, and satisfy non-negativity constraints $g \geq 0$ and $f^j \geq 0 \ \forall \ j$. The government budget constraint is therefore given by:

$$\sum_{j \notin S} \mu^j \cdot r^j + \mu^s \cdot f^s + g \leq R(\tau) \tag{9.2}$$

where $R(\tau) = \tau \cdot \theta(\tau) \cdot \sum_{j \notin S} \mu^j$ is the government's tax revenue when the tax rate is τ.

The Politics

The two political parties, P_1 and P_2, compete during elections to win a majority of votes and choose the policy vector $p = [\tau, g, f^j]$. Any member of the political parties, μ^j for $j = P_1, P_2$ can be a candidate. The political party that wins office chooses policies to maximize the welfare of its members (core constituents) subject to a re-election

[15] The characterization of this group as swing voters is consistent with several different characterizations in the literature of what it means to be "swing." First, swing voters in this model are indifferent between voting for or against an incumbent government, based upon comparing the benefits of economic policy against a reservation utility (as in Persson et al., 2007). Second, swing voters in this model are not ideologically attached to political parties, and vote only the basis of evaluating general public policies of incumbent governments (as in Lindbeck and Weibull, 1987; Dixit and Londregan, 1995, 1996; and much of the political science literature). Third, some models define swing voters as those whose ballots ultimately determine the outcome of elections (as in Feddersen and Pesendorfer, 1998), which also happens in the equilibrium in this model.

constraint (to be derived below), in addition to the budget constraint specified in equation (9.2) above. The objective function of party j in government is given by:

$$\max_{\{\tau,g,f^j\}} \mu^j[y^j - \tau + r^j + H(g)] + B \tag{9.3}$$

B represents the rents or benefits (outside of fiscal policy) from holding office, which are shared equally among all members of the party. Note that swing voters and opposition party supporters do not enter the government's objective function. Any transfers to them would be determined by their role in the re-election constraint, to be derived below. Political parties in this model are therefore both partisan and opportunistic. They cater to the interests of their core constituents once in office, but also choose policies to try to win elections and gain office. The core supporters μ^j of political party j always vote for the party to which they are attached, consistent with the party's objective of maximizing the welfare of its supporters subject to re-election and budget constraints.

The unorganized or swing voters cast their ballot for the incumbent government if their welfare under government policy, $H(g) + f^s$, is higher than or equal to a reservation utility parameter ω; otherwise they vote for the opposition. The swing voters' reservation utility parameter ω is distributed on the support $[\underline{\omega}, \overline{\omega}]$, with density f and cumulative F which are common knowledge.[16]

When the incumbent implements the policy $p = [\tau, g, f^j]$ it can expect to receive $\mu^S F(H(g) + f^s)$ of swing voters' ballots. The remaining swing voters $\mu^S(1 - F(H(g) + f^s))$ will punish the incumbent and vote for the opposition. The incumbent government party $j \in G$ therefore receives $\mu^G + \mu^S F(H(g) + f^s)$ of the votes. The reelection constraint is given by:

$$F(H(g) + f^s) > \frac{\mu^S - \Delta\mu^G}{2\mu^S} = \lambda \quad \text{or} \quad H(g) + f^s \geq F^{-1}(\lambda) \tag{9.4}$$

Where $\Delta\mu^G = (\mu^G - \mu^{-G})$ is the difference in size of the core constituents of the two political parties. λ is the *minimum swing votes* the incumbent government needs to win re-election.

The Political Distortion

In the absence of political considerations, a utilitarian social planner would solve only the public goods and taxation problem, setting all targeted transfers to zero. The public good optimization problem is therefore:

$$\max_{\{\tau,g,f^j\}_{j\in G}} H(g) + \sum_{j\notin S} \mu^j \cdot [y^j - \tau] \tag{9.5}$$

subject to

[16] We assume that $\underline{\omega} \geq 0$ i.e. the swing voters expect to be at least as well off as under laissez-faire with no taxation and no public goods or spending targeted to them.

$$g \leq R(\tau) = \tau \cdot \theta(\tau) \cdot \sum_{j \notin S} \mu^j, \quad g \geq 0, \text{and} \quad 0 \leq \tau \leq y. \tag{9.6}$$

The solution is familiar, given by: $H'(g^*) = \left(\partial[\theta(\tau)\cdot\tau]/\partial\tau\right)^{-1} = 1$, $R(\tau^*) = g^*$. The level of public goods supplied in the utilitarian optimum equates marginal social benefit of the public good to its marginal social cost of production. The utilitarian government raises just enough taxes to finance the production of the public good, spending nothing on targeted transfers to organized interest groups or individual swing voters.[17]

When political considerations are taken into account, the incumbent political party will deviate from this optimum and aim to provide targeted transfers to its core constituents, and perhaps also to some swing voters to win elections. The extent to which it is able to capture public benefits for its core supporters depends upon its prospects for gaining public office, which in turn depends upon how demanding swing voters are, or the function $F(\omega)$ chosen by nature.[18]

We now derive the *preferred* levels of the tax, the public good, and targeted rents of an incumbent political party, denoted by τ^{*G}, g^{*G}, and r^{*G} respectively, or the policy package incumbents would implement if their re-election constraint were ignored or not binding. A government's optimization of the welfare of its core constituents consists of a multi-step procedure. First, it chooses the tax rate that maximizes the disposable income of its constituents to whom all tax proceeds are redistributed:[19]

$$\max_{\{\tau\}_{j \in G}} y^j - \tau + \alpha \cdot \theta(\tau)\tau, \textit{where } \alpha^G = \sum_{j \notin S} \mu^j / \mu^G. \tag{9.7}$$

The first-order condition for the above maximization, where τ^{*G} denotes the preferred tax rate, satisfies $\alpha^G \cdot [\theta'(\tau^{*G}) \cdot \tau^{*G} + \theta(\tau^{*G})] = 1$ or $R'(\tau^{*G}) = \mu^G$.

Second, the government chooses that optimal level of the public good that would be financed by its constituents alone, equating the marginal benefit and costs of the public good accruing only to its constituents, or $H'(g^{*G}) = 1/\mu^G$. Note that this level of public good is lower than the utilitarian social planner's optimum.

Finally, it redistributes the total tax revenue, net of public good spending, amongst its constituents, giving no specific transfers to the members of the opposition party or to swing voters. The government's constituents thus receive $r^{j^{*G}} \equiv r^{*G} = [R(\tau^{*G}) - g^{*G}]/\mu^G$

17 If the objective of the social planner is redistribution, to equalize welfare, or to guarantee a minimum level of welfare for the poorest group, then private transfers to the poorest may emerge in equilibrium depending on the gains to welfare from public goods versus private transfers.

18 In our model, if voters could cooperate and choose the distribution of reservation utilities (as in Persson et al., 2000) they would set it in a way to extract the maximum amount of public good from whatever government is in place. This assumption is, however, unrealistic since it requires a high level of information. It is also inconsistent with our modeling of swing voters as unorganized, and therefore unable to coordinate. We instead consider atomistic voters who cannot communicate or cooperate. Each swing voter will then independently set her reservation utility or will be assigned one by nature.

19 The simultaneous use of inefficient transfers to and taxes on the same group was a puzzling feature of African fiscal policies, highlighted in Bates' (1981) classic study of political economy. In our model transfers are redistributive, to lower the net tax burden on the incumbent political group. Taxes across groups are uniform, the underlying rationale being to avoid additional distortions to revenue generation from economic decision-making by the rival groups.

as specific transfer, which gives them a consumption level of $c^{j^{*G}} = y - \tau^{*G} + r^{*G}$, $j\epsilon G$. The other groups not represented in the government do not receive any rents, i.e. $r^{*j\notin G} \equiv 0$, and have a final consumption of

$$c^{*j\notin G} = y - \tau^{*G}.$$ [20]

The incumbent government can choose its preferred policy package when its preferred level of public good is sufficient to win the minimum swing votes needed for electoral victory, or $F(H(g^{*G})) \geq \lambda$. It would also choose this when re-election is entirely out of reach, which happens when swing voters are too demanding and the minimum swing votes required for victory cannot be obtained even by spending all revenues on them at the maximum tax rate $\tau^{\max}$. That is, governments anticipate defeat in an upcoming election, and implement predatory policy (their most preferred policy).

Incumbent Government's Constrained Choice Under Re-election

Suppose that the distribution of reservation utilities is such that $F(H(g^{*G})) < \lambda < F(H(g^{\max}))$. The government can then either increase the level of the public good or provide targeted transfers to swing voters until it receives the minimum swing votes λ. The decision to re-allocate resources away from the preferred allocation, in which the core constituents of the incumbent party receive private rents, to the public good versus the private transfer would depend on the relative expected vote returns from the two types of instruments. The incumbent would attempt to find the cheapest possible strategy to win the minimum swing votes needed. Here we examine decentralization as a strategic political instrument in this context.

The first critical assumption we make to build the argument is that the vote return from shifting resources at the margin to targeted transfers to some swing voters is greater than the vote return from increasing the public good, at the preferred public good level of the incumbent. That is,

$$\frac{\partial F(H(g^{*G}) + f^s)}{\partial g} < \frac{\partial F(H(g^{*G}) + f^s)}{\partial f^s} \tag{9.8}$$

If the incumbent party chooses to seek re-election, it would provide private transfers to swing voters just up to the point where it meets the re-election constraint. The constrained optimal amount of private transfers to swing voters for a government seeking re-election is therefore given by f^{s*} where $F(H(g^{*G}) + f^{s*})) = \lambda$. The government would attempt to finance the provision of these transfers by diverting tax revenues collected through its preferred rate τ^{*G} from rents for its constituents. Assuming sufficient

[20] We assume throughout that $R(\tau^{*G}) > g^{*G}\ \forall_j$. This assumption means that the preferred tax rate of the government generates at least enough revenue to pay for its preferred level of public good. This assumption puts an upper bound on the inefficiency of taxation. If we do not impose it, the government's optimal tax rate does not change but the amount of public good provided becomes $g^{*G} = Max\{H'^{-1}(1/\mu^G), R(\tau^{*G})\}$ which may entail some rationing.

revenues, the central politician would continue to keep the tax rate at τ^{*G} and to provide g^{*G}, but would reduce the targeted rents to its constituents to $r^{j**G} = r^{*G} - f^{s*}$.

Decentralization Under Heterogeneity of Preferences?

Within this political economy framework, would a central political incumbent choose to decentralize the authority to raise revenues under the standard technical rationale for decentralization—heterogeneity of preferences over public goods? Suppose there are n localities such that $H'^{n}(g)$ varies across n, that is the marginal utility from the public good varies across localities. Under the assumption that g is divisible into g^n (such as schools, health centers, etc.), benevolent decentralization by a central social planner would involve the creation of n local governments, and decentralization of decision-making to these local governments over g^n and τ^n. Benevolent local governments would in turn select local levels of taxation to finance locally preferred levels of the public good. However, such decentralization involves giving up taxation rights by the central incumbent, and risks greater tax rates and redistribution to rival interest groups by rival political parties that come into power at local levels. For such decentralization to happen, it would need conditions on the likelihood of the ruling political party controlling local governments, as in the analysis of O'Neill (2003).

Decentralization Under Local Vote Mobilization?

Now suppose local elections enable the identification of local leaders with social networks within which vote buying is more effective than through centralized "party machines." This is the second critical assumption for the arguments offered in this chapter.

Consider the following form of decentralization: (1) announcement of the decentralization of local grants, $D^n \epsilon (0, R(\tau))$, determined for each locality at the discretion of the central government for poverty alleviation programs for which the beneficiaries will be identified by locally elected governments; (2) local elections occur to select the candidate who will subsequently determine f^{nj}, $j \epsilon$ 1,2,S, and the outcome of the first local elections is determined by a coin toss; (3) the locally elected leader receives D^n, and allocates it to f^{nj} to maximize the utility of his/her core supporters subject to a budget and re-election constraint.[21]

First, under decentralization, in equilibrium $D^n{}_{n \notin G} = 0$ for those localities where the citizen-candidate who wins elections belongs to the opposition party.[22] To determine grants to the localities where its party affiliates win office, the central incumbent party

[21] Tax decentralization is not an option because it would lead to loss of central incumbent control over the revenues collected by opposition party local governments.

[22] The actions of the state government of Andhra Pradesh in India in the late 1990s have been interpreted in this light—because the elected leaders of village governments were not aligned with the state ruling party, the state party bypassed these local governments and gave program transfers directly to other forms of community organization—user committees—that it was better able to control (Powis, 2003; Manor, 2004).

goes through the following exercise: it first chooses its unconstrained (by re-election) most preferred tax rate and public good level; it then estimates how many swing votes it can get with its preferred level of public goods, and how many more it needs to win re-election. If it has sufficient swing votes at its preferred policy, there is no benefit from decentralization.

If the swing votes are not sufficient, $F(H(g^{*G}))< \lambda$, the central politician could provide grants $D^* = \sum_{n \epsilon G} D^n = [F^{-1}(\lambda) - H(g^{*G})]$ to its affiliated localities to buy votes through direct transfers to those swing voters, μ^{*s},whose reservation utility is given by $F^{-1}(\lambda) \geq \omega^*>H(g^{*G})$. These swing voters cast their vote in the next elections (both local and central) in favor of the party of the local incumbent who provides them with transfers $f^s = \frac{[F^{-1}(\lambda)-H(g^{*G})]}{\mu^{*s}}$.[23]

Assuming sufficient revenues, the central politician would continue to keep the tax rate at τ^{*G}, and provide g^{*G}, but would reduce the targeted rents to its constituents to $r^{jDG} = r^{*G} - D^{*G}$.

What would the local politicians belonging to the group μ^G do upon receiving grants D^n? Since their objective is the same as the incumbent political party G; that is, to maximize the utility of core constituents subject to a re-election constraint, they will spend the entire grant on buying the swing votes needed for their party to win office both locally and centrally.[24]

If local elected leaders are more efficient and effective than local party operatives at identifying and winning the cheapest swing votes, then the local spending needed to win the minimum swing votes would be less than the additional transfers provided by party operatives (in the absence of decentralization): $D^{*G} < f^{s*}$. Decentralization of grants for beneficiary selection of targeted transfers would therefore be selected by the central political incumbent if it were cheaper to buy votes from the poorest voters through the advantages of local-election vote mobilization than through centralized party machines.

Acknowledgements

The author thanks Tim Besley and Jean-Paul Faguet for inviting this chapter, and for their valuable comments, and also an anonymous referee for their very useful suggestions. The opinions and conclusions expressed here are those of the authors and not those of the World Bank or its Executive Directors.

[23] We assume at this point that the number of localities n^G is sufficient to contain the μ^{*s} swing voters.

[24] The local party leader receives the group-targeted transfers and shares in the general benefits of his/her party holding office.

References

Acharya, S., 2004. "India's growth prospects revisited." *Economic and Political Weekly*, October 9, 4,537–42.

Ahmad, E. and M. Garcia-Escribano, 2006. "Fiscal Decentralization and Public Subnational Financial Management in Peru." IMF Working Paper, WP/06/120, IMF, Washington, DC.

Alesina, A., and Perotti, R., 1995. "Fiscal expansions and adjustments in OECD countries." *Economic Policy*, 10(21), 205–48.

Aiyer, Mani Shankar, 2009. "Inclusive Growth Through Inclusive Governance." Conference Paper, Initiative for Policy Dialogue, Decentralization Task Force Meeting, Columbia University, New York. <http://www0.gsb.columbia.edu/ipd/pub/Aiyar_inclusive_growth.pdf>.

Alderman, H., 2002. "Do Local Officials Know Something We Don't? Decentralization of Targeted Transfers in Albania." *Journal of Public Economics*, 83(3): 375–404.

Ambrosanio, M. F. and M. Bordignon, 2006. "Normative Versus Positive Theories of Revenue Assignments in Federations." In E. Ahmad and G. Brosio (eds.) *Handbook of Fiscal Federalism*, Cheltenham, UK: Edward Elgar.

Araujo, M. C., Ferreira, F. H., Lanjouw, P., and Özler, B., 2008. "Local inequality and project choice: Theory and evidence from Ecuador." Journal of Public Economics, 92(5).

Baland, Jean Marie and Jean-Philippe Platteau, 1999. "The Ambiguous Impact of Inequality on Local Resource Management." *World Development* 27(5): 773–88.

Banerjee, A., R. Banerji, E. Duflo, R. Glennerster, D. Keniston, S. Khemani, and M. Shotland, 2007. "Can Information Campaigns Raise Awareness and Local Participation in Primary Education?" *Economic and Political Weekly*, April 14, 42(15): 1365–72.

Banerjee, A., R. Banerji, E. Duflo, R. Glennerster, and S. Khemani, 2010. "Pitfalls of Participatory Programs: Evidence from a Randomized Evaluation in Education in India." *American Economic Journal: Economic Policy*, 2(1): 1–30.

Bardhan, P., 2002. "Decentralization of Governance and Development." *Journal of Economic Perspectives* 16(4): 185–205.

Bardhan, P., and Mookherjee, D., 2007a. "Decentralization, corruption and government accountability." In Rose-Ackerman, Susan (ed.), *International Handbook on the Economics of Corruption*, 6, 161–88. Northampton, Massachusetts: Edward Elgar Publishing.

Bardhan, P., S. Mitra, D. Mookherjee, and A. Sarkar, 2007. "Local Democracy in Rural West Bengal: Political Participation and Targeting of Public Services." Working Paper, UC-Berkeley, Department of Economics.

Bardhan, Pranab, and Dilip Mookherjee, 2000. "Capture and Governance at Local and National Levels." *American Economic Review*, 90(2): 135–9.

Bardhan, Pranab, and Dilip Mookherjee, 2005. "Decentralizing Antipoverty Program Delivery in Developing Countries." *Journal of Public Economics*, 89: 675–704.

Bates, Robert H., *Markets and States in Tropical Africa: The Political Basis of Agricultural Policies. Vol. 1.* Berkeley, CA: Univ of California Press, 1981.

Besley, Timothy, Rohini Pande, Lupin Rahman, and Vijayendra Rao, 2004. "The Politics of Public Good Provision: Evidence from Indian Local Governments." *Journal of the European Economic Association*, April–May 2004.

Boex, J. and J. Martinez-Vazquez, 2005. "The Determinants of The Incidence of International Grants: A Survey of the International Experience." Working Paper 05-09, Andrew Young School of Policy Studies, Georgia State University, Atlanta, Georgia.

Brusco, V., M. Nazareno and S. Stokes, 2004. "Vote Buying in Argentina." *Latin American Research Review*, 39(2):66–88.

Burki, Shaid Javed, Guillermo Perry, and William Dillinger, 1999. *Beyond the Center: Decentralizing the State*. World Bank: Washington, DC.

Chaudhuri, S., 2006. "What Difference Does a Constitutional Amendment Make? The 1994 Panchayati Raj Act and the Attempt to Revitalize Rural Local Government in India." In P. Bardhan and D. Mookherjee (eds.) *Decentralization and Local Governance in Developing Countries: A Comparative Perspective*. Cambridge, Mass.: MIT Press.

Cheema, Ali, and Shandana Khan Mohmand, 2008. "Decentralization and Inequality in Pakistan: Bridging the Gap?" *Devolution and Governance: Reforms in Pakistan*. Oxford: Oxford University Press.

Cremer, J. and T. Palfrey, 1996. "In or Out? Centralization by Majority Vote." *European Economic Review*, 40, 43–60.

De Dios, Emmanuel, 2007. "Local Politics and Local Economy." In Arsenio M. Balisacan and Hal Hill (eds.) *The Dynamics of Regional Development—The Philippines in East Asia*, Manila, Philippines: Ateneo De Manila University Press.

DellaVigna, Stefano, and Matthew Gentzkow, 2009. *Persuasion: Empirical Evidence*. No. w15298. National Bureau of Economic Research.

Devarajan, S., Khemani, S., and Shah, S., 2009. "The politics of partial decentralization." In Ahmad, E. and Brosio, G. *Does Decentralization Enhance Service Delivery and Poverty Reduction?* Edward Elgar, 79–101.

Dickovick, J. T., 2007. "Municipalization as Central Government Strategy: Central-Regional-Local Politics in Peru, Brazil, and South Africa." *Publius: The Journal of Federalism*, 37(1): 1–25.

Dixit, Avinash, and John Londregan. "The determinants of success of special interests in redistributive politics." *Journal of Politics* 58 (1996): 1132–55.

Faguet, J.P., 2000. "Decentralization and Local Government Performance: Improving Public Service Provision in Bolivia," *Revista de Economía del Rosario*, 3(1): 127–76.

Faguet, J.P., 2004. "Why So Much Centralization? A Model of Primitive Centripetal Accumulation." STICERD DEDPS No.43, London School of Economics.

Faguet, J.P. and F.B. Wietzke, 2006. "Social Funds and Decentralization: Optimal Institutional Design." *Public Administration and Development*, 26(4): 303–15.

Feddersen, Timothy J., and Wolfgang Pesendorfer. "The swing voter's curse." *American Economic Review* (1996): 408–24.

Ferraz, C. and F. Finan, 2008. "Exposing Corrupt Politicians: the effect of Brazil's Publicly Released Audits on Electoral Outcomes." *Quarterly Journal of Economics*, 123(2): 703–45.

Finan, F. and L. Schechter, 2010. "Vote-buying and Reciprocity." Mimeo, Department of Economics. Berkeley, USA: University of California, <http://www.econ.berkeley.edu/~ffinan/Finan_VB.pdf>.

Foster, A. and M. Rosenzweig, 2001. "Democratization, Decentralization, and the Distribution of Local Public Goods in a Poor Rural Economy." Working Paper, Brown University, <http://adfdell.pstc.brown.edu/papers/democ.pdf>.

Galasso, E., & Ravallion, M., 2005. "Decentralized targeting of an antipoverty program." Journal of Public Economics, 89(4), 705–27.

Green, Elliott. "Decentralization and political opposition in contemporary Africa: evidence from Sudan and Ethiopia." *Democratization* 18.5 (2011): 1087–105.

Harding, Robin, 2008. "Vote Buying Across Africa." Mimeo. Department of Political Science, New York University.

Keefer, Philip, and Stuti Khemani, 2009. "When do legislators pass on pork? The role of political parties in determining legislator effort." *American Political Science Review* 103.01: 99–112.

Khemani, S., 2013. "Buying Votes versus Supplying Public Services: Political Incentives to Under-Invest in Pro-poor Policies." Working paper no. 6339, Development Research Group, The World Bank, Washington, DC.

Khemani, S., 2006a. "Local Government Accountability for Health Service Delivery in Nigeria." *Journal of African Economies*, June 2006, 15(2): 285–312.

Khemani, S., 2006b. "The Political Economy of Fiscal Equalization Transfers." In Roy Bahl, Jorge Martinez and Robert Searle (eds) *Fiscal Capacity Equalization and Intergovernmental Transfers*. New York, N.Y.: Springer Publications.

Khemani, S. and W. Wane, 2008. "Populist Fiscal Policy." Policy Research Working Paper No. 4762, Development Research Group, The World Bank, Washington, DC.

Labonne, J. and R. Chase, 2008. "Do Community-Driven Development Projects Enhance Social Capital? Evidence from the Philippines." Policy Research Working Paper No. 4678, Development Research Group, The World Bank, Washington, DC.

Lindbeck, Assar, and Jörgen W. Weibull, 1987. "Balanced-budget redistribution as the outcome of political competition." *Public choice* 52.3: 273–97.

Lizzeri, A. and N. Persico, 2004. "Why Did the Elites Extend the Suffrage? Democracy and the Scope of Government, with an Application to Britain's 'Age of Reform'." *Quarterly Journal of Economics*, 119(2): 707–65.

Lockwood, B., 2004. "Decentralization via Federal and Unitary Referenda." *Journal of Public Economic Theory*, 6: 313–37.

Manor, J., 2004. "User Committees: A potentially Damaging Second Wave of Decentralization?" Special Spring 2004 issue of *European Journal of Development Research*, eds. J. C. Ribot and A.M. Larson, Volume 16, Number 1, Chapter 11.

Mansuri, G., and Rao, V., 2004. "Community-based and -driven development: A critical review." *The World Bank Research Observer, 19*(1), 1–39.

Mohanty, M., Mathew, G., Baum, R., and Ma, R. (eds.), 2007. Grass-*Roots Democracy in* India *and* China*: The Right to Participate*. New Delhi: SAGE Publications.

O'Neill, K., 2003. "Decentralization as an Electoral Strategy." *Comparative Political Studies*, 36(9): 1068–91.

Oates. W., 1972. *Fiscal Federalism*, New York: Harcourt-Brace.

Oberholzer-Gee, F. and K. S. Strumpf, 2002. "Endogenous Policy Decentralization: Testing the Central Tenet of Economic Federalism." *Journal of Political Economy*, 110: 1–36.

Panizza, U., 1999. "On the Determinants of Fiscal Centralization: Theory and Evidence." *Journal of Public Economics*, 74: 97–140.

Persson, Torsten and Guido Tabellini, 2000. *Political Economics: Explaining Public Policy*. Cambridge, Mass.: The MIT Press.

Persson, T., Roland, G., & Tabellini, G., 2007. "Electoral rules and government spending in parliamentary democracies." *Quarterly Journal of Political Science*, 2(2), 155–88.

Powis, B., 2003. "Grass Roots Politics and the 'Second Wave of Decentralisation' in Andhra Pradesh." *Economic & Political Weekly* (28 June).

Ravallion, Martin, 1999. "Are poorer states worse at targeting their poor?" *Economics Letters* 65.3: 373–7.

Redoano, M. and K. Scharf, 2004. "The Political Economy of Policy Centralization: Direct versus Representative Democracy." *Journal of Public Economics*, 88: 799–817.

Robinson, James A., and Ragnar Torvik, 2009. *The Real Swing Voter's Curse*. No. w14799. National Bureau of Economic Research.

Rocamora, Joel, 2004. "Formal Democracy and its Alternatives in the Philippines." *Democracy and civil society in Asia* 2: 196–221.

Sanchez de Lozada, G., 2000. Letter to Mr. Eduardo Aninat. <http://www0.gsb.columbia.edu/ipd/pub/SanchezLozada.pdf>.

Stokes, Susan, 2005. "Perverse Accountability: A Formal Model of Machine Politics with Evidence from Argentina." *American Political Science Review*, 99(03): 315–25.

Tendler, J., 1997. *Good Government in the Tropics*. Baltimore, Md.: Johns Hopkins University Press.

Tiebout, C. M., 1956. "A Pure Theory of Local Expenditures." *Journal of Political Economy*, 65(5): 416–24.

Varshney, Ashutosh, 2000. "Why Have Poor Democracies Not Eliminated Poverty?" *Asian Survey* Vol XL, No. 5, September/October 2000, 718–36.

World Bank, 2003. *Restoring Fiscal Discipline for Poverty Reduction in Peru: A Public Expenditure Review*. The World Bank, Washington, DC.

World Bank, 2008. *Spending for Development: Making the Most of Indonesia's New Opportunities, Indonesia Public Expenditure Review*. The World Bank, Washington, DC.

Part III

Decentralization and Local Service Provision

10

Does Yardstick Competition Influence Local Government Fiscal Behavior in the Philippines?

Joseph J. Capuno, Stella A. Quimbo, Aleli D. Kraft, Carlos Antonio R. Tan, Jr, and Vigile Marie B. Fabella

10.1 Introduction

On why local governments in some developing countries have not become responsive under decentralization, several reasons have been cited, including mismatches in the devolution of expenditure and revenue functions, unfunded mandates, and weak local capacity to deliver services or absorb additional fiscal resources (see, for example, Bird and Vaillancourt, 1998). Others point to the inherent weaknesses in these countries' electoral institutions and other accountability mechanisms, such as limited and delayed public access to appropriate information, which enable the winning political candidate to renege on his or her campaign promises (Bardhan and Mookherjee, 2006; Bardhan, 2002; Faguet 2004; Keefer and Khemani, 2004). Thus, various measures to improve the design and implementation of decentralization programs, with increasing emphasis on strengthening transparency and democratic participation, have been advocated (e.g., World Bank, 2004).

Indeed, where access to information has been expanded, whether through the usual mass media or the public dissemination of satisfaction surveys, public service delivery has been seen to improve (e.g., Paul, 1998; Reinikka and Svensson, 2003; Ravindra, 2004; Deininger and Mpuga, 2005). Arguably, one strategy that local voters can use to overcome information asymmetry is to compare their local government's performance with that of surrounding localities with similar socioeconomic conditions (Faguet and Wietzke, 2006). If the other localities are able to provide better public services for the same level of taxes or collect lower taxes for the same level of public provisions, then voters can make informed decisions in re-electing their local officials. To win their voters' support, local governments in turn will attempt to outperform their neighboring localities. Since Besley and Case's research (1995b), evidence of the effects of this so-called yardstick competition among local governments on their fiscal decisions has been found in other developed countries (see e.g., Revelli and Tovmo, 2007; Rincke, 2009; Allers and Elhorst, 2005).While the general results point to the positive impact of relative performance assessment on local government fiscal behavior, Revelli (2005) also raised the possibility that previous findings are unable to identify the effects of yardstick competition from other forms of local government interactions. For example, the observed correlation between the public provisions of a local government and that of its neighbors may be due to expenditure spillovers or tax competition and not because local voters compel their leaders to improve. Akin to the reflection problem (Manski, 1993), the identification of the underlying reason for the observed correlation between local fiscal decisions is important for their divergent policy implications. Where the correlation is due to yardstick competition, stimulating greater expenditure in one locality have the same effects on another. But when it is due to, say, expenditure spillover, stimulating the fiscal spending in one locality may encourage free-riding in another.

In this chapter, we investigate whether voters' comparative assessment of local government performance affects their own local government's fiscal behavior in a developing country setting, where presumably the formal accountability mechanisms are weaker and the local elites continue to dominate local politics. The issue is especially pertinent in the Philippines given the wide divergence in regional growth and local government performance in the last twenty years of decentralization (Silva, 2005; Manasan, 2007; Llanto, 2012). Despite the devolution of more expenditure functions and greater shares in the internal tax revenues as mandated under the Local Government Code of 1991, most local government units (provinces, cities, municipalities, villages) are found inadequate in their delivery of basic services (Azfar et al., 2000; Diokno, 2012). While several jurisdictions are found innovative (Galing Pook Foundation, 2006), the spread of innovations is slow, with the multitude of localities lagging behind (Capuno, 2007). While the Code mandates the establishment of several local consultative bodies, shorter-term limits for elected officials, and the institutionalization of a system of recall of local officials, some have argued that political dynasties remain entrenched under decentralization (Rivera, 1999; Coronel et al., 2004; Rivera, 2011).

Since 1991, there have been policies adopted to improve the availability and access to information on local governments. Besides fiscal revenues and expenditure data, more than thirty performance monitoring systems for local government units (LGUs) have been introduced (Capuno, 2007). Several of these systems are used as basis for bestowing awards or recognitions or for determining grants or aids. While most of these data are available online, not many households have access to the internet, nor are they likely to attempt to sort and understand the available fiscal figures. It is more likely that households observe and then compare their LGU against those in the neighboring localities in terms of service provision. While it is not possible with the available data to test directly if voters indeed make comparative assessments, we provide indirect evidence of this by investigating how the fiscal decisions of one LGU are affected by the fiscal decisions of its neighboring LGUs.

Using a panel dataset from cities and municipalities in the Philippines for 2001, 2004, 2007, and 2010, we investigate whether yardstick competition—using the average spending of surrounding LGUs as a benchmark—influence a local government's own spending for local public services or the mobilization of revenues from local sources. To identify the effects of yardstick competition, we use the variations in term limit status of incumbent mayors and their membership in political clans. The idea is that incumbents who are still eligible to run may have a higher discount factor for the value of pleasing their constituents. This hypothesis is derived from the two-period model of an incumbent political agent presented in section 10.2. In section 10.3 we describe our empirical strategy for verifying this hypothesis. We present evidence of the effect of yardstick competition in section 10.4, and discuss these results further and their policy implications in the last section.

10.2 A Model of Incumbent Behavior

Following political agency models of electoral accountability (e.g., Barro, 1973; Ferejohn, 1986; Rogoff, 1990; Persson and Tabellini, 2002), we present in this section a two-period model of an incumbent local chief executive (city or municipal mayor) who desires to stay in office to appropriate rents or enjoy the perks of the position. The mayor makes fiscal decisions affecting the welfare of the voters through the provision of local public goods and the collection of local taxes. The local government uses its tax revenues and fiscal transfers from the central government to finance its expenditures. A part of the local government budget goes to overhead expenditures like new municipal halls, more vehicles, and additional support staff that benefit the office holders more than the local constituents. We assume that the incumbent mayor effectively controls the budget allocations and knows the true cost of public provisions, which the voters can only approximate from the observed fiscal decisions. Modelling local fiscal decisions from the point of view of the incumbent mayor seems appropriate in the case of the Philippines for two reasons.

First, the decentralization programs gave fiscal autonomy to LGUs and control over the fiscal decision-making processes to local chief executives. Second, due to weaknesses in transparency and accountability mechanisms, voters can only imperfectly monitor their local governments. This could allow the local officials undue to have control over the local governments (Lacaba, 1995; Sidel, 1997).

The mayor is able to take advantage of the information asymmetry because institutional weaknesses render any campaign promise for efficient or equitable spending not credible. Following the literature on yardstick competition (e.g., Besley and Case, 1995b; Bordignon, Cerniglia, and Revelli, 2004; Revelli, 2005), we assume that the uninformed but rational voters employ performance yardsticks to curb unnecessary public spending. In deciding to re-elect the incumbent mayor, voters assess their mayor's performance relative to that of a previous incumbent or to those in the neighboring jurisdictions. Through yardstick competition, the incumbent is thus motivated to improve her performance in the current term to secure more rents in her succeeding term in office. She is less motivated to do so, however during her last term when the possibility of future rents is nil (Besley and Case, 1995a, 1995b).

Consider then an incumbent leader who makes a fiscal decision in the first period to improve her chances of getting re-elected for another term, which is going to be her last. Let U_t be the incumbent's utility from office in period t, t =1, 2. Further, assume that she derives positive but diminishing marginal utility from rents (or ego-rents), R, while in office. Her total utility is then the sum of her utility in the first period and the discounted value of her expected utility in the second period. That is,

$$U = U_1(R_1) + \delta\pi U_2(R_2), \tag{10.1}$$

where δ is her discount factor, π is the probability of re-election, and $0 \leq \delta, \pi \leq 1$. An incumbent who already faces a term limit in period 1 may be specified as somebody who totally discounts the future (i.e., δ=0).

In period t, the incumbent faces the following local government budget constraint,

$$I_t + T_t = pG_t + R_t, \tag{10.2}$$

where I is a given amount of central fiscal transfers, T is local tax revenues, G is a local public good, p is the unit price of the local public good, and R is the amount of fiscal resources used for the incumbent's rents in office. In each period, the central fiscal transfers are assumed to be strictly positive, while the amount of local revenues, public goods, and rents are each assumed to be non-negative (i.e., $I_t > 0, T_t \geq 0, G_t \geq 0, R_t \geq 0$). The local tax revenues (T) comprise lump-sum taxes (τ) imposed on each of the N citizen-voters in the locality.

A representative voter derives utility from G and a private good X. To maximize his utility, he allocates his given income (y) net of lump-sum taxes

(τ) on the private good, whose unit price is set to one. While a voter may want a higher G for a given τ he remits or a lower τ for the level of G provided, he has only imperfect information about p, which gives the incumbent the opportunity to increase R. To influence G (and, indirectly, R), assume that voters in locality i assess their own incumbent's performance against the average public provisions of the J neighboring jurisdictions (G^0), which is defined as

$$G^0 = \sum_{j=1}^{J} G_j/(J-1), \text{ where } j \neq i \text{ and } j, i = 1, 2, 3, \ldots, J.$$

Assume that there is an institutionally set tax ceiling of $\bar{\tau}>0$, and $\bar{\tau} \geq \tau$.[1] Further, the total cost of providing G^0, given τ and I, is assumed to be affordable in each period, i.e., $I_t + \bar{T} - pG^0 \geq 0$ where $\bar{T} = N\bar{\tau}$. As an incentive for seeking another term, let the incumbent's total utility over two periods exceed that of the maximum rents possible in the first period. That is, for $0<\delta \leq 1$,

$$U_1(I_1 + T_1 - pG^0) + \delta\pi U_2(I_2 + T_2) > U_1(I_1 + \bar{T}). \quad (10.3)$$

To secure her re-election and then the second-period rents, she has to provide G at minimal taxes to voters, given the average public provision in the neighboring jurisdictions. Let the relationship between public provisions and taxes, and the probability of re-election, be denoted by the following function:

$$\pi = \pi(G, \tau, G^0), \; 0 \leq \pi \leq 1, \; \pi_G > 0, \; \pi_\tau < 0, \pi_{G^0} < 0. \quad (10.4)$$

In words, the chances of the incumbent getting re-elected improve with greater provisions of local public goods or with reductions in local taxes, other things being constant. However, she cannot just provide any G or collect any t. She has to be mindful of the public provisions in the surrounding jurisdictions to improve her chances of another term. In particular, her chances of getting re-elected fall as the public provision in the neighboring jurisdiction rises, other things being constant.[2]

To maximize her utility (10.1), the incumbent then chooses the optimal level of G and T, subject to the fiscal budget constraint (10.2), and given the benchmark G^0 and ceiling $\bar{\tau}$. In the second period, after which she is not allowed to run for the same office anymore, the incumbent will maximize her rents by providing a minimum G (possibly zero) and imposing $\bar{\tau}$.[3] Hence, her choice problem reduces to

[1] In reality, the minimum G and maximum τ are institutionally set. For example, the local chief executive cannot appropriate for herself the entire local government budget without facing administrative or legal sanctions.

[2] Further, let the probability function be linear in each argument such that but that $\pi_{GG} = 0, \pi_{\tau\tau} = 0$, and $\pi_{G^0G^0} = 0$; but that $\pi_{GG^0} < 0$ and $\pi_{\tau G^0} < 0$.

[3] That $\tau_2 = \bar{\tau}$ follows from the assumption that the marginal utility of fiscal revenues is positive, which also implies that budget constraint is satisfied as an equality in equilibrium.

$$\text{Max.}_{\{G,\tau\}} U = U_1(I_1 + T_1 - pG_1) + \delta\pi(G_1, \tau_1, G^0)U_2(I_2 + \bar{T}). \qquad (10.5)$$

The necessary conditions for a maximum are:

$$U'_{G_1} = U'_{1G_1}(-p) + \pi'_{G_1}\delta U_2 = 0,$$

$$U'_{\tau_1} = U'_{1\tau_1}(N) + \pi'_{\tau_1}\delta U_2 = 0.$$

To maximize her utility, the first equation states that the incumbent mayor should provide an additional unit of public good up to the point where the increment in the expected utility of second-period rents offsets the loss in the marginal utility of first-period rents (brought about by the greater public provision); while the second equation states that the mayor should increase the tax rate up to the point where the reduction in the expected utility of second-period rents is offset by the increase in marginal utility of first-period rents (brought about by higher tax collections).

Let the solutions to the above pair of equations be denoted by the following functions G^* and τ^*:

$$G^* = G(G^0, \delta, \bar{\tau}, I_1, I_2, p, N), \qquad (10.6')$$

$$\tau^* = \tau(G^0, \delta, \bar{\tau}, I_1, I_2, p, N). \qquad (10.6'')$$

Depending on the value of the discount factor, the model yields two sets of testable hypotheses regarding the effect of yardstick competition on local provision (i.e., $\partial G^*/\partial G^0$) and revenue mobilization (i.e., $\partial\tau^*/\partial G^0$). In the first case where δ=0, the incumbent will simply maximize her first-period rent by setting τ to the maximum possible value and G to the minimum possible value. Consequently, she will not be influenced by the fiscal decisions of the other mayors, i.e.,

$$\frac{\partial G^*}{\partial G^0} = 0, \quad \frac{\partial \tau^*}{\partial G^0} = 0\,.$$

In the other case where δ>0, the incumbent seeking another term will be induced to adjust G^*, τ^*, or both if G^0 changes. To illustrate, substitute G^* and τ^* in the first-order conditions and then differentiate the resulting pair of equations with respect to G^0 to get,

$$-pU''_{GG^0}\left[N\frac{\partial\tau}{\partial G^0} - p\frac{\partial G}{\partial G^0}\right]dG^0 + \delta U_2\pi''_{GG^0}\left[\frac{\partial G}{\partial G^0} + \frac{\partial\tau}{\partial G^0} + 1\right]dG^0 = 0, \qquad (10.7')$$

$$NU''_{\tau G^0}\left[N\frac{\partial\tau}{\partial G^0} - p\frac{\partial G}{\partial G^0}\right]dG^0 + \delta U_2\pi''_{\tau G^0}\left[\frac{\partial G}{\partial G^0} + \frac{\partial\tau}{\partial G^0} + 1\right]dG^0 = 0. \qquad (10.7'')$$

Given the assumptions about the shapes of the utility function and the probability of election function, and that $dG^0>0$, it is clear from these two equations that $\partial G/\partial G^0$ and $\partial\tau/\partial G^0$ cannot be equal to zero simultaneously. If $\partial G/\partial G^0>0$, then the incumbent official, in order to finance the extra spending, may raise the tax rate (i.e., $\partial\tau/\partial G^0>0$). Alternatively, she may reduce rents to keep the tax rate constant or lower. This can be shown by plugging in (10.6′) and (10.6″) into (10.2), expressing R in terms of the other variables, and then differentiating the resulting equation (i.e., $R^* = R(G^0, \delta, \bar{\tau}, I_1, I_2, p, N)$) with respect to G^0 to get

$$\frac{dR}{dG^0} = N\frac{\partial\tau}{\partial G^0} - p\frac{\partial G}{\partial G^0} \overset{>}{\underset{<}{=}} 0.$$

The equation above is simply the first bracketed term in (10.7′) or (10.7″). If $\delta=0$, then dR/dG^0 must be equal to zero to be able to solve (10.7′) and (10.7″) simultaneously. By the same argument, if $\delta>0$ then dR/dG^0 must be greater or less than zero. From these comparative statics, it is clear that the value of the discount factor is critical in determining the effects of yardstick competition on local fiscal decisions.

10.3 Empirical Model and Data

10.3.1 *Empirical Model*

To determine the effects of yardstick competition and other factors on local fiscal decisions, we estimate equations (10.6′) and (10.6″) using the following regression equations:

$$G_{it} = \alpha_i + \alpha_1 G^0_{it} + \alpha_2(G^0_{it} \times D_{it}) + \alpha_3 D_{it} + \boldsymbol{I}'_{it}\boldsymbol{\alpha}_4 + \boldsymbol{P}'_{it}\boldsymbol{\alpha}_5 + \boldsymbol{N}'_{it}\boldsymbol{\alpha}_6 + \boldsymbol{Y}'_t\boldsymbol{\alpha}_7 + e_{it},$$

$$T_{it} = \beta_i + \beta_1 G^0_{it} + \beta_2(G^0_{it} \times D_{it}) + \beta_3 D_{it} + \boldsymbol{I}'_{it}\boldsymbol{\beta}_4 + \boldsymbol{P}'_{it}\boldsymbol{\beta}_5 + \boldsymbol{N}'_{it}\boldsymbol{\beta}_6 + \boldsymbol{Y}'_t\boldsymbol{\beta}_7 + v_{it},$$

where G_{it} and T_{it} are the total expenditures (net of rents from office) and total local revenues, respectively, of the ith local government unit (city or municipality) in the tth year. The yardstick variable is G^0 and the indicator for discount factor is D. The vector $\boldsymbol{I}$ includes central fiscal transfers and other subsidies extended to the local government. To capture spatial variations in prices of local public provision, $\boldsymbol{P}$ is a vector of binary indicators for cities and other highly urbanized jurisdictions. To control for the size and wealth of the local tax base, the vector $\boldsymbol{N}$ includes income class indicators of the local governments. Finally, vector $\boldsymbol{Y}$ includes dummy variables for the years 2004, 2007, and 2010.

The αs and βs, with the bold letters as vectors, are regression coefficients. The error terms e and v represent the unobservable factors which may influence G and T respectively. We assume that e and v are normally distributed and uncorrelated with the other dependent variables, i.e., $cov(G, v) = 0$ and $cov(T, e) = 0$. We estimate each regression equation separately using panel data estimation methods.

The key parameters of interest are the coefficients of G^0 and of its interaction with D. We test if the estimates will be different and consistent with our hypotheses as D switches from 0 to 1 (i.e., low or high discount factor).

10.3.2 *Data*

To estimate the parameters, we assembled a panel dataset of 1,514 municipalities and cities in the Philippines (but excluding those in the Autonomous Region of Muslim Mindanao)[4] for the election years 2001, 2004, 2007, and 2010. We culled our local government fiscal data from the Bureau of Local Government Finance and the Commission on Audit; the income and local government classification from the Department of the Interior and Local Government; and the population, poverty,[5] and price data from the National Statistical Coordination Board and National Statistics Office. Data on the number of families enrolled by the national government and other public and private sponsors are taken from the Philippine Health Insurance Corporation. The indicators of term limit and political dynasties were constructed from data obtained from the Commission on Elections.

Due to missing data, our regression sample only has a total of 5,770 observations—about 3.8 observations per local government unit. Where LGUs have incomplete data, this is mostly for 2010. We compared the mean characteristics of these LGUs with that of those with complete data and found no systematic differences in terms of last term, dynasty and other key variables.

10.3.3 *Variables*

Table 10.1 contains the list of regression variables and their definitions. The dependent variable G is measured with *total expenditures net of general public services*, which refers to the local government's total spending on social, economic, and debt payments and other services that have direct impact on

[4] The Autonomous Region of Muslim Mindanao was excluded because it has a different governance structure from the rest of the regions in the country.

[5] There are no official estimates of poor families for the years in our study. For 2004, we used the same estimates found in the official small-area poverty estimates for 2003. For 2001, 2007, and 2010, we multiplied the official poverty rates for 2003 of each local government against its official projected population in 2001, 2007, and 2010.

local welfare. It excludes the outlays on general public services, which include the offices of the mayor, legislative council, assessor, budget and treasury, planning and development, civil registrar, and other centralized services.[6] The other dependent variable is *local revenues*, defined as income from local sources such as real property taxes, regulatory fees, rentals, service charges, and extraordinary receipts and borrowings. Another measure of public provisions, *social and economic services* is the local government expenditures on social services (health, education, social welfare, housing, labor, and employment) and on economic services (public infrastructure, agriculture, trade and industry, and economic enterprises).[7]

There are two yardstick variables: *yardstick_total expenditures* and *yardstick_social and economic services*. The former is the average total expenditures net of general public services of all other LGUs within the province's geographical boundary. The latter is the average expenditures on social services and economic services of the same surrounding LGUs. In the Philippines, cities and municipalities are classified as either component LGUs or independent LGUs. Component LGUs are under the administrative control of the provincial governments while the independent cities and the so-called highly urbanized LGUs are autonomous. Effectively each yardstick variable then renders the average LGU relatively small to influence all of its neighbors, and thus minimizes the possibility of reverse causality.

The discount factor is represented by two proxy indicators. The first indicator is *last term*, which takes on a value of 1 if the incumbent mayor is on her third consecutive term in office and 0 otherwise. Under Philippine laws, a local elected official can occupy the same office for up to three consecutive three-year terms only, and only after a hiatus of one term can she vie for the same position again. The second indicator is an interaction between the variables *last term* and *dynasty*, where the latter is a binary indicator of the incumbent's membership in a local political clan. Presumably, clan membership extends the political horizon of a last-term incumbent mayor. In the Philippines' context, however, clan membership may also reflect the stock of political capital, which may create an incentive for clan members to abuse their term in office. Were this to happen, the dynasty variable would then exhibit a negative effect instead. To distinguish a few incumbent mayors who

[6] According to Manasan and Chatterjee (2003), general public services accounted for an average of about 40 percent of total expenditures of all local governments in the country during the periods 1985–91 and 1993–2000. Later figures from the Bureau of Local Government Finance reveal that the percentage share of general public services in the total municipal spending in each year has risen from 57 in 2001 to 65 in 2010. For cities, the percentage share has likewise risen from about 41 to 58 over the same decade.

[7] Faguet and Sánchez (2014) argue that education, health, and other social services account for the majority of local expenditure across developing countries.

Table 10.1. Variable definitions.

Variable	Definition
Total expenditures net of general public services	Total expenditures of the local government net of expenditures on general public services, per capita (in 2001 pesos)
Social and economic services	Total expenditures on social and economic services, per capita (in 2001 pesos)
Local revenues	Total revenues from local sources including real property taxes, fees and charges, borrowings, extraordinary receipts, and inter-local transfers, per capita (in 2001 pesos)
Yardstick—total expenditures	Average expenditures of the local government net of expenditures on general public services per capita of all other cities and municipalities in the province (in 2001 pesos)
Yardstick—social and economic services	Average expenditures on social and economic services per capita of all other cities and municipalities in the province (in 2001 pesos)
Last term	=1 if incumbent mayor is on his/her third consecutive term in office, 0 otherwise
Dynasty	= 1 if incumbent mayor is related by blood or marriage to a previous or current mayor, governor, or member of Congress, in the same province, 0 otherwise
Yardstick_total expenditures × last term	Interaction of last term and average expenditures of the local government net of expenditures on general public services per capita of all other cities and municipalities in the province (in 2001 pesos)
Yardstick_total expenditures × last term × dynasty	Interaction of last term, dynasty, and average expenditures of the local government net of expenditures on general public services per capita of all other cities and municipalities in the province (in 2001 pesos)
Yardstick_social and economic services × last term	Interaction of last term and average expenditures on social and economic services per capita of all other cities and municipalities in the province (in 2001 pesos)
Yardstick_social and economic services × Last term × dynasty	Interaction of last term, dynasty, and average expenditures on social and economic services per capita of all other cities and municipalities in the province (in 2001 pesos)
Average _IRA	Average internal revenue allotments per capita of all other cities and municipalities in the province (in 2001 pesos)
Extended term	=1 if incumbent mayor is beyond his/her third consecutive term in office, 0 otherwise
Fiscal transfers	Total internal revenue allotment and shares in national wealth received from the national government, per capita (in 2001 pesos)
Non-LGU insurance coverage rate	Proportion of poor families enrolled by the national government, national legislative officials, and private sponsors in the PhilHealth Sponsored Program
Component city	=1 if classified as a component city of a province, 0 otherwise
Highly urbanized LGU	=1 if classified as a highly urbanized local government or independent city, 0 otherwise
Middle income class	=1 if local government belongs to thirrd or fourth income class, 0 otherwise

Low income class	=1 if local government belongs to fifth or sixth income class, 0 otherwise
Year 2004	=1 if year is 2004, 0 otherwise
Year 2007	=1 if year is 2007, 0 otherwise
Year 2010	=1 if year is 2010, 0 otherwise

managed to stay in power for more than nine consecutive years, a dummy variable *extended term* is included.[8]

Local government revenues from external sources are captured by two variables. The first variable, *fiscal transfers*, pertains to the LGU's share in the national government's revenues from internal taxes (called the internal revenue allotment) and from the development of mineral and other natural resources located in the LGU's jurisdiction.[9] The second variable, *non-LGU insurance coverage rate*, is defined as the proportion of poor families in the locality that the national government, national legislative officials, and private sponsors unilaterally enrolled in the country's social health insurance program. Effectively, the LGU thus received a subsidy that partially relieved them of their responsibilities to enroll the same group as mandated under the National Health Insurance Act of 1995.[10] Another fiscal variable is the *average_IRA*, used as an instrument in testing for endogeneity of the yardstick variables. It is defined as the average internal revenue allotment (IRA) provided by the national government to the surrounding LGUs. All fiscal variables are measured in real per capita terms (in 2001 pesos).

In the absence of the actual prices of local public goods, we account for the possible spatial differences between cities or highly urbanized municipalities and other areas with the binary indicators *component city* and *highly urbanized LGU*. A component city shares with the provincial government its real property tax revenues and, in return, benefits from province-provided public services. A highly urbanized LGU—a municipality or an independent city—is administratively and fiscally independent of any provincial government.

To account for the differences in the local tax bases, LGUs are also grouped according to their official income classification. Specifically, an LGU is *middle income class* if it belongs to the third or fourth income class, or *low income class* if it

[8] For example, a former mayor of the town of Mabalacat in the province of Pampanga effectively served a third consecutive term when his previous election to office was eventually nullified after a protracted legal proceeding. He was allowed to run again after the third term and won three more consecutive terms thereafter.

[9] As measured here, the number of *fiscal transfers* in a given year is also a good proxy for the next year's transfers since the principal central fiscal grant—the internal revenue allotment—is based on a fixed formula and distributed periodically and automatically to local governments (Guevara, 2000).

[10] Under the so-called Plan GMA, the national government enrolled 5 million families in 2004, 2.5 million families in 2005, and another 2.5 million families in 2006 in the social health insurance program (Manasan, 2011).

belongs instead to the fifth or sixth income class. These LGUs have less-developed economies relative to those in the first or second income classes. Finally, dummy variables for the years 2004, 2007, and 2010 are introduced to control for any unobserved time-varying factors that affected local fiscal behavior. Election years are chosen to avoid confounding the results with possible political budget cycles in annual data series. Also, elections are like a common shock to all LGUs that their constituents easily observe to assess their relative responses.

10.3.4 *Descriptive Statistics*

The descriptive statistics of the regression variables are shown in Table 10.2. The sample comprises 5,770 observations and the average total expenditures net of general public services and average expenditures on social services are 5.35 pesos and 2.16 pesos, respectively. The average yardstick_total expenditures and yardstick_social and economic services are 12.19 pesos and 2.13 pesos, respectively.

The average local revenue is about 2.34 pesos, while the average of fiscal transfers is nearly five times as much (11.14 pesos). The other subsidy received by local governments comes in the proportion of poor households sponsored into the country's social health insurance program. The non-LGU sponsors have extended coverage up to nearly 40 per cent of the target population on average. However, there were LGUs where the coverage was more than 100 per cent of the estimated number of poor families.

Of the then incumbent mayors, about 22 per cent were on their last term and 33 per cent belonged to political dynasties. About one per cent of them were on

Table 10.2. Descriptive statistics (*N*=5,770).

Variable	Mean	Std. dev.	Min.	Max.
Total expenditures net of general public services	5.35	5.79	0.04	260.23
Social and economic services	2.16	2.58	0	69.62
Local revenues	2.34	4.93	0.003	111.78
Yardstick_total expenditures	12.19	6.93	2.49	80.59
Yardstick_social and economic services	2.13	1.13	0.46	15.32
Last term	0.221	0.415	0	1
Dynasty	0.332	0.471	0	1
Average _IRA	10.92	7.20	2.32	84.44
Extended term	0.011	0.104	0	1
Fiscal transfers	11.14	10.83	1.49	431.10
Non-LGU insurance coverage rate	0.396	0.889	0	33.873
Component city	0.048	0.213	0	1
Highly urbanized LGU	0.196	0.139	0	1
Middle income class	0.466	0.499	0	1
Low income class	0.287	0.452	0	1
Year 2004	0.262	0.440	0	1
Year 2007	0.245	0.430	0	1
Year 2010	0.232	0.422	0	1

extended term. Less than five per cent of the observations are component cities, while nearly 20 per cent of them are highly urbanized local governments or independent cities. Each year accounts for roughly a quarter of the observations. There are slightly fewer observations in 2010 due to missing fiscal data.

10.3.5 *Specification Tests*

To distinguish yardstick competition models from other models of spatial interactions among local governments, Revelli (2005) underscored the importance of tests that would identify common reactions to unobserved stimuli and possible reverse causality. In our theoretical model, yardstick competition is identified by the sharp difference in fiscal behavior when the incumbent's discount factor switches to zero or positive. To better understand the nature of local government interactions in the Philippines, we thus tried four regression specifications for each of the three dependent variables. Each model specification would have one of two yardstick variables (yardstick_total expenditures and yardstick_social and economic services), interacted with one of the two indicators of discount factors (last term and last term × dynasty), but all the other regressors are the same for all specifications. The different specifications allow us to determine exactly on which fiscal performance indicators the LGUs are being compared, and for them to respond differently based on their political horizons to common external influences (such as the provincial government). For each model, we then tested for possible omitted variable bias, the endogeneity of the yarsdstick variable, and the joint significance of all the coefficients of the same yardstick variable.

Specifically, we tested if the omitted variables might be LGU-specific using Hausman tests for fixed effects versus random effects in panel data models. Note that when the yardstick variable is interacted with last term and dynasty, the number of observations for each combination (of the three variables) becomes fewer. This makes it difficult to estimate the standard errors of the differences in the estimated coefficients under fixed-effects model and random-effects model needed to perform the Hausman test. In this case, we estimate and report the coefficients using fixed effects, which are still consistent even if the true model is a random-effects model. Given the results for the other specifications, however, we think the fixed-effects model is the appropriate one in these cases.

The endogeneity of the yardstick variable is examined using the Wu–Hausman test. Following the procedure in Cameron and Trivedi (2005), we performed the test by first regressing the yardstick variable against the same set of exogenous regressors used in the four models and one instrumental variable, the average_IRA. We then obtained the residuals of this regression run and used them as an additional regressor in the main models. If the estimated coefficient of the residual is statistically insignificant, the Wu–Hausman test indicates that the original yardstick variable is not endogenous. Besides performing this test, there are two reasons why the yardstick variable is unlikely to be endogenous. First, it includes the expenditures of all surrounding LGUs and even those autonomous of the province. Second, most local governments are heavily dependent on their internal revenue allotment which is determined using a fixed formula based on the local government level, number of LGUs at each level, and the local government's share of the total population and land area. If the yardstick variable is not endogenous, this avoids the problem of reverse causality (i.e., the reference LGU is actually influencing its neighbors).

Also, we performed an *F*-test on all coefficients of the yardstick variable to see whether yardstick competition and term limits jointly matter in explaining local fiscal behavior. Finally, we obtained the marginal effects of the yardstick variable and discount factor indicators to check their consistency with our model's hypotheses.

10.4 Analysis of Results

10.4.1 *Total Expenditures Net of General Public Services*

Table 10.3 shows the regression results for the total expenditures net of general public services using LGU fixed-effects panel data estimation model and after checking for the endogeneity of the yardstick variable. The use of the fixed-effects model is borne by the results of the Hausman tests reported in the bottom half of the table. Also in the bottom half of the table, the Wu–Hausman tests indicate that neither yardstick_total expenditures nor yardstick_social and economic services are endogenous.

In model specifications 1 and 2, none of the coefficients of the yardstick_total expenditures (alone and when interacted with last term and dynasty) is statistically significant. In models 3 and 4, however, the own coefficients of yardstick_social and economic services are both negative and highly statistically significant. The coefficients of the interaction terms are still not significant. Model 3 is the only specification with interaction (yardstick_social and economic services × last term) that reveals joint significance of the yardstick variable and this interaction term, as borne by the results of the *F*-test reported in the bottom row. These results indicate that LGUs are compared by their constituents in terms of social and economic services, rather than just any type of public spending.

Consistent across all specifications, the variables last term, dynasty, and extended term do not manifest any independent effects on total expenditures net of general public services. In contrast, fiscal transfers and non-LGU insurance coverage rate both show strongly positive influence on local spending.

Table 10.3. Panel data regressions of total expenditures net of general public services (N=5,770).

Independent variables	Model 1		Model 2		Model 3		Model 4	
	Coef.	Rob. std. errors	Coef.	Rob. std. errors	Coef.	Rob. std. errors	Coef.	Rob. std. errors
Yardstick_total expenditures	−0.023	0.018	−0.025	0.020				
Yardstick_total expenditures × last term	0.005	0.019	0.006	0.020				
Yardstick_total expenditures × dynasty			0.011	0.033				
Yardstick_total expenditures × last term × dynasty			0.019	0.052				
Yardstick_social and economic services					−0.353**	0.153	−0.341*	0.178
Yardstick_social and economic services × last term					−0.037	0.197	−0.052	0.191
Yardstick_social and economic services × dynasty							−0.030	0.219
Yardstick_social and economic services × Last term × dynasty							−0.038	0.356
Last term	−0.061	0.219	−0.082	0.250	0.070	0.384	0.070	0.390
Dynasty	0.125	0.105	−0.006	0.370	0.128	0.104	0.173	0.434
Extended term	−1.118	0.883	−1.111	0.886	−1.114	0.899	−1.119	0.899
Fiscal transfers	0.441***	0.054	0.440***	0.054	0.450***	0.053	0.450***	0.053
Non–LGU insurance coverage rate	1.015***	0.244	1.017***	0.244	0.945***	0.228	0.943***	0.228
Highly urbanized LGU	0.435	0.530	0.431	0.541	0.540	0.503	0.555	0.497
Component city	0.800**	0.392	0.795**	0.394	0.801**	0.392	0.796**	0.395
Middle income class	−0.311**	0.131	−0.311**	0.131	−0.313**	0.129	−0.314**	0.129
Low income class	−0.484***	0.164	−0.485***	0.165	−0.487***	0.163	−0.488***	0.164
Year 2004	−1.351***	0.363	−1.351***	0.364	−1.427***	0.372	−1.426***	0.372
Year 2007	−0.219	0.155	−0.219	0.155	−0.392**	0.178	−0.394**	0.178
Year 2010	−2.642***	0.253	−2.639***	0.253	−2.558***	0.243	−2.561***	0.243
Constant	1.539***	0.493	1.570***	0.502	1.979***	0.536	1.963***	0.566
R^2 (overall)	0.6382		0.6385		0.6366		0.6366	
F–statistic	41.01		35.30		56.08		54.45	
Prob>F	0.00		0.00		0.00		0.00	

(continued)

Table 10.3. Continued

Independent variables	Model 1		Model 2		Model 3		Model 4	
	Coef.	Rob. std. errors	Coef.	Rob. std. errors	Coef.	Rob. std. errors	Coef.	Rob. std. errors
Hausman test: LGU fixed–effects								
χ^2–statistic	104.42		n.a.		123.91		n.a.	
Prob>χ^2	0.00				0.00			
Wu–Hausman Test of endogeneity of yardstick variable [a]	NO		NO		NO		NO	
Joint test: Yardstick variable (and interaction terms)								
F–statistic	0.79		0.46		2.87		1.74	
Prob>*F*	0.4534		0.7636		0.0571		0.1444	

Notes: ***$p<0.01$, **$p<0.05$,*$p<0.10$

[a] Using average_IRA as identifying instrument, the Wu-Hausman test indicates that the yardstick variable is not endogenous.

n.a. means the Hausman test is not applied. The reported coefficients in the table are estimated using LGU fixed effects.

Perhaps this can be expected, since most local governments are heavily dependent on their internal revenue allotments. Also consistent across all models, component city has positive and significant effects. The positive effect may reflect that public provision could be cheaper (on a per capita basis) in urbanized areas due to economies of scale and easier access to market inputs. Unlike a component city, a highly urbanized LGU shows positive but insignificant effects.

Perhaps as expected, the middle income class and low income class are both negative and significant. These only indicate that LGUs in the third to sixth income classes tend to spend less than their richer counterparts in the first and second income classes. Finally, years 2004 and 2010 are both negative and significant, while year 2007 is insignificant. This suggests a lower total spending net of general public services in 2004 and 2010 relative to 2001.

10.4.2 *Expenditures on Social and Economics Services*

Table 10.4 show the regression results for the expenditures on social and economic services. The coefficients and standard errors are also obtained using the LGU fixed-effects model, following the results of the Hausman test. We likewise confirmed the yardstick_social and economic services is not endogenous.

Compared to the previous results, there is stronger evidence here of the effects of yardstick competition. Both yardstick variables on their own show positive and statistically significant coefficients across different specifications. However, the coefficients are highly significant and larger when the yardstick variable is based on expenditures on social and economic services alone than when it is based on total expenditures net of general public services. Further, the results of the *F*-tests (bottom row) reveal joint significance of the yardstick variable and its interaction with the last-term indicator for the discount factor. Again, the results are consistent with those in Table 10.3 in that LGUs are more sensitive to comparisons in their outlays for social and economic services.

Some of the results are quite different from those in the previous table. In this case, non-LGU insurance coverage rate is not significant anymore, although fiscal transfers are still consistently positive and significant. The component city remains positive and significant. But now, highly urbanized LGUs are also positive and significant, while both middle income class and low income class are negative and insignificant. Finally, all three year-dummy variables are negative and significant, indicating lower LGU spending on social and economic services relative to that in 2001.

Table 10.4. Panel data regressions of expenditures on social and economic services (N=5,770).

Independent variables	Model 1		Model 2		Model 3		Model 4	
	Coef.	Rob. std. errors	Coef.	Rob. std. errors	Coef.	Rob. std. errors	Coef.	Rob. std. errors
Yardstick_total expenditures	0.029**	0.013	0.025*	0.014				
Yardstick_total expenditures × last term	−0.002	0.017	−0.002	0.016				
Yardstick_total expenditures × dynasty			0.023	0.029				
Yardstick_total expenditures × last term × dynasty			0.041	0.052				
Yardstick_social and economic services					0.340***	0.108	0.327***	0.123
Yardstick_social and economic services × last term					0.080	0.191	0.034	0.161
Yardstick_social and economic services × dynasty							0.038	0.176
Yardstick_social and economic services × last term × Dynasty							0.230	0.385
Last term	0.012	0.185	−0.065	0.228	−0.166	0.360	−0.181	0.367
Dynasty	0.113	0.079	−0.210	0.333	0.106	0.078	−0.044	0.364
Extended term	−0.494	0.421	−0.479	0.424	−0.506	0.415	−0.521	0.419
Fiscal transfers	0.181***	0.016	0.181***	0.016	0.172***	0.014	0.172***	0.014
Non-LGU insurance coverage rate	−0.127	0.096	−0.124	0.096	−0.061	0.090	−0.063	0.091
Highly urbanized LGU	0.880***	0.238	0.873***	0.225	0.776***	0.229	0.785***	0.228
Component city	0.398**	0.174	0.366**	0.178	0.395**	0.181	0.362*	0.187
Middle income class	−0.025	0.074	−0.028	0.074	−0.022	0.074	−0.025	0.073
Low income class	−0.083	0.098	−0.090	0.097	−0.079	0.098	−0.086	0.097
Year 2004	−0.542***	0.114	−0.543***	0.115	−0.458***	0.126	−0.454***	0.126
Year 2007	−0.776***	0.070	−0.780***	0.071	−0.589***	0.064	−0.590***	0.065
Year 2010	−0.272***	0.074	−0.269***	0.074	−0.348***	0.076	−0.353***	0.077
Constant	0.200	0.269	0.269	0.266	−0.146	0.325	−0.085	0.341
R^2 (overall)	0.4363		0.4370		0.4433		0.4443	
F-statistic	65.02		76.55		194.66		538.29	
Prob>F	0.00		0.00.		0.00		0.00	
Hausman test: LGU fixed-effects			n.a.				n.a.	
χ^2-statistic	108.29				125.39			
Prob>χ^2	0.00				0.00			
Wu–Hausman Test of endogeneity of yardstick variable[a]	NO		NO		NO		NO	
Joint test: Yardstick variable (and interaction terms)								
F-statistic	2.97		1.46		5.27		2.75	
Prob>F	0.0518		0.2111		0.0052		0.0271	

Notes: ***p<0.01, **p<0.05, *p<0.10

[a] Using average_IRA as identifying instrument, the Wu-Hausman test indicates that the yardstick variable is not endogenous.

n.a. means the Hausman test is not applied. The reported coefficients in the table are estimated using LGU-fixed effects.

10.4.3 *Local Revenues*

Table 10.5 shows the regression results for local revenues, which are also estimated using LGU fixed effects and after confirming that the yardstick variable is exogenous. Consistent across all models, the yardstick variables are not statistically significant. This indicates that local revenue mobilization is not sensitive to expenditure comparisons. This is borne further by the low R^2 (0.064–0.066), which suggests that other factors (not included in the models) explain the larger part of the variations in local revenues. Moreover, the results of the *F*-tests on the yardstick variables and their interaction terms (bottom row) suggest that the null hypothesis (of zero joint effect) cannot be rejected.

There also other unexpected results. First, both fiscal transfers and non-LGU insurance coverage rate consistently have positive and highly significant effects. Also, highly urbanized LGUs, middle income class, and low income class have positive and significant coefficients. Finally, only Year 2004 among the year dummies has a significant negative coefficient.

10.4.4 *Marginal Effects*

Recall that the theoretical model has sharp predictions about the effects of yardstick competition when the discount factor switches from zero to positive. To verify them, we obtain the full marginal effects of the yardstick variables, which include its own direct effect and indirect effects (through the interaction terms) by switching the values of last term and dynasty. The results are reported in Table 10.6.

The top row (Case 1) roughly corresponds to a situation where the incumbent faces term limit and has a very short political horizon (i.e., she does not belong to a political dynasty). Our theory predicts in this case that yardstick competition would have nil effect on spending or revenue mobilization since the incumbent cares only about the rents in her current and final term. Indeed there is no effect on local revenue mobilization. However, there is some evidence of positive effect on spending on social and economic services, and negative effect of total spending net of general public services.

The positive effect on social and economic outlays could imply that the incumbent, while facing term limit, actually wants to leave a legacy for which she will be remembered if she runs for the same office after the mandatory one-term hiatus. This supposition of a legacy motivation is partly supported by the results in Case 2 (second row). In this case the incumbent also faces term limit, but she is a clan member. In this case, yardstick competition has nil effect on social and economic spending. This suggests that the incumbent may not care about leaving a legacy since she can depend on her clan in future

Table 10.5. Panel data regressions of local revenues (*N*=5,770).

Independent variables	Model 1		Model 2		Model 3		Model 4	
	Coef.	Rob. std. errors	Coef.	Rob. std. errors	Coef.	Rob. std. errors	Coef.	Rob. std. errors
Yardstick_total expenditures	−0.0001	0.018	−0.002	0.023				
Yardstick_total expenditures × last term	−0.003	0.012	−0.003	0.016				
Yardstick_total expenditures × dynasty			0.009	0.032				
Yardstick_total expenditures × last term × dynasty			0.014	0.041				
Yardstick_social and economic services					0.085	0.180	0.081	0.236
Yardstick_social and economic services × last term					−0.059	0.125	−0.076	0.135
Yardstick_social and economic services × dynasty							0.010	0.213
Yardstick_social and economic services × last term × dynasty							−0.008	0.287
Last term	0.045	0.165	0.014	0.188	0.132	0.249	0.127	0.258
Dynasty	0.160	0.156	0.029	0.368	0.162	0.155	0.114	0.404
Extended term	−0.189	0.230	−0.183	0.232	−0.181	0.230	−0.187	0.233
Fiscal transfers	0.193***	0.026	0.193***	0.026	0.191***	0.026	0.191***	0.026
Non-LGU insurance coverage rate	0.434***	0.126	0.436***	0.127	0.450***	0.121	0.449***	0.121
Highly urbanized LGU	1.774***	0.321	1.771***	0.333	1.758***	0.341	1.763***	0.325
Component city	0.283	0.258	0.270	0.262	0.283	0.258	0.270	0.259
Middle income class	0.332**	0.144	0.332**	0.144	0.331**	0.144	0.330**	0.144
Low income class	0.357*	0.196	0.354*	0.194	0.355*	0.195	0.352*	0.194
Year 2004	−0.525***	0.187	−0.525***	0.188	−0.516**	0.202	−0.514**	0.203
Year 2007	−0.002	0.100	−0.003	0.100	0.023	0.110	0.023	0.108
Year 2010	0.103	0.151	0.104	0.151	0.080	0.153	0.078	0.154
Constant	−0.234	0.373	−0.206	0.421	−0.403	0.499	−0.384	0.598
R^2 (overall)	0.0640		0.0650		0.0657		0.0657	
F-statistic	14.81		12.95		13.87		12.52	
Prob>*F*	0.00		0.00		0.00		0.00	
Hausman test: LGU fixed-effects χ^2-statistic	331.19		n.a.		332.81		n.a.	
Prob>χ^2	0.00				0.00			
Wu–Hausman Test of endogeneity of yardstick variable[a]	NO		NO		NO		NO	
Joint test: Yardstick variable (and interaction terms)								
F-statistic	0.06		0.23		0.14		0.24	
Prob>*F*	0.9440		0.9230		0.8728		0.9144	

Notes: ***$p<0.01$, **$p<0.05$, *$p<0.10$

[a] Using average_IRA as identifying instrument, the Wu-Hausman test indicates that the yardstick variable is not endogenous.

Table 10.6. Marginal effects of yardstick, last-term, and dynasty variables.

Cases	Total expenditures net of general public services		Expenditures on social and economic services		Local revenues	
	Marginal effects	Rob. std. errors	Marginal effects	Rob. std. errors	Marginal effects	Rob. std. errors
Case 1: (last term = 1) or (last term = 1 and dynasty = 0)						
Yardstick_total expenditures × last term (Model 1)	−0.017	0.022	0.0002	0.009	−0.003	0.012
Yardstick_total expenditures × last term × dynasty (Model 2)	−0.018	0.021	0.023*	0.013	−0.005	0.013
Yardstick_social and economic services × last term (Model 3)	−0.389*	0.224	0.291	0.188	0.026	0.138
Yardstick_social and economic services × last term × dynasty (Model 4)	−0.393*	0.212	0.361**	0.152	0.005	0.158
Case 2: (last term =1) or (last term =1 and dynasty=1)						
Yardstick_total expenditures × last term (Model 1)	−0.017	0.022	0.0002	0.009	−0.003	0.012
Yardstick_total expenditures × last term × dynasty (Model 2)	−0.006	0.049	0.066	0.049	0.013	0.030
Yardstick_social and economic services × last term (Model 3)	−0.389*	0.224	0.291	0.188	0.026	0.138
Yardstick_social and economic services × last term × dynasty (Model 4)	−0.379	0.324	0.557	0.356	0.073	0.175
Case 3: (last term = 0) or (last term = 0 and dynasty = 0)						
Yardstick_total expenditures × last term (Model 1)	−0.023	0.018	−0.007	0.009	−0.0001	0.018
Yardstick_total expenditures × last term × dynasty (Model 2)	−0.025	0.020	0.025*	0.014	−0.002	0.023
Yardstick_social and economic services × last term (Model 3)	−0.353**	0.153	0.233***	0.079	0.085	0.180
Yardstick_social and economic services × last term × dynasty (Model 4)	−0.341*	0.178	0.327***	0.123	0.081	0.236
Case 4: (last term = 0) or (last term = 0 and dynasty = 1)						
Yardstick_total expenditures × last term (Model 1)	0.023	0.018	−0.007	0.009	−0.0001	0.018
Yardstick_total expenditures × last term × synasty (Model 2)	−0.014	0.032	0.048*	0.028	0.008	0.021
Yardstick_social and economic services × last term (Model 3)	−0.353**	0.153	0.233***	0.079	0.085	0.180
Yardstick_social and economic services × last term × dynasty (Model 4)	−0.371*	0.200	0.365**	0.160	0.091	0.148

Note: ***$p<0.01$, **$p<0.05$, *$p<0.10$

elections. The dynasty variable in this sense might partly reflect the stock of political capital perhaps built by other clan members who previously held elective offices.

Case 3 (third row) corresponds to the case where the incumbent does not yet face term limit and has no political clan. The prediction here is that yardstick competition would have a positive effect, since the incumbent would want to be perceived as a good performer to win another term. In this case, we find yardstick_social and economic services to have positive and significant marginal effects on expenditures on social and economic services. The effect is slightly bigger when incumbent is also a member of political dynasty (0.365 in Case 4, model 4) than when she is not (0.327 in Case 3, model 4) . This corresponds to the situation where clan membership extends the political horizon of the incumbent that renders her more sensitive to peer comparisons.

In all cases, we find local revenue mobilization to be consistently unresponsive to yardstick competition. This could be due to the fact that most LGUs are heavily reliant on central fiscal transfers. Also, not many LGUs have vibrant local economies. Also, yardstick competition has negative effects on total expenditures net of general public services. Recall that the residual outlays comprise spending on social and economic services and on debt payments and other extraordinary expenses outlays. The negative effect then means that LGUs are spending less on debt payments and other expenses, since they also tend to spend more on social and economic services.

10.5 Discussion and Conclusion

To the question on whether decentralization in developing countries can improve the delivery of public services given the generally weak accountability mechanisms in these places, we find some evidence in the Philippines that yardstick competition has the desired impact. The results have important policy implications since decentralization in the Philippines, like in other developing countries, is believed to have entrenched elite control of local governments. Since the Local Government Code was enacted in 1991, members of political clans have continued to occupy local elective positions despite the improvements in electoral institutions, which include a system of recall for the people to remove from office any elected official in which they have lost confidence and the computerization of ballot counting. Plausibly, however, the same reforms that expanded democratic spaces and the adoption of various local government performance indicators and award schemes may have influenced how the people perceive, if not actually monitor, their local governments.

In this chapter, we have investigated the case where voters do not know the unit costs (or prices) of public services and therefore do not know the maximum affordable levels of public provision with which to assess the performance of their incumbent mayors. Instead, the voters are assumed to observe and compare the level of public provisions of their own local governments and that of the neighboring localities. If the incumbent mayors are sensitive to voters' comparisons, then their fiscal decisions will be correlated. However, an observed correlation does not necessarily indicate yardstick competition. To identify the effects of yardstick competition, we have compared local fiscal decisions when incumbent mayors face and do not yet face mandatory term limits in a panel of cities and municipalities in four election years. Here, we find evidence that public service delivery in neighboring jurisdictions influences the local government's own performance. In particular, when the incumbent mayor is not yet on her last term, the local government's provision of social and economic services rises with the mean expenditures on the same services of its neighbors within the province. When she is on her last term and is a member of political clan, the local provision of the same services is uninfluenced by the neighbors' public provisions. The effect is positive only when the last-term mayor is not a clan member, possibly because she wants to leave a legacy. These results support the hypothesis that electoral pressures can and do make local officials responsive to their constituents' needs. The implication then is that widening access to information about the performance of other local governments, especially those in nearby localities, can influence how the people will assess their own local government, which will then induce the desired response from the latter.

Our results also reveal some nuanced characteristics of the nature of yardstick competition in the Philippines. First, performance in terms of provision of social and economic services is what matters, not total spending per se. This seems sensible since health, education, social welfare, employment, and infrastructure services bear directly on the welfare of the constituents. Second, political dynasties can either extend the political horizon or endow political capital, which may lead to different responses to yardstick competition. This is consistent with the view that political dynasties persist in the Philippines because they substitute for dysfunctional political parties (De Dios, 2007), and that it is the absence of rival political dynasties rather than clan membership per se that seems inimical to local development spending (Solon, Fabella, and Capuno, 2009).

Finally, our results suggest issues for further research. In particular, the negative relationship between an LGU's own total expenditure net of general public services and that of its neighbors, regardless of the incumbent's term limit status, suggests free riding among local governments. If this were the case, then the policy prescription is not necessarily more information to voters, but rather corrective fiscal transfers. Another unexpected result is the positive effect of fiscal transfers on local revenue mobilization. Using shorter time periods and different estimation methods, previous studies found that the internal revenue allotment disincentivizes real property tax collections of local governments in the Philippines. Finally, it remains to be seen whether responses to yardstick comparisons actually determine election or re-election outcomes.

Acknowldegements

This research is part of the Health Equity and Financial Protection in Asia (HEFPA) Project, with funding support from the European Union (EU-FP7 research grant HEALTH-F2-2009-223166-HEFPA). An earlier version of this chapter appeared as UPSE Discussion Paper No. 2012–08 with the title "Perks and Public Provisions: Effects of Yardstick Competition on Local Government Fiscal Behavior in the Philippines." We gratefully acknowledge the overall technical and moral support of Adam Wagstaff, Eddy van Doorslaer, Owen O'Donnell, and other members of the HEFPA consortium, and comments and suggestions from J.P. Faguet. Last, we also thank Filipinas Bundoc, Rhea Molato, Noel Del Castillo, and Kate Farrales for their excellent research assistance. All errors are ours.

References

Allers, M. and Elhorst, J., 2005. "Tax Mimicking and Yardstick Competition among Local Governments in the Netherlands." *International Tax and Public Finance* 12(4): 493–513.

Azfar, O., Gurgur, T., Kähkönen, S., Lanyi, A., and Meagher, A., 2000. "Decentralization and Governance: An empirical Investigation of Public Service Delivery in the Philippines." Discussion Paper IRIS Center, University of Maryland, Baltimore, USA.

Bardhan, P., 2002. "Decentralization of Governance and Development." *Journal of Economic Perspectives* 16(4): 185–205.

Bardhan, P. and Mookherjee, D., 2006. *Decentralization and Local Governance in Developing Countries: A Comparative Perspective*. Cambridge, Mass.: MIT press.

Barro, R., 1973. "The Control of Politicians: An Economic Model." *Public Choice* 14: 19–42.

Besley, T. and Case, A., 1995a. "Does Electoral Accountability Affect Economic Policy Choices? Evidence from Gubernatorial Term Limits." *Quarterly Journal of Economics* 110(3):769–98.

Besley, T. and Case, A., 1995b. "Incumbent Behavior: Vote Seeking, Tax Setting and Yardstick Competition." *American Economic Review* 85(1): 25–45.

Bird, R. and Vaillancourt, F., 1998. *Fiscal Decentralization in Developing Countries*. Cambridge, UK: Cambridge University Press.

Bordignon, M., Cerniglia, F., and Revelli, F., 2004. "Yardstick Competition in Intergovernmental Relationships: Theory and Empirical Predictions." *Economics Letters* 83: 325–33.

Cameron, A. C. and Trivedi, P., 2005. *Microeconometrics: Methods and Applications*. Cambridge, UK: Cambridge University Press.

Capuno, J. J., 2007. "The Quality of Local Governance and Development under Decentralization." In Balisacan, A.M. and Hill, H. (eds.), *The Dynamics of Regional Development: The Philippines in East Asia*. Cheltenham, UK: Edward Elgar, pp. 204–45.

Coronel, S., Chua, Y.T., Rimban, L., and Cruz, B. B., 2004. *The Rulemakers. How the Wealthy and Well-Born Dominate Congress*. Quezon City, Philippines: Philippine Center for Investigative Journalism.

De Dios, E. S., 2007. "Local Politics and Local Economy." In Balisacan, A.M. and Hill, H. (eds.), *The Dynamics of Regional Development: The Philippines in East Asia*. Cheltenham, UK: Edward Elgar, pp. 157–203.

Deininger, K., and Mpuga, P., 2005. "Does Greater Accountability Improve the Quality of Public Service Delivery? Evidence from Uganda." *World Development* 33(1): 171–91.

Diokno, B. E., 2012. "Fiscal Decentralization After 20 Years: What Have We Learned? Where Do We Go From Here?" *Philippine Review of Economics* 49(1): 9–26.

Faguet, J.P., 2004. "Why So Much Centralization? A Model of Primitive Centripetal Accumulation." STICERD DEDPS No.43, London School of Economics.

Faguet, J.P. and F. Sánchez, 2014. "Decentralization and Access to Social Services in Colombia." *Public Choice*, 160(1–2): 227–49. DOI 10.1007/s11127-013-0077-7.

Faguet, J.P. and F.B. Wietzke, 2006. "Social Funds and Decentralization: Optimal Institutional Design." *Public Administration and Development*, 26(4): 303–15.

Ferejohn, J., 1986. Incumbent performance and electoral control. *Public Choice* 50:5–26.

Galing Pook Foundation, 2006. *Kaban Galing: A Case Bank of Innovative and Exemplary Practices in Local Governance*. Galing Pook Foundation: Makati City, Philippines.

Guevara, M. W., 2000. "Decentralization and Economic Development: The Philippine Experience." *Hitotsubashi Journal of Economics* 41: 97–109.

Keefer, P. and Khemani, S., 2004. "Why do the Poor Receive Poor Services?" *Economic and Political Weekly*, 28 February 2004, 935–43.

Lacaba, J., (ed.), 1995. *Boss: 5 Case Studies of Local Politics in the Philippines*. Quezon City, Philippines: Philippine Center for Investigative Journalism.

Llanto, G., 2012. "The Assignment of Functions and Intergovernmental Fiscal Relations in the Philippines: 20 Years after Decentralization." *Philippine Review of Economics* 49(1): 37–80.

Manasan, R. G., 2007. "Decentralization and the financing of regional development." In Balisacan, A.M. and Hill, H. (eds.), *The Dynamics of Regional Development: The Philippines in East Asia*. Cheltenham, UK: Edward Elgar, pp. 275–315.

Manasan, R. G., 2011. "Expanding Social Health Insurance Coverage: New Issues and Challenges." PIDS Discussion Paper No. 2011–21, Makati, Philippines. Philippine Institute for Development Studies.

Manasan, R. G. and Chatterjee, S., 2003. "Regional development." In Balisacan, A.M. and Hill, H. (eds.), *The Philippine Economy: Development, Policies and Challenges*. Quezon City, Philippines: Ateneo de Manila University Press, pp. 342–80.

Manski, C. F., 1993. "Identification of Endogenous Social Effect: The Reflection Problem." *Review of Economic Studies* 60(3): 531–42.

Paul, S., 1998. "Making Voice Work: The Report Card on Bangalore's Public Service." World Bank Policy Research Working Paper 1921, World Bank, Washington, DC.

Persson, T. and Tabellini, G., 2002. *Political Economics: Explaining Economic Policy*. Cambridge, Mass.: The MIT Press.

Ravindra, A., 2004. "An Assessment of the Impact of Bangalore Citizen Report Cards on the Performance of Public Services." ECD Working Paper 12, Operations Evaluation Department, World Bank, Washington, DC.

Reinikka, R. and Svensson, J., 2003. "The Power of Information: Evidence From a Newspaper Campaign to Reduce Capture." Policy Research Working Paper Series 3239, World Bank, Washington, DC.

Revelli, F., 2005. "On Spatial Public Finance Empirics." *International Tax and Public Finance* 12: 475–92.

Revelli, F. and Tovmo, P., 2007. "Revealed Yardstick Competition: Local Government Efficiency Patterns in Norway." *Journal of Urban Economics* 62: 121–34.

Rincke, J., 2009. "Yardstick Competition and Public Sector Innovation." *International Tax and Public Finance* 16(3): 337–61.

Rivera, T., 1999. "How Fare the Clans? Poverty and Elite Reproduction in the Philippines." Paper presented at the annual conference of the Philippine Political Science Association, 23–24 July, University of the Philippines, Diliman, Quezon City, Philippines.

Rivera, T., 2011. "In Search of Credible Elections and Parties: The Philippine Paradox." In Miranda, F.B., Rivera, T.C., Ronas, M.C. and Holmes, R.D., *Chasing the Wind: Assessing Philippine Democracy*. Quezon City, Philippines: Commission on Human Rights, pp. 46–94.

Rogoff, K., 1990. "Equilibrium Political Budget Cycles." *American Economic Review* 80: 21–36.

Sidel, J., 1997. "Philippine Politics in Town, District, and Province: Bossism in Cavite and Cebu." *The Journal of Asian Studies* 56(4): 947–66.

Silva, J.A., 2005. "Devolution and Regional Disparities in the Philippines: Is there a Connection?" *Environment and Planning C: Government and Policy* 23(3): 399–417.

Solon, J.O.C., Fabella, R.V., and Capuno, J.J., 2009. "Is Local Development Good Politics? Local Development Expenditures and the Re-Election of Governors in the Philippines in the 1990s." *Asian Journal of Political Science* 17(3): 265–84.

World Bank, 2004. *World Development Report 2004*. Washington, DC: The World Bank.

11

Area-Based Competitions and Awards as a Motivational Tool for Public Service Provision

The Experience of Xining, China

Bingqin Li and Yongmei Zhang

11.1 Introduction

There are many situations in which one authority ("the center") is interested in promoting a certain policy in many local governments ("the local authorities"), and is facing the following three challenges at the same time: (1) local officials are not intrinsically motivated, and the center does not have the power to force them to make the policy a priority; (2) success requires the cooperation of the general public, including individuals or businesses, who are also not intrinsically motivated; and (3) successful enforcement requires local knowledge and initiatives.[1] Public environment is one policy area that faces these kinds of challenges not only in China, but also in many other countries. Competition and awards that are based on judicial areas are often used to deal with the problems. However, how they work and why they can help to achieve the goals of the center are rarely discussed carefully. In Europe, recent examples include the competition for European City of Culture and, in Britain, the City in Bloom and Garden Village competitions. In Singapore, in the housing sector, there is the Island-Wide Cleanest Estate competition. The competition for hosting the Olympic Games is a worldwide example. In

[1] Birney (2014) analyzes the problem of local authority shirking and predation in a context of significant levels of discretion for China. Faguet (2004), Faguet and Wietzke (2006), and Faguet and Sánchez (2014) discuss different aspects of this dynamic in detail for other countries.

China there are many examples, one of the most important of which is the "Hygienic City" campaign. It has been running for many years. The experiences and lessons from China can be useful in understanding the impact of this type of policy tool.

In most previous studies, these competitions or awards are analyzed as strategies for place marketing (Sjoholt, 1999) or the contribution of culture to urban regeneration or development (Sassatelli, 2002; Balsas, 2004; Evans and Shaw, 2004). However, we are interested in looking at how *area-based* competition may fit into the ongoing debates over how to improve public services. This chapter discusses the advantages and disadvantages of area-based competition and awards as a policy tool, and thus spells out under what circumstances policy makers may consider using area-based competition and awards, and under what circumstances a more traditional tool such as targeting is more appropriate.

The chapter is organized as follows. In Section 11.2 we examine different models of motivation in public services. Section 11.3 discusses the model of area-based competition and awards. In Section 11.4 we look at a particular case, the Hygienic City Campaign in China. This case has been chosen as it represents a particular large-scale, multi-leveled scheme which has been running for more than twenty years. Section 11.5 illustrates how local authorities have responded to the incentives of such a campaign in Xining City. Finally, we consider what lessons could be drawn from this case study if it were to be applied to other situations.

11.2 Public Sector Motivation

The multi-dimensional challenges discussed earlier are often studied separately in the literature, each holding a large body of theories and studies. There is little attention given to bringing them together and outlining the connections between these strands of theories. However, in a principal–agent relationship, it is not uncommon that a principal will need to face all the challenges at the same time and will find each of the tools discussed in the literature insufficient to tackle the problems. Therefore, a more holistic approach is often called for to tackle public management.

11.2.1 *Motivating Public Sector Employees*

Improving the motivation of service providers in the public sector can be implemented through a positive approach, i.e. to reward best performances, or a negative approach, i.e. to make the non-performers suffer from the consequences. There are a number of tools that are associated with these two approaches to motivate public sector employees.

The first tool is using performance-related pay (PRP, or merit pay) to motivate staff members. This is largely a positive approach in which better performance is rewarded financially. This model assumes that individuals try to maximize their income, so they would be eager to improve performance if they can earn more money as a result of better performance. This has been increasingly used as a tool of motivation in the management of the public sector in many countries. There is evidence showing modest improvement in the services concerned, such as that presented in the survey of performance-related pay in the education system in Britain (Marsden and French, 1998; Burgess et al., 2001) and in the healthcare system in Italy(Adinolfi, 1998). However, the outcomes are not as good as the theorists would like and, on the contrary, have incited criticism. First, the impact of PRP is very difficult to observe. Because of the complexity of public sector jobs—which often involve many departments having almost incomparable positions—little systematic information can be obtained effectively. As a result, the measurement of performance is often poorly designed (Buchan and Thompson, 1993; Arrowsmith et al., 2001). The result is that reward schemes tend to be viewed as unfair and divisive by the public sector employees (Marsden and Richardson, 1992; Marsden and Belfield, 2007). Also, even when differences in performance can be properly measured, the differential pay is also criticized for not being significant enough to compensate for the difference in work contribution (Forest, 2008). As a result, PRP can potentially affect staff morale (Marsden and Richardson, 1994). Similar results have been found in the evaluation of PRP in public services in France, Britain, and the United States (Forest, 2008).

In some occasions, PRP may generate perverse incentives and crowd out the altruistic behavior of some public sector employees (Frey and Oberholzer-Gee, 1997; Frey and Jegen, 2001). Liu and Mills (2005) examined PRP for healthcare professionals in China and found that doctors would provide unnecessary care in order to increase their income. In Britain, there are also findings showing doctors or teachers who used to work overtime voluntarily may decide not to do so if they are not paid for the extra hours or if they think the extra pay is not high enough (Marsden, 2000).

A second set of tools comprises: (1) targets with associated penalties, or (2) a benchmarking system in which the providers are compared to comparable private sector providers (Martin, 2000). The idea behind these tools is to hold the service providers accountable for the outcomes. This can be made into to a negative approach dependent on individuals' fear to lose out either financially or in terms of their future career, or a positive approach in which those who meet targets or reach performance benchmark levels are rewarded. These tools seek to emulate the *effects* of private sector competition, without any *actual* competition (Glennerster, 1991; Le Grand, 1991; Grimshaw, et al., 2002). Targets and benchmarks can be effective in achieving specific goals.

They can offer a good reference point for people to strive for, and are particularly good at maintaining a minimum standard in the related area (Kouzmin et al. 1999). Also, unlike individually based performance pay, rewards for targets based on the principle of 'winner takes all' tend not to involve disputes around whether the reward or punishment is sufficient to cover specific activities (Propper and Wilson, 2003). Of course, they also face criticism. One problem is that service providers have no incentives to do more than the necessary minimum to achieve their targets (John, et al., 2004). Also, targets and benchmarks do not necessarily encourage innovations and may even *reduce* the public sector's ability and willingness to innovate (Le Grand, 2006b). In this sense, if targets and benchmarks are very detailed and staged, it would automatically generate a detailed agenda of enforcement which can focus service providers' attention on the targeted areas and become rigid and less responsive to user needs (Flynn, 1986). The second problem is that, in terms of effectiveness, the negative approach will require the center to have the capacity to impose effective sanctions. Restricting funding is a particularly effective sanction. However, when the center does not control local funding, sanctions are unlikely to be nearly as effective (Boyne, 1996). The third problem, which relates to the first, is that in a targeting or benchmarking system, it is often the case that only the indicators that are measured by principals affect the behavior of agents (Bevan and Hood, 2006). The behavior of local residents and businesses and other members of society, however, tends to remain unchanged. Furthermore, consumer feedback may be ignored if the complaints are not part of the targets, and if the agents are actively manipulating the system (Croxson and Atkinson, 2001; Bruns, et al., 2004). For example, Ravallion (2007) used evidence from poverty reduction in China to argue that "standard measures of targeting are found to be uninformative, or even deceptive, about impacts on poverty and cost-effectiveness in reducing poverty." In many projects operated by the World Bank, there has been a shift from targeting towards more holistic assessments (Mansuri and Rao, 2004).

These motivational tools have a central theme: to align the interests of the principal and agents so that the latter may be able to act in the interests of the former. However, as discussed, the shortcomings of these tools cannot guarantee that the service providers can be properly monitored and motivated. As a result, the benefits gained may be cancelled out by the costs.

11.2.2 *Encouraging Users to Motivate Public Sector Performances*

The introduction of user choice is an attempt to increase the capacity of performance monitoring by turning users into principals. It takes care of more aspects of the services than the straightforward motivational tools discussed earlier. It is not only a motivational tool for service providers, but also a tool to empower users (Barnes and Walker 1996; Le Grand 2006a). First, users can vote with their feet if they are not happy with the services, putting pressure on the service providers to improve them. This is similar to the theories on competitive market in the private economy. Second, in order to make choices, users have to learn about the services and take greater interest in understanding and monitoring them. As a result, users are more actively engaged (Fotaki, 1999; Le Grand 2007; Matosevic, et al., 2008). However, for the motivation and empowerment to be realized, there are a number of conditions to be met: (1) Users are either fund holders themselves or their coming and going may change the funding position of the service providers; (2) The users need real alternatives to turn to when they need to choose; (3) The costs for users to shift to different service providers are not prohibitive; (4) Users have the ability to make choices, not only in terms of financial costs, but also in terms of other factors such as knowledge, information, and physical ability (Greve, 2009). However, in practice, these conditions can be hard to meet in public sector services. First, some service providers have a natural monopoly, so users have no alternatives even if they are not satisfied with the service (Boyne, 1996).

In some services a natural monopoly can be overcome by enabling the consumer to use service providers further away from home (McGuire et al., 1987). This can be realized when there are affordable means of transportation to make these distant choices possible. Time is also a factor that needs to be taken into consideration. Even if transportation and time are not a problem, there are still many services in which a natural monopoly cannot easily be broken; environmental and community services are obvious examples. Unless residents are prepared to move their home to another area, the service providers may face no effective pressure from consumer exit. After all, consumer exit is "passive." Service users are not real stakeholders, have no obligation to help improve services, and feel no sense of loyalty. In fact, users lacking loyalty is important for them to be able to put effective pressure on providers (Hirschman, 1980). In this sense, user choice encourages a split between service providers and users. This may not matter in many situations, but it is definitely a problem when the outcomes that the service deliverers desire require user contribution or cooperation. For example, a clean environment requires that local residents help maintain it.

Another way to involve users is via competition between political parties in the local democracy (Boyne, 1996). However, elections often involve many issues at the same time; if a certain service is not on the political agenda it may have little effect on the result of an election, and user choice cannot be exercised effectively in relation to each individual service.

Another tool for involving user participation is user voice. Here, users do not simply leave when they are not satisfied with services;[2] they can voice their complaints so that the service providers can improve accordingly (Hirschman, 1980). Voice can function in two ways. First, voices can provide inspiration for initiatives to make the service providers more efficient and responsive. Second, improved accountability can itself make users more satisfied with the services. However, for voice to work, service providers have to have the motivation to listen to user complaints or suggestions. Also, users need to be interested in their voice being heard. Unfortunately, this is not always the case. Making use of voice takes time and confidence. It is likely to be hijacked by the articulate middle class and work against the interests of the poor. In this sense, compared to voice, choice is a more equitable solution (Le Grand, 2006b), and we turn to this now.

11.2.3 *Combining Voice and Choice—Unsolved Problems*

To overcome the shortcomings of voice, choice (or exit) is often used alongside it. This means users can leave if their voice is not heard. Hirschman (1970) does not support this practice. He suggests that exit can potentially undermine voice because if people have the ability to leave, they may not be interested in making their voices heard. But despite of its widespread acceptance, this criticism is not always supported by evidence (Dowding and John, 2008). Williams and Rossiter (2004) examine the experience in education and healthcare in different countries and show that the "introduction of effective voice mechanisms alongside choice mechanisms should limit movement of users between providers." In this sense, choice may be able to reinforce the effect of voice.[3]

Various forms of (quasi-) market competition featuring competition between providers can be good tools for combining choice and voice. However, they all have limits; the following criteria need to be satisfied first before market competition can function adequately.

First, users should be educated and know what they can demand. However, this is not always the case; users can be ignorant. They do not know what to anticipate, what to choose, and what to voice. Existing studies suggest that user ignorance may exist for several reasons: (1) Users do not have sufficient information. This may be resolved if an independent body can broadcast the

[2] Obviously, local democracy may also be considered to be user voice, but in this section we only discuss voices that are directly addressed to service providers.

[3] Faguet and Ali's (2009) findings from Bangladesh support the importance of voice and exit in making local government responsive. Channa and Faguet's (2012) survey of international experiments in decentralization provides evidence on the importance of electoral exit as a tool for motivating public officials.

necessary information (Beales et al., 1981; Scannell 1989) or regulations can be used to require information provision by the service providers; (2) Users may not be able to make judgements, even when they have sufficient information. This can either be a result of physical conditions or a lack of ability to process the information given. Literature on the practice of involving user participation in decision-making in the healthcare sector has shown that patient ignorance, mental and physical imbalance, and shyness prevented them from participating effectively (Sainio, Eriksson, and Lauri, 2001). (3) Users simply do not demand certain services or have no idea what they should get from the service providers. For example, not all children hope to go to university, or people living in rural areas may not want certain public services that are necessary for those living in cities. This may also happen to newly arrived immigrants coming from different cultural, social, and economic backgrounds.

Second, service providers may not educate the users to demand more. This can result from two factors. First, from the perspective of service providers, the better educated the users are, the more likely they are to identify problems with services. Therefore, it is rational for service providers to provide less information about a service. As we have discussed, the regulator or an independent body putting information in the public domain may resolve this problem. However, when users do not know about the existence of certain services, they may not look out for the information in the first place. Learning to demand these types of services may be more difficult than learning to demand a TV set. For example, good public hygiene may not be very obvious to many people. If a person has never traveled to a clean place, even if he/she is told that it is necessary for a public space to be clean, he/she may not be able to visualize a desirable outcome. When this is the situation, the policy makers face a dilemma. On one hand, the potential service users do not have the motivation to demand a service. On the other, service providers do not have the incentive to provide it either.

Third, taking one step back, it may not always be a result of service providers' lacking in incentives that the services or information are not provided. Local service providers themselves (even if always well-intentioned) may not be inspired themselves. This issue may be more serious in countries where regional disparity is very serious and the local service providers may not be aware of better practices or know how to achieve the desired outcomes that the center has asked for.

A further question is, if there is no demand for the service, then why is there a need to provide it at all? The kinds of services that may suffer from these problems are those that relate to the public environment, public health, and, in some countries or communities, education. However, the non-existence of demand may have negative externalities and in the long run generate social costs for the other members of society. Therefore, it is important to be able to "inspire" or educate users and at the same time motivate service providers to provide the services which are not demanded by the public. Then how can this be achieved?

11.3 Area-Based Competition and Awards

The earlier analyses suggest that a quasi-market system based on competition between service providers cannot help improve services when there is weak demand for service improvement that maybe useful for the community. Therefore, policy tools that can help align the interests of service providers not only with those of the center/regulators, but also with users, become crucial.

Area-based competitions and awards mean that local governments or service providers working for different areas compete for a prize that the regulators or higher authorities offer. In an area-based competition, participants from different areas compete against each other to become the best performer. Awards can be slightly different from those of competition in that everyone that passes the threshold can be a winner.

The difference between area-based competition and provider-based competition is that the former offers a mechanism to motivate a service provider that enjoys local monopoly. By putting it in competition with other areas, the local service provider is turned into a "representative" of the area. If properly crafted, winning the competition can boost local support. The mechanism is that in the competition, people living or associated with a certain area share a local identity. Once people in the local area acknowledge this identity, they will be proud if their own "team" wins or is rewarded in the end. In this sense, motivation schemes that try to build on local identity can potentially turn the originally alienated service providers and users into members of the same team, whoshare the same goal and therefore may make joint efforts for mutual benefit. Also, as the higher authorities/the center set the criteria for winning the competitions, the local team of service providers and users may cooperate to achieve these goals. In this way, the interests of the three parties—the center, the local authorities/service providers, and the users—are in line with each other.

Theoretically, such a mechanism can deal with the problems discussed earlier for the following reasons. First, because the competition helps to define the identity and generate a sense of community, service users may potentially be proud when their area wins. As a result, they may be happy to contribute when necessary, even in a personal capacity. Second, service providers who may benefit from user contribution may be more willing to educate users so that the users do not by any means affect the performances negatively, even if they cannot contribute. Therefore, service providers are willing to share information with users. Third, because the service providers are competing against other areas, it is important for them to understand what the criteria for winning are and in what ways the competitors are doing better. This motivates the service providers and users to aspire to better performance and overcome the problems of low demand. Finally, because of the honor associated with winning and the greater awareness of the benefits of services concerned, the prize awarded to the winners does not have to be high enough to cover the costs of running the campaign. This means that the organizers of the campaigns do not have to devote a lot of resources.

In the following sections, we will use the case of Chinese public hygiene campaigns to examine whether what the theory predicted has turned out to be the case.

11.4 Area-Based Competition (ABC) for Public Hygiene in China

In China, ABCs are frequently used as a motivational tool. While it has been dismissed as a Communist-style political campaign (Zhang and Li, 2011), the impact of this type of motivation, the reasons for its popularity, and the mechanisms through which the motivation works deserve a closer look. Its ability to take advantage of identity to align the interests of the center, local authorities/service providers, and users may contribute to the existing motivation literature.

China has a highly fragmented local government system, with a large number of local authorities, and several layers of government between the center and street-level authorities.[4] This makes it extremely difficult to motivate the local authorities. In the history of imperial dynasties, the Emperor's power travelled down through the administration system, but would not go lower than the county level. Local administration was not controlled by the center. This meant that when local government did not aspire to good governance, local services could deteriorate. ABCs were introduced during the

[4] The Chinese government has a five-layer government system: (1) central government; (2) provinces, autonomous regions, cities under the direct control of the central government (thirty-four authorities at this level); (3) regional, league, autonomous state, regional city (333 authorities at this level); (4) county, autonomous county, Qi, autonomous Qi, county level city (2,859 authorities at this level); and (5) village, minority village, township (40,813 authorities at this level). At the central level there are a number of authorities that deal with different aspects of society, for example, Ministry of Health, Ministry of Education.... Local governments, except for those at the bottom, i.e. village and township level, usually mirror the structure of the central authorities. As a result, even if we look only at the provincial level, there are thirty-four local authorities that work in the same area. One layer down, there will be 333 local authorities working in the same area nationwide.

Central Planning era (1949–78) and continued to evolve after the economic reform started.

ABCs are usually initiated by higher authorities. Participants are lower authorities. Participation can either be voluntary or compulsory depending on its design. It can be about a single policy goal, for example, GDP growth, foreign investment growth, or university entrance rate of high schools. It can also be a complex task that will involve a whole range of goals and targets. In the following part of this chapter, we use one of the largest-scale and oldest ABCs in China, the Hygienic City Campaign, to see how the center, local authorities, and users have been brought together to improve public hygiene.

11.4.1 *The Hygienic City Campaigns*

Public hygiene is a policy area that involves the problems we have discussed above. First, local authorities do not necessarily prioritize public hygiene and public environment. In the wealthier cities and popular tourist destinations, public hygiene has improved greatly in recent years, and the general public is more aware of the importance of keeping the public environment clean. In other areas, local officials may not consider that public hygiene can contribute to economic growth, and therefore treat it as a cost item. Consequently, the costs should be reduced. Also, it may be that local officials are unaware that hygiene standards should be improved. After all, they are likely to have grown up in such an environment (Shen, 2004). Second, public hygiene suffers from low consumer demand. In many parts of the country, people do not appreciate efforts to maintain good public hygiene (Xi et al., 1998). Therefore, local people may not demand an improved public environment. What is more, maintaining good public cleanliness requires the collaboration of local people. If they do not appreciate it, their behavior, such as littering, spitting, or waste dumping can make it very difficult for local authorities to improve the situation.

ABCs were introduced in the 1950s to clean up the environment. They were stopped during the Cultural Revolution but resumed in 1978. In 1989, the State Council decided to organize a campaign to reward the cleanest cities, so as to solve the motivation problem and stimulate public support (1989). The Hygienic City campaign was born.

Hygienic City is a combination of targets and competition. The targets include a series of standards for quality of environment, service sector hygiene, and bug control. The participants are geographically defined. There are campaigns for cities, urban districts, and townships/villages. Participants need to satisfy a range of targets to be evaluated by the campaign organizer's inspectors. Campaigns take place at regional, provincial, and national levels. For a participant to enter a higher level of competition, it needs to win at the lower level and be recommended by the governing authorities to move on to the next level. Finally, at the national level, winners receive the title of Hygienic City and awards from the National Patriotic Committee (now the Disease Prevention and Control Bureau of the Ministry of Health). Their achievements and efforts are also published in the national media. Local businesses, public agencies, and individuals who are considered to have made outstanding contributions during the competition are awarded by the local authorities (National Patriotic Committee PRC, 1989). In the early stages there were less than ten winners at the national level each year. More recently, there have been only two or three winners each year.

11.4.2 *Incentives to Participate*

It is important to know that participation in these campaigns is voluntary. Why, then, do local authorities participate at all?

First, if local authorities achieve good results in the campaigns, the officials are likely to have a better opportunity to get promoted (National Patriotic Committee, PRC, 1989). Cases in which some mayors have gained significant political capital through their achievements in improving city hygiene are well publicized by the organizers of the campaigns. In order to ensure the campaign receives local support, the mayor of a city often promises promotions or awards to lower-level officials in return for help in achieving the desired outcomes (Dai and Wang, 2007).

Second, to boost performances the higher authorities (e.g. provincial government) that recommended a local authority (e.g. city government) to participate in the campaign may agree to cover some of the costs of the campaign. Financial incentives, along with the honor of being recommended, are attractive enough for the local officials to decide to participate.

11.5 Case Study of Xining

In this section, we use the case of Xining, the capital city of Qinghai Province in West China to illustrate how an originally less inspired local government responded to the incentives of ABCs. Xining is a relatively poor city in China. Being an inland province, Qinghai's economic development is well behind that of the eastern provinces. Xining's rapid growth began only recently when the national policy to "Develop the West" was introduced. We do not think the case of Xining is representative of all cities in China, but it is true that this city suffered from all the problems we discussed earlier at the same time. Therefore, it can serve as a good example of how these difficulties may be addressed through the Hygienic City campaign.

The data used in this chapter was collected by the authors on 19–20 October 2008, during the final inspection period of the competition. Four types of information were collected: (1) official documents, (2) official statistics, (3) the authors' observations during the field trip, and (4) two surveys involving thirty-two street vendors and ninety-nine people in the street. The official documents and statistics help us to see whether the campaign has helped focus the attention of local authorities and generate significant investment in public hygiene. The surveys were designed to help us see whether the public education goals of the competition had been realized and whether the public were supportive of the competition.

We interviewed street vendors because they always work in the public space, and were thus a prime target for the public hygiene campaign. We sent the interviewers to the two largest street markets in Xining: Minzhu Road market and Shuijing Lane market. The sampling method was equal distance selection of the first one out of every five vendors. Six out of the thirty-two vendors normally operated in other areas, but were asked by local officials to move from their original business site to one of the two organized markets. A drawback with this sampling method was that we could only capture people who were relocated to new business sites but not those who were driven out of business because it was not practical for them to move to the new site. Therefore, it may be possible that the level of support we got through this sampling was higher than would have been the case if the people who were driven out of business had also been included. However, if people were driven out of business, this should in principle have been captured in the survey of individuals.

The individuals interviewed were selected at six different sites where streets crossed each other in the city center. The interviewees were divided into three age groups: younger than 30, 31–60, and 61 and above. The ratio of the age groups was 3:5:2. The sex ratio was 52 men to 48 women.[5] Each of the six interviewers[6] stopped passers-by, and carried out the interviews after confirming that the candidates met the two sampling criteria. Ideally, it would have been better to carry out some in-depth interviews at people's homes, but this would have been difficult as the timing of our research was quite sensitive and interviews of this type need to be arranged via community leaders. Considering that all the communities were nominated for the final stage of the competition,[7] interviews in the presence of community leaders

[5] The age and sex ratios used in the sampling are calculated according to the numbers published in the Xining Statistical Yearbook, 2007.

[6] The interviewers were master's students from the Sociology Department of Lanzhou University. They had received training before the interviews.

[7] Our presence in some neighborhoods as strangers in several local communities during this period had caused alert from the community leaders, as we were told later that the locals thought we were central government inspectors in disguise.

could be be strongly biased. In this sense, stopping people randomly in the street and carrying out anonymous surveys, though not ideal, provided an opportunity to obtain information offering more insights on the issues at hand.

The official data and documents were mainly used to show the workload and outcome of the campaign. To make sure that we did not only receive the documents that are presented to the inspectors which might only show nice stories, we collected documents and official speeches to local residents before the final campaign began. These were speeches pleading for greater efforts from the general public and private businesses. Therefore, some of the key difficulties during the earlier part of the campaign are highlighted. We tried to check between different documents for consistency, so that we would not get a beautified image of the campaign.

11.5.1 *Physical Changes Brought by the Campaign*

Xining decided to participate in the Hygienic City campaign in 1999. According to the description of some local residents we interviewed, the streets were poorly maintained. Piles of garbage could be seen everywhere. People threw litter and spat in the street without hesitation. According to the Xining government (2008), more than 80 per cent of the small businesses in the service sector suffered from low-quality hygiene facilities and poor cleaning. Few farmers' markets had covers. The plan to meet the basic requirements to join the Hygienic City competition was finalized in 2003. Since then, a series of local hygiene campaigns have been implemented. In 2005, the city won the title of Provincial Hygienic City. In 2008, it finally reached the minimum requirements for entering the national competition. In June 2008, the final campaign for the competition started. From 19 to 21 September, 2008, Xining was inspected by officials from the National Patriotic Hygiene Committee. In accordance with the design of the competition, the inspectors came in disguise and collected evidence independently. The result was that Xining passed the initial stage of the campaign and was allowed to go through to the formal assessment in October 2008. The October results were not satisfactory; however, the city then entered for a second assessment in 2009 and received the title in the end.

After the campaign, dry pit toilets were renovated. Sixty-five farmers' markets were formally organized. Some farmers who used to pile up goods on the pavements received their own stalls, and others were allocated space inside covered markets. Street vendors were licensed and required to help keep the markets clean. Small businesses improved significantly in their pollution control, sewage processing, waste disposal, noise reduction, ability to guarantee food safety, and also fire protection. Places that particularly attracted insects and rats were cleaned up. Moreover, the amount of green space per person in the urban public area increased from 2.3 m^2 per person in 1995 to 7.57 m^2 in 2008.

Some of these achievements were direct outcomes of following the campaign guidelines.[8] There were clear targets to meet. Households, estates, and businesses were required to take care of the space in front of their doors. Property owners were fined if they allowed graffiti and illegal advertisements to remain for more than fourteen hours. Shop signs and business façades were supposed to be cleaned regularly or even renovated. Drinking taps and toilets which had been accessible to state enterprise employees only were opened to the public. Small-business owners, especially those in the food and catering sector, had to follow strict hygiene criteria.

These outcomes depend on the local governments' awareness, ability, and willingness to enforce the policies. Local officials have to study the requirements of the campaigns very carefully and try to enforce them. The format of area-based campaign holds the local authorities accountable for their performance, making them keen to enforce the criteria as the state suggests.

11.5.2 *"Teaming Up" with the Public*

At the start of the campaign, people were reluctant to support it. People were detached and thought it was the responsibility of the government. Businesses defaulted on the promises they made, and earlier inspection results were very poor. The local government realized that it had to rely on public support to be able to achieve the desired results. The cleanliness of the public environment can only be improved and maintained if individuals changed their behavior and stopped littering and spitting in the streets and polluting the environment, and instead did their bit to keep the public environment clean. The experience of earlier public hygiene campaigns showed that small fines were largely ineffective, and that significant behavioral change only followed once public hygiene became a value espoused by the local people.

An effort to resort to "patriotism," highlighting competitiveness against rival places, was evident in Xining and became observable during the final campaign period. There were special newspaper columns, TV programs, and telephone hotlines to spread the news, distribute information about the campaign, and report complaints. Students were lectured on the campaign, and teachers organized meetings with parents to distribute the information. In residential areas there were community-based performances, leaflets were distributed, advertising boards were used, exhibitions were staged in galleries, and public participation was sought. A special website was also established.

[8] A detailed introduction of the requirements at different levels of the campaigns can be found in Zhang and Li (2011a).

Gradually, more people began to appreciate the campaign. One key result was an increase in the number of volunteers, who came from all different sectors of society. Our interviews show that at the time of the inspection all ninety-nine individual interviewees had heard of the campaign. Sixty-seven were aware of the purpose of the campaign; fifty-three of the fifty-six people who understood the motivation for the competition believed that it was intended to improve the living environment and image of Xining. Only three people were cynical and felt the competition was all about making the local government look good. Twenty-two of the thirty-two street vendors interviewed knew what the competition was intended to achieve, and twenty knew why Xining needed to compete. It seems that the public were aware of the ongoing campaign and quite a large proportion of them took part. On the other hand, most people's understanding of the campaign was not very detailed.

Apart from handing out information, the education campaign also used strategies to build up the "team spirit," employing slogans such as "I love Xining," "Let's run the campaign together," "Cleaner Xining will give visitors a good impression," etc. In a sense, these campaigns helped to define the physical boundary between the city and other competitors and the "mental" boundary between Xining residents and outsiders. It nurtured a sense of pride among local residents and intended to motivate them to make their contribution to the campaign. We could see that numerous people from all backgrounds were involved in the campaign. Employers, neighborhood committees, and schools also organized small groups of volunteers to clean up public spaces, hand out leaflets, and put on street performances. Among the ninety-nine individuals interviewed, sixty-seven had actually taken part in one or more of the activities that were part of the competition. Twenty-four of the thirty-two small business interviewees had participated in one or more of the activities.

Despite these efforts, the level of public support as measured by the level of participation, i.e. the proportion of people taking part in one or more of the activities during the campaign, was less than 70 per cent. In winning cities this proportion was usually above 75 per cent. The Xining government attributed this relative lack of success to not using sufficiently innovative methods to motivate the general public. Although a lot of information was provided, people in Xining did not pay as much attention to this as the government would have liked (2008). This turned out to be a big disappointment not only for the government, but also for the local people. After further efforts, the city finally fulfilled the criteria and there was a strong sense of celebration.

11.5.3 *Learning from Others and Developing Local Strategies*

The competitiveness of the campaign also encouraged city officials to look out for good examples from previous winners and visit other competitors to learn from their experiences in order to copy good practices. They participated in training programs offered by the campaign organizers and collected the past winners' campaign documents.

The campaign generated a sense of urgency. The government officials became much more open to suggestions and criticisms. They were eager to hear about good practices and suggestions for improvement and to adapt existing practices to fit local circumstances. The approach was pragmatic and aimed at problem-solving.

A key issue faced by Xining was that it was not possible for this city to spend as much money as the richer cities. As a result, it needed to identify its own strengths and take advantage of these. The city worked out that it had a much higher rate of green space per person, but needed to focus more on cleaning up the city. Relatively speaking, it was easier to mobilize volunteers in Xining than in more developed cities. These strategies helped the city to compete while spending less.

11.5.4 *Localized Finance*

As discussed earlier, city officials, if not especially motivated, may not realize the value in spending a lot of money on cleaning the environment. If there were no competitive campaign like this, they would not prioritize funding for it. With the campaign, the spending on city hygiene was unprecedented.

Most of the money for participating in the national campaign came from the public sector: the provincial government, departments in the local government, district authorities, and state-owned enterprises. According to the statistics kept by the Xining government, the Qinghai (provincial) government set aside 800 million yuan to improve infrastructure and promote general social development. Some of this money was used for building small-scale urban construction projects and an infrastructure for improving the environment. The Transportation Department of the provincial government allocated 40 million yuan for regenerating the backstreets of Xining. The Health Department contributed 10 million yuan specifically for cleaning the city. Xining government, comprising several departments, contributed 435 million yuan in 2008. The district authorities and state enterprises contributed more than 150 million yuan. The details are shown in Table 11.1.

The reason given by the officials for spending so much money also confirms the theory. It is about local pride and the pride of the officials. A document published by the Patriotic Hygienic Campaign Committee of Qinghai Province (2008) stressed that Xining as the capital city of Qinghai serves as a window to the outside world. Participating in the competition could improve the city's hygiene and at the same time set an example to other cities in the province. What is more, it could boost the image of the whole province

Table 11.1. Spending by the Xining government and district authorities.

Funding source	Usage	Amount (million yuan)	Notes
Administration Bureau	City cleaning	54.24	
Transportation Bureau	Small-scale infrastructure construction	318.54	
Bureau of Commerce	Regeneration of farmers' market	51.01	
Bureau of Forestry	Green Space Improvement	11.50	
Subtotal		435.29	
Districts			
East District		55.62	
Central District		46.14	
West District		14.13	Promised to invest 23.32m
North District		23.63	
Dongchuan Industrial Park		12.54	
Other		9.25	
Total		596.60 million yuan	

Source: Xining government, statistics for the funding of the 2008 Hygienic City campaign

nationally and impress potential investors. Not only the city thought so; the provincial government that recommended that the city participate as a representative of the province also felt the need to support the city. As a municipal official, who wanted to remain anonymous, (20 October, 2008) commented to the researchers:

> Once we decided to participate, we just could not afford to be mediocre. I do not think we would have been punished for not winning. Actually for Xining, even if we only spent the money allocated by the province and did not make contributions ourselves, we could get by. But we (officials) also have pride. Once we participate, we want to do well and we do not want to lose face in front of other provinces.

Individuals and private businesses were another important source of funding. Their contribution took different forms:

(1) *Donations, usually organized at the community level.* For example, market vendors contributed money to thank the cleaners who worked in their market. Residents contributed money to reward the street cleaners of their own neighborhoods.[9]

(2) *Payment for services and facilities.* Individual businesses were required to update their facilities or pay for services offered by the authorities. The amount could be large, as when investing in new ventilation and

[9] "Donation" is the term used in the official documents. However, we do not rule out the possibility of cases of compulsory contributions, or voluntary contributions but under government or peer pressure.

sewage systems, or it could be small, as in improving the aesthetics of their stalls.

(3) Some private businesses were required to *open their private facilities to the general public*, in particular their toilets and water taps (Xining government, PRC, 2008).

11.5.5 *Problems that Appeared during Xining's Campaign*

The atmosphere in the final stages of the competition was intense, particularly so when the inspectors came. All activities that could have affected the results were put on hold. This had significant costs. There were many inconveniences for local residents and businesses. For example, informal street markets were closed down, and street vendors and shoppers had to move to organized markets. Among the street vendors we interviewed, six out of the thirty-two had to move, and eight reported that the competition had had a negative impact on their business. Because the traffic was under heavy control, some small businesses found it difficult to secure their supplies, and business costs were much higher than usual. Twenty-nine interviewees reported that the competition made their life less convenient. The most discussed inconvenience was grocery shopping, mainly because of the closure of the informal street markets. In addition, markets were required to close earlier than usual.

A second problem was the very high frequency of inspections of small businesses. In some places, inspectors exhibited a condescending attitude and totally disregarded the practicality of proposed improvements. The inevitable result was resentment felt by small business owners. The intensity of inspections justifies the doubts expressed by a number of interviewees in Xining as to whether the level of effort is sustainable. In some cases businesses cynically played the system by not offering toilets to customers, thereby making it easier for the restaurants to keep the toilet facilities clean.

A third problem is that many resources were used for arguably unrelated urban modernization projects. This observation can be confirmed by the transcribed speech of Mayor Yulin Luo in Xining Communist Party Committee Office (2008). According to him, one of five steps to improve Xining in the future months of the campaign was to accelerate the demolition of old neighborhoods, the implication being that older houses were associated with poor hygiene. Instead of cleaning up these neighborhoods, they should be demolished. However, Xining has been regenerated to such an extent in the last decade that the whole city is almost newly built. Even before the campaign it was very difficult to find houses built before the 1980s. During the campaign, houses built in the 1980s and 1990s became targets for demolition. In this chapter we will not engage with the debate concerning the impact of such frequent demolition of neighborhoods on people's livelihoods. Nevertheless, it is apparent that the goal of improving public hygiene has been entangled with the attempt to modernize the city. However, it is difficult to blame the city authorities for this. In the campaign document published by the organizers, the term "beautifying" was used several times (National Patriotic Committee, PRC, 1989). The danger of such vagueness in the design of the campaign is that beautifying a city can take up resources that could be spent on improving basic services. For a city which is already relatively under-resourced, the costs of the competition could be exceptionally high.

11.6 Conclusion

Local governments' participation may derive from different motivations. These include the intrinsic motivation to improve services, and personal career development. In terms of trying to make use of these motivations, area-based competitions (ABCs) are no different from other types of competition. What does make them different is that they are able to mobilize local authorities and service providers as well as service users by aligning the interests of all three. What we could see in Xining's case was that local governments, including the provincial government, city government, and district authorities, were all keen for the city to perform well in the campaign. They indeed prioritized the campaign and spent large amounts of money on making improvements, especially during the final stage. The relationship between the users and the government was also transformed. The public did not only treat the campaign as a government project; they began to consider themselves members of a team and were willing to make efforts to support the campaign. This is because ABCs can help form a group identity for members of local society and encourage user participation. What we saw in Xining is that both local officials and residents started to view other cities as competitors, and users, officials, and service providers were willing to work together as a team to achieve the common goal: winning the campaign. As a result, the decoupled relationship between service providers and users in the consumer choice model was avoided. Because user voice can help local authorities win, local authorities are more willing to listen to suggestions and are more open to innovative ideas that can help the city gain an advantage. They may also be an important source for local innovations.

As predicted by the theory, the educational effects of ABCs are very strong. The learning experience has several dimensions. First, participation in competition is a learning-by-doing process. Through the feedback received from the competition organizers and the experiences of other cities, Xining's leadership realized their own weaknesses and set out new working plans for the next round of inspection (Xining Communist Party Committee Office, 2008).

Second, cities are encouraged to learn from each other and good practices spread and are adopted faster than during non-competition periods. Third, the dedicated campaigns through public media and the school system became sessions of intensive education. The direct benefit is that local residents get to know what is possible, and hopefully in the future they can start to demand an improved public environment or voice their dissatisfaction.

With these advantages, the ABCs are very good at dealing with uninspired local authorities and service users, and overcome problems caused by low demand for desirable services.

Boyne (1996) studies competitions between local authorities in Britain and concludes that a large number of authorities are required to ensure competitions are truly competitive. Also, because a competition is typically run at a particular time, there is a risk that improvements will not persist beyond the time in which the competition is judged. What is more, the performance of participants has to be judged, and in situations of asymmetric information, there may be opportunities for rent seeking and corruption. Our studies do not contradict his findings. In addition, it is important to point out that as there is no clear signal in the system to show how good is good enough, competitors may compete to outdo each other, i.e. spending ever more money and devoting ever more time to achieve better results than their rivals. What we can see is a tendency to over-demand and over-invest. The following points are of note:

- When the campaign is highly prioritized, the level of attention and resources mobilized may not be sustainable in the long run.
- When the number of competitions increases, it becomes burdensome for one local area to handle several competitions at the same time. This has happened in China. The massive increase in the number of ABCs has exhausted local authorities and residents. The central government ended up carrying out large-scale crackdowns in 1996 and 2006 in order to reduce the number of competitions. In 2007, 1,705 national-level competitions were cancelled, as well as more than 90 per cent of competitions organized at the local level. However, as predicted by past experience, because of their effectiveness as motivational tools, the number of competitions tended to creep up again over time.
- Overly enthusiastic officials are able to abuse public support. When the government starts to take public support for granted and begins to work single-mindedly on the competition without taking into account the potential costs to the public, this risks alienating supporters.

There is no built-in mechanism in the Chinese system to stop over-zealous participation. Therefore, ABCs, even those with positive outcomes, became increasingly controversial. However, given that it is the center rather the market that decides what is desirable, it is very difficult to "cap" performance.

Acknowledgement

The authors of this chapter would like to thank Mr. Yongji Zhang from the Office of Qinghai Provincial Government for his general support during our fieldwork.

References

Adinolfi, P., 1998. "Performance-related pay for health service professionals: the Italian experience." *Health services management research: an official journal of the Association of University Programs in Health Administration/HSMC, AUPHA* 11:211.

Arrowsmith, J., S. French, M. Gilman, and R. Richardson, 2001. "Performance-related pay in health care." *Journal of health services research & policy* 6:114.

Balsas, C. J. L., (2004) "City Centre Regeneration in the Context of the 2001 European Capital of Culture in Porto, Portugal." *Local Economy,* vol 19, no 4: 396–410.

Barnes, M. and A. Walker, 1996. "Consumerism versus empowerment: a principled approach to the involvement of older service users." *Policy & Politics* 24: 375–93.

Beales, H., M. B. Mazis, S. C. Salop, and R. Staelin, 1981. "Consumer search and public policy." *The Journal of Consumer Research* 8: 11–22.

Bevan, G. and Hood, C., (2006) "What's Measured Is What Matters: Targets and Gaming in the English Public Health Care System." *Public Administration* vol 84, no 3: 517–38.

Birney, M., 2014. "Decentralization and Veiled Corruption under China's 'Rule of Mandates'." *World Development* 53: 55–67. <http://dx.doi.org/10.1016/j.worlddev.2013.01.006>.

Boyne, G. A., 1996. "Competition and Local Government: A Public Choice Perspective." *Urban Studies,* vol 33, no 4: 703–21.

Bruns, B. et al., 2004. "From Voice to Empowerment: Rerouting Irrigation Reform in Indonesia." In Alex Bolding (ed.), *The Politics of Irrigation Reform: Contested Policy Formulation and Implementation in Asia, Africa, and Latin America,* chap. 5, pp. 145–65. London: Ashgate Publishing.

Buchan, J. and M. Thompson, 1993. "Pay and nursing performance." *Health Manpower Management* 19: 2.

Burgess, S., B. Croxson, P. Gregg, and C. Propper, 2001. "The intricacies of the relationship between pay and performance for teachers: do teachers respond to performance related pay schemes?" University of Bristol, Centre for Market and Public Organisation, CMPO Working Paper Series No. 01/35.

Channa, A. and J.P. Faguet, 2012. "Decentralization of Health and Education in Developing Countries: A Quality-Adjusted Review of the Empirical Literature." LSE/STICERD Working Paper No. EOPP 38.

Croxson, B. and A. Atkinson, 2001. "Incentives in secondary schools: the impact of the Performance Threshold." University of Bristol, Centre for Market and Public Organisation. CMPO Working Paper Series No. 01/45.

Dai, L. and Wang, W., 2007. "Some Suggestions on the Campaigns for National Hygienic Cities (Guanyu Woshi Chuangjian Guojia Weisheng Cheng Huodong De Jidian Jianyi)." *Daqing Social Science (Daqing Shehui Kexue)* 4: 54–9.

Dowding, K. and P. John, 2008. "The Three Exit, Three Voice and Loyalty Framework: A Test with Survey Data on Local Services." *Political Studies—Oxford* 56: 288.

Evans, G. and Shaw, P., 2004. "The Contribution of Culture to Regeneration in the UK: A Review of Evidence." *London: Department for Culture Media and Sport Retrieved August,* 5: 4708–8386.

Faguet, J.P., 2004. "Why So Much Centralization? A Model of Primitive Centripetal Accumulation." STICERD DEDPS No.43, London School of Economics.

Faguet, J.P. and Z. Ali, 2009. "Making Reform Work: Institutions, Dispositions and the Improving Health of Bangladesh." *World Development.* 37: 208–18.

Faguet, J.P. and F. Sánchez, 2014. "Decentralization and Access to Social Services in Colombia." *Public Choice,* 160(1–2): 227–49. DOI 10.1007/s11127-013-0077-7.

Faguet, J.P. and F.B. Wietzke, 2006. "Social Funds and Decentralization: Optimal Institutional Design." *Public Administration and Development,* 26(4): 303–15.

Flynn, N., 1986. "Performance measurement in public sector services." *Policy & Politics* 14: 389–404.

Forest, Virginie, 2008. "Performance-related pay and work motivation: theoretical and empirical perspectives for the French civil service." *International review of administrative sciences* 74: 325–39.

Fotaki, M., 1999. "The Impact of Market Oriented Reforms on Choice and Information: A Case Study of Cataract Surgery in Outer London and Stockholm." *Social Science & Medicine,* vol 48, no 10: 1415–32.

Frey, B. S. and R. Jegen, 2001. "Motivation crowding theory." *Journal of Economic Surveys* 15: 589–611.

Frey, B. S. and F. Oberholzer-Gee, 1997. "The cost of price incentives: An empirical analysis of motivation crowding-out." *The American Economic Review,* vol. 84, No. 4: 746–55.

Glennerster, H., 1991. "Quasi-Markets for Education?" *The Economic Journal,* vol 101, no 408: 1268–76.

Greve, B., 2009. "Can Choice in Welfare States Be Equitable?" *Social Policy & Administration* 43: 543–56.

Grimshaw, D. et al., 2002. "Going Privately: Partnership and Outsourcing in UK Public Services." *Public Administration,* vol 80, no 3: 475–502.

Hirschman, A. O., 1980. " 'Exit, Voice, and Loyalty': Further Reflections and a Survey of Recent Contributions." *The Milbank Memorial Fund Quarterly. Health and Society* 58: 430–53.

Hirschman, A. O., 1970. *Exit, voice, and loyalty: Responses to decline in firms, organizations, and states.* Cambridge, MA: Harvard University Press.

John, P. et al., 2004. "The Bidding Game: Competitive Funding Regimes and the Political Targeting of Urban Programme Schemes." *British Journal of Political Science,* vol 34, no 3: 405–28.

Kouzmin, A., E. Loffler, H. Klages, and N. Korac-Kakabadse, 1999. "Benchmarking and performance measurement in public sectors." *International Journal of Public Sector Management* 12: 121–44.

Le Grand, J., 2006a. "The Blair Legacy? Choice and competition in public services." Transcript of Public Lecture. London School of Economics, 21 February 2006:

<http://www.lse.ac.uk/collections/LSEHealthAndSocialCare/documents/ByProfessorJulianLeGrand.pdf>.

Le Grand, J., 2006b. "Equality and choice in public services." *Social Research: An International Quarterly* 73: 695–710.

Le Grand, J., 1991. "Quasi-Markets and Social Policy." *The Economic Journal,* vol 101, no 408: 1256–67.

Le Grand, J., 2007. *The other invisible hand: delivering public services through choice and competition.* Princeton, NJ: Princeton University Press.

Li, B. and An, X., 2009. *Migration and Small Towns in China–Power Hierarchy and Resource Allocation.* London: International Institute and Environment and Development (IIED), vol. 16.

Liu, X. and A. Mills, 2005. "The effect of performance-related pay of hospital doctors on hospital behaviour: a case study from Shandong, China." *Human Resources for Health* 3(11): 1–12.

Mansuri, G. and V. Rao, 2004. "Community-based and-driven development: A critical review." *The World Bank Research Observer* 19: 1.

Marsden, D., 2000. "Teachers Before the Threshold." *CEP Discussion Papers.*

Marsden, D. and R. Belfield, 2007. "Pay for performance where output is hard to measure: the case of performance pay for school teachers." *Advances in Industrial and Labor Relations* 15: 1–37.

Marsden, D. and S. French, 1998. *What a Performance: Performance Related Pay in the Public Services.* Centre for Economic Performance, London School of Economics and Political Science, London, UK.

Marsden, D. and R. Richardson, 1992. "Motivation and performance related pay in the public sector: a case study of the inland revenue." CEP discussion paper, 75. Centre for Economic Performance, London School of Economics and Political Science, London, UK.

Marsden, D. and R. Richardson, 1994. "Performing for pay? The effects of merit pay on motivation in a public service." *British Journal of Industrial Relations* 32: 243–61.

Martin, S., 2000. "Implementing 'best Value': Local Public Services in Transition." *Public Administration,* vol 78, no 1: 209–27.

Matosevic, T. et al., 2008. "Motivation and Commissioning: Perceived and Expressed Motivations of Care Home Providers." *Social Policy & Administration, vol* 42, no 3: 228–47.

McGuire, R. A. et al., 1987. "The Determinants of the Choice between Public and Private Production of a Publicly Funded Service." *Public Choice,* vol 54, no 3: 211–30.

National Patriotic Committee, PRC, 1989. "Notice on the National Hygienic City Campaign (Guanyu Kaizhan Chuangjian Guojia Weisheng Chengshi Huodong De Tongzhi)." 2360148903 .

Patriotic Hygienic Campaign Committee of Qinghai Province, 2008. "Notice on Offering Further Help to Xining to Prepare for the National Hygienic City Campaign (Guanyu Jingyibu Peihe Xiningshi Zuohao Chuangjian Guojia Weisheng Chengshi Gongzuo De Tongzhi)." Qinghaiwei (2008) No. 12, 23/09/2008.

Propper, C. and D. Wilson, 2003. "The use and usefulness of performance measures in the public sector." *Oxford Review of Economic Policy* 19: 250.

Ravallion, Martin, 2007. "How Relevant is Targeting to the Success of an Antipoverty Program?" World Bank Policy Research Working Paper Series. Available at SSRN: <http://ssrn.com/abstract=1029500>.

Sainio, C., E. Eriksson, and S. Lauri, 2001. "Patient participation in decision making about care: The cancer patient's point of view." *Cancer Nursing* 24: 172.

Sassatelli, M., 2002. "Imagined Europe: The Shaping of a European Cultural Identity through Eu Cultural Policy." *European Journal of Social Theory,* Vol 5, No 4: 435–51.

Scannell, P., 1989. "Public service broadcasting and modem public life." *Media, Culture and Society* 11: 135–66.

Shen, R., 2004. "Alternatives to Improve the Ability of Public Provision by the Government (Tigao Zhengfu Gonggong Fuwu Nengli De Xuanze)." *China Public Administration (zhongguo xingzheng guanli),* no 223: 29–32.

Sjoholt, P., 1999. "Culture as a Strategic Development Device: The Role of 'European Cities of Culture', with Particular Reference to Bergen." *European Urban and Regional Studies,* vol 6, no 4: 339–47.

State Council, PRC, 1989. "'Decisions on Improving the Work for Patriotic Hygiene' (Guanyu Jiaqiang Aiguo Weisheng Yundong De Jueding)." State Council (1989), Document No. 22.

Williams, J., and A. Rossiter, 2004. Choice: The Evidence. *The Operation of Choice Systems in Practice: National and International Evidence.* London: Social Market Foundation.

Xi X., Fan L., and Deng, X., 1998. "Public Environment Awareness in China: An Analysis of the Results of Public Surveys." Project report, National Research Centre for Science and Technology for Development, Ministry of Science and Technology, Beijing, December.

Xining Communist Party Committee Office, 2008. "Xining Communiqués," 21.

Xining government, PRC, 2008. "Statistics for the Funding of 2008 Hygienic City Campaign (2008 Nian Chuangwei Gongzuo Quanshi Zijin Touru Qingkuang Tongji)." unpublished.

Zhang, Y., and B. Li, 2011. "Motivating service improvement with award and competition: hygienic city campaigns in China." *Environment and urbanization* 23(1): 41–56.

12

Empirical Studies of an Approach to Decentralization

"Decision Space" in Decentralized Health Systems

Thomas J. Bossert

12.1 An Innovative Approach to Decentralization

One of the central problems of the analysis of decentralization has been the difficulty of defining the complex elements that make up the concept. Much of the theory of decentralization does not disaggregate the concept sufficiently to help answer the policy question of whether decentralization is a good way to achieve policy objectives (Channa and Faguet, 2012). Rather, most analysts present rational choice or other ideologically bound arguments for why local choice is likely to be a good, or bad, way to achieve objectives or to respond to local decisions about priorities. In an attempt to address this issue, in the late 1990s the author reviewed different theories and evidence on decentralization and proposed an approach that focuses on the amount of choice that local officials have over a series of different functions and applied the concept to the case of the health system in Colombia (Bossert, 1998). I reviewed the major approaches to decentralization, including the public administration approach, local public choice, social capital, and principal agent theories and proposed a more complex approach, based in part on principal agent theory, that describes decentralization as a set of rules about local choice and incentives that the central authorities use to encourage local decision-makers to make choices that are likely to achieve the objectives of the central authorities. The approach defined the "decision space" or local discretion allowed by the central government for functions and sub-functions about financing, service delivery, human resources, and governance.

This approach has several advantages. It proposes that decentralization is fundamentally about shifting choice from central authorities to local authorities (Faguet and Wietzke, 2006). The choice allowed is not a single block but rather a range of discretion allowed over different functions. Therefore, some systems will allow more choice over budgets and financing, while others will allow more choice over hiring and firing, and other functions. Furthermore, as systems change, the range of choice may change for some functions and not for others. This is a more realistic way of viewing the complexity of real experience than the usual dichotomous descriptions in which systems are defined as decentralized or centralized (or in some cases, recentralizing).[1] However, the objective of defining decentralization in this way is not just for more complex typologizing. It proposes specific definitions of what the range of choice might be—using health sector functions as an example—with the hope that in defining empirically the complex types of decision space, we could then test whether more local choice for some functions would result in better health system performance. This last objective has proven to be the most challenging.

This chapter surveys the theoretical and empirical developments in the study of decision space carried out by our team at Harvard T.H. Chan School of Public Health, as they have evolved from the first studies we implemented to the present. It first reviews a comparative desk study of formal decision space in four countries to demonstrate the utility of the framework, and additional studies to evaluate the impact of decentralization in Zambia, Chile, Bolivia, and Colombia; these were the first assessments of the impact of decentralization on the equity of allocations of financial resources. A second phase was a series of empirical studies in Nicaragua and Morocco to examine the actual choices that local officials reported they made; what we called "informal decision space," which showed variations not apparent with the formal assignments of roles and responsibilities. In a third phase of research we combined assessments of informal decision space with information on the local capacities and accountability of health officials to locally elected officials in Pakistan, India, and Vietnam. Finally, a comparative desk analysis of decentralization using a modified decision space framework revisited the issues of decision space, capacity, and accountability in a broader range of countries. This review is followed here by

[1] There are other functional definitions that have been developed both generally and specifically in the health sector. For general functional definitions, see: Gershberg, A. I., 1998. "Decentralisation, Recentralisation and Performance Accountability: Building an Operationally Useful Framework for Analysis." *Development Policy Review,* 16(4), 405. For specific functional definitions for health, see: Peckham, S., Exworthy, M., Powell, M., and Greener, I. A. N., 2008. "Decentralizing health services in the UK: a new conceptual framework." *Public Administration,* 86(2), 559–80. See also Paul L. Hutchinson and Anne K. LaFond, 2004. *Monitoring and Evaluation of Decentralization Reforms in Developing Country Health Sectors.* Bethesda, MD: The Partners for Health Reform*plus* Project, Abt Associates Inc.

recommendations for future policies on decentralization and a call for additional research in this topic.

12.2 Initial Empirical Applications of the "Decision Space" Approach

Using the "decision space" approach, the author, along with colleagues and students at the Harvard T.H. Chan School of Public Health, began a series of studies to analyze empirical cases of decentralization. We first applied the framework to a comparative analysis of secondary sources on four countries that in the early 2000s had reputations for being decentralized: Ghana, Zambia, Uganda, and the Philippines (Bossert and Beauvais, 2002). The study produced a comparative "map" of decision space (Table 12.1) classifying (based on criteria established in the original *Social Science and Medicine* article[2]) the different degrees of formal choice for each function for each country and demonstrating considerable variation among countries and among functions.

However, a review of the available evidence did not allow us to determine the relationship between decision space and performance. While there was evidence of differences in financing, service delivery, and human resources, attributing these differences to the degree of decentralization was not possible. In the end this study showed that the approach could distinguish the different degrees of decision space among the four countries and showed how complex the empirical problem of assessing impact on performance was.

In a follow up study of Zambia, for which we were able to do primary research, we analyzed data from before and after decentralization and found positive effects on allocation of resources to and within districts based on a strong application of a well-designed formula based on population size and hospital beds, and on carefully monitored expenditures by the Central Board of Health (Bossert, Chitah, and Bowser, 2003). Wealthier districts were, however, able to mobilize more resources than the poorer districts, suggesting that inequities would widen in the future. The study found no distinguishable difference in health performance after decentralization as measured by utilization of health services, immunization coverage, and family planning activities.

During the early 2000s we also studied three countries in Latin America which had a reputation for having the most decentralized health systems at

[2] The scores for "narrow," "moderate," and "wide" varied for each function. For instance, for revenue in financing, the greater degree of local financing constituted wider decision space; for salaries for human resources, "narrow" would be defined by national civil service rules, "wide" would not limit local choice on salaries, and "moderate" would be a limited range of choice about salaries (see Bossert, 1998).

Table 12.1. Comparative decision space for Ghana, Zambia, Uganda, and the Philippines.

Functions	Range of Choice		
	Narrow	Moderate	Wide
Financing			
Sources of revenue	Zambia	Ghana Uganda	Philippines
Expenditures		All four	
Income from fees		Ghana Zambia Uganda	Philippines
Service organization			
Hospital autonomy	Ghana Zambia	Uganda	Philippines
Insurance plans	Ghana Uganda		Zambia Philippines
Payment mechanisms	Ghana Uganda	Philippines	Zambia
Contracts with private providers		Ghana Zambia Philippines	Uganda
Human Resources:			
Salaries	AllfFour		
Contracts	Ghana	Philippines	Zambia Uganda
Civil service	Ghana	Zambia Uganda Philippines	
Access rules	Ghana	Zambia Uganda Philippines	
Governance			
Local government	Ghana Zambia		Uganda Philippines
Facility boards	All four		
Health offices	Ghana Philippines	Zambia Uganda	
Community participation	Ghana Uganda	Zambia Philippines	
Country Totals			
Ghana	11	4	0
Zambia	5	7	3
Uganda	5	7	3
Philippines	3	7	5

Source: Bossert and Beauvais (2002).

the time: Chile, Bolivia, and Colombia (Bossert, Larrañaga, and Ruiz Meir, 2000). The study found that in the Latin American cases, as in the African and Asian cases, there was considerable variation in decision space among countries and among functions within countries. It also found that over time decision space was reduced for some key functions—such as human resources salaries and earmarking of financial allocations. Even in these countries with a reputation for decentralization, many functions remained highly centralized (in decision space terms, "narrow" choice for local officials).

This study also found the clearest evidence that the process of decentralization had, surprisingly, led to increased equity of allocations (Bossert et al., 2003b). In the Chilean and Colombian cases, for which the financial data was most reliable, the study found that over time since decentralization the gap between the wealthiest municipalities and the poorest was significantly reduced—both for intergovernmental transfers from central government and for locally generated tax revenues assigned to health (see Table 12.2). While the intergovernmental transfers in Colombia, for instance, had favored the wealthiest quintile of municipalities with six times higher per capita allocations before decentralization, the application of a population based formula for allocations that was imposed by decentralization legislation, resulted in almost equal allocations from the central government. The surprise was that the gap between rich and poor in terms of their own source revenues allocated to health also declined—from a difference of almost 42 times higher per capita expenditures in health to only 12 times higher. Decentralization appears to have encouraged poorer localities to take financial responsibility for health seriously, and the wealthier did not keep pace with the increases assigned by the poor. While the rich still assigned more of their local resources than did the poor, decentralization actually narrowed the gap, flying in the face of theoretical expectations.

This series of studies focused on the formal range of choice allowed local governments and demonstrated that the decision space approach had value in describing the full range of functions that could be decentralized to local governments. In the case of Chile and Colombia, it also lent evidence to the

Table 12.2. Colombia: average external and own source revenues per capita by income decile.

	1994		1995		1996		1997	
Deciles	External	Own	External	Own	External	Own	External	Own
1 poor	7.1	0.2	10.9	0.2	22.4	0.9	54.6	2.1
2	10.7	0.5	12.0	0.8	22.8	1.2	56.2	2.9
3	10.5	1.2	15.3	1.4	25.4	3.2	59.1	7.1
4	14.8	2.2	19.4	2.4	26.6	4.7	54.4	9.6
5	16.9	2.6	24.3	4.3	28.8	7.6	62.4	13.9
6	28.1	4.1	27.1	6.0	38.0	12.8	60.0	18.1
7	24.5	4.1	36.0	7.9	47.2	14.7	67.3	20.3
8	25.7	4.1	41.6	8.0	45.8	13.4	67.3	21.2
9	37.8	6.7	52.4	10.0	56.0	18.1	64.7	23.4
10 rich	43.4	8.3	58.7	14.0	52.7	21.2	64.6	25.0
Avg.	21.9	3.4	29.7	5.4	36.6	9.8	61.1	14.4
10th/1st	6.11	41.5	5.38	70.0	2.35	23.55	1.18	11.9

Source: Bossert, et al. (2003b).

argument that formal decentralization could improve equity—at least equity in allocations of financial resources. However, the authors were uneasy with the limited ability to assess the actual range of choice that was exercised by local officials. Were they simply following the directives of higher officials as they had under centralized authority, or were they exercising fully the range of choice formally granted by central authorities?

12.3 Focus on Variations within Formal Decision Space: Informal Decision Space

It soon became apparent that the formal legal and regulatory rules about decision space did not really define the actual practice of officials. In interviews with officials we consistently found that some made more use of the range of choice they formally had while others limited their choices to earlier centralized decisions or were unaware of the range of choices they could use. In some cases, officials indeed made more choices than they were "allowed" and got away with it because of a lack of centralized monitoring or enforcement. We decided then to develop survey instruments to ask local officials what kinds of choices they had actually made in the past year. Other surveys (for instance the original Decentralization Mapping Tool of Management Science for Health) had attempted to assess local officials' attitudes toward decentralization. These instruments, however, were largely open-ended, or vague enough to allow for very subjective responses. It was felt that open-ended questions tended to reflect the different abilities or desires of respondents and were not as comparable as questions asking directly if they had actually made specific choices about different functions.

Developing appropriate questions for surveys of officials was tricky business, because it meant that the survey instruments would have to be developed with a group of informants who knew what choices were likely to be made in order to develop closed-ended questions that would be meaningful and discriminate different degrees of choice within the country context. It also meant that we would be limited in our ability to make comparative analysis across countries with different levels of formal choice. We developed and tested these survey instruments in Nicaragua and Morocco.

The Nicaragua surveys helped define the decision space that was available in a system that had evolved with few clearly defined rules so that less was known by policy makers about what decision space was actually in practice (Bossert, Bowser, and Corea, 2001). The study of the decision space at the district (*SILAIS*) level suggested that officials had a moderate range of choice over central government-funded expenditures, over their own source revenues collected at the facilities, and over assignments and transfers of human resources and community participation. For other functions the central Ministry of Health defined the choices without allowing local discretion. We were not able to find relationships between decision space over these functions and any of a series of relatively reliable performance indicators. However, the study did analyze funding shortages, inequities of allocation among districts, and high rotation rates of human resources, and made recommendations for policy changes including a "needs based" formula and longer-term assignments to reduce the change in local staffing, especially of managers.

In Morocco we found that the formal decision space was generally very narrow—not unusual for former French colonies with their history of highly centralized bureaucracies—but that there was variation in the amount of decision space that the district *délégués* reported in actual practice (Bossert et al., 2003a). The questions asked specifically if they made choices that were allowed, and also if they needed higher approval for choices that they made and whether these choices were approved, to get a sense of how wide their judgement was respected by higher authorities. Those *délégués* who reported higher decision space and less rejections from superiors for choices in specific functions tended to allocate more resources to administration and training than directly to priority maternal and child health programs and immunizations. This was not seen as a positive outcome and suggested that stricter allocation monitoring was needed.

In a more specific application of decision space analysis, we were asked to do an applied research project for a USAID-funded logistics system project to assess the impact of decentralization on health logistic systems in low-income countries (Bossert, Bowser, and Amenyah, 2007). This project gave us an opportunity to apply decision space analysis to a situation in which the project was collecting detailed measures of performance. Working with logistics system experts we were able to define fourteen different logistics functions that might be decentralized—from forecasting needs through to the delivery of drugs to the patient—and to develop specific questions for two different health systems: Guatemala and Ghana. At the same time as we did our surveys, the project used its standardized questionnaire about the performance of the logistics system—asking questions about key issues such as stock outs, inventory methods, cold chain maintenance, etc. We were able to identify performance indicators for most of the fourteen functions that could be decentralized and to show that some of the decentralized functions were associated with higher (and others with lower) levels of performance in both countries. We concluded that for logistics system functions there was evidence in both countries suggesting that better performance could be achieved if inventory control and logistics information systems were centralized while planning and budgeting was decentralized. Both these findings made logical sense in that allowing variation in such technically rigid functions as inventory control and information system formats would result in poor quality logistics, while local knowledge of needs and finances would strengthen planning and budgeting. In Guatemala, an unusual form of procurement allowed local officials to procure medicines directly from producers for fixed low prices determined by a competitive national process called "open contracting." This suggests that under conditions of open contracting, more local decision-making might result in better performance.

These studies of informal decision space led to the conclusion that there was a range of choice within the formal decision space that was likely to have an impact on how effective decentralization would be (see also Faguet and Ali, 2009). If some officials did not take advantage of the full range of choice, as they responded to their local conditions and situation, decentralization would not have the theoretical advantage claimed by advocates. This difference also had implications for the policy of defining decentralization in ways to promote better performance, based on local decision-making. However, it was also clear that there were other factors that would contribute to better performance, namely the capacities of local administrations to design and implement health programs and the responsiveness or accountability of health officials to locally elected officials.

12.4 Widening the Scope of Analysis: Decision Space, Capacities, and Accountability

In response to growing attention to health system strengthening and to a growing literature on governance and accountability, we decided to expand our conceptual framework to include two additional dimensions to complement our initial focus on decision space and performance.

It was clear that our earlier focus on decision space would not account for the differences in the capacities of those making decisions—in terms of personal skills and knowledge, and institutional factors such as staffing patterns and funding. In addition, since many forms of decentralization imply a dual principal agent situation—health administrators respond both to the central government and to the locally elected officials—a form called, in the classic literature on decentralization, "devolution," in contrast to "deconcentration," within the ministry of health—we wanted to examine the accountability of local health officials to the guidance and priorities of locally elected officials (Rondinelli, 1981).

One of the critical objections to decentralization has been the argument that the skills and knowledge of decision-makers and the staffing levels in localities are often too weak to make and implement good decisions about health service issues. (In some cases this argument is an equity argument, emphasizing the differences in skills and staffing between wealthy and poor communities.) Others suggest that the difference in funding levels from one locality to another might explain the difference in the ability to make good decisions at the local level.

Since many decentralized health systems emerge from a centralized bureaucracy and introduce new authority and responsibility for locally elected officials—charging them with the responsibility of defining local priorities and mobilizing additional local resources—we sought to assess the accountability of health administrators at local levels to the elected officials at those levels (Brinkerhoff, 2004; Shah, 2006; Yilmaz, Beris, and Serrano-Berthet, 2008).

Opportunities to examine these dimensions appeared in USAID and World Bank projects in Pakistan, India, and Vietnam. Modifying the survey instruments used in Nicaragua and Morocco and adding questions about the dimensions of institutional and individual capacity and accountability to local officials, we implemented surveys specific to the conditions in selected districts in Pakistan, districts in three states in India, and at the provincial level in Vietnam.

The study in Pakistan was the first attempt to assess decision space, capacities, and accountability together (Bossert and Mitchell, 2011). The administrative organization of Pakistan involves national, provincial, and district administrative units with a uniform civil service that involves both general administrators and health-specific administrators. At the district level there are locally elected officials, *Nazim*, who have a role in local decision-making. The survey asked ninety-one officials, including the two types of administrators and the *Nazim*, questions about decision space, capacities, and accountability specific to their roles in seventeen districts.

The questions about decision space focused on four key functional areas (strategic and operational planning, budgeting, human resources, and service organization/delivery), and the questions on capacity asked about resources available, skills and experience, and processes. Questions about accountability attempted to assess how much the *Nazim* were involved in decision-making and how responsive local administrators were to the *Nazim's* priorities. In this study we converted the responses into quantifiable indices in order to test the significance of relationships. The responses were coded on a three-point Likert scale into narrow, moderate, or wide decision space or high, medium, or low capacity or accountability. These responses were then standardized by respondent type and summarized into two indices: one for responses to functional issues by individuals and one for responses to those issues across all respondents in a district.

We found that there were strong positive correlations among the different dimensions of decentralization—those who reported high levels of decision space in a specific function also reported high levels of capacities and accountability for that function.(see Table 12.3) For instance, if a district had high decision space for strategic and operational planning they also had high decision space for service organization and delivery (p= 0.43 at 5 per cent level of significance).

We also found that those who had high levels of one dimension in one function also had high levels in other functions—high decision space for all functions was correlated with high capacity and high accountability (see Table 12.4). For instance, officials with high decision space for strategic and operational planning also had high levels of capacity for that function (p = 0.41 at 5 per cent level of significance).

To further test the relationship of the dimension of capacity we assessed the personal experience of the respondents and found correlations between years of service and an index of decision space—longer-serving officials reported wider decision space—and more capacities (as measured by the index of capacities in the survey) (see Table 12.5) Those with more training also reported more capacities. Interestingly there was no relationship with accountability.

This study demonstrated, as had the earlier studies, that there was a wide variation of responses about the informal decision space, even within a

Table 12.3. Cross-function correlations within dimensions of decentralization.

Function 1	Function 2	DS		CAP		ACC	
		ρ	N	*ρ*	N	*ρ*	N
SOP &	BUD	0.21	59	0.20	36	0.15	16
	HR	0.21	59	0.27	36	0.00	16
	SOD	0.43**	44	0.43*	21		
BUD &	HR	0.22*	75	0.35**	60	0.10	32
	SOD	0.35**	44	0.31**	44		
HR &	SOD	0.14	44	0.42**	44	0.37**	44

Notes: * $p < 0.10$; ** $p < 0.05$; DS = decision space; CAP = capacities; ACC = accountability; SOP = strategic and operational planning; BUD = budgeting; HR = human resources; SOD = service organization and delivery.

Table 12.4. Within-function correlations between dimensions of decentralization.

Function	DS/CAP		CAP/ACC		DS/ACC	
	ρ	N	*ρ*	N	*ρ*	N
SOP	0.41**	35	0.47*	15	0.10	15
BUD	0.32**	75	0.14	31	0.19	31
HR	0.11	60	0.02	60	−0.20	60
SOD	0.07	44	0.04	44	0.32**	44
ALL	0.39**	75	0.23*	75	0.02	75

Notes: * $p < 0.10$; ** $p < 0.05$; DS = decision space; CAP = capacities; ACC = accountability; SOP = strategic and operational planning; BUD = budgeting; HR = human resources; SOD = service organization and delivery.

Table 12.5. Correlations between decentralization and respondent experience/capacity.

Dimension	Training scale		Years of service		Years at post	
	ρ	N	*ρ*	N	*ρ*	N
DS	0.25	44	0.26 **	74	0.04	75
CAP	0.30 **	44	0.24 **	74	−0.01	75
ACC	0.15	44	0.18	74	0.03	75

Notes: * $p < 0.10$; ** $p < 0.05$; DS = decision space; CAP = capacities; ACC = accountability; SOP = strategic and operational planning; BUD = budgeting; HR = human resources; SOD = service organization and delivery.

Source: Bossert and Mitchell (2011).

relatively uniform civil service context based on a British model of administration. It also showed that there were significant synergies among the three key dimensions—decision space, capacity, and accountability. The least strong relationship was with accountability, which is not surprising given the lack of long experience with civil servants being responsive to local authorities. This synergy among the dimensions is an important finding suggesting, although not demonstrating causally, that policies to strengthen one of the dimensions might lead to improvements in the other dimensions. We also found that the choice allowed in human resources decisions—hiring, firing, and transfers—was extremely limited, and that this limitation was viewed by respondents as not reflecting their capacities in this area.

In an unusual opportunity, we followed up the original 2006 study with a capacity-building intervention and a follow-up study in 2009. The follow-up study is based on surveys administered to local health sector decision-makers in fifteen districts in Pakistan—ten of which received capacity-building assistance from a USAID-funded maternal and child health project, called PAIMAN, and five similar control districts which had no capacity-building interventions (Bossert and Mitchell, 2011). While local authorities in both districts reported using more of their discretionary powers (i.e., "decision space") by 2009, institutional capacities in PAIMAN districts improved to a higher degree than in comparison districts. Officials in neither set of districts reported significant changes in their accountability to elected local officials, although those districts with more decision space and institutional capacities did mobilize greater local support for health programs. As in the earlier study, we found that there were strong synergies among the dimensions of decentralization for different health sector functions. This study extended those findings to show that stronger institutional capacities and wider decision space were associated with improvements in health coverage and in better administration of the health system. These findings, again, were from some of the few studies of decentralization that show how capacity-building interventions to improve decentralization at the district level may contribute to improved decision-making abilities and, in turn, improved health system performance.

We modified the instruments of the Pakistan study to implement similar surveys in three states in India—Uttar Pradesh, Orissa, and West Bengal (Bossert et al., 2008; Bossert et al., 2010). The methodology was similar to that of Pakistan and the findings were similar. The Indian system granted greater authority to the states than had Pakistani provinces (at the time—since the study was completed Pakistan has devolved most responsibilities to the provinces), so there is potential for greater variation among the states in India, and the elected local officials in the *panchiat raj* institutions (PRIs) were likely to be more reflective of electoral politics than were the *Nazim* of districts in Pakistan. The dynamics of the interplay of decision space, capacities, and accountability at the district level were found to be similar. In all three states, we found significant variation in decision space, capacities, and accountability as reported by the officials interviewed. For instance, the results in six districts studied in West Bengal are presented in Figure 12.1 below.

In all three states, synergies among the dimensions of decision space, capacities, and accountability were also demonstrated, although to different degrees of correlation and significance for specific functions. The least-strong relationship was with accountability—reflecting the same situation in Pakistan, and reflecting again the historical experience of civil servants not being responsive to local authorities. We also found that limitations in human resources were perceived as a major constraint on effective management at local levels.

While the Vietnam study focused on provincial-level decentralization rather than that at the district level, the study found similar results to the findings in Pakistan and India (Bossert, Mitchell, and Blanchet, 2010). While the political system in Vietnam was different from that of Pakistan and India, the dynamics of relationships among the dimensions of decentralization did not seem to be affected by a system dominated by a single political party. We again found significant variations in informal decision space, capacities, and accountability, and also significant synergies between the three dimensions. Again, accountability was the least-strong dimension, and human resources perceived as the most restricting functional area, although the policy of allowing local contracting has mitigated this constraint. In Vietnam, central allocations to poorer provinces was a clear national policy that had the implication that the wealthier provinces exercised greater decision space, likely because they contributed more of their own-source revenues, than did the poorer provinces which were more dependent on central government transfers.

This series of studies confirmed the utility of examining decision space, capacities, and accountability in a way that explored the interactions among

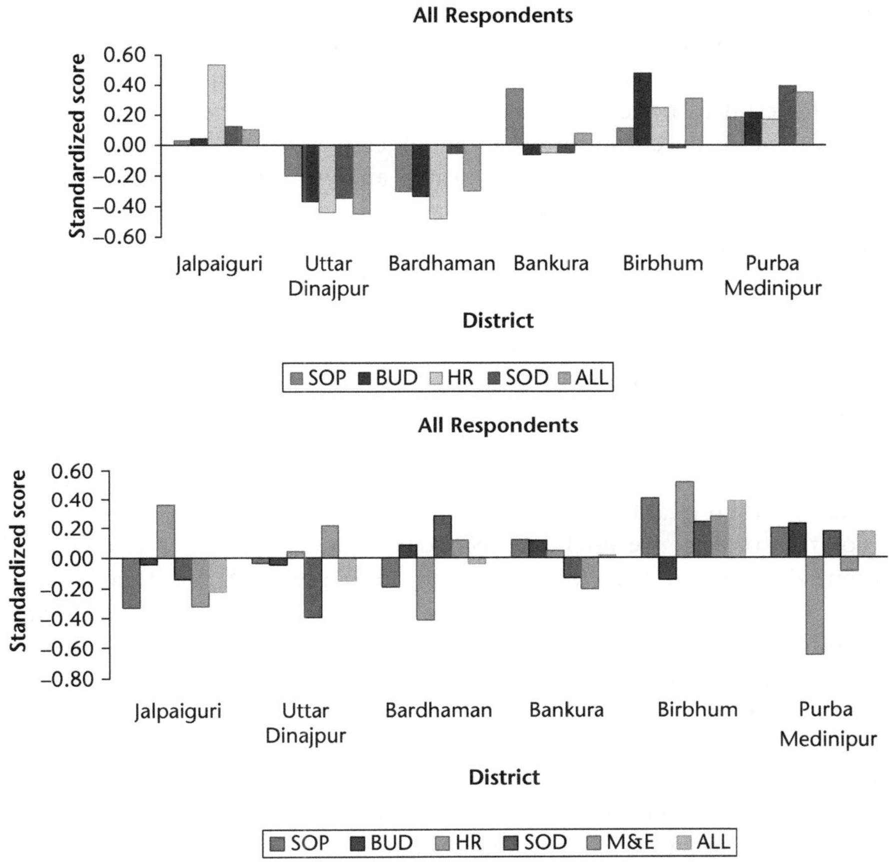

Figure 12.1. Decision Space and Capacities Scores in Six Districts of West Bengal, India

Note: SOP = Strategic/Operational Planning; BUD = Budgeting; HR = Human Resources; SOD = Service Delivery/Organization; M&E = Monitoring and Evaluation

Source: Bossert, et. al. (2008).

the three dimensions. In the study of Pakistan, it also provided evidence of how a single intervention in capacity-building could strengthen the performance of the system, and the advantages of synergies among the dimensions.

12.5 Governance and Sector Interests

In some recent work we have become aware of a significant difference in the way we approach and seek to evaluate decentralization from those who identify themselves as governance experts (Mitchell and Bossert, 2010). The growing interest in governance among major development donors has given rise to analysts who examine decentralization from a normative perspective based on theory (going back at least to de Tocqueville) and advocacy that more decentralized governance is likely, at least in the long term, to result in better democracies and in better policies. From this perspective, more decentralization is an objective to be sought by general policies, although the more sophisticated analysts also warn that the type of decentralization needed would have to avoid problems of capture, corruption, and inequities of resources. In terms of objectives, this perspective is quite different from ours. We start with the proposition that we want to know the best form of decentralization for achieving the objectives of a health system. For us the performance that measures the effectiveness of decentralization is primarily whether and how decentralized systems achieve better health outcomes. However, we are also concerned that health policy reduce the financial risk of illness, and generate patient and public satisfaction with health services in a manner that is equitable, efficient, and marked by high quality (Roberts et al., 2008).

For this project, we analyzed secondary sources for six case studies of decentralization, in Asia (India, Pakistan, Philippines), Africa (Uganda) and Latin America (Bolivia, Chile) to assess differences in decision space and accountability for policy recommendations for World Bank officials. We summarized the decision space of the six cases as follows in Table 12.6.

For capacities, the cases suggested that specific capacities be assessed in terms of present capacity for implementation—for instance, use of contracting when existing capacity does not exist—as well as using decentralization as a means of strengthening longer-term capacity.

For accountability we identified several mechanisms that appeared to improve both civic and social accountability which went beyond the focus only on accountability toward elected local officials to see if accountability to community organizations was effective (Table 12.7).

This study was a review of existing literature and, in contrast to our earlier work on this wider type of analysis, was not the result of primary research using a consistent methodology. This study did, however, demonstrate that the combined study of formal decision space, capacities, and accountability could be informative, even if it was not based on a survey of officials—making the study of complex decentralization factors feasible for desk study methods.

12.6 Policy Recommendations

In general we found that the decision space at local levels was still quite restricted, even in countries with reputations for being very decentralized.

Table 12.6. Decision space for six-country study.

Function	Exercise of local discretion			Drivers of local-level authority
	Low	Med	High	
Administrative Decentralization				
Required programs	India Pakistan Uganda	Bolivia Chile	Philippines	India, Pakistan, Uganda: high conditionality on central fiscal transfers shape programmatic implementation. Bolivia, Chile: insurance-related mandates provide some programmatic mandates. Philippines: minimal central programmatic mandates
Hospital autonomy	Chile Pakistan Uganda	India	Bolivia Philippines	Chile, Pakistan, Uganda: secondary and/or tertiary care outside of scope of health sector decentralization. India: hospital autonomy conducted on state-by-state basis Bolivia, Philippines: local government ownership and/or management of hospitals provides wide discretion.
Insurance Plans	Bolivia Chile Pakistan Uganda	India Philippines		Bolivia, Chile: centrally defined/administered plans. Pakistan, Uganda: lack of large-scale insurance mechanisms. India: some use of community-based health insurance. Philippines: centralization over many elements (e.g., administration; premium collection) coupled with local choice over selected plan elements (e.g., enrollment of the poor).
Contracting (with organizations)	Chile India Uganda	Bolivia Pakistan Philippines		Chile, India, Uganda: little local-level ability to contract. Bolivia, Pakistan: contracting allowed upon central approval. Philippines: relatively wide ability to contract at an organizational level (but not yet well developed in practice).
Procurement	Bolivia India Pakistan Uganda	Chile	Philippines	Bolivia, India, Pakistan, Uganda: most elements standardized at national level (e.g., drug lists, prices). Chile: local choice for hospitals using public/private suppliers. Philippines: existence of numerous local procurement systems.
Civil Service (salaries)	Bolivia Chile India			All countries: continued reliance on centrally set civil service salary grades.

(continued)

Table 12.6. Continued

Function	Exercise of local discretion			Drivers of local-level authority
	Low	Med	High	
	Pakistan Philippines Uganda			
Civil Service (other HRM* functions)	Bolivia India Pakistan	Chile	Philippines Uganda	Bolivia: public sector personnel not devolved. India, Pakistan: continued local government deference to civil service administrators. Chile: discretion limited to primary care sector. Philippines, Uganda: wide local discretion exists.
Contracting (with individuals)	Bolivia Chile India Pakistan Uganda	Philippines		Bolivia, Chile, India, Pakistan, Uganda: little locally initiated contracting for services in public facilities. Philippines: local contracting allowed below level of physician.
Fiscal Decentralization **Expenditures/Revenues**	India Pakistan Uganda	Bolivia Chile Philippines		India, Pakistan, Uganda: comparatively high conditionality on central transfers/low local capacity and few own-source revenues. Bolivia, Chile, Philippines: comparatively low conditionality on central transfers/higher levels of own-source revenues.

Source: Mitchell and Bossert (2010).

Table 12.7. Accountability and decentralization in six-country study.

Function	Public Accountability	Social Accountability
Administrative Decentralization		
Norms/programs	• Minimum technical standards (e.g., staff establishments)	• Area-wide performance agreements/rankings (Bolivia)
Hospital autonomy	• Limited autonomy to certain hospital functions (Philippines) • Performance agreements for nationally important indicators (e.g., immunization coverage)	• Hospital boards (with government representation) (India) • Facility/provider report cards (Bolivia)
Insurance plans	• Use matching grants to encourage some components (e.g., enrollment of subsidized beneficiaries)	• Community-based financing
Contracting (with organizations)	• Permit local contracting under case-by-case approval from central government (Bolivia)	• Institutionalized community identification and implementation of projects (e.g., CCBs in Pakistan)
Procurement	• Retain strict standards for uniform functions (e.g., inventory control)/allow greater discretion over variable functions (e.g., budgeting)	• Institutionalized transparency (e.g., information dissemination on prices) with purchasing decision left to localities (Chile)
Human Resources		
Civil service	• Allow increased short-term contracting of some professionals to increase flexibility	• Provider/facility report cards (Uganda)
Contracting (with individuals)	• Allow increased short-term contracting of some professionals to increase flexibility	• Provider/facility report cards (Uganda)
Fiscal Decentralization		
Expenditures/ revenues	• Match expenditure to revenue assignments	• Participatory budgeting (Uganda) • Performance agreements (Uganda, Bolivia)

Source: Bossert and Mitchell (2009).

We found that there was considerable variation in decision space between different countries and within countries in the decision space between different functions. The recent studies of decision space, capacities, and accountability show relatively consistent synergies among the three dimensions in three different country contexts (Pakistan, India, and Vietnam) and similar weakness of accountability and limitations on human resources decisions.

The decision space studies have in general supported the idea that it is not so much *whether* policy makers choose to design and implement decentralization but *how* they do so. While we only have some sophisticated studies demonstrating the effects of some processes of decentralization, these studies do show that, under certain conditions, some forms of decentralization can improve equity of access and logistics systems performance. In general, since in several countries we find that decision space and capacity are linked, policies to increase decision space should be accompanied with programs to improve local capacities. The relationship with accountability, although not as strong, also suggests that mechanisms for local accountability can improve decentralization—even in countries where local elite capture may be rampant. The current low levels of decision space in many countries also suggest that there is considerable room for experimentation in wider decision space than most countries currently allow.

The studies of decentralization that used the decision space approach led to some specific recommendations for policy in each country. For Nicaragua and Morocco we were able to recommend expansion of decision space for specific functions that were seen by respondents as particularly constraining. We were able to make specific recommendations for capacity building in different functional areas by district in Pakistan and India and by province in Vietnam.

These studies suggest that decentralization policies be developed in ways that can incrementally increase the range of local choice for officials, who can be responsive to local needs and priorities and at the same time improve overall health system performance and equity. This can best be achieved if a wider decision space is accompanied by capacity building at the local level, and by some increase in accountability of health officials to elected local officials. Especially important are increasing institutional capacities through additional staffing, well-designed and specific management training programs, and technical assistance support for logistics and information systems—a potent combination likely to improve health systems performance. We also found that targeting districts with low levels of capacities could be a way of improving the equity of performance across districts.

The experience in the countries in our earlier studies, especially Chile and Colombia, suggests a process of incrementally increasing decision space while at the same time providing additional resources, either through resource generation by local authorities, or through greater intergovernmental transfers, or both.

The possibility of improved synergies shown especially in the Pakistan study encourages us to recommend interventions in the capacity-building area that can also be related to greater use of decision space and more responsiveness to local authorities. They also allow us to recommend specific widening of decision space from the often quite restricted narrow range, in order to facilitate: greater local discretion over how to allocate own funds; more control over human resources, especially incentives for better performance; a greater ability to focus organizational resources on priority health problems and to make decisions to make services available at more appropriate times for patients; and greater local participation in the governance of health services. It is also likely that central authorities should retain control over norms and standards for the quality of services and for equity of access to services. While expanding choice for human resources—a constraint that several studies found particularly important—policies of decentralization should, nevertheless, also retain some control over human resources to assure that hiring, firing, and incentives decisions are made based on merit rather than patronage or individual caprice.

We have some evidence that greater responsiveness to local authorities, especially if they are held accountable by effective elections, is likely to improve performance. The mechanisms of accountability that require some oversight by local authorities and grant them some control of local budgets, as well as some granting of direct community participation through local health committees or social audits, also seem to have an important role, although our studies do not find this as significant as capacity-building and decision space adjustments (see also Faguet, 2014).

12.7 Where to go from Here

The empirical research suggests that decentralization is extremely complex both conceptually and in practice, and that much more work is necessary to develop clear and comparative criteria for defining the phenomenon. We are not satisfied with the general approaches which use simple dichotomous definitions of decentralization. We have tried to define it as choices made by local officials and have used two methods of defining that decision space of choice: the regulations and laws defining "formal" decision space, and the use of "informal" decision space that is reported by respondents to closed-ended surveys. There are problems with these approaches. Laws and regulations often do not reflect actual use and therefore might over- or under-estimate the amount of local choice that is practised. However, reports by officials may be influenced by reluctance to report what is not in the formal rules, or by ignorance, misunderstanding, or self-aggrandizement. These are general problems of any survey so it is important to continue to validate the approach in places where some observation by outsiders is also possible. Perhaps more important, the need to tailor each survey instrument to the likely reasonable responses within the country context, and to the situation of each type of official respondent, means that comparative analysis across countries is extremely limited. Although we have used relatively similar instruments in Pakistan and the three states in India, the variations in conditions make it hard to say that there is more use of informal decision space for any specific functions in one or another state or country.

The empirical work we have done has also given rise to some preliminary findings that partly suggest how decentralization is related to performance—with findings that decentralization processes have brought increased equity of allocations in some contexts, and that in some cases those officials who take greater advantage of the decision space that they are allowed can make better choices if they have more capacity and more accountability. However, we are still far from our initial objective of finding evidence of what type of decentralization should be recommended for achieving better health system outcomes. It is likely that better performance depends on a combination of contextual factors about the overall governance and economic systems, including specific details of the processes of accountability, as well as details of the rules of decision space and the institutional and personal capacity of local decision-makers.

However, to determine what these factors are and when to increase decision space and/or develop system-strengthening capacity-building programs with scientific confidence would require a research agenda tied to the implementation of a decentralization policy that would allow random assignment of changes in decision space, capacity, and accountability. The before-and-after studies that we have carried out and the observational studies of point-in-time associations do not control for other factors that might influence observed performance differences. For instance, changes in decision space in Colombia and Chile were made at the same time as other changes in insurance programs which might also have influenced health outcomes, and for that reason we focused only on allocation decisions not likely to be affected by an insurance program.

While random control trials are the gold standard for evaluating the impact of interventions, in the case of decentralization especially they are likely to be most difficult to implement. Few countries are willing to implement a complex intervention like decentralization in a phased manner amenable to randomized trials (a rare exception being the random trial evaluation of Mexico's complex social insurance program, see King et al., 2009). It would be a rare policy maker that would be willing to allow researchers to randomly assign which districts will receive greater decision space and which will not, even if the trial was only to last a year or so before rolling out decentralization to the control districts.

In the absence of opportunities for randomized trials, continuing efforts to evaluate decentralization by examining performance indicators from before and after initiation of changes in local decision-making authority is probably the only method we will have.

The effort to evaluate the advisability of different degrees of decision space, different levels of local capacity, and different responsiveness to elected local officials is likely to be worth it. Without empirical evidence of the results of policy choices about decentralization, we are likely to continue to miss out on strongly supported recommendations for future policy, and to continue to hear recommendations coming from untested theories and from advocates either for or against decentralization.

References

Bossert, T., 1998. "Analyzing the decentralization of health in developing countries: decision space, innovation and performance." *Social Science and Medicine* 47: 1513–27.

Bossert, T. J. and Joel C. Beauvais, 2002. "Decentralization of health systems in Ghana, Zambia, Uganda and the Philippines: a comparative analysis of decision space." *Health Policy and Planning* 17(1): 14–31.

Bossert, T. J., Diana M. Bowser, and Johnnie K. Amenyah, 2007. "Is decentralization good for logistics systems? Evidence on essential medicine logistics in Ghana and Guatemala." *Health Policy and Planning,* 22: 73–82.

Bossert, T., Diana Bowser, and Leonor Corea, 2001. *Studies of decentralization of the health system in Nicaragua: Final Report.* Boston, MA: Harvard School of Public Health and Management Sciences for Health.

Bossert, T., Volcan Cakir, Diana Bowser, and Andrew Mitchell, 2003a. *Morocco Decentralization Study: Summary of Preliminary Findings.* Boston, MA: Harvard School of Public Health and John Snow Incorporated.

Bossert, T., Mukosha Bona Chitah, and Diana M. Bowser, 2003. "Decentralization in Zambia: Resource Allocation and District Performance." *Health Policy and Planning* 18 (4): 3, 587–669.

Bossert, T., Osvaldo Larrañaga, and Fernando Ruiz Meir, 2000. "Decentralization of health systems in Latin America." *Pan American Journal of Public Health* Vol. 8, Nos. 1/2: 84–92.

Bossert, T. J., Osvaldo Larrañaga, Ursula Giedion, Jose Arbelaez, and Diana Bowser, 2003b. "Decentralization and Equity of Resource Allocation: Evidence from Colombia and Chile." *Bulletin of World Health Organization,* 81 (2) pp. 95–100.

Bossert, T. J., and Andrew D. Mitchell, 2011. "Health Sector Decentralization and local decision-making: Decision Space, Institutional Capacities and Accountability in Pakistan." *Social Science and Medicine* 72, pp. 39–48.

Bossert, T. J., and Andrew Mitchell, 2009. "Background Note on Sectoral Decentralization and Local Governance for an Economic and Sector Work (ESW): Health Sector." Boston, MA: Harvard School of Public Health and World Bank.

Bossert, T., Andrew Mitchell, and Nathan Blanchet, 2010. Governance and Decentralization of Health Systems in Vietnam: Analysis of Provincial Organization, Decision Space/Accountability and Capacity. Washington, DC: World Bank.

Bossert, T., Andrew Mitchell, Prarthna Dayal, and Madhu Sharma, 2008. Decentralization of Health in the Indian States of Uttar Pradesh and Orissa: Analysis of Decision Space, Capacities and Accountability. World Bank, February 2008.

Bossert, T., Andrew Mitchell, Sumit Mazumdar, and Paolo Belli, 2010. Decentralization of Health in the Indian State of West Bengal: Analysis of Decision Space, Institutional Capacities and Accountability. World Bank, January 2010.

Brinkerhoff, D. W., 2004. "Accountability and health systems: toward conceptual clarity and policy relevance." *Health Policy and Planning* 19(6): 371–9.

Channa, A. and J.P. Faguet, 2012. "Decentralization of Health and Education in Developing Countries: A Quality-Adjusted Review of the Empirical Literature." LSE/STICERD Working Paper No. EOPP 38.

Faguet, J.P., 2014. "Can Sub-National Autonomy Strengthen Democracy in Bolivia?" *Publius: The Journal of Federalism*, 44(1): 51–81.

Faguet, J.P. and Z. Ali, 2009. "Making Reform Work: Institutions, Dispositions and the Improving Health of Bangladesh." *World Development*. 37: 208–18.

Faguet, J.P. and F.B. Wietzke, 2006. "Social Funds and Decentralization: Optimal Institutional Design." *Public Administration and Development*, 26(4): 303–15.

Gershberg, A. I., 1998. "Decentralisation, Recentralisation and Performance Accountability: Building an Operationally Useful Framework for Analysis." *Development Policy Review*, 16(4), 405.

Hutchinson, P. L. and LaFond, A. K., 2004. *Monitoring and Evaluation of Decentralization Reforms in Developing Country Health Sectors*. Bethesda, MD: The Partners for Health Reform*plus* Project, Abt Associates Inc.

King, G., Gakidou, E., Imai, K., Lakin, j., Moore, R. T., Nall, C., Ravishankar, N., Vargas, M., Téllez-Rojo, M. M., Hernández Ávila, J. E., Hernández Ávila, M., and Hernández Llamas, H., 2009. "Public policy for the poor? A randomised assessment of the Mexican universal health insurance programme." *The Lancet*, 373: 1,447–54.

Mitchell, A. and Bossert, T., 2010. 'Decentralisation, governance and health-system performance: "where you stand depends on where you sit".' *Development Policy Review*, Vol. 28, No.6: 669–91.

Peckham, S., Exworthy, M., Powell, M., and Greener, I. A. N., 2008. "Decentralizing health services in the UK: a new conceptual framework." *Public Administration*, 86(2), 559–80.

Roberts, M., Hsiao, W., Reich, M., and Berman, P., 2008. *Getting Health Reform Right*. London and New York: Oxford University Press.

Rondinelli, D., 1981. "Government decentralization in comparative perspective: Theory and practice in developing countries." *International Review of Administrative Science* 47: 133–45.

Shah, A., 2006. *Local governance in developing countries*. Washington, DC: World Bank.

Yilmaz, S., Berris, Y., and Serrano-Berthet, R., 2008. Local Government Discretion and Accountability: A Diagnostic Framework for Local Governance. Washington, DC: World Bank.

13

Political Participation, Clientelism, and Targeting of Local Government Programs

Results from a Rural Household Survey in West Bengal, India

Pranab Bardhan, Sandip Mitra, Dilip Mookherjee, and Abhirup Sarkar

13.1 Introduction

Much attention has been devoted in recent years to decentralized development strategies in poor countries, in the hope that this will enhance efficiency and accountability in delivery of public services (see, for example, the 2004 *World Development Report*). Whether this hope will be realized depends in large part on the functioning of local democracy in less-developed countries.

Accountability pressures depend on the pressures imposed on elected officials by citizens through the way they vote, exercise voice, and receive information about the actions of officials. If a large fraction of citizens either do not express their opinions or lack proper information or understanding of policy issues, a democracy will create no incentives for politicians to espouse or implement policies in the public interest. Governments can then become corrupt and be captured by special interest groups, without facing any threat of displacement. Uneven patterns of political participation or political awareness across different socio-economic groups may thus be a powerful cause of perpetuation of social and economic inequalities.

The extent to which this is true in any given context needs to be studied empirically. How do patterns of political participation (e.g., election turnout, and political and civic meetings), awareness, and exposure to media or related sources of information concerning government programs and policies vary across socio-economic categories? In particular, do households owning little land or belonging to low social status groups participate significantly less in local politics? Do local governments distribute public services equitably within their jurisdictions? How do service delivery patterns vary with citizen participation in civic meetings which provide an opportunity for citizens to air grievances, question elected officials, and debate local policies? Do service delivery patterns affect the way citizens vote subsequently? In particular, what kinds of delivery patterns increase chances of re-election of incumbent governments? Empirical analyses of these kinds of questions are relatively scarce, particularly in the context of developing countries. With few exceptions (such as Baiochhi et al. (2006) or Krishna (2006)), most studies of patterns of political participation do not examine targeting of services across different socio-economic categories and the links between them.

This chapter presents an empirical analysis of patterns of political participation (turnout, awareness, attendance at political and civic meetings, involvement in political campaigns, voting) in local governance across socio-economic categories in rural West Bengal, a state in eastern India with over 80 million residents. We relate these to targeting of services administered by local governments. We also examine ways that citizens voted for different parties in a poll we administered (with secret ballots), and how these related to benefits they received from local governments. We discuss possible implications of these results concerning the nature of accountability pressure imposed on local governments in rural West Bengal over the past three decades.

The analysis is based on data collected from a household survey conducted in 2004 in a sample of eighty-nine villages drawn from fifteen major agricultural districts in West Bengal. This state provides a suitable context for study for a variety of reasons. It has had a relatively long experience with local democracy spanning three decades, unlike other Indian states. Starting in 1977, West Bengal created a three-tier system of local governments, with officials at each tier directly elected in elections held every five years. The state government subsequently devolved to the local governments significant responsibility for selecting beneficiaries of various developmental and welfare programs, such as land reforms, subsidized credit, agricultural seeds and fertilizers, local infrastructure projects, subsidized food and fuel, low-income housing and sanitation, disaster relief, and old-age and widows' pensions. The size of resources available for different programs percolated down from state ministries through different tiers of the local governments down to the lowest level called *gram panchayats* (GPs). Each GP typically has a jurisdiction covering ten to fifteen villages, each of which elects a representative to the governing council of the GP. Actions of the GP are discussed in annual *gram sabha* (or village assembly) meetings where residents can raise questions for elected GP officials to answer publicly.

Moreover, West Bengal is unique insofar as a coalition of Left parties has been repeatedly re-elected across six successive elections with an absolute majority, whereas other Indian states have witnessed incumbents losing elections regularly. However, the dominance of the Left in recent elections has been declining. The source of the political durability of the Left Front in West Bengal is an intriguing question, as is the question of why it appears to be increasingly challenged in recent years. Has the durable political success of the Left in West Bengal resulted from its actions to relieve rural poverty via land reforms and broad-based distribution of benefits from development programs? Or does it reflect a strategy of clientelism which favored particular narrow groups and services to the exclusion of many others?

Details of the surveys are described in Section 13.2. Ours is a cross-sectional analysis in which inference of causality may sometimes be problematic. The correlations in some cases are to be properly viewed as descriptive facts. For example, when political participation as an explanatory variable may itself be endogenous, we summarize our main results on correlation without going into the details of the statistical regressions. Nevertheless, we believe that the underlying issues are important enough that such facts and their consistency with different hypotheses are of considerable interest. In other cases such endogeneity is less of a problem and causal inferences can be made. We shall also seek to corroborate these findings with others based on longitudinal village studies (e.g., with Bardhan and Mookherjee (2006) who studied the same set of villages from 1978 to 1998 using different data sources).

Section 13.3 examines patterns of political participation and awareness of citizens, and how they relate to measures of socio-economic status. We examine both their average levels and distribution across measures of socio-economic status. With few exceptions, we find that average levels of political participation in elections, village meetings, and political campaigns, as well as awareness of programs administered by GPs, were high. We find no evidence of any significant variation of participation rates or awareness between either landowning or low-caste status of households. The main determining factors were education, gender, and immigrant status, rather than land or caste. These results are similar to findings for other Indian states (e.g., for Rajasthan and Madhya Pradesh in Krishna (2006)) and many Latin American countries (Gaviria et al., 2002).

Section 13.4 studies targeting of benefits disbursed by local governments. This can be classified into the division of targeted of resources: (a) *within* a village by the concerned local governments, and (b) *across* villages and corresponding local governments by upper levels. The former is subject to more direct pressures of democracy, given the high levels of information within communities of the needs and entitlements of different residents. The latter involves negotiation between elected GP officials, elected officials at higher levels of the local government system at the block and district levels, and members of the state bureaucracy. The nature of democracy is less direct in the latter, and the allocation process less transparent. Differences between targeting performance of different levels of government have important implications for decentralization: arguments in favor of decentralization are strengthened if lower-level governments achieve superior targeting.

Within villages we find (with a few exceptions) little evidence of systematic biases in the distribution of public services on the basis of agricultural landownership, caste, gender, education, or immigrant status. Moreover, there was no bias in favor of those voting for the party with a majority of seats in the GP. Nor was there a bias in favor of those actively involved in political campaigns. Therefore there is no evidence that local governments at the lowest level discriminated on the basis of wealth, education, caste, or political partisanship in allocating benefits within villages.

Across villages, however, we find considerable biases, against villages with a high proportion of landless households: such villages received fewer benefits per household from upper-level governments. Villages with greater land inequality allocated a significantly lower share of benefits to the scheduled castes (SC) and scheduled tribes (ST). Members of these groups have been historically disadvantaged in terms of their social and economic status. These results suggest greater accountability at the lowest level of local governments (GPs), compared with higher levels of government located at the block or district levels. These results match those of Bardhan and Mookherjee (2006), based on a different data set (village panel data collected directly from the records of local governments).[1]

We subsequently examine how benefit delivery patterns were related to attendance and participation rates in the village *gram sabha* (GS), a key forum within these villages for citizens to meet at least twice a year, raise questions to be answered by elected GP officials, and discuss activities of the GP. We find evidence that villages with greater GS participation were also those which delivered more benefits to the landless and SC/ST population. And villages with lower incidence of landlessness and ST presence exhibited greater GS participation. This is consistent with the hypothesis that village

[1] The analysis of that paper is based on information about various benefit programs from the records of local governments themselves, which contain names of beneficiaries and the nature and timing of benefits. The socio-economic characteristics of the beneficiaries were obtained from an independent indirect (third-party) household survey, in which some prominent village citizens were asked to identify land, caste, education, and occupation details of each household in the village in 1978 and 1998. In contrast, the analysis of this chapter is based on a one-off direct household survey carried out in 2004, where each household was asked to report the benefits it had received in past years.

meetings formed a channel of accountability of GPs to the poor and low-caste groups. It does not, of course, provide evidence of a causal impact of village meetings on targeting—the results are equally consistent with the hypothesis that village meeting participation and targeting both reflected the effect of deeper, unobserved characteristics of the community reflecting its 'social capital'.

Section 13.5 examines voting patterns in order to better understand the nature of electoral pressures, and sources of incumbency advantage of the Left. At the end of our survey, we conducted a secret ballot of respondents across major political parties active in the local area. We report how different kinds of benefits received, as well as measures of improvement of economic status since 1978, were correlated with the tendency for the respondent to cast a vote in favor of the local incumbent. We find that the likelihood a given respondent voted for the Left Front coalition in our survey was correlated with benefits received from programs administered by previous Left Front-dominated local governments. However, not all benefits nor all forms of improvement in economic status mattered equally. Receipt of recurring short-term benefits rather than one-time benefits or infrastructural improvements affected voting patterns. Improvements in income or housing per se did not matter, but improvements in agricultural landownership did. Help provided by GPs dominated by the Left Front in the past with respect to easing difficulties faced in one's occupation, or in times of personal emergency—classic symptoms of clientelism—were also significantly correlated with voting in favor of the Left Front. Controlling for these factors, as well as other personal characteristics, poorer and SC/ST groups within a village were more inclined to vote in favor of the Left Front. The support for the Left was also greater in areas with a higher incidence of agricultural occupations, controlling for other household and community characteristics.

These findings are consistent with the hypothesis that the continued domination of local government (*panchayat*) elections by the Left Front over five successive election terms owed partly to dispensation of recurring short-term benefit programs (such as IRDP, credit, minikits (kits containing agricultural seeds and fertilizers), and employment and relief programs) by Left-dominated GPs to weaker sections of the community. Personalized help and short-term benefits had a stronger effect on voter support, compared with infrastructural improvements or more substantial one-time benefits (such as receiving a land title, or getting a tenancy contract registered). The results also help explain why the political success of the Left (measured by vote or seat shares) in local government elections has been declining in recent years: rising population pressure, stagnation in agricultural yields, and increasing urbanization have brought about a decline in agricultural land owned per capita and in the importance of agricultural occupations. At the same time, rising education and living standards have raised awareness and aspirations of citizens, and reduced their vulnerability to personal shocks and subsequent dependence on local governments for help in coping with such shocks.

It is, however, difficult to draw any definitive inferences concerning the role of clientelism vis-à-vis effective governance, while there is evidence of both. Proponents of the latter could argue that anti-poverty and relief programs have been distributed mostly to poorer, vulnerable sections of the population; and these sections have responded by voting in favor of the Left. There is no evidence that supporters of rival parties were excluded from benefits allocated, or of favoritism towards active political campaigners. On the other hand, there are also a number of symptoms of clientelism: voting tended to be more responsive to help provided in times of personal difficulty or receipt of recurring short-term private benefit programs, rather than one-time, long-term benefits or provision of local public goods. Local democracy in West Bengal has been vibrant and participative, and exhibited symptoms of clientelism in some dimensions (e.g., its focus on recurring, short term private benefits), effective governance in some other dimensions (intra-village allocation across socio-economic categories), and elite capture in yet other dimensions (e.g., inter-village allocations).

13.2 Survey Details

Our surveys were carried out during 2003–5. They involved 2,410 households in a sample of eighty-nine villages in West Bengal. The village sample is a subsample of an original stratified random sample of villages selected from all major agricultural districts of the state (only Kolkata and Darjeeling are excluded) by the Socio-Economic Evaluation Branch of the Department of Agriculture, Government of West Bengal, for the purpose of calculating cost of cultivation of major crops in the state between 1981 and 1996. In order to facilitate comparisons with their work, we use exactly the same sample of villages as Bardhan and Mookherjee (2004 and 2006, containing a more detailed description of the sampling procedure used). A random sample of blocks was selected in each district, and within each block one village was selected randomly, followed by random selection of another village within an eight-kilometer radius. Our survey teams visited these villages between 2003 and 2005, carried out a listing of landholdings of every household, then selected a stratified random sample (stratifying by landownership) of approximately twenty-five households per village (with the precise number varying with the number of households in each village). Two additional households were selected randomly from middle and large landowning categories respectively, owning five to ten acres acres and more than ten acres of cultivable land.

This was to ensure positive representation of these groups, which are small in number in many villages. The stratification of the sample of households was based on a prior census of all households in each village, in which demographic and landownership details were collected in a door-to-door survey.

Representatives (typically the head) of selected households were subsequently administered a survey questionnaire consisting of their demographics, land, economic status, economic activities, benefits received from various development programs administered by GPs, involvement in activities pertaining to local governments, and political and local community organizations. Response rates were high: only fifteen households out of 2,400 of those originally selected did not agree to participate, and were replaced by randomly selected substitutes. At the end of the survey we asked each respondent to cast a ballot into a box, where they ticked off a political party of their choice best representing their party preferences for election of GP officials. Ballots were anonymous, with no markers for identity of the voter. Voters were assured that the ballots would be opened only by us once we had returned to the research center in Kolkata, and the outcomes would not be disclosed to anyone apart from the authors of the research project. The response rate was predictably lower: 310 household representatives out of the entire sample of 2,410 refused to cast a ballot. A similar method is used by the National Election Surveys, but in most of them the focus is on national or provincial elections rather than local *panchayat* elections or processes of local governance. Studies of political participation in local governments have been carried out for three districts each of Rajasthan and Madhya Pradesh by Krishna (2006), and two Karnataka districts by Crook and Manor (1998). Ghatak and Ghatak (2002) have studied participation in village meetings (*gram sansads*) in a sample of twenty villages in Birbhum district of West Bengal.

13.3 Political Participation and Awareness

Table 13.1 describes household characteristics in our sample. Approximately half of all households were landless; another quarter were marginal owners with less than 1.25 acres of agricultural land. The interviews were conducted usually with the household head, 90 per cent of which were male. Education measured by highest years of schooling across all household members rose from an average of 6.6 years among the landless to 13.9 years among the biggest landowners with more than 10 acres of agricultural land. One-third belonged to scheduled castes (SCs) and 3.4 per cent to scheduled tribes (STs). The proportion of SCs is negatively correlated with landholding, but this is not evident for STs. Excepting the landless, more than two-thirds were engaged in agriculture as their primary occupation, and less than one-fifth

Table 13.1. Sample characteristics: household heads.

Agricultural land ownership	Age	% Male	Maximum education in household	% SC	% ST	% Agriculture occupation	% Immigrants
Landless	45	88	6.6	35	2.4	26	40
0–1.5 acres	48	88	7.8	34	4.9	65	17
1.5–2.5 acres	56	92	10.8	15	7.4	82	19
2.5–5 acres	58	93	11.1	24	3.1	72	10
5–10 acres	60	89	12.5	22	4.1	66	12
10 acres and above	59	100	13.9	24	6.9	72	14
ALL	49	89	8.0	32	3.4	47	28

had migrated into these villages since 1967. The landless in contrast were predominantly engaged in non-agricultural occupations, and two-fifths were newcomers.

Reported registration and turnout were near universal (above 98 per cent) for all except the landless (88–89 per cent): it is likely these have been subject to some degree of over-reporting. The aggregate voter turnout rate was similar to that reported (95 per cent) in Madhya Pradesh and Rajasthan by Krishna. Among the landless, more than a tenth said they were not registered or did not vote. A larger fraction (15 per cent) among the landless and marginal landowners also reported disturbances at or near the polling booth, or declined to answer this question, compared with 6–9 per cent among the rest.[2] Table 13.2 reports conditional logit regressions for registration, turnout, and disturbances (either reported or declined to answer), with village fixed effects. Within villages, it shows that lower registration and turnout among the landless resulted from a combination of factors apart from their lack of ownership of land: higher incidence of immigrants, non-agricultural occupations, and lower education were correlated with low registration and turnout. We shall see in this chapter that voters with low socio-economic characteristics (SECs) were more inclined to vote in favor of the Left Front, so these patterns of turnout and registration worked to the disadvantage of the Left. At the same time, it may have reduced accountability of elected officials towards the landless vis-à-vis other classes. But the difference in reported registration rates and turnouts was modest, more similar to European patterns than the

[2] Only four households in the entire sample reported not being able to cast their vote because of fear of disturbances, or because they discovered their vote had already been cast by someone else, or because they had to wait too long at the polling booth. So we describe instead their response to the question whether they faced any difficulties or disturbances when they went to vote (which does not seem to have prevented them from casting their vote). About 5 per cent of households reported facing difficulties or disturbances in and around voting booths, and nearly 200 households did not respond to this question. This suggests that there is some substance to allegations in the media concerning incidence of polling disturbances, but it affected a small proportion of households (between 5 and 12 per cent), and did not affect their ability to vote.

Table 13.2. Logit regressions: voter registration/turnout/disturbance (all regressions with village fixed effects).

	Voter Registration	Voter Turnout	Disturbance
Agricultural land	1.40**	0.36	0.05
	(0.70)	(0.24)	(0.05)
Other land	1.77	0.19	−0.88*
	(2.70)	(0.46)	(0.47)
Agriculture occupation	17.44***	0.96***	−0.51***
	(0.25)	(0.27)	(0.16)
Immigrant	−2.67***	−2.75***	−0.24
	(0.26)	(0.27)	(0.18)
Max education level in household	0.12***	0.12***	−0.03
	(0.03)	(0.04)	(0.02)
ST	1.23	1.10	0.72
	(0.06)	(1.05)	(0.52)
SC	−0.70***	−0.66***	0.10
	(0.20)	(0.21)	(0.19)
Male	−0.45	−0.70**	0.08
	(0.33)	(0.35)	(0.27)
Age	0.03***	0.12***	−0.00
	(0.008)	(0.04)	(0.03)
No. of observations	2,237	2,237	1,997
pseudo-R^2/p-value	0.36/0.00	0.36/0.00	0.013

Notes: All three regressions also include interactions of North Bengal dummy with male, agricultural land, SC, and ST only.
* significant at 10%; ** significant at 5%; *** significant at 1%

steep asymmetries in the United States (Przeworski, 2006). With regard to voting disturbances, there was no clear correlation with socio-economic status. Nor was there any tendency for polling disturbances to affect Left-leaning voters more or less than Congress-leaning voters.

We now turn to attendance in political meetings such as rallies, organized by political parties. Attendance rates were quite high, averaging 48 per cent across the population—much higher than the corresponding attendance rate of 33 per cent reported for Rajasthan and MP (Krishna, 2006). Attendance rates were above 40 per cent for every land class, rising to 65 per cent among big landowners. This is more likely to owe to higher education among the landed: the regression in the first column of Table 3 shows that attendance rates rose with education levels and fell with landownership, once we control for education and other characteristics. Moreover they were higher among SC and ST households, after controlling for land, education and other characteristics. As expected, males, non-immigrants, and those engaged in agricultural occupations were more likely to attend.

Table 13.3 also reports on a more active form of political participation: in political campaigns. Approximately 26 per cent of all households were engaged in campaigns. This is similar to the Karnataka districts studied by Crook and Manor (1998) (where it was 23 per cent), but lower than the Rajasthan and MP districts studied by Krishna (2006) (where it was 43 per cent). In our sample this

Table 13.3. Political activity regressions: attendance, participation, and contribution (conditional logits).

	Attendance (village fixed effects)	Campaign participation (village fixed effects)	Contribution to political campaigns (no village fixed effects)	Contribution to political campaigns (village fixed effects)
Agricultural land	−0.076***	−0.038	0.049	0.065*
	(0.028)	(0.026)	(0.032)	(0.038)
Other land	0.141	−0.031	0.458**	0.231
	(0.101)	(0.089)	(0.216)	(0.171)
Agriculture occupation	0.240**	0.139	0.150	−0.044
	(0.105)	(0.114)	(0.101)	(0.123)
Immigrant	−0.274**	−0.344***	0.102	0.028
	(0.111)	(0.125)	(0.106)	(0.129)
Max education level in household	0.044***	0.067***	0.096***	0.103***
	(0.013)	(0.014)	(0.012)	(0.015)
ST	1.237***	−0.492	0.781**	0.206
	(0.374)	(0.355)	(0.309)	(0.407)
SC	0.567***	0.208*	0.601***	0.079
	(0.134)	(0.124)	(0.124)	(0.152)
Male	0.407**	0.448**	0.371**	0.435**
	(0.185)	(0.192)	(0.152)	(0.196)
Age	0.010	−0.006	−0.001	0.065**
	(0.019)	(0.021)	(0.003)	(0.022)
Other land* North Bengal dummy	−0.187	0.219	−0.747**	−0.701*
	(0.238)	(0.322)	(0.324)	(0.374)
SC* North Bengal dummy			−0.605***	−0.138
			(0.224)	(0.296)
Male* North Bengal dummy			−2.145***	−1.297
			(0.615)	(0.846)
Agriculture land* North Bengal dummy			0.206***	0.120
			(0.070)	(0.085)
No. of observations	2,384/87	2,353/84	2,400	
Pseudo-R^2/p-value			0.06/0.00	

Note: * significant at 10%; ** significant at 5%; *** significant at 1%.

proportion was distributed quite evenly across different land classes, with the lowest proportion being 23 per cent among the landless, and the highest participation rate being 38 per cent among the biggest landowners. The regression results in Table 13.3 show no correlation with land or occupation, after controlling for other characteristics. It is interesting to note that the SC households are significantly more involved in campaigns, corroborating accounts of the increasingly active role played by some SC groups by Ruud (1999). A similar finding is reported for Karnataka, Rajasthan, and Madhya Pradesh by Crook and Manor (1998), and Krishna (2006) respectively. As with all other measures of participation, males and more educated heads were significantly more likely to be involved, and immigrants less likely to be involved.

Finally, a staggering 69 per cent of households reported making financial contributions to political campaigns, with the lowest proportion being 61 per cent among the landless, rising from 74 per cent among marginal landowners to 93 per cent among the biggest. The regressions show some but limited association with land owned, and a stronger association with education. This confirms the impression of many observers that a majority of the village population contributes regularly to political parties. Most households contribute small amounts, using this to signal their loyalty to the parties, representing a coping strategy in a highly politicized environment involving patron–client relationships. Here we shall provide evidence consistent with this hypothesis of clientelism.

Table 13.4 describes reported attendance and participation rates in village meetings (*gram sabhas*) that discuss matters relating to local government activities. One-third of all households reported attending these within the previous three years, compared with 17 per cent in the Karnataka districts studied by Crook and Manor (1998). Attendance rates exhibit some unevenness across land classes, rising from 33 per cent among the landless to 44 per cent among marginal landowners and 50 per cent for those with between 1.25 and 2.5 acres, and falling thereafter to between 35 and 44 per cent among those owning more land. The regressions in Table 13.4 show little association with land or caste status, but are correlated with education and immigrant status.

Our survey included questions about the nature of active participation in *gram sabhas*: whether respondents were accustomed to standing up to speak or ask questions. These participation rates rose from 6.5 per cent among the landless, to between 14 and 19 per cent among marginal, small and medium landowners, and 38 per cent among big landowners. Hence there is some unevenness in active participation in the village meetings only at the extreme ends of the economic spectrum. However, the regressions in Table 13.4 show the only significant predictors of active involvement in *gram sabhas* to be education, gender, and immigrant status. For the vast majority of landowning households (i.e., excluding the top 1 per cent of the population owning more than 10 acres of agricultural land) the likelihood of speaking in *gram sabhas* hardly varied. Moreover, SC/ST households were just as likely to speak up as non-SC/ST households.

We now turn to evidence concerning political awareness. Table 13.5 deals with responses to questions pertaining to regularly watching (or hearing) political or economics news on TV (or radio). TV news exposure was positively associated with land status, as one might expect. The proportion rose from 31 per cent among the landless, to 72 per cent among big landowners. Table 13.5 shows it was significantly negatively associated with agricultural

Table 13.4. *Gram sabha* attendance and participation regressions (conditional logits with village fixed effects).

	Gram sabha attendance conditional logit	*Gram sabha* participation conditional logit
Agricultural land	−0.015	0.041
	(0.029)	(0.036)
Other land	0.035	0.044
	(0.090)	(0.109)
Agriculture occupation	0.260	0.100
	(0.110)	(0.164)
Immigrant	−0.469***	−0.713***
	(0.120)	(0.194)
Max education level in household	0.024*	0.160***
	(0.014)	(0.021)
ST	0.487	0.153
	(0.349)	(0.588)
SC	0.049	0.237
	(0.140)	(0.217)
Male	1.052***	1.301***
	(0.232)	(0.479)
Age	0.072***	0.067*
	(0.022)	(0.076)
Other land* North Bengal dummy	0.093	0.177
	(0.280)	(0.235)
SC* North Bengal dummy	−0.096	0.195
	(0.270)	(0.373)
ST* North Bengal dummy	−0.147	0.492
	(0.661)	(1.080)
Agriculture land* North Bengal dummy	−0.085	−0.132**
	(0.054)	(0.065)
No. of observations	2,191/85	2,158/69
Pseudo-R^2/p-value	/0.00	/0.00

Notes: Std. errors are reported in parentheses.
***, **, and * denote significant at 1%, 5%, and 10% respectively. Table includes age-squared data.

occupation and ST/SC status, and positively with education and male gender. With regard to radio news, the overall proportion was similar to TV (about 33 per cent), but was much more even across socio-economic categories. Only education and gender were significantly correlated with exposure to radio news.

Next, consider principal sources of information concerning GP activities apart from the media. These are remarkably similar across different land classes, with the exception of the top 1 per cent that owned more than 10 acres. Between 43 and 48 per cent got information from elected GP officials; between 29 and 38 per cent from friends, relatives, or neighbors; and between 18 and 25 per cent from political party activists. *Gram sabhas* and government bureaucrats did not have any significant role as information providers. The regression results shown in Table 13.5 indicate almost no pattern of variation with SECs, except for a slight tendency for more-educated heads to rely less on

Table 13.5. Information sources (multinomial logits).

	Panchayat members	Political party activists	Friends/relatives/ neighbors
Agricultural land	0.228	0.237	0.282
	(0.175)	(0.176)	(0.176)
Other land	3.956	4.039	3.610
	(3.856)	(3.857)	(3.858)
Agriculture occupation	−0.039	0.149	0.137
	(0.459)	(0.464)	(0.462)
Immigrant	0.656	0.592	1.056
	(0.567)	(0.574)	(0.569)
Max education level in household	−0.079	−0.129**	−0.128***
	(0.057)	(0.057)	(0.057)
ST	−0.423	−0.434	0.016
	(1.064)	(1.080)	(1.062)
SC	0.021	0.084	0.050
	(0.472)	(0.478)	(0.475)
Male	0.340	0.202	−0.616
	(0.767)	(0.778)	(0.704)
Other land* North Bengal dummy	−4.437	−4.489	−3.339
	(3.962)	(3.979)	(3.951)

Note: (n=1991, pseudo R^2 =0.026)

informal sources (family, friends, or party activists). These results imply homogeneous access to information concerning GP activities across various socio-economic categories within villages.

Finally we consider awareness of development or anti-poverty programs administered by GPs. On average, less than 20 per cent in most classes were aware of these programs, which seems quite low (and probably reflects the small scale of these programs: the average proportion of households that reported receiving benefits from any single program did not exceed 4 per cent; and only in three or four programs did reported benefit rates exceed 1 per cent). The raw averages show some tendency for the top 1 per cent of the population to be more aware, and the landless to be less aware, but otherwise awareness tends to vary little across land classes. The regression results in Table 13.6 show that, after controlling for education, immigrant status, and gender, those with less land were more likely to be aware. SC and ST heads were likely to be just as aware as anyone else, and in some cases (employment programs for STs and housing programs for SCs) were likely to be significantly more aware. Across different programs there was a tendency for awareness to vary with need and/or entitlement: landless households were more aware of loan and employment programs earmarked for the landless; marginal landowners more aware of loan and seed programs that only they would find useful.

In summary, rates of political participation appeared high on average, and did not vary much with socio-economic characteristics such as land and caste, with some exceptions: lower voter turnouts and participation in *gram sabhas*

Table 13.6. Information regarding GP-administered development programs (conditional logit with village fixed effects).

	Current GP programs	New GP programs	Past loan program	Seed program	Employment programs	Construction/ housing programs
Agricultural land	0.044	0.050	−0.054*	−0.002	−0.030	−0.068**
	(0.041)	(0.036)	(0.032)	(0.033)	(0.038)	(0.033)
Other land	0.066	0.053	−0.130	0.030	−0.067	−0.077
	(0.114)	(0.115)	(0.110)	(0.103)	(0.126)	(0.105)
Agriculture occupation	0.054	0.045	0.455***	0.986***	0.083	0.274**
	(0.176)	(0.164)	(0.132)	(0.160)	(0.157)	(0.126)
Immigrant	−0.527***	−0.516***	−0.521***	−0.706***	−0.339*	−0.419***
	(0.196)	(0.188)	(0.152)	(0.197)	(0.177)	(0.140)
Max education level in household	0.180***	0.123***	0.040**	0.120***	0.045**	0.016
	(0.024)	(0.022)	(0.016)	(0.020)	(0.020)	(0.016)
ST	0.856*	0.268	−0.123	0.371	0.802**	0.341
	(0.477)	(0.433)	(0.340)	(0.394)	(0.365)	(0.320)
SC	−0.011	−0.021	−0.170	0.173	0.241	0.279**
	(0.197)	(0.182)	(0.148)	(0.178)	(0.173)	(0.136)
Male	1.167***	1.606***	0.629**	−0.011	0.224	0.257
	(0.409)	(0.470)	(0.246)	(0.286)	(0.262)	(0.212)
Age	0.043	0.049	0.081***	0.036	0.013	0.035
	(0.038)	(0.036)	(0.028)	(0.032)	(0.031)	(0.025)
Other land* North Bengal dummy	−4.420	−0.859	−0.864	−0.613	0.018	0.042
	(2.809)	(0.630)	(0.784)	(0.547)	(0.449)	(0.354)
No. of observations	1,685/43	1,891/58	2,218/76	2,113/72	2,086/70	2,308/82
p-value	0.0	0.0	0.0	0.0	0.0	0.0

Notes: Std. errors are reported in parentheses.
***, **, and * denote significant at 1%, 5%, and 10% respectively. Table includes age-squared data.

among the landless and SC/ST groups. They did, however, vary significantly with education, gender, and immigrant status. Controlling for these, there was little evidence of political marginalization or exclusion of weaker socio-economic groups. Marginal landowners, and SC or ST populations seemed well integrated into local political life, often participating more vigorously than others, with access to similar information flows concerning GP activities. Only immigrants, women, and those with low education seemed significantly less involved and aware.

13.4 Targeting Patterns and *Gram Sabha* Attendance

In this section we consider the distribution of benefits within and across villages, the extent to which they were targeted at poor and SC/ST groups, and how these targeting patterns varied with one form of political participation—attendance and participation in *gram sabhas*. Since we are relying on a one-time household survey, we have carried out some cross-village regressions of targeting with political participation. As we have mentioned before, such cross-section regressions are fraught with all the customary qualifications: they do not establish causation, and may reflect the joint effect of unobserved community characteristics. So we will report verbally some of the results of the statistical analysis, just as one way of checking whether the evidence is consistent with the hypothesis that political participation affects accountability of elected government officials. One additional value of the exercise is that data concerning allocation of benefits of various public services is often lacking, while evidence on political participation is more easily available (e.g., attendance rates in civic and political meetings). The results can inform us on the extent to which attendance rates may be taken to be an indicator or proxy of how well the democratic process is functioning with regard to service delivery.

Table 13.7 provides averages of various benefit programs (house, water, employment, minikits, IRDP, roads, relief against disasters, relief against old-age or widow status, and ration card) that households reported receiving over the periods 1978–98 and over 1998–2005. We report these two periods separately, as the reported benefits for the earlier period may be subject to greater recall bias. We see that the proportions reporting receiving benefits of most kinds were substantially higher for the later period. We therefore use reported benefits for the 1998–2005 period subsequently in our analysis of targeting. Table 13.7 shows that a large fraction of village households benefited from

Table 13.7. Average percentage of households receiving different kinds of benefits, for the periods 1978–97 and 1998–2005.

	House	Water	Employment	Minikits	IRDP	Road	Relief	Ration card
% HH Received benefit (1978–97)	1.29	23.78	1.67	2.42	6.66	9.7	1.64	27.16
% HH Received benefit (1998–2005)	3.0	23.41	5.21	5.0	2.33	32.11	11.91	12.33
Fraction of benefits accruing to SC/ST (1978–97)	67.74	32.22	0.40	32.76	0.45	33.48	45.71	33.44
Fraction of benefits accruing to SC/ST (1998–2004)	52.77	37.72	49.41	46.67	55.36	32.68	35.66	32.43
Fraction of benefits accruing to landless (1978–97)	64.5	49.39	52.5	15.51	48.13	49.78	57.14	46.32
Fraction of benefits accruing to landless (1998–2005)	65.28	53.5	44.89	12.5	46.43	43.84	68.5	43.92

Notes: House denotes that a house was built for a low-income household by the GP. Water denotes access to drinking water, usually through a water tap in the neighborhood. Employment denotes employment in a local infrastructure program administered by the GP. Minikits are kits containing agricultural seeds and fertilizers. IRDP denotes low-interest loans disbursed by state banks. Road denotes a road built in the village. Relief denotes pensions or disaster support. Ration card denotes a card that entitles the holder to receive subsidized food and fuel through the public distribution system.

various programs during the 1998–2005 period. The largest benefits were reported for roads (32 per cent) and water (24 per cent). Ration card and relief programs were reported by 12 per cent, minikits and employment by 5 per cent, and IRDP loans and housing by 2–3 per cent.

Table 13.7 also indicates the high proportion of these benefits that were allocated to landless and SC/ST categories, consistent with the results in Bardhan and Mookherjee (2006) based on data collected for 1978–98 from local government records. Between 50- and 67 per cent of houses constructed by the GP benefited SC/ST households, who collectively comprised less than 40 per cent of the population. For other programs (with the single exception of minikit allocation to the landless) the proportion of landless and SC/ST households reported receiving benefits was approximately similar to or higher than their demographic weight.

Table 13.8 examines determinants of the number of benefits (aggregating across different programs) received by a household over the period 1998–2003, controlling for village fixed effects. This indicates the nature of intra-village targeting. The first column shows that those with more non-agricultural land were likely to receive more benefits. Apart from this, there was no tendency for GPs to discriminate on the basis of education, caste, or agricultural land. There was no noticeable bias against the poor, against women-headed households, or against immigrants. In villages with higher attendance rates in the *gram sabha*, there was smaller bias in favor of those owning non-agricultural land, and there was better treatment of the SC households.

Table 13.8. Intra-village targeting (OLS regression with village fixed effects).

	Number of GP benefits received by household
Education	−0.2 (0.04)
SC dummy	−0.37 (0.36)
ST dummy	1.41 (1.02)
Non agricultural land owned	0.70* (0.37)
Agricultural land owned	−0.03 (0.07)
GS attendance rate * education	−0.08 (0.12)
GS attendance rate * SC	1.98** (1.01)
GS attendance rate * ST	−1.67 (2.95)
GS attendance rate * Non-agricultural land	−1.84* (0.98)
GS attendance rate * agricultural land	0.09 (0.19)
N, p-value	2176, 0.000

Note: Controls include age, gender, occupation, immigrant dummy, and interactions. Standard errors in parentheses.
* significant at 10%; ** significant at 5%; *** significant at 1%.

Table 13.9 explores the possible role of political partisanship in distribution of benefits, distinguishing further between swing voters and those voting consistently for one party over successive elections. In the next section we shall see that almost half the sample reported voting for the Left in all past elections: we call these *Left-secure voters*. A substantially smaller fraction had voted consistently for non-Left parties in all past elections: we refer to them as *non-Left-secure voters*. Those changing their allegiance are denoted *non-secure voters*. Conceivably, the Left may seek to woo swing voters and favor them relative to Left-secure voters in the distribution of benefits. Alternatively, voters that have been treated worse by a Left-controlled GP may be more inclined to switch allegiance to a non-Left party, so Left-secure voters may have been treated better than swing voters. Moreover, a party controlling a GP

Table 13.9. Intra-village targeting, including swing, left-secure, and non-left-secure dummy (OLS regression with village fixed effects).

	Number of GP benefits received by household
Education	−0.025
	(0.045)
SC	−0.456
	(0.366)
ST	1.323
	(1.024)
Non-agricultural land	0.704*
	(0.376)
Agricultural land	−0.055
	(0.078)
Education*GS attendance	−0.089
	(0.126)
SC*GS attendance	2.008**
	(1.014)
ST*GS attendance	−1.824
	(2.933)
Non-agricultural land* GS attendance	−1.819*
	(0.981)
Agricultural land* GS attendance	0.129
	(0.194)
Winning party Left and Left-secure voter	−0.044
	(0.137)
Winning party Left and non-Left-secure voter	0.288
	(0.349)
Winning party non-Left and Left-secure voter	0.361
	(0.276)
Winning party non-Left and non-Left-secure voter	−0.022
	(0.179)
Observations	2252
Numeric code of each village	73

Notes: standard errors in parentheses.
* significant at 10 %; ** significant at 5%; *** significant at 1%. Other controls include age, occupation, male, immigrant dummy, and their interactions

Table 13.10. Cross-village regression of intra-village targeting ratios. Dependent variable: share of GP benefits 1998–2003 going to specified group in the village.

	Landless % share	SC/ST % share
GS attendance	−0.35**	−0.32**
	(0.15)	(0.12)
GS attendance * % landless	1.69***	
	(0.41)	
% landless	−0.05	
	(0.20)	
% SC (LL)	−0.01	
	(0.06)	
% ST (LL)	−0.13	
	(0.10)	
Land Gini	−0.03	−0.57***
	(0.24)	(0.21)
Education Gini	0.33	
	(0.22)	
GS attendance * % SC landless		6.02***
		(2.28)
GS attendance * % ST landless		2.19***
		(0.45)
N, R-squared	88, 0.55	88, 0.32

Note: Controls include village average for land and education. Standard errors in parentheses.
* significant at 10%; ** significant at 5%; *** significant at 1%.

may discriminate against voters committed to the rival party, relative to swing or its own secure constituency. Four additional variables are included in the regression, based on the combination of majority party in the GP (Left, or non-Left), and whether the voter is a Left-secure or non-Left-secure voter. None of these turn out to be statistically significant, while other coefficients are unchanged compared with Table 13.8. Hence there appears to be no evidence of any partisan treatment by either Left-controlled or non-Left-controlled GPs.

Table 13.10 examines how intra-village targeting ratios (aggregating across all benefits) for the period 1998–2003 were correlated with *gram sabha* attendance rates across villages, besides measures of inequality in land and education (controlling for the demographic weights of the landless and SC/ST groups, and average land holdings and education in the village). A higher demographic weight of the landless indicates a higher incidence of landlessness in the village, given the average landholding in the village—i.e., greater poverty.[3] Note that if per capita benefits received by members of a particular group do

[3] In Bardhan and Mookherjee (2006), increasing landlessness was associated with significantly lower wage rates for agricultural workers, controlling for village fixed effects and other time-varying village characteristics (such as rainfall, population density, agricultural yields, and other measures of land distribution).

not vary with the relative size of the group, the share of this group as a whole will increase proportionally with the demographic weight of the group. If the per capita benefit accruing to the landless rises with the extent of landlessness, the targeting share of the landless will decrease in demographic weight. The first column shows an insignificant association of the targeting share of the landless with their demographic weight—suggesting that their per capita benefits were declining significantly with the extent of landlessness. Moreover, there was a significant positive interaction between GS attendance rates and the demographic weight of the landless. This suggests that per capita benefits were significantly higher in villages with higher GS attendance rates. Otherwise, the targeting share did not co-vary with land or education inequality.

The second column provides corresponding results for the targeting share of the SC/ST group. Consistent with the results in Bardhan and Mookherjee (2006), but based on an entirely different source and nature of data for the same villages covering the period 1978–98, we find a significant negative association with land inequality.[4] We also find a significant positive interaction between GS attendance rates and the demographic weights of these groups.

Table 13.11 examines the pattern of inter-village allocation of benefits. The dependent variable is the number of benefits received per household (aggregating across all programs) in a village over the period 1998–2003. Villages with a larger proportion of the landless received significantly *smaller* benefits, indicating a perverse pattern of targeting by higher-level governments. This is also consistent with the results in Bardhan and Mookherjee (2006). Combined with Table 13.10, this indicates lower government accountability to the poor in villages with greater poverty: a village with more landless households got fewer resources from upper-level governments. And of the resources they obtained, they allocated a lower share to the landless. We do not see signs of any significant bias in cross-village allocations with respect to the proportion of SC/ST groups.

The second column in Table 13.11 includes the share of the Left Front in local government seats during the 1998–2003 period, and the third column also adds the square of this share. There is a significant U-shaped relation with the extent of Left domination of the local government with a turning point at around 57 per cent. This suggests a tendency to allocate more resources to GPs where the Left Front was solidly entrenched (i.e, had a two-third majority or

[4] That paper was based on data concerning distribution of IRDP credit, minikits, and employment from local government sources, and pertained to regressions of the targeting ratio for SC/STs on time-varying measures of land distribution in the village, controlling for village fixed effects.

Table 13.11. Inter-village targeting regressions.

	(1)	(2)	(3)
	Number of benefits per household	Number of benefits per household	Number of benefits per household
Proportion landless	−0.980**	−1.099***	−1.076***
	(0.391)	(0.400)	(0.385)
Proportion SC	−0.133	−0.188	−0.180
	(0.385)	(0.385)	(0.370)
Proportion ST	0.015	−0.062	0.163
	(0.527)	(0.527)	(0.513)
Left share 1998–2003		−1.124	−10.738***
		(0.715)	(3.517)
Left share squared			9.475***
			(3.400)
Constant	1.666***	2.285***	4.541***
	(0.227)	(0.454)	(0.920)
Observations	89	88	88
R-squared	0.08	0.10	0.18

Note: Standard errors in parentheses. * significant at 10%; ** significant at 5%; *** significant at 1%

higher), compared with those more evenly contested. Hence there seems to be evidence of political partisanship in the inter-village allocation, in contrast to intra-village allocations.

Table 13.12 examines how inter-village allocations varied with GS attendance rates within those villages. If we differentiate between villages with high and low attendance rates of the poor (the second column of Table 13.12), the inter-village biases become even more sharply evident. Among villages with low attendance rates, those with more landless or SC households received significantly fewer benefits. In addition, villages with greater inequality in education were favored. These biases were substantially smaller in villages with high GS attendance rates of poor households.

Hence the results indicate that *gram sabha* attendance rates were positively correlated with targeting in favor of landless and SC groups. Could *gram sabha* participation represent a channel through which inequalities in land or social status were associated with poorer targeting? Recall from Table 13.4 that attendance rates were not significantly associated with land or caste at the household level. Table 13.13 examines how attendance and participation rates were correlated with village characteristics (across villages). Villages with a higher landlessness and ST presence exhibited lower attendance rates, irrespective of whether we control for district fixed effects. Controlling for this, land or education inequality was not significantly associated with attendance rates.

In summary, *gram sabha* attendance rates were positively correlated with measures of targeting to vulnerable sections of the population. They were also

Table 13.12. Inter-village targeting, inequality, and *gram sabha* attendance. Dependent variable: number of GP benefits per household in village, 1998–2003.

	Using GS attendance rate of all	Using GS attendance rate of poor
GS attendance	1.95	2.20
	(1.95)	(1.96)
GS attendance * % landless	0.72	5.78
	(2.63)	(7.93)
% landless	−2.23	−2.70**
	(1.36)	(1.15)
% SC	−0.41	−1.76**
	(1.06)	(0.88)
% ST	0.18	−0.78
	(0.96)	(0.73)
Land Gini	1.32	1.80
	(1.54)	(1.48)
Education Gini	5.01**	5.82***
	(2.21)	(1.90)
GS attendance * % SC	2.81	5.04**
	(2.49)	(2.49)
GS attendance * % ST	−2.78	2.41
	(3.41)	(4.86)
GS attendance * education Gini	−11.04**	−16.69***
	(5.25)	(5.67)
N, R-Squared	88, 0.21	88, 0.25

Note: Controls include average land and education. Standard errors in parentheses.
* significant at 10%; ** significant at 5%; *** significant at 1%.

Table 13.13. GS attendance/speech rates: cross-village regression.

	Attendance (OLS)	Attendance (district FE)	Speech (OLS)	Speech (district FE)
% landless	−0.48**	−0.36*	−0.06	−0.03
	(0.16)	(0.20)	(0.10)	(0.11)
% SC	0.05	−0.01	−0.05	−0.12**
	(0.07)	(0.09)	(0.04)	(0.05)
% ST	−0.30**	−0.38***	−0.11*	−0.17**
	(0.10)	(0.12)	(0.06)	(0.07)
Land Gini	0.35	0.27	0.11	0.21
	(0.29)	(0.32)	(0.18)	(0.19)
Education Gini	−0.12	−0.10	−0.13	−0.09
	(0.21)	(0.24)	(0.13)	(0.14)
N, R-squared	88, 0.20	88, 0.18	88, 0.06	88, 0.18

Note: Controls include average land and education. Standard errors in parentheses.
* significant at 10%; ** significant at 5%; *** significant at 1%.

negatively correlated with landlessness and ST presence. Hence *gram sabha* participation represented a possible channel by which inequality in land and in social status translated into lower accountability of *panchayat* officials to the landless and SC/ST groups.

13.5 Voting Patterns

We now analyze voting patterns across different political parties in the secret ballot we administered at the end of the household survey. Each respondent was asked to select from symbols representing different parties used in elections, and cast the ballot into a sealed box. Ballots were marked by a code number for each respondent and opened later, and recorded in data sheets. A similar procedure has been used in National Election Surveys in India.

Approximately two-thirds of small, marginal, and landless households voted in favor of a Left Front party; the remainder voted for either the Indian National Congress (INC) or its recent offshoot the Trinamul Congress (TNC). Among medium and large landowning families the proportion voting Left was slightly above 50 per cent, and among the big landowners this proportion dropped below 50 per cent, with a correspondingly higher share for the INC/TNC.

The election statistics for these villages shows that the Left won an average of 57 per cent of votes cast in GP elections in the three election years of 1978, 1983, and 1988. This subsequently fell to 55 per cent in 1993 and 49 per cent in 1998. Their share in GP seats varied between 75 and 71 per cent in the first three elections, falling thereafter to 68 per cent and 56 per cent. These figures indicate a strong dominance of the Left Front which began to wane in the early 1990s (though it rose again in 2003). A panel regression of GP seat share of the Left in Bardhan and Mookherjee (2010) shows a strong positive incumbency effect (captured by lagged Left seat share), controlling for village land and occupational and caste distribution, apart from variables representing strength of the Left at the district, state, and national levels.

The continued domination of the Left Front during this period owed partly to its large loyal base of voters; 45 per cent of respondents reported that they vote the same way as their fathers, while an even higher proportion (67 per cent) reported voting for the same party for the last 25 years. The proportion that voted for Left Front parties in our ballot was 65 per cent. Among those voting Left, the proportions of loyal voters were slightly higher than in the entire population: 48 per cent reported voting like their father, and 76 per cent reported having voted consistently for the same party for the last 25 years. This implies that approximately half of all voters had been loyal to the Left over the quarter-century leading up to the survey.

Table 13.14 presents regressions predicting whether a respondent voted for a Left Front party in our ballot, on the basis of number of reported benefits and their timing, apart from various household characteristics. Receipt of benefits is interacted with the seat share of the Left Front in the year that the benefits were received, since the 'gratitude' of the voter would be likely to be directed to the party in power in the local government at that time. We separate the

Table 13.14. Logit regressions for left vote dummy on number of benefits received (1998–2003), improvement in standard of living, and GP help.

	No. of benefits	No. of benefits (with village fixed effects)
Personal benefits *Left share[1]	0.153**	0.147*
	(0.071)	(0.079)
Acquaintance benefits * left share	−0.060	−0.084
	(0.042)	(0.055)
Proportion of village benefits * Left share	0.059	
	(0.278)	
GP help with occupation * Left share	0.167	0.441**
	(0.161)	(0.185)
GP help in disturbances * Left share	0.377***	0.260
	(0.132)	(0.158)
Improvement in income over 1978–2004 * average Left share[2]	0.014	0.020
	(0.012)	(0.014)
Improvement in number of rooms in the house 1978–2004 * Left share	0.035	0.082
	(0.078)	(0.091)
Improvement in house type 1978–2004 * average Left share	0.120	0.118
	(0.184)	(0.201)
Increase in agricultural Land 1978–2004 * average left share	0.054**	0.096***
	(0.023)	(0.028)
Agricultural land	−0.079***	−0.137***
	(0.026)	(0.031)
Other land	−0.194**	−0.150*
	(0.088)	(0.091)
Education	−0.034**	−0.028
	(0.015)	(0.017)
ST	0.895**	0.999**
	(0.349)	(0.488)
SC	0.398***	0.408***
	(0.122)	(0.144)
Agricultural occupation	0.262**	0.014
	(0.117)	(0.135)
Immigrant	0.155	0.170
	(0.139)	(0.151)
Observations	1695	1637

Note: Regressions include gender, age, and its square as additional controls.Standard errors in parentheses.
* significant at 10%; ** significant at 5%; *** significant at 1%.
[1] Left share in the time block that the benefit was received. [2] Average Left share, 1978 to 2004.

role of benefits received by the household in question from those received by friends or kin, and the proportion of households in the village as a whole that received benefits. We also include help provided by the GP to the household in connection with difficulties faced by the latter in their occupation, and in times of disturbances or personal emergency. The precise year that such benefits were provided was not recorded, so these are interacted with the average Left share over the entire period 1978–2004, to indicate the support among voters that such forms of personal help may have generated for the Left Front. The regression also controls for various indicators of personal economic improvement for the period 1978–2005, all of which are interacted with the average Left share: percentage change in incomes, changes in type of housing, in the number of rooms, and in agricultural land owned.

The regressions show the number of personal benefits received from Left-dominated GPs was significantly related to the likelihood of voting for the Left. This is true within as well as across villages; the coefficient changes little with the incorporation of village fixed effects. Higher benefits received by the village as a whole or by friends and family did not matter, controlling for own benefits. The second notable result is the importance of help received from the GP in connection with ones' occupation (within the village) and in times of personal difficulty (across villages). Third, changes in personal economic circumstances measured by income or housing were not significant, but changes in agricultural land were. Those whose landownership increased (respectively decreased) at times when the GP was dominated by the Left were more inclined to vote in favor of the Left. Apart from these factors, support for the Left was negatively related to land and education status, and positively related to SC/ST status. Age, gender, and immigrant status per se did not matter. Agricultural occupations were significant only in the regression without village fixed effects, implying that this was a relevant community rather than household characteristic: regions relying more on agricultural occupations were characterized by greater support for the Left.

In order to investigate the interpretation of the preceding results as symptoms of clientelism, Table 13.15 separates benefits further into two different categories: one-time and recurring benefits. Clientelism involves an implicit *quid pro quo*, an exchange of (recurring) favors for (recurring) political support. The latter category of benefits includes IRDP loans, minikits, and employment and relief programs, while the former includes the rest. Some programs are inherently one-time, such as land reform benefits, building of houses, provision of toilets, or installation of drinking water taps in the neighborhood. Others are ambiguous, such as road programs. We include roads in the one-time category partly because that seems more appropriate, besides the fact that the one-time category includes programs of a more infrastructural, local public good nature. We also ran the regressions including roads in the recurring category and found the results largely unchanged.

Table 13.15 shows that only the recurring benefits received from Left-dominated GPs were associated with higher support for the Left. Moreover, controlling for one's own receipt of recurring benefits, increased recurring benefits received by kin from Left-dominated GPs reduced support for the Left. These results suggest that personalized exchanges of short-term benefits played a significant role in electoral support for the Left—those aware of benefits received by others rather than oneself from Left-dominated GPs were less inclined to vote for the Left. Furthermore, the importance of recurring rather than one-time benefits suggest the importance of an implicit *quid pro quo*

Table 13.15. Logit regressions for Left vote, with respect to number of benefits received (one-time versus recurring benefits, 1998–2003), improvement in standard of living and GP help.

	No village fixed effects	With village fixed effects
No. of personal benefits (one-time) * Left share	0.066	0.044
	(0.087)	(0.095)
Number of friends/family benefits received (one time) * Left share	−0.019	−0.038
	(0.059)	(0.073)
Number of personal benefits received (recurring) * Left share	0.468***	0.403**
	(0.152)	(0.165)
Number of friends/family benefits received (recurring) * Left share	−0.151	−0.277*
	(0.137)	(0.160)
Proportion of benefits received in the Village * Left share	0.099	
	(0.284)	
GP Help with Occupation * average Left share	0.132	0.410**
	(0.162)	(0.186)
GP Help during disturbance * average Left share	0.396***	0.284*
	(0.132)	(0.159)
Improvement in income over 1978–2004 * average Left share	0.014	0.020
	(0.012)	(0.014)
Improvement in number of rooms in the house over 1978–2004 * average Left share	0.024	0.076
	(0.076)	(0.089)
Improvement in house type over 1978–2004 * average Left share	0.136	0.128
	(0.185)	(0.202)
Improvement in agriculture over 1978–2004 * average Left share	0.053**	0.093***
	(0.023)	(0.028)
Agricultural land owned	−0.078***	−0.136***
	(0.026)	(0.031)
Other land owned	−0.202**	−0.159*
	(0.088)	(0.091)
Education	−0.037**	−0.030*
	(0.015)	(0.017)
ST	0.916***	0.986**
	(0.349)	(0.485)
SC	0.376***	0.397***
	(0.123)	(0.145)
Agricultural sector occupation	0.255**	−0.003
	(0.117)	(0.135)
Immigrant	0.171	0.172
	(0.140)	(0.152)
Observations	1695	1637

Note: Additional controls include gender and age of household head. Standard errors in parentheses.
* Significant at 10%; ** significant at 5%; *** significant at 1%.

between beneficiaries and the party perceived to be dispensing the benefits. The results also suggest that electoral accountability pressures would have operated more with regard to distribution of recurring rather than one-time private or local public good benefits.

Table 13.16 explores determinants of whether a voter tended to vote consistently for the Left or its opponents across successive elections. We have seen above that almost half of the respondents were Left-secure voters, constituting

Table 13.16. Logit regressions for secure, Left-secure and non-Left-secure voter dummies on household and village characteristics.

	(1)	(2)	(3)	(4)	(5)	(6)
	Secure voter	Secure voter (VFE)	Left-secure voter	Left-secure voter (VFE)	Non-Left secure voter	Non-Left secure voter (VFE)
Max education in household	−0.02*	−0.02*	−0.03**	−0.03**	0.01	0.02
	(0.01)	(0.01)	(0.01)	(0.01)	(0.02)	(0.02)
ST dummy	0.25	0.28	0.80***	0.94***	−1.15**	−1.30***
	(0.32)	(0.32)	(0.29)	(0.31)	(0.45)	(0.47)
SC dummy	0.25**	0.26**	0.44***	0.47***	−0.38**	−0.39***
	(0.12)	(0.12)	(0.11)	(0.11)	(0.15)	(0.15)
Agriculture occupation	−0.08	−0.07	0.11	0.07	−0.23*	−0.16
	(0.11)	(0.11)	(0.10)	(0.11)	(0.12)	(0.13)
Immigrant	−0.26**	−0.28**	0.04	0.08	−0.48***	−0.56***
	(0.11)	(0.12)	(0.11)	(0.11)	(0.15)	(0.16)
Panchayat help in disturbance	0.17*	0.25**	0.24**	0.31***	−0.12	−0.11
	(0.10)	(0.11)	(0.09)	(0.11)	(0.12)	(0.13)
Panchayat help with occupation	0.01	0.07	0.07	0.27**	−0.11	−0.32**
	(0.12)	(0.13)	(0.11)	(0.13)	(0.14)	(0.16)
Other land owned	−0.14*	−0.17**	−0.06	−0.07	−0.13	−0.16
	(0.08)	(0.08)	(0.08)	(0.09)	(0.11)	(0.11)
Agricultural land owned	−0.07***	−0.07***	−0.15***	−0.15***	0.08***	0.08***
	(0.02)	(0.03)	(0.03)	(0.03)	(0.03)	(0.03)
Village land Gini	−2.14***		−1.73***		−0.28	
	(0.49)		(0.45)		(0.55)	
Village education Gini	−0.96		−1.24		0.52	
	(0.96)		(0.88)		(1.10)	
Village education proportion	−0.16***		−0.12**		−0.05	
	(0.06)		(0.05)		(0.07)	
Village SC proportion	0.10		0.16		−0.10	
	(0.25)		(0.23)		(0.29)	
Village ST proportion	1.25*		0.41		0.82	
	(0.70)		(0.57)		(0.66)	
Constant	4.53***		2.99***		−1.04	
	(1.10)		(1.01)		(1.25)	
Observations	2215	2189	2215	2208	2215	2110

Note: Additional controls include gender and age of household head. VFE denotes village fixed effects included. Standard errors in parentheses.
* significant at 10%; ** significant at 5%; *** significant at 1%.

a secure 'vote-bank' for the Left. Columns 3 and 4 present a logit for whether a respondent was a Left-secure voter, Columns 5 and 6 for a secure non-Left voter, and columns 1 and 2 for whether the household was a secure voter for either Left or non-Left. There is a strong positive association of SC, ST status, and help received from GP in times of disturbance with Left-secure. Conversely, there is a strong negative association of SC/ST with non-Left secure, and a positive association with land owned. Immigrants were less inclined to be secure voters for either party, or to be secure non-Left supporters. 'Swing' voting was more likely among those with more education and more land, who were non-SC or immigrants, and who received less help from GPs. Among village attributes relevant in predicting secure Left support, high land inequality and low education spread were negatively correlated. Hence Table 13.16 shows that the Left was more likely to have a secure vote-bank among poorer, lower-caste, less educated sections of the population, and in villages with lower land inequality. This is consistent with explanations for stable support of the Left in terms of vulnerability and lack of education among poor, lower-caste sections, and in their reliance on local governments for personal help. In villages with lower land inequality, the Left was more successful in mobilizing these groups.

13.6 Summary

Our results can be summarized as follows. West Bengal villages are characterized by high levels of political participation: 50 per cent of households attend political meetings, 25 per cent participate in political campaigns, 70 per cent contribute to political campaigns, 37 per cent attend *gram sabha* meetings, and 11 per cent ask questions at these meetings. By comparison, in Karnataka districts studied by Crook and Manor (1998), 23 per cent were involved in campaigns, 17 per cent attended *gram sabhas*, and 6.5 per cent asked questions. So reported participation rates are higher in West Bengal in many respects. Moreover, one-third of West Bengal households report watching political and economic news on the TV and on radio. Forty per cent obtain news about activities of the GPs from the GP directly, indicating a high level of personal contact.

With the exception of education, gender, and immigrant status, reported participation rates vary remarkably little with socio-economic status. Weaker sections of the population, defined by land or caste status, participate at rates similar to those of the remaining population, and have access to similar information channels. There is negligible evidence of exclusion or marginalization of these sections from the local political process.[5] The importance of education in predicting political participation suggests the possible role of education policy in strengthening local democracy. Of course, this is only suggestive as it is based on cross-sectional rather than longitudinal evidence: it

[5] The only exception was with regard to voter registration, where landownership was positively correlated with the likelihood of being registered, and 12 per cent of the landless were not registered.

is equally possible that it reflects unobserved traits that correlate with both education and political participation.

Ninety-five per cent households reported absence of disturbances or irregularities in local elections. Ninety-nine per cent of those registered turned out to vote, and almost no voters reported failure to cast their vote owing to disturbances. This compares favorably with the Karnataka districts studied by Crook and Manor, where 95 per cent reported believing elections were fair.

The allocation of benefits within villages displayed almost no association with wealth, caste, education, or gender of household head. Nor was there any evidence of exclusion of those supporting the rival of the locally dominant party. There is no evidence that GPs dominated by either Left or non-Left party discriminated on the basis of political partisanship: secure voters for either party and swing voters did not receive significantly different benefits, controlling for their individual characteristics. The only exception was a positive association between attendance in *gram sabhas* and benefits received. There was also some tendency for villages with greater land inequality to allocate fewer benefits to SC/ST groups. Across villages, there was evidence of targeting biases against landless and low-caste households. The contrast of intra-village targeting with inter-village targeting is striking, matching findings of Bardhan and Mookherjee (2004, 2006) based on different datasets. The high level of intra-village targeting to vulnerable socio-economic groups and lack of political partisanship most likely reflects a high level of accountability of the lowest rung of local government officials to the local community. In turn this seems related to the high and even rates of political participation and awareness of different socio-economic groups in the activities of the local GP and *gram sabha* meetings. This is encouraging news for decentralization advocates: governments at the lowest layer seemed less prone to 'capture' by local socio-economic elites than were governments at upper levels.

With regard to voting patterns, we found electoral support for incumbent parties among households was related to the benefits they received from GPs dominated by the incumbent in the past. This is unlikely to reflect voter gratitude per se, because it pertained only to recurring benefits such as credit, minikits, employment, relief payments, and help received from the GP in times of personal need. One-time benefits from road and water projects or from land reforms were not associated with electoral support. This is suggestive of personalized clientelistic relationships with political parties as a source of ensuring continued political support. Such clientelism can distort the democratic process and shift local government allocation from long-term investment in local public goods to short-term private goods and services. On the other hand, as explained, there is no evidence that these benefits were concentrated narrowly to favor particular groups within the village, which suggests that clientelism may not have been the only source of support for the

Left. Finally, one reason for the continued political success of the Left in rural West Bengal until recently is the existence of a large fraction of committed Left supporters, almost one-half of the total population. With such a secure vote base, the ability of the Left to garner majority control of GPs requires attracting a fraction of the swing voters that constitute one-third of voters.

Secure support for the Left was concentrated among SC and ST groups, those with less land and education, and those relying on support from GPs in times of personal emergency. This fact can also be viewed in different ways. Supporters of the Left Front could argue that the political durability of the Left owed to the support it has provided to poor and more vulnerable sections of the rural population. Critics could interpret the same facts as implying that continued political dominance of the Left will require perpetuation of vulnerability of these groups.[6] In either case, the results indicate that some causes of the increasingly contested nature of local government elections over the past decade lie in the decline in agricultural occupations, reduced economic vulnerability, and rising levels of education and aspiration among the poor. It seems likely that these long-term factors, along with contingent events, may have contributed to the declining fortunes of the incumbent Left government in local elections in recent years.

Acknowledgements

We thank: the MacArthur Foundation, the Indian Statistical Institute, and WIDER for funding this research; seminar participants at the Center for Studies in Social Science, Kolkata and Institute for Policy Dialogue at Columbia University for useful comments; and Jean-Paul Faguet and an anonymous referee for expositional suggestions.

References

Baiochhi, Gianpaolo, Patrick Heller, Shubham Chaudhuri, and Marcelo Silva, 2006. "Evaluating Empowerment: Participatory Budgeting in Brazilian Muncipalities." Mimeo, Department of Politics, University of Massachusetts, Amherst.

Bardhan, Pranab and Dilip Mookherjee, 2010. "Ideology Versus Electoral Competition in Redistributive Politics: Land Reform in West Bengal." Working Paper, 2005, Boston University; revised version published in *American Economic Review*, September 2010.

[6] The latter statement does need to be qualified by the fact that increases in agricultural land over time in Left-dominated villages by a given household translated into a greater likelihood of voting for the Left. In contrast, cross-sectional variations of voting patterns indicate a general tendency for wealthier, better-educated people to vote against the Left.

Bardhan, Pranab and Dilip Mookherjee, 2004. "Poverty Alleviation Efforts of West Bengal Panchayats." *Economic and Political Weekly*, 28 February, 965–74.

Bardhan, Pranab and Dilip Mookherjee, 2006. "Pro-Poor Targeting and Accountability of Local Governments in West Bengal." *Journal of Development Economics*, 79(2): 303–27.

Crook, Richard and James Manor, 1998. *Democracy and Decentralisation in South Asia and West Africa*. Cambridge, UK: Cambridge University Press.

Gaviria, Alejandro, Ugo Panizzia and Jessica Seddon, 2002. "Economic, Social and Demographic Determinants of Political Participation in Latin America: Evidence from the 1990s." Working Paper no. 472, Research Department, Inter-American Development Bank, Washington DC.

Ghatak, M. and M. Ghatak, 2002. "Recent Reforms in the Panchayat System in West Bengal: Towards Greater Participatory Governance." *Economic and Political Weekly*, 5 January, 45–58.

Krishna, Anirudh, 2006. "Poverty and Democratic Participation Reconsidered: Evidence from the Local Level in India."*Comparative Politics*, Vol. 38, No. 4 (July): 439–58.

Przeworski, Adam, 2006. "Constraints and Choices: Electoral Participation in Historical Perspective." Mimeo, New York University Department of Politics.

Ruud, A., 1999. "From Untouchable to Communist: Wealth, Power and Status among Supporters of the Communist Party (Marxist) in Rural West Bengal." In B. Rogaly, B. Harriss-White, and S. Bose (eds.), *Sonar Bangla? Agricultural Growth and Agrarian Change in West Bengal and Bangladesh*. New Delhi: Sage Publications, and London: Thousand Oaks.

World Development Report, 2004. *Making Services Work for Poor People*. Washington DC: World Bank.

Index

Page numbers in italics refer to figures and tables.